Editor's Note

I compare the author's family history to Whitman's great book, *Leaves of Grass*. This, because Whitman wrote and revised his poems during the better part of the 19th century, and consciously thought of his poems as unfolding in tandem with the American project itself, the United States being, in his words, "essentially our greatest poem." Like his book, her family's history begins nearly with the beginning of the country itself, in its colonial period, and continues on to this very moment, encompassing the country's entire history, and being present at many of its pivotal moments.

There is a strong feminist component to the author's book. Though the patriarchs of her family have frequently written about themselves and their ancestors, no woman has yet done so until now. It's clearly integral to the book to tell her family's story through the figures of its prominent women, and this unprecedented perspective provides some important visibility to them, which might be thought of as "reinserting" them into the historical record. Also important is the fact that these women's own voices are heard, through her extensive use of letters and other personal documents. Thus she is not speaking for them, so much as providing the space for them to speak directly to the reader. But lastly, it seems like a tremendous gesture that the first all-encompassing history of her family should be written by a woman, who in so doing not only meets the standard set by her ancestors to produce such a text, but also exceeds it, since her text focuses not merely on one figure or time, but rather accounts for everyone, assembling all the various stories and figures together. Everyone else has provided necessary threads, but she has woven them into a grand narrative tapestry.

— Matt Pieknik

The Lodge Women, Their Men and Their Times

For Dorine
Best Wishes
Emily Lodge
March, 2014

EMILY LODGE

Cover photo: Elizabeth Mathilda Frelinghuysen Davis Lodge (Bessy)

Printed in the United States of America.

First Edition.

ISBN 9780615937717

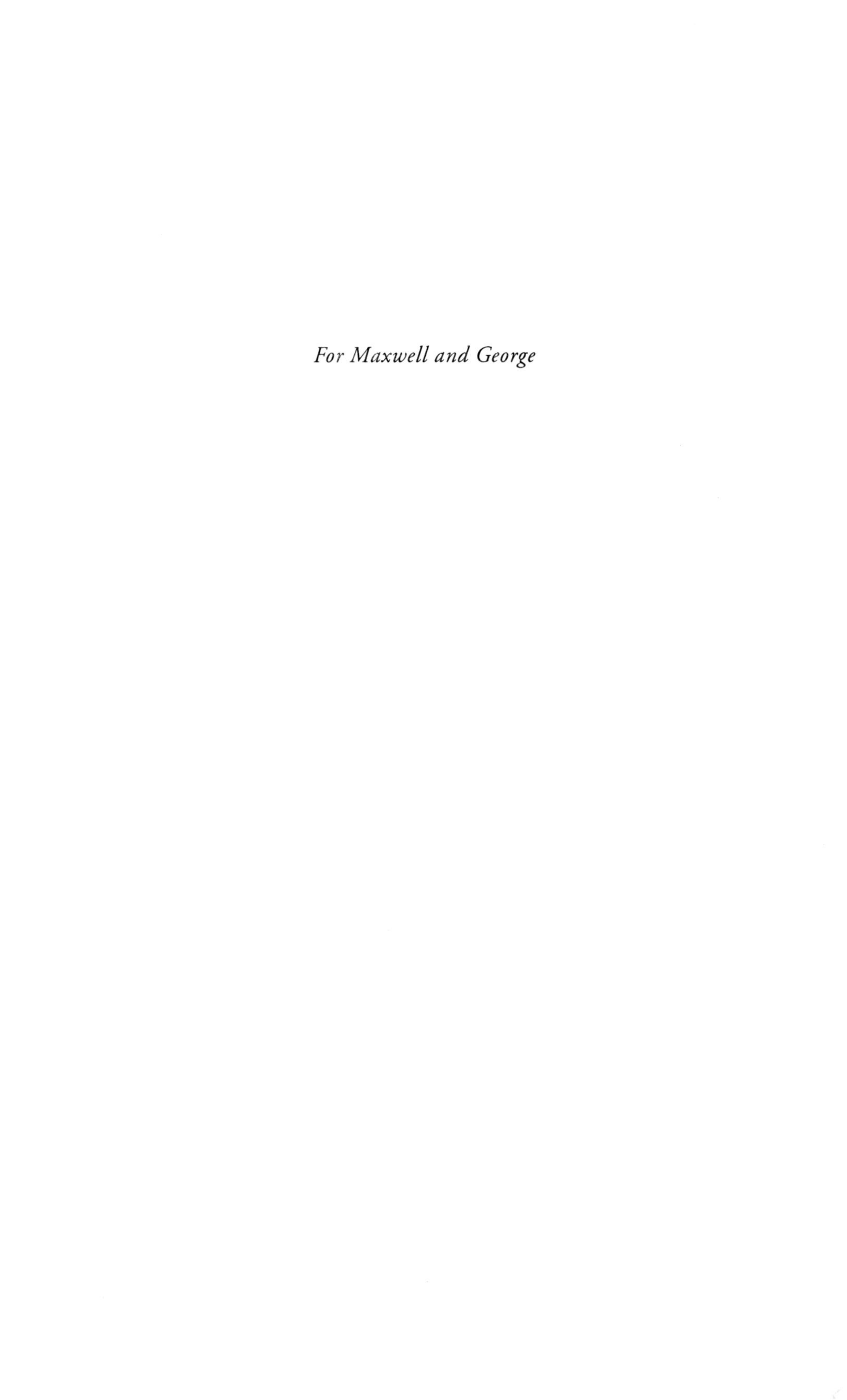

For Maxwell and George

Acknowledgments

With special thanks to my husband, Robert R. Pingeon, and our children, Maxwell and George, whose unwavering love and devotion made it possible for me to complete this work; also to my father, George Cabot Lodge for his numerous comments; my uncle, Henry Sears Lodge and his wife, Eleanita, whose brilliance and humor made the story come alive; to my late great Aunt Helena and her daughter, Elisabeth and grandchildren, Jean-Marc and Anne, without whose understanding, memories and anecdotes this history could not have been written.

I am grateful to my step-mother, Susan Powers Lodge, for her encouragement, and my sisters, Nancy and Dossy for their vivid memories and support; and also to my brothers, Cabot, George and David. For the invaluable help of a great gentleman, the late Stuart Preston, historian and former art critic for the New York Times, whose gentle guidance and profound insight into the period was of inestimable value. I am also grateful for the insights of the late Louis Auchincloss, the late John A. Garraty, and Patricia O'Toole; for the hard work and patience of my editor, Sally Arteseros and agent, the late Charles Everitt; to Matt Pieknik, copy editor and Beth Steidle, designer; and for the advice of Julie Winn, Robin Platt, Irene Stillman, and Elizabeth Graver. I am also indebted to the great actress and my dear friend, Olivia de Havilland, for the book's title. My thanks also go to Wallace Dailey and Heather Cole at the Theodore Roosevelt Collection of the Houghton Library, Harvard University, Holly Snyder, the Brown University Library and especially to Peter Drummey, and the entire staff of the Massachusetts Historical Society, for allowing me into the inner recesses of the Lodge and the Adams collections, and for their constant attentiveness, professionalism and support over the last decade and a half.

I have dedicated this book to our two sons, Maxwell and George, who having lived abroad all their lives, will learn more about their family. It is a tribute to my grandmother, Emily Sears Lodge, whose namesake I am. My beloved grandfather, Henry Cabot Lodge, was the person who guided me to take an interest in family history.

Contents

Prologue

If one asked me to what do I think one must principally attribute the singular prosperity and growing force of this people, I would answer that it is to the superiority of its women.

—Alexis de Tocqueville, *De la Démocratie en Amérique*

When I was living in Paris as a young mother, I was able to make trips to see Great Aunt Helena, the one whom I felt could unlock the mystery of the Lodge women and in particular, her mother, Elizabeth Frelinghuysen Davis Lodge, Bessy [cover photo], as she was generally known. On the train ride between Paris and Brussels, I watched the telephone poles tick by like the days, months and years of compiling research about thirteen generations of family history. Thanks to her cues and those of her children and grandchildren, as well as the stories of her nephews—my father and uncle—and many others, generations of family history have opened out like the folds of an accordion file.

Helena was always glad to see me. I had loved her brother, my grandfather, and I marveled at her resemblance to him in appearance and in forms of speech—old-fashioned English, flashes of enthusiasm, love of laughter and family, and perfect attention to detail—be it in conversation or at her immaculate table with silver and porcelain and white lace on polished mahogany. She underscored the importance of privacy, one of the central codes of the Lodge women, but also the importance of sympathy. As she looked into my questioning eyes and observed my patient and unswerving devotion to my research, she simply sighed and said, "You are so like *her*," referring to her mother, Bessy.

"Don't you see, they would have taken you right in," she said, implying that I was one of these women, and that I wanted to be taken in—and perhaps, that being taken in would somehow put me off my task. The paradox of the Lodge women—intensely private women who were also described by the men who knew them as "dauntless," "forbidding," or "terrifyingly powerful"—had a distinctly foreign ring. In this society, there are three times when a woman's name should appear in print; at birth, marriage, and death. Yet what if their deeds in service to their country rivaled those of their husbands? Finally, in grudging enthusiasm for my quest, Helena concluded, "To understand them, just think of your grandmother," referring to my grandmother, Emily Esther Sears. "She was just like them. *They were good wives.*"

Telling the story of the Lodge women proved impossible without their impressive men. In part I, the Senator and Mrs. Henry Cabot Lodge, Sr., Bessy's in-laws, dominate the picture as two Americans who stood at the pinnacle of power at the turn of the last century. Both the Senator and his wife, Nannie Lodge, expected and received deference, and Nannie tolerated what Henry Adams once called Cabot's "gargantuan selfishness." If Anna Cabot Lodge, the Senator's mother, instilled intense pride in her son for her paternal grandfather, George Cabot—a privateer in the American Revolution and a founder of the American Navy—Nannie made him a success. In part II, the Bay Lodges—the rebel poet son, George Cabot Lodge (1873-1909), and his beautiful wife, Bessy—take center stage. They were at odds with the Gilded Age, and conflicted about their relationship with the powerful Senator. Nannie inspired her son George, nicknamed "Bay" (as in "Ba-by") by his elder sister, Constance, to become a poet.

One glimpses the mysterious fascination of the Lodge women and their small, coveted world, in the independence and grandeur of a John Singer Sargent portrait or a Mary Cassatt reading to the children. Their authority seemed almost sacred and was often more powerful than that accorded to men. The mystery of the sacred feminine, engrained in our collective imagination from Venus to the cult of the Virgin, found expression in the Protestant ethic, self-reliance, and independent thought. Little is known about early American women; common knowledge has it that the culture of independent, educated women began in the twentieth century with Virginia Woolf and her essay, "A Room of One's Own." Yet the eighteenth and nineteenth century Lodge women were intellectuals and diplomats, not only engaging in sophisticated networking to further their husbands' careers but also acting as "ministers without portfolio" in their own right.

Among the photographs on the wall of the spiral staircase in my grandparents' house, the gleaming smile of an exquisite woman in a white dress embroidered with diamonds brilliantly stood out—Bessy, photographed in 1897.[1] Whenever I asked my grandfather about his mother there was a mysterious pause and then a quiet response, "She had a difficult life." Bessy seemed different from the other women who mostly stood behind the Lodge men. She bravely fought for what she believed in even if it was unpopular within the family. She didn't always play the game. She was a purist. The central tension of the book and its climax comes in Paris, 1912-14, between the Senator and his daughter-in-law, when he literally had her brought back to America. Henry Adams had begged Bessy to allow him to tell her story (to no avail); Henry James and Edith Wharton befriended both Mrs. Lodges (Nannie and Bessy); distinguished people doted on them and some fell in love with them. The Lodge women publicly avowed their immense ignorance. They would have said they were too lazy to write a book but they privately rewrote everything their men wrote. Behind their meek words stand women of iron who worked hard to become knowledgeable, who not only ruled from behind the scenes but made America greater for the men they loved.[2]

---

[1] Cover photo.

[2] The genealogical chart of my grandfather, Henry Cabot Lodge, helped me to create the family trees on the following pages.

THE LODGES

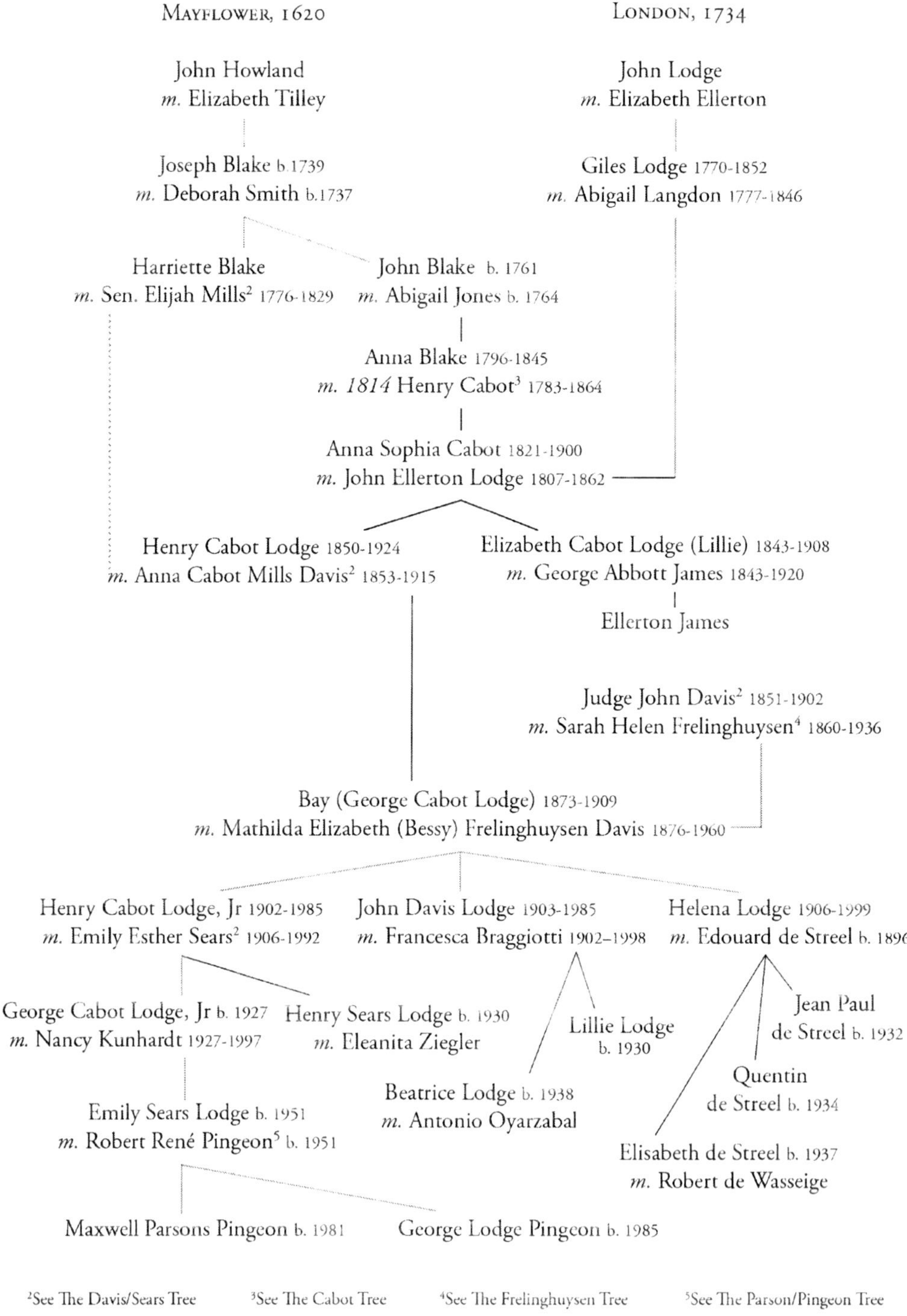

MAYFLOWER, 1620
LONDON, 1734
John Howland
m. Elizabeth Tilley
John Lodge
m. Elizabeth Ellerton
Joseph Blake b.1739
m. Deborah Smith b.1737
Giles Lodge 1770-1852
m. Abigail Langdon 1777-1846
Harriette Blake
m. Sen. Elijah Mills[2] 1776-1829
John Blake b. 1761
m. Abigail Jones b. 1764
Anna Blake 1796-1845
m. 1814 Henry Cabot[3] 1783-1864
Anna Sophia Cabot 1821-1900
m. John Ellerton Lodge 1807-1862
Henry Cabot Lodge 1850-1924
m. Anna Cabot Mills Davis[2] 1853-1915
Elizabeth Cabot Lodge (Lillie) 1843-1908
m. George Abbott James 1843-1920
Ellerton James
Judge John Davis[2] 1851-1902
m. Sarah Helen Frelinghuysen[4] 1860-1936
Bay (George Cabot Lodge) 1873-1909
m. Mathilda Elizabeth (Bessy) Frelinghuysen Davis 1876-1960
Henry Cabot Lodge, Jr 1902-1985
m. Emily Esther Sears[2] 1906-1992
John Davis Lodge 1903-1985
m. Francesca Braggiotti 1902–1998
Helena Lodge 1906-1999
m. Edouard de Streel b. 1896
George Cabot Lodge, Jr b. 1927
m. Nancy Kunhardt 1927-1997
Henry Sears Lodge b. 1930
m. Eleanita Ziegler
Lillie Lodge
b. 1930
Jean Paul
de Streel b. 1932
Quentin
de Streel b. 1934
Beatrice Lodge b. 1938
m. Antonio Oyarzabal
Emily Sears Lodge b. 1951
m. Robert René Pingeon[5] b. 1951
Elisabeth de Streel b. 1937
m. Robert de Wasseige
Maxwell Parsons Pingeon b. 1981
George Lodge Pingeon b. 1985

[2]See The Davis/Sears Tree [3]See The Cabot Tree [4]See The Frelinghuysen Tree [5]See The Parson/Pingeon Tree

THE DAVIS/SEARS FAMILY

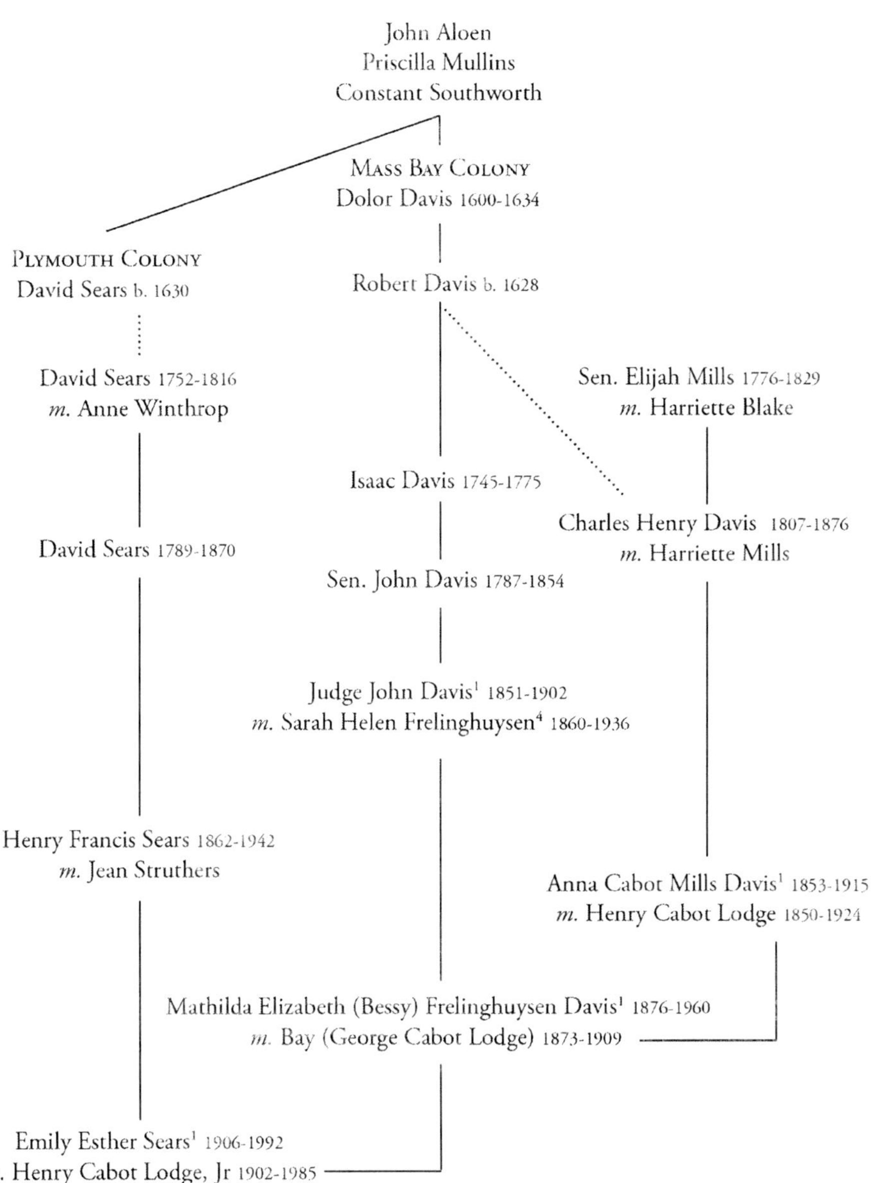
MAYFLOWER, 1620
John Aloen
Priscilla Mullins
Constant Southworth
MASS BAY COLONY
Dolor Davis 1600-1634
PLYMOUTH COLONY
David Sears b. 1630
Robert Davis b. 1628
David Sears 1752-1816
m. Anne Winthrop
Sen. Elijah Mills 1776-1829
m. Harriette Blake
Isaac Davis 1745-1775
Charles Henry Davis 1807-1876
m. Harriette Mills
David Sears 1789-1870
Sen. John Davis 1787-1854
Judge John Davis[1] 1851-1902
m. Sarah Helen Frelinghuysen[4] 1860-1936
Henry Francis Sears 1862-1942
m. Jean Struthers
Anna Cabot Mills Davis[1] 1853-1915
m. Henry Cabot Lodge 1850-1924
Mathilda Elizabeth (Bessy) Frelinghuysen Davis[1] 1876-1960
m. Bay (George Cabot Lodge) 1873-1909
Emily Esther Sears[1] 1906-1992
m. Henry Cabot Lodge, Jr 1902-1985

[1]See The Lodges Tree [4]See The Frelinghuysen Tree

THE CABOTS

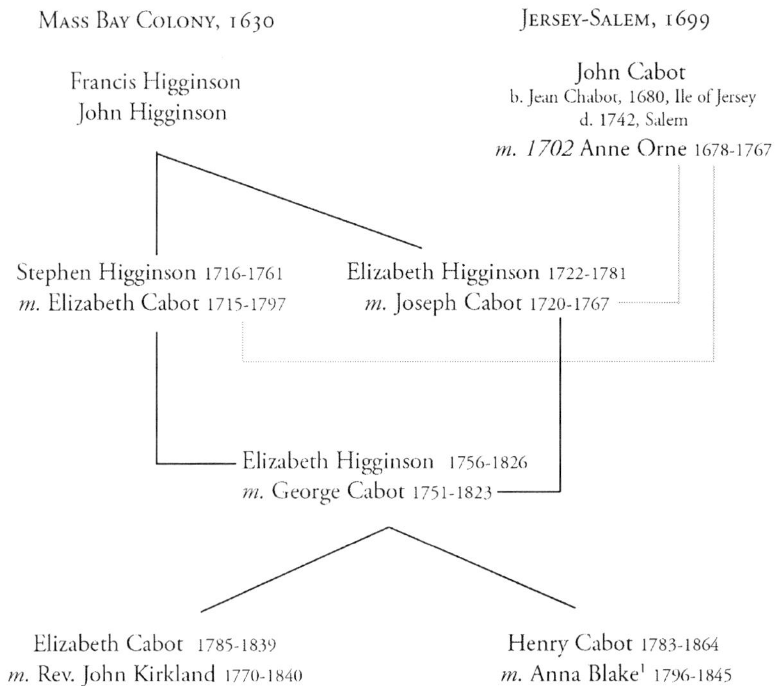

Mass Bay Colony, 1630
Jersey-Salem, 1699
Francis Higginson
John Higginson
John Cabot
b. Jean Chabot, 1680, Ile of Jersey
d. 1742, Salem
m. 1702 Anne Orne 1678-1767
Stephen Higginson 1716-1761
m. Elizabeth Cabot 1715-1797
Elizabeth Higginson 1722-1781
m. Joseph Cabot 1720-1767
Elizabeth Higginson 1756-1826
m. George Cabot 1751-1823
Elizabeth Cabot 1785-1839
m. Rev. John Kirkland 1770-1840
Henry Cabot 1783-1864
m. Anna Blake[1] 1796-1845

[1]See The Lodges Tree

THE FRELINGHUYSENS

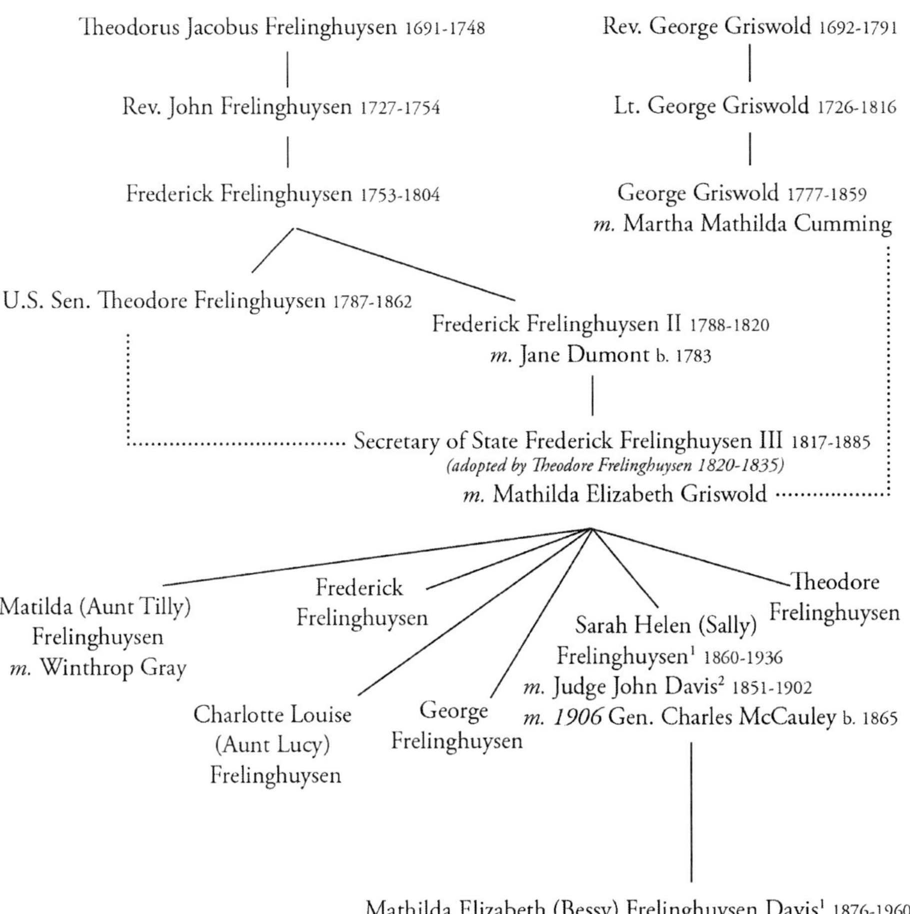

Geertie de NYC, 1685
Theodorus Jacobus Frelinghuysen 1691-1748
Rev. George Griswold 1692-1791
Rev. John Frelinghuysen 1727-1754
Lt. George Griswold 1726-1816
Frederick Frelinghuysen 1753-1804
George Griswold 1777-1859
m. Martha Mathilda Cumming
U.S. Sen. Theodore Frelinghuysen 1787-1862
Frederick Frelinghuysen II 1788-1820
m. Jane Dumont b. 1783
Secretary of State Frederick Frelinghuysen III 1817-1885
(adopted by Theodore Frelinghuysen 1820-1835)
m. Mathilda Elizabeth Griswold
Matilda (Aunt Tilly) Frelinghuysen
m. Winthrop Gray
Frederick Frelinghuysen
Charlotte Louise (Aunt Lucy) Frelinghuysen
George Frelinghuysen
Sarah Helen (Sally) Frelinghuysen[1] 1860-1936
m. Judge John Davis[2] 1851-1902
m. 1906 Gen. Charles McCauley b. 1865
Theodore Frelinghuysen
Mathilda Elizabeth (Bessy) Frelinghuysen Davis[1] 1876-1960
m. Bay (George Cabot Lodge) 1873-1909

[1]See The Lodges Tree [2]See The Davis/Sears Tree

THE PARSONS/PINGEONS

Plymouth Colony

Gov. William Bradford 1589/90-1657
m. Alice Carpenter b. 1670

|

William Bradford Jr 1624-1703/04
m. Alice Richards 1627-1671

|

Hannah Bradford 1662-1738
m. Joshua Ripley 1658-1739

|

Alice Ripley 1683-1730
m. Samuel Edgerton 1670-1748

|

Joshua Edgerton 1707/08-1779
m. Ruth Kingsbury 1712/13-1769

|

Eleazer Edgerton 1748-1820
m. Sarah Hyde 1754-1824

|

Uriah Edgerton 1780-1868
m. Lydia Fay 1778-1838

|

Caroline Althea Edgerton 1813-1900
m. Norman Bingham Hinsdill 1811-1840

|

Ellen Edgerton Hinsdill 1835-1896
m. James Russell Parsons 1830-1899

|

James Russell Parsons Jr 1861-1905
m. Frances Theodora Smith 1861-1952

|

James Russell Parsons III 1896-1970
m. Margaret Alice Chubb 1901-1976

|

Frances Theodora Parsons 1926-1999
m. René Andre Henri Pingeon 1918-

|

Robert René
Pingeon[1] 1951-
m. Emily Lodge

Maxwell Pingeon | George Pingeon 1985-

[1]See The Lodges Tree

Part 1

Chapter I

Ancestral Portraits

George Cabot

In 1699, three brothers—Jean, François, and Georges Chabot—emigrated from the Ile of Jersey off the coast of Normandy to Salem, Massachusetts. "Les trois chabots," in the Jersey phrase, were fishing merchants, probably seeking the quantities of cod off the Georges Banks.[3] The Cabots were so renowned that "cabotage" in French is the word for coastal trade or shipping. *The Life and Letters of George Cabot*, the first of the Senator's twenty-nine histories, written just after college and dedicated to his mother, traces the family's origins. Upon arrival in Salem, the three Chabot anglicized their name to Cabot. The crest of that great French family, Rohan-Chabot—three red fish on a yellow background—almost identical to that of Georges, François, and Jean Cabot—is the crest of Cabot House at Harvard University.[4]

Henry Cabot Lodge writes:

> Among the names on the 'auncient role,' given by Stow,[5] of "the chiefe Noblemen & Gentlemen, which came into England with William the Conqueror," is that of Cabot.... Modern research has traced the numerous branches of the Cabot family back to one stem, which has flourished in the Island of Jersey.... It is mere conjecture to connect William's follower with those of like name in the Channel Islands; but

---

[3] Samuel Eliot Morison, *Maritime History of Massachusetts, 1783-1860* (Boston: Houghton Mifflin, 1921), 13-14.

[4] The Cabot coat of arms bore the inscription, "Semper Cor Caput Cabot." Vicomte Olivier Rohan-Chabot, a descendant, and one of the organizers of the Friends of Versailles, told me, "If you can show me the crest, I can show you how you can trace your ancestry to Charlemagne."

[5] John Stow, *Annales, or a General Chronicle of England* (London, 1631), 107. The original title reads, "Cognomina Conquisitorum Angliae cum Domino Gulielmo Duce Normanniae et Conquisitore Angliae."

the conjecture has the merit of probability, since the Normans had possessed the Island long before the memorable year 1066. Many centuries intervened before the world heard of another Cabot... the great navigators, John and Sebastian.... To the connection of John and Sebastian Cabot[6] with the discovery of this continent is probably due the claim of descent from them that has been made by American Cabots, but for which there is no sufficient foundation. The only evidence ever adduced in its support has been a chance resemblance in face and feature, on an heirloom... a mourning ring, over two hundred years old, with the name "Sebastian Cabot" engraved upon it, now in the possession of the late C.C. Foster of Cambridge....

The Cabots, like their northern ancestors, were a wandering race; and, as the channel island offered no field for advancement, the more adventurous spirits were driven out into the world to seek their fortune. The nationality even of John Cabot, the discoverer, is still uncertain for modern investigation has cast doubt upon the usually accepted story of his Venetian birth.[7] His course of life and personal characteristics would lead us to suppose him of the island race; and this supposition is converted into certainty by the identity of arms and motto, as borne by the French descendants of the discoverer, with those of the Jersey family.[8] Armorial de Languedoc states the Jersey and American Cabots to be of the same family as the navigators. Such a relationship is purely theoretical. About 1699, the registry of deeds at St. Heliers bears witness that the three sons sold a large amount of real estate and soon afterward, they emigrated to America. The New England family came from Jersey, where there are two parishes still inhabited almost exclusively by Cabots, not unlike a Scottish clan. The coat of arms of the Jersey family is perfectly defined and well-known. The device is three fishes, or, in the Jersey phrase, "trois chabots." The fishes are found crossed with the Rohan arms, when one of that great family married a Chabot of Poitou, and one of the most distinguished branches of the same

---

[6] John Cabot and his son Sebastian, the Venetian navigators, engaged by the English Court in the Fifteenth century to continue to find a path to the Orient, followed the path of Christopher Columbus to the New World.

[7] Rawdon Brown, *Calendar of State Papers in the Archives of Venice*, 1202-1509, §§ 743 and 753; Nicholls, *Life of Sebastian Cabot* (London: Nicholls, 1869).

[8] Armorial de Languedoc, L. de la Roque, Tome II, 163. The French Cabots trace their descent from Louis, John Cabot's second son. M. de la Roque says Sebastian died without issue, but gives no proof of this assertion. He also states the Jersey and American Cabots to be of the same family as the navigators. The identity of arms and motto can leave but little doubt on this last point.

family is Rohan-Chabot.[9] The arms of the Poitou Chabots and the Jersey Chabots are almost identical, and they probably had a common origin. They were born by an Italian Cardinal of the last century and they are still preserved unaltered by the family in America.The Cabots of St. Trinity have been linked with both the Chabots of Poitou and the Cabots of Normandy. Some time in the latter half of the seventeenth century, François Cabot, of St. Trinity, a large landowner and wealthy man, married Suzanne Gruchy. In 1677, a son of theirs was baptized George in the St. Heliers Church; whose records show that three years later another son received the name of Jean. There was also an older son, whose baptism is not recorded, named François.[10]

By 1766, New England fisheries reached their peak. From 1740 to the Revolution, Boston declined slightly in population but the smaller seaports increased in size. "A glance at the Georgian mansions of Michael Dalton and Jonathan Jackson at Newburyport; of John Heard at Ipswich; of Winthrop Sargent at Gloucester; of George Cabot at Beverly... will convince the most skeptical that wealth and good taste came out of the sea, into these little towns.... Marblehead in 1744 had ninety vessels in active service, two hundred acres covered with fish-flakes, and an annual catch worth £34,000. In 1765, with just under five thousand inhabitants, it was the sixth town in the thirteen colonies; behind Newport, but ahead of Salem, Baltimore and Albany."[11]

The Senator was careful to say of his ancestors that they were "public-spirited [merchants] without self-advertisement." Before the end of the eighteenth century, Boston and Salem were no mere market towns for salt fish and country produce but *entre-pôts* of world commerce.[12] "The most formidable rival to Boston in the contest for oriental wealth lay but sixteen miles "to the east'd," as we say on the Massachusetts coast when we mean north. Salem, with a little under eight thousand

[9] See Etat Présent de la Noblesse Française. Bachelin de Florenne, art. *Rohan-Chabot,* 4eme ed., (1873-1874), 1601.

[10] Of François nothing is known after his arrival in America, except the bare fact that he was a ship-owner and merchant with his brother George, the latter a tax-payer in Salem in 1700, and was also described as a joiner (a mason). Soon after his arrival George Cabot (John Cabot's brother) made a good marriage, obtaining the hand of Abigail Marston of Salem, whose father built the first brick house in Salem, the mason and builder of which was George Cabot. The presumption is strong that the first George Cabot was a jack of all trades and master of none... for at his death his brother John administered *de bonis non.*

[11] Morison, 22.

[12] Ibid., 161.

inhabitants, was the sixth city in the United States in 1790."[13]

George Cabot's grandparents—John Cabot and Anna Orne, masons in Salem—had a named son, Joseph, who married Elizabeth Higginson, a descendant of Francis Higginson, first minister of the Massachusetts Bay Colony (1630); they had nine sons and two daughters. The seventh child and fifth son, George Cabot, was born on January 16, 1751. George displayed such proficiency in his studies that in 1766 his father sent him to Harvard College, even though the custom was that only the eldest son usually went to school.

George Cabot was tall, more than six feet, large and powerfully built, handsome and with an expression of dignity and repose. He had a low, musical voice, but one of great power. His manners were gentle and courteous, and he wore his hair without powder, drawn back, and tied in a queue. He dressed in black in knee britches with silk stockings. Two years after George entered college, his father died. At eighteen, says historian Daniel Boorstin, George was commander of a codfishing vessel.[14] Samuel Eliot Morison states that in eighteenth century America, going into business meant going to sea on the parental ship, "or, if they cared not for business, to Harvard College."[15] In fact, George's case was the opposite: he cared not for the rarified Harvard environment and chose to follow his ambition at sea, although this did not keep him from studying Greek, Latin, French, Spanish, metaphysics and political economy onboard.

George Cabot. Photograph of the painting courtesy of George Cabot Lodge, Jr.

> Expelled from Harvard for disciplinary reasons, George Cabot went to sea aboard his [brother-in-law, Joseph Lee's] ship to tame his erratic nature and

[13] Ibid., 79.
[14] Daniel Boorstin, *The National Experience* (New York, NY, Vintage, 1965), 7.
[15] Morison, 25.

> learn the business. As a trader before the American Revolution, George Cabot earned a reputation for aggressiveness. When war broke out, he exploited it as a privateer. Rich before the age of thirty, Cabot entered politics after the Revolution, first as a founder of the North Shore Essex Junto and later as United States Senator from Massachusetts. Cabot strongly endorsed Alexander Hamilton's economic policies and through associations with Hamilton, Washington, John Adams and Fisher Ames, he influenced the policies of the Federalist Party. When the power of the Federalists waned, George Cabot feared the subjugation of New England interests to those of the South and West. His consequent involvement in the Hartford Convention of 1814 elicited angry reproach from his old ally (John) Adams: 'He wants to be president of New England, sir.'[16]

George Cabot became a privateer, transforming his fishing vessels into vessels of war, and profiting from the arrangement with a "letter of marque" from George Washington to raid British ships. The colonies had no navy, so Congress gave private merchants the right to take any British ship and split the profits with the Continental Congress; the American navy was born and the family profited handsomely.

> Six hundred and twenty-six letters of marque were issued to Massachusetts vessels by the Continental Congress, and some thousand more by the General Court. Privateers... a form of legalized piracy... were of little use in naval operations... but they were of very greatest service in preying on the enemy's commerce, intercepting his communications with America, carrying terror and destruction into the very chops of the Channel, and supplying the patriot army with munitions, stores and clothing at Johnny Bull's expense. From an economic and social viewpoint, privateering employed the fishermen and all those who depended on shipping; taught daring seamanship, and strengthened our maritime aptitude and tradition.[17]

---

[16] Karl Schriftgiesser, *The Gentleman from Massachusetts: Henry Cabot Lodge* (Boston: Little, Brown, 1944), 11. Quoted in John W. Crowley, *The Education of George Cabot Lodge*, (Bloomington: Indiana University Press, 1970). At the Hartford Convention (1814-15), Federalists met to discuss President Jefferson's anti-foreign trade measures with Great Britain in 1807 and 1809, and the unpopular War of 1812 with New England giving the federal government minimal support. They also discussed the Louisiana Purchase, and their opposition to the growing congressional influence of the southern and western states. The extremists' proposals of secession from the union and a separate peace with Great Britain never became a major focus of debate at the convention.

[17] Morison, 29-30.

What made George Cabot's ships special was their versatility; the designs of his merchant ships were easily adapted to the requirements of war, as the drawings and sketches in the family collection demonstrate. "Privateers required speed; and the Massachusetts builders, observing, it is said, the scientifically designed vessels of our French allies, did away with high quarterdecks, eased water-lines, and substituted a nearly U-shaped cross-section for the barrel-shaped bottom and unseemly tumble-home of the old-style ships. Commerce continued with the West Indies, France and Spain in letter of marque ships, armed merchantmen with a license to take prizes on the side.... On the back side of Cape Cod, whalemen with swivel-armed boats kept watch over Nantucket and Vineyard Sounds, the sea-lane to the British base in New York. With an impudent daring that astounded the enemy, they swooped down on his vessels when becalmed."[18]

During the Revolution, George Cabot and his brothers operated an extensive and profitable privateering business out of Bilbao, Spain, and between 1775 and 1780, George Cabot became the richest man in New England. In Essex County (of which the town of Beverly is part), a loyalist named Curwen wrote in her journal: "The Cabots of Beverly who, you know, had but five years ago a very moderate share of property, are now said to be by far the most wealthy in New England."[19] The English had a price on George Cabot's head—in other words, they wanted him hanged.

Colonel John Trumbull says in his reminiscences that he took passage at Bilbao for Beverly in 1781 in *The Cicero*, a fine letter of marque ship of twenty guns and one hundred and twenty men, commanded by Captain Hill, belonging to the house of Cabot. When Colonel Trumbull joined the ship, she had with her a British Lisbon packet of sixteen guns which she had just taken as a prize. On his arrival at Beverly, Colonel Trumbull saw eleven privateers lying in the harbor all finer than *The Cicero* and all belonging to the Cabots. The following year the same writer speaks of being in Beverly again and adds that not one of the privateers was seen in the harbor. All had been lost and the Cabots did not have a single letter of marque ship afloat. Many of these vessels belonged to John and Andrew who, like their brother George, were also Beverly merchants.[20]

---

[18] Ibid., 29.
[19] Henry Cabot Lodge, *The Life and Letters of George Cabot*, (Boston: Little, Brown, 1878), 13.
[20] Ibid., 13, 14; Trumbull, *Reminiscences*, 84. Sketches exist in the archives—George Cabot's doodling of his ships—as illustrations.

Chastellux, in *Travels in North America* notes:

> The town of Beverly began to flourish greatly toward the conclusion of the war by the extraordinary spirit of enterprise and success of Messrs. Cabot, gentlemen of strong understanding and the most liberal minds, well-adapted to the most enlarged commercial undertakings and the business of government. Two of their privateers had the good fortune to capture in the European seas, a few weeks previous to the peace, several ships to the value of at least 100,000 pounds sterling.[21]

As Daniel Boortstin writes, "The sea was a path direct from Old and New England, from Babylon to Zion. It was both a waterway from colony to mother country and a gulf that separated colonists from poverty, decadence and dynastic conflict. It was the highway to the world.... The commerce of the sea demanded versatility. It called for quick decisions and the willingness to jettison unprofitable cargo." The New England "versatiles" as he called them, traded in tea, copal for varnish, rubber, sandalwood, otterskin, linseed oil, and peppercorns.[22] In 1784, one of George Cabot's ships carried the first American flag to St. Petersburg in Russia. "Since New England had no ancient trading companies nor any rigid tradition of adventure, her enterprise was controlled by upstart Cabots, Jacksons, Lees, Higginsons and Perkinses, ingenious at finding their own markets and making their own ways."

In 1774, George Cabot married another Elizabeth Higginson (1756-1826), also a direct descendant, sixth generation of Reverend Francis Higginson, and her husband's double first cousin. Five of their eight children died young. Only two survived to adulthood their sixth, Henry, who lived to eighty-one years (1783-1864), and their eighth child, Elizabeth (1785-1839).[23] The name of George's daughter, Elizabeth, who later married a president of Harvard University, was discovered in the Higginson, not the Lodge, family papers. Her mother, Mrs. George Cabot, born Elizabeth Higginson, was a brilliant and attractive woman but her health weakened with the death of each child. There is one excellent record of her character, a tribute written

---

[21] François-Jean de Chastellux, *Travels in North-America, in the Years 1780, 1781, and 1782*, vol. II, trans. George Grieve (London, 1787), 252, 253.

[22] Boorstein, 5-9.

[23] Source: Massachusetts Historical Society. The children were: George (1775-1788); Charles (1777-1811); Elizabeth (1779-1780); Henry (1780-1783); Elizabeth (1782-1783); Henry (1783-1864); Edward (1784-1803); Elizabeth (1785-1839).

by her nephew, John Lowell, to her father, Stephen Higginson, at her death, July 17, 1826. Because of the historical rarity of a personal account of an eighteenth century American woman, it is quoted in full:

> It is not the course of the world to estimate justly female merit. The present age is somewhat more correct in this respect; but still many an accomplished woman, with high and elevated powers, passes off the stage with little notice, while a man of far inferior natural powers, from the adventitious circumstance of his having held offices which a female of great talents would have better sustained, fills the world for a time with his posthumous praises. I do not quarrel with this state of public feeling, because it was part of the wide system of Providence that the province of the two sexes should be separate. Still, however, that same Providence occasionally permits that some gifted females should appear, who seem by their talents calculated to rule rather than obey. Of this last description was our revered departed friend.
>
> She had **all the firmness, vigor, resolution, penetration, capacity to form and express her thoughts in a strong, clear and masculine style, which are found in men of the firmest, boldest and most elevated temperament and mind. If she had been called like (Queen) Elizabeth (I) to stations of great power, she would have been like her, prudent, energetic, and commanding. She had none of the advantages of early education afforded so bountifully to the young ladies of the present age**[24]; but she surpassed *all* of them in the acuteness of her observation, in the knowledge of human nature, and in her powers of expressing and defending the opinions which she formed. Without systematic knowledge, her mind was filled with information on every topic interesting to us in this world. No doubt she derived great benefit from the intercourse with one of the most luminous minds of the age with whom for nearly fifty years she

[24] Emma Willard (1787-1870) in 1821 founded the first school for women's higher education, The Troy Female Seminary in Troy, New York, renamed the Emma Willard School in 1895. In 1819, she wrote a pamphlet entitled "A Plan for Improving Female Education," proposing public funding, equal to men's schools. She believed women should be taught world politics, philosophy, and mathematics, then primarily male subjects. Emma Willard told the New York legislature that the education of women "has been too exclusively directed to fit them for displaying to advantage the charms of youth and beauty." The problem, she said, was that "the taste of men, whatever it might happen to be, has been made into a standard for the formation of the female character." Reason and religion teach us, she said, that "we too are primary existences... not the satellites of men." Mount Holyoke, est. 1837, was the first women's college and served as a model for the other "Seven Sisters," one of which was Wellesley, est. 1870, Nannie's alma mater.

> was associated (her husband, George). With these great qualities, for great they were, she had a full share of all the virtues of her sex. Her firmness and resolution were mingled with kindness and tenderness and affection for her own children and numerous friends.[25]

Elizabeth Cabot was often with child during the American Revolution. She kept the family books, cared for her young family and in anticipation of George's return, paced the widow's walk on top of the house at Beverly whose lawn reached down to the harbor, one year full of ships and the next year empty. Her husband had been born at a time when talent met with opportunity.

Between 1780 and 1788, there were no political parties in the U.S. The war had just ceased, and in the fledgling legislatures all had been Whigs or patriots. Holding together the country fell on the shoulders of President George Washington. In January of 1781 Cabot served on the subcommittees of the state constitutional convention and he was one of what was described as the "Essex Junto" which held political power in Massachusetts for more than a quarter century. The (future) Senator gave an honest depiction of them:

> The men of Essex were descendants of those who, in the dark days of 1629, followed Endicott [John, English colonial magistrate and governor of the Massachusetts Bay Colony, led the first expedition of sixty men to what would come Salem] into the wilderness. They were of the oldest Puritan stock. Strong, honest, in many cases of an almost reckless courage, they were sagacious in civil and bold in military life. But their intellectual vigor and clear perceptions were in many instances combined with great mental narrowness and rigidity.[26]

Shortly after the new constitution went into effect, Cabot was chosen as a State Senator from Essex County. In the winter of 1782, there were violent debates in the Senate and the Assembly during which, Chastellux commented, "Cabot, a very sensible man and a rich merchant of Beverly, distinguished himself on this occasion by a speech full of eloquence and wit." Although urged to continue in office, he declined re-election in 1783. In 1784, he became a director of the Bank of Massachusetts and was involved in the development of the Beverly Cotton manufactory. The young nation was developing independence in building her own looms to produce cotton. In 1789, George Cabot invited President

[25] Henry Cabot Lodge, *Life and Letters*, 12.
[26] Ibid., 18.

George Washington to stop at his house for rest and refreshment, while the latter was on a visit to Massachusetts and New Hampshire. The story of their breakfast together, documented in the President's diary, lived long in the history of the family. George Cabot's letter:

> Beverly
> October 24, 1789
> *Sir:*
> The public papers having announced "that the President of the United States is on his way to Portsmouth in New Hampshire," it immediately occurred to me that your route would be through *this village*, and that you might find it convenient to stop here and take a little rest: should this prove to be the case, permit me, Sir, to hope for your acceptance of such accommodation and refreshment as can be furnished in my humble dwelling, where two or three beds would be at your disposal.
> I am fully aware that by indulging this hope I expose myself to the imputation of vanity as well as ambition and therefore should hardly dare to have my conduct tried by the cool maxims of the head alone, but would rather refer it to the dictates of my heart, which, in the most affecting concerns of life, I believe to be a sure guide to what is right.
>
> I have the honor, Sir, to be with sentiments of the most profound respect your devoted and humble servant.
>
> *George Cabot*

From George Washington's diary:

> Oct. 30, 1789
> After passing Beverley 2 Miles we come to the Cotton Manufactury [sic] which seems to be carrying on with Spirit by the Mr. Cabots (principally). In this Manufactory they have the New Invented Carding and Spinning Machines—one of the first supplies the work; and four of the latter; one of which spins 84 threads at a time by one person.[27]

In June 1791, George Cabot was chosen without opposition to be U.S. Senator from Massachusetts to succeed Tristram Dalton, the other Massachusetts Senator at this time being Caleb Strong. When Cabot

---

[27] The Beverly Cotton Manufactory was established in 1787-88 with John Cabot and Joshua Fisher as managers and George and Andrew Cabot as leading stockholders. In its early years the factory received considerable encouragement from the state legislature—a grant of land in 1789 and a state lottery in 1791. It was incorporated Feb. 3, 1789. Source: *Life and Letters of George Cabot.*

took his seat, the Federalist Party had begun to crystallize and had become supporters of the government. Jefferson on his return from Europe had practically come out as chief of the opposition. Although he continued to hold the first cabinet office and was still a nominal supporter of the administration, he later branded Adams and Hamilton with the stigma of monarchism. Cabot served on the committee on the mint, on appropriations and on the committee for establishing a consular system. He was a free-trade advocate believing in moderate use of protection in exceptional cases, especially tariffs on cotton.

In 1795, at age forty-four, Cabot resigned from the Senate to lead "a perfect retired life." With a sufficient fortune, he left Beverly for Brookline, Massachusetts, to a comfortable house that stood by a narrow country lane. It was named "Greenhill" and is still standing. Cabot had hardly returned to Brookline when he was recalled to Philadelphia for the ratification of the Jay Treaty, which effected a peace with England that Cabot vehemently supported.

In that year, during the Reign of Terror, America did not have diplomatic relations with France.[28] If President Washington could not receive Gênet, the French envoy, since it would mean tacit acceptance of the slaughter or imprisonment of friends, sometimes heroes, of America, neither could he receive young Lafayette, the son of the hero of the American Revolution, who fled to the United States for safety when the elder Lafayette was imprisoned in Austria. At the same time, Washington's deep affection for his comrade in arms urged him to do everything for the son. In this dilemma, Washington determined to entrust the care of young Lafayette, then in Boston, under the assumed name of Motier, to George Cabot. Cabot, whose French was flawless, became Lafayette's son's guardian in America at a time when President Washington hesitated to assist the young Lafayette openly. He wrote to young Lafayette, explaining his own difficult position and the reasons for his leaving such a matter to another's care. President Washington also wrote to Cabot:

WASHINGTON TO CABOT

(Private and Confidential)

Philadelphia, 7th Sept., 1795
DEAR SIR,
The enclosed letters (which after reading, be so good as to return to me)

[28] See appendix for more on Gênet and Jefferson.

> will be the best apology I can offer for the liberty I am about to take, and for the trouble, if you comply with my request, it must necessarily give.
>
> To express all the sensibility which has been excited in my breast by the receipt of young Fayette's letter, from the recollection of his father's merits, services and suffering, from my friendship for him, and from my wishes to become a friend and father to his son, are unnecessary.[29]

When Gênet, the French minister, discovered Lafayette in Cambridge and attempted to use him to gain access to the President, the boy and his tutor were quickly sent on to New York where, even then, anonymity was more easily guaranteed than in Cambridge. Cabot relinquished his charge to his friend Alexander Hamilton, who at the request of the President, watched over the young exile until the time arrived when he could with safety enter the President's family.

A country residence in Brookline meant complete separation from life in Boston, five miles away, and separation from members of his family obliged Cabot to live in the city. Charles, his eldest son, had gone to sea and long voyages to the East Indies permitted rare and distant visits home. This caused Mr. and Mrs. Cabot to cling even more closely to their other children. Henry (1783-1864) and Edward (1784-1803) were, respectively, in a law office and a counting house in Boston and unable to be with their parents except for Sundays.

George and Mrs. Cabot's daughter, Elizabeth (1785-1839), was only mentioned in the Senator's memoir because she was the impetus for Cabot's decision to move to Boston. George Cabot did not think that his only daughter, then just entering womanhood, should for six months of the year be entirely cut off from all society. With great reluctance he sold his farm and, in early 1803, moved to Boston where he passed the rest of his life. Elizabeth married Reverend John Kirkland (1770-1840), fifteen years her senior and the future president of Harvard University (1810-1828).[30] Cabot's youngest son, Edward, died at age nineteen in the same year, and six months later occurred the tragic and untimely death of Alexander Hamilton, an intimate friend and the last hope for the Federalist Party.

In 1797, at the moment when John Adams succeeded General Washington to the Presidency, Cabot understood that the Essex Junto had opposed Adams' election because of his pride, his vanity, and his

---

[29] President Washington's entire letter is appendixed.

[30] Thomas Wentworth Higginson, *Descendants of the Reverend Francis Higginson, First "Teacher" in the Massachusetts Bay Colony of Salem, Massachusetts and Author of "New-England's Plantation"* (Private printing, 1910).

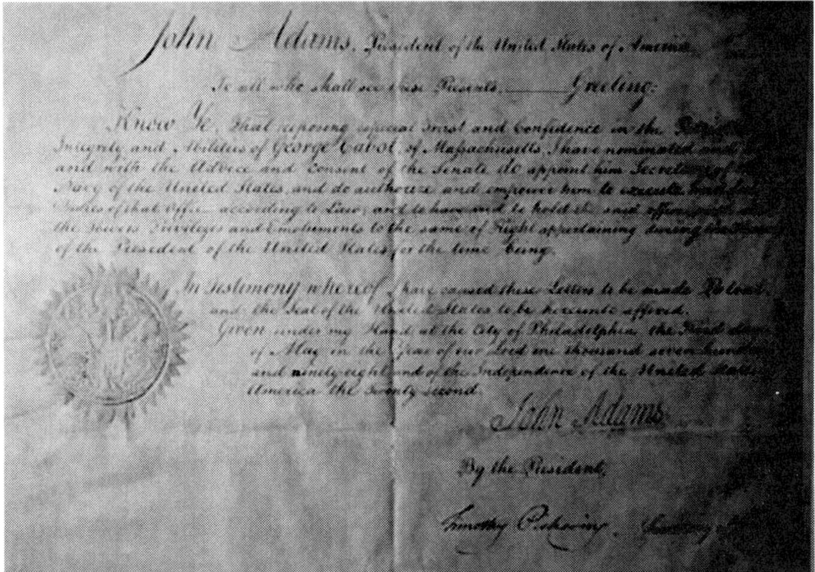

John Adams, President of the United States of America,

To all who shall see these Presents, Greeting:

Know Ye, That reposing special Trust and Confidence in the Patriotism, Integrity and Abilities of George Cabot of Massachusetts I have nominated and by and with the Advice and Consent of the Senate do appoint him Secretary of the Navy of the United States, and do authorize and empower him to execute and fulfil the Duties of that Office according to Law; and to have and to hold the said office with all the Powers, Privileges and Emoluments to the same of Right appertaining during the pleasure of the President of the United States for the time being.

In Testimony whereof I have caused these Letters to be made Patent and the Seal of the United States to be hereunto affixed. Given under my Hand at the City of Philadelphia the [illegible] day of May in the Year of our Lord one thousand seven hundred and ninety eight and of the Independence of the United States of America the twenty second.

John Adams

By the President,

Timothy Pickering, Secretary

Photograph of Adams' appointment of Cabot to Secretary of the Navy, courtesy of George Cabot Lodge, Jr.

eccentricities.[31] Nevertheless, interestingly, in 1798, President John Adams nominated the "Boston Patriot," George Cabot, to be Secretary of the Navy (perhaps because as a privateer, he had helped to create the American Navy), but according to the letters of Colonel Pickering, Cabot declined the honor and retired to a life of letters.[32]

A patriot of the Revolution, Cabot was also one of the most ardent advocates of the Constitution. Quoting a 1843 speech Daniel Webster gave before the New England Society of New York, the Senator recalls, "The mention of the father of my friend, Mr. Goodhue, brings to mind the memory of his great colleague, the early associate of Hamilton and [Fisher] Ames, trusted and beloved by Washington, consulted on all occasions, connected with the administration of the finances; the establishment of the treasury department, the imposition of the first rates of duty and with every thing that belonged to the commercial system of the United States—George Cabot of Massachusetts."[33] In *Life and Letters*, the Senator seems to share George Cabot's aversion to pure democracy and to favor a governing class:

---

[31] From The National Intelligencer, 1806. Quoted in Lodge, *The Life and Letters of George Cabot Lodge*, 21.

[32] Henry Cabot Lodge, in *The Life and Letters of George Cabot*, maintains that Cabot held the post for one month then retired to intellectual pursuits. See appendix for his essays.

[33] Lodge, *Early Memories*, 10.

Like Hamilton, (Cabot) desired a government possessing both vigor and energy and though he believed an infusion of democracy essential, he thought a governing class likewise essential to success. Bitterly opposed to all the doctrines of the French Revolution, his natural aversion to a pure democracy was thereby increased.... He sincerely believed that no pure democracy could long be successful or could sufficiently protect the rights of property and of the individual. In the election of Jefferson he believed that the ascendancy of pure democratic theories was assured and that this evil was radical.

Cabot since 1804 had occupied in his party a position similar to that of Jefferson in the Republican Party after 1808. From Brookline, as from Monticello, the active party leaders received letters that spoke with authority. Easily the intellectual leader of his party since the death of Hamilton, George Cabot in his study at Brookline, saw what no other Federalist had the wisdom to see, that a page of democratic evolution had been turned and the days of democratic ascendancy had passed, never to return.[34]

[34] Morison, quoted in Lodge, *Early Memories*, 9.

Anna Sophia Blake and Henry Cabot

MASSACHUSETTS SOCIETY OF MAYFLOWER DESCENDANTS 1620-1920

1. John Howland married Elizabeth Tilley; both were *Mayflower* passengers.
2. Their daughter Hope Howland married John Chipman.
3. Their son John Chipman married Mary Skiff.
4. Their daughter Bethiah Chipman married Samuel Smith.
5. Their daughter Deborah Smith married Joseph Blake.
6. Their son John Welland Blake married Abigail Jones.
7. Their daughter **Anna Sophia Blake married Henry Cabot.**
8. Their daughter Anna Sophia Cabot married John E. Lodge.
9. Their son Henry Cabot Lodge married Anna Cabot Mills Davis [Nannie].
10. Their son George Cabot Lodge married Elizabeth Davis [Bessy].
11. Their son Henry Cabot Lodge married Emily Sears.
12. Their son George Cabot Lodge married Nancy Kunhardt.
13. Their daughter Emily Sears Lodge married Robert René Pingeon.

The Lodge family is descended from *The Mayflower* through Anna Sophia Blake (1796-1845). Henry Cabot (1783-1864), George Cabot's son, was not an obvious choice for Anna Blake, as is evident in these pleading letters from her father, John Blake (b.1761), urging eighteen-year-old Anna to take Henry, then thirty-one, more seriously. Henry, whose looks were not his strong point, was a lawyer and man of letters with a lively interest in literature and theater, and a lifelong friend of Daniel Webster. In this letter of February 4th, 1814, Anna's father encourages his daughter to stay in Boston with her aunt in order to see more of Henry:

> I derive great pleasure my daughter from the repeated evidence your late letters give me of a very becoming and laudable stability of character and of settled opinion in the all important *affair of love*. Could

Henry Cabot in his later years.

> I from any circumstance have cherished a belief when you left home that your acquaintance with Mr. H.C. would be renewed and that you should for a week, be, en famille, in the domicile of the father, having a confidence in your taste for *refined* society, I should readily have anticipated the result would be exactly what it is. Whether you shall seek an opportunity to return with Mrs. Chapin or not, is a point upon which I am at this moment, totally unprepared to *advise*, much more, to *direct*. You appear to be so very happy with your Boston friends, and have so long been immersed in this dreadful solitary residence, that I cannot find it in my heart, much as I feel the want of your society, to curtail your visit.

In her March 1814 letter, Aunt Harriet Blake Mills (John Blake's sister) of Northampton, Massachusetts, implies that Anna and Henry have become engaged and urges her niece not to prolong the engagement. (*Their grandchildren*, Anna Cabot Mills Davis and Henry Cabot Lodge, respectively, were later to marry.)

> ...You will remember Mr. Cabot is no common lover—I hope and think you will not be disposed to protract your union beyond the two or three weeks we talked of when I last saw you as I believe that period better suited to his convenience as well as more agreeable to his wishes than any other. Mr. Cabot has been kind enough to cheer me in my solitude by spending part of every evening with us. Every interview I have with this said friend of yours serves to elicit his virtues and admirable qualities.... I tell you now you are one of the most fortunate (and will be happiest) woman in Christendom.

This endearing love letter of March 2, 1814, demonstrates that Henry Cabot was more in love than Miss Blake:

> *My Dear Anna,*
> I have of late been so habituated to the delights of your society that although five days have scarcely elapsed since your departure from Boston, even this short interval has been more than sufficient to put my patience to a severe trial—indeed, I should be inconsolable under my present privation if the animating recollection that we are soon to be united by an indissoluble tie did not frequently recur to fill my heart with exquisite delights. This alternate state of hope and solicitude, perhaps inseparable from ardent affection in the absence of its objects,

you can render more tolerable by permitting no opportunity of writing to pass unimproved—do not fail dearest girl to inform me at the least twice in a week of every circumstance however trivial which affects your health or happiness—how did you bear your journey? How find your friends—are you happy at present and in anticipation of the future? Has your partiality for Boston friends experienced no abatement from time and absence? Are your sentiments on a particular topick [sic] as favorable as when we parted? To these and many other enquiries the answers would be most interesting—.

I am much occupied by my insurance establishment that I have made but two very short visits to Mrs. Blake (Mrs. Joseph Blake of Boston, Anna's grandmother) since Saturday morning—She feels the loss of her husband's society much more keenly than when she had the support of Mrs. Mills and yourself—She will write to you by tomorrow's mail—All the members of our family have enjoined upon me to transmit to you their kindest regards—I have only time to conjure you to encourage and cherish a reciprocal affection for him who lives but in the hope of making you happy.

Yrs with unabated love
H.C.

Henry entered Harvard in the Class of 1800, but did not graduate because, true to the family's rebellious spirit, he became involved in a dispute about rancid butter in the cafeteria. What is obvious from the Senator's *Early Memories* is that his maternal grandfather was immensely rich, generous,and assiduously modest:

I looked up to him with awe, for he impressed me with an air of distinction which I could not have defined then, but which I fully realize now. I do not know why I had that feeling of awe, because he was always most gentle in his manner, and as he had a way, if I asked him for money, of pulling out a handful of change and letting me take my choice among the coins I felt a peculiar affection for a person addicted to a method of giving quite unexampled in my experience. I used to try his patience, I fear, by urging him to tell me how he hid under the sideboard and watched Washington at breakfast with his father when the President stopped at my great-grandfather's house in Beverly, on his journey through New England in 1789.... I have always liked since to think, as I have recalled this trifling anecdote, that I have known and talked with some one who had seen Washington. But this was the only

> incident of the past I ever extracted from my grandfather. I used to importune him to tell me stories of the distant time when he was a boy and especially all about his father. I remember well his kindly refusal and his then adding: **"My boy, we do not talk about family in this country. It is enough for you to know that your grandfather is an honest man."**[35]

Anna Blake and Henry Cabot were married in the spring of 1814. Anna Blake Cabot gave birth to their first child, Elizabeth (1817-1833), three years later, and in 1821 to a second girl, Anna (1821-1900), the future mother of the Senator. In June of 1823, two months after the death of her father-in-law, George Cabot, the young couple went to live abroad for a year—in Naples, Venice and Rome.

The Senator often debated with his friend, Margaret (Mrs. Winthrop) Chanler, where conversation was better—in Rome or in America. The Senator could not bring himself to admit that a Catholic society would have an edge over a Protestant one. Iris Origo's "apercu" in her biography of the poet Giacomo Leopardi lends color to that debate and to the society in which the Senator's maternal grandmother lived in 1823. Leopardi was not invited to the great houses, whereas Italian Counts, Dukes, and Princes vied for the privilege of showing Mrs. Cabot their "pictures" by Michelangelo and Leonardo da Vinci at the Palazzos Doria and Colonna. "Many foreign ladies had married into the great Roman families and to their salons there now came scholars such as Niebuhr, artists like Thorwalden, sightseers and writers like Stendhal.... I have not seen in the whole of Europe any drawing rooms preferable to the Roman ones; it is impossible to gather together a hundred people, all indifferent to each other, who would give each other greater mutual pleasure; is not that the perfection of society?"[36] The irony that Mrs. Cabot's social success far surpassed that of the great poet at the time was that seventy years later Bay Lodge, her great grandson, dedicated his first volume of poetry, *The Song of the Wave*, to Leopardi's memory.

Anna Blake Cabot, at twenty-seven, was a uniquely gifted musician who played the piano, and composed both duets with harp and musical plays for her friends. She also lunched and dined with the Caetani, the Colonnas, and Count Apponyi, and regularly attended concerts

---

[35] Lodge, *Early Memories*, 40-42. Author's emphasis. Margaret Chanler, author of *Roman Spring*, her memoir.
[36] Iris Origo, *Leopardi: A Study in Solitude* (London: Hamish Hamilton, Ltd., 1953), 70.

and the opera with them. Her comments about art in public and private collections are lively and original, and it is evident from her travel journals that she had great charm and humor. Her amusing observations and her complaints about various ailments—a pimple on the left cheek, ear-aches, tight boots—indicate that she took care of herself and was a little vain. Oddly, there is only one mention of "Mr. Cabot" but it would have been unthinkable at the time for her to travel alone. As glimpsed below, Anna's travel journals, are unique in the annals of "womens' history."[37]

July—*Engaged an apartment in Vico Freddo 37 (Rome) from Princess Caetani.*

Sunday, July 21—*Went to see Duke of Casperano's pictures.*

22nd—*Dined with Princess Caetani, removed my effects with some regret from Vico Freddo, 37. After dinner, received certain direful warnings from an old stump of a tooth. Ventured however in the evening to St. Carlos to hear Spontini's Vestate. Obliged to leave the theatre with violent paroxysms of a toothache.*

29th—*Has seized my whole face. Took two glasses of sulfur water.*

31—*Cheek swelled even into deformity. Obliged to wear a piece of flannel over it although the thermometer is about eighty in the shade. Thunderstorms, every peal as loud as an explosion of a powder magazine or somewhat more noisy perhaps.*

1—*August*

2nd—*Finished correcting the introduction to* Berenice. *[She wrote an opera based on Racine's play.] Began Dante. Felt myself well enough to go to St. Carlos.*

5th—*Worse. Teatro di Fiorentina.*

6th—*Return of the King. Illumination, beautiful effect.*

Ten years after her year in Italy, Anna's first daughter, Elizabeth, sixteen, (1833) died, plunging Anna into a depression. Some speculate that that was the year Anna's portrait was painted, either in London or by an Italian artist.[38] The portrait shows her in black, holding a letter, with a glove on the floor, implying loss. A closer look shows a portrait of a man in the upper left corner. The family interpretation of the painting is that of a romantic loss rather than a familial one; her husband outlived her.

At Anna Blake Cabot's death in 1845, at the age of forty-nine, her

[37] The entire text of the travel journal is appendixed.

[38] Property of Helena's grand-daughter, Anne de Wasseige, Brussels.

obituary in a Boston newspaper relates the important effect she had on the people around her:

> No one approached her who did not also admire her; no one knew her, who did not love her, saw the pure and generous feelings and acts. Seldom has nature been more lavish in endowment. To personal beauty was united grace that threw a charm around beauty. The outward was in unison with the inward.... The basis of her character was love. Her heart was filled with kind emotions—kind looks, kind words, kind actions—and in the consciousness of her own moral rectitude she gave no heed to slander. She possessed an energy of will and firmness of purpose which would have distinguished a man, but withal so tempered by sweetness and softness in expression, that in being earnest and ardent, she never ceased to be feminine. In her perceptions she was exquisitely delicate; in her views, enlarged; in her judgments, just. She had the truest sense of beauty. She looked disease and its follower, death, in the face with cheerfulness.

Anna Blake Cabot.

The Senator recalls:

My grandmother Cabot died before I was born but she was one of the women who make such a deep impression upon those about them that I have always felt as if I had known her. Not only in the family, but from all my grandfather's old friends, I used to hear continually, until the last one who remembered her had passed from the stage, of her beauty and grace, her abiding charm and fascinating qualities. Venerable gentlemen, when I had grown up, used to tell me of her many attractions with such emphasis and insistence that I frequently had an uneasy feeling at the back of my mind that they were thinking how unlike she was to some of her grandchildren. None the less, it was pleasant to hear such things said of her, her bust by Greenough and her portrait painted by an English artist when she was in Europe in 1837 certainly, so far as they can, bear out the tradition.[39]

[39] Lodge, *Early Memories*, 7-8.

The Lodges

"Why was maritime Massachusetts so prominent," asks Samuel Morison, "in the American Revolution? ...American democracy was not born in the cabin of The Mayflower *or in a Boston town meeting, but on the farming, fighting frontier of all the colonies, New England included. Seaboard Massachusetts has never known such a thing as social democracy; and in seaboard Massachusetts, as elsewhere, inequalities in wealth have made political democracy a sham. Few town meetings have been held near tidewater where the voice of ship-owner, merchant, or master mariner did not carry more weight than that of fisherman, counting-room clerk, or common sea-man. Society in seaboard New England was carefully stratified, and the Revolution brought little change save in personnel. The 'quality' dressed differently from the poor and middle classes, lived in finer houses, expected and received deference, and 'ran' their communities because they controlled the working capital of ships and goods. The only difference from old-world society lay in the facility in passing from one class to another.... The sea is no wet-nurse to democracy. Authority and privilege are her twin foster-children. Instant and unquestioning obedience to master is the rule of the sea; and your typical sea-captain would make it the rule of the land if he could."* [40]

Historians have remarked on the twin strains of autocracy and democracy in American culture. Boston's "aristocratic republicans"[41] thought they were purer than Europeans, more incorruptible than kings, and heir to the golden democracies of Athens and Rome, when philosopher-kings ruled the world. The Bostonians of the autocratic tradition were educators—sometimes nauseatingly so. The eighteenth and nineteenth century American certainly would not have gone to Chicago or St. Louis or San Francisco for high culture. They took "the grand European tour" through Paris, London, Berlin, Leipzig, Salz-

[40] Morison, 23-24.

[41] Historian, *New York Times* art critic, and editor Stuart Preston used this phrase for the Lodges.

burg, Vienna, St. Petersburg, Rome, Naples, and Venice. Although they went to Europe, they despised both monarchy and democracy unless it included leadership by an elite, a noble male elite. Service was another principle—the belief in a governing class, common in Boston society, meant they felt obliged to serve the nation.

The first Lodge arrived in America in 1792. Giles (1770-1852) was twenty-one when his voyage began between Liverpool and Santo Domingo where he acted as an agent for his brothers who owned a sugar plantation. When he discovered that there was a slave rebellion on the family estate, he managed to get off the ship at Boston and had the good fortune to meet Abigail Langdon, the daughter of Mary and John Langdon, the latter a captain in the Continental Army during the Revolution. Giles Lodge was a "holy terror," as my Uncle Harry put it, and one can catch some of his meanness in the "hard little portrait," as the Senator once described it. In 1800, Giles, like the Cabots before him, was marrying "up," right into the heart of the new American society.[42] Legend has it that Giles, in a fit of temper in 1823, slapped his sixteen-year-old son John across the face whereupon John went to sea as a cabin boy and never spoke to his father again.

John Ellerton was a voracious reader and a curious fellow who learned fast. By the time he was twenty-one, he was skipper of a clipper ship bound for Canton. From his logs, we know something of his skill. A clipper ship captain had to know much of commerce,

Giles Lodge and Abigail Lodge, courtesy of my brother, Henry Cabot Lodge, III. By Rembrandt Peale.

[42] A deed from Anna Sophia Cabot's scrapbook places Giles Lodge on Milk St. in Boston in 1810.

commodity prices, and exchange rates. He had considerable latitude in what he loaded and sold. Once going around Cape Horn, his ship was badly damaged, its masts and rigging carried away by huge seas. Under jury rig, he kept going, arriving in Canton six months late. Along the way, he had to subdue a mutinous mate with a belaying pin. He arrived in China during the off-season so his cargo brought an exceptionally large sum. He sold his ship, bought another one and sailed for home with a full load of tea. When he arrived in Boston it was again off-season so his tea brought a high price. By the time he was thirty years old, he had retired from the sea to build his own ships, *The Fly Away, Don Quixote, Sancho Panza, Argonaut* and *Storm King*, among others. Samuel Eliot Morison records that *Argonaut* had paid for herself before she cast off her lines for her maiden voyage.

John Ellerton Lodge.

In 1842, when she was twenty-one, Anna Cabot (1821-1900) married John Ellerton Lodge (1807-1862). Although they were relative newcomers to Boston, the Lodges through their alliance with the Cabots and thanks to their own enterprise, established themselves at the center of Boston society. In wedding a clipper ship captain, Anna was choosing someone very much like her grandfather, George Cabot.

Anna Cabot Lodge, the Senator's mother, was an heiress, granddaughter of George Cabot, the richest man in eighteenth century Massachusetts, and daughter of a celebrated beauty, Anna Blake Cabot. Her thick leather scrapbook with the metal buckle gives the historian a unique and intimate glimpse of mid-nineteenth century America and provides the key to an understanding of her son, the Senator's pride. Anna's scrapbook places her within a microcosmic community of Boston—it contains the pen Nathaniel Hawthorne used to write *The Scarlet Letter*,[43] and letters of acceptance to dinner from Ralph Waldo Emerson, Henry Wadsworth

---

[43] Hawthorne had given it to the clerk with whom he worked in the customs house and the clerk, an admirer of the Senator's civil service reform legislation, gave it to the Senator.

Longfellow, and Senator Charles Sumner. A letter from Anna's cousin Thomas Higginson, describing a young poet named Emily Dickinson, encloses copies of two poems: "Of all the sounds dispatched abroad" and "Some keep the Sabbath going to church."[44]

The scrapbook contains a gray suede glove with Lafayette's portrait on it, from the time when he took his tour of America in 1820, and various memorabilia relating to John Kirkland.[45] Every detail of her son Cabot's life is recorded, from his school reports to the menus of the dinners he attended, to her gifts to him of valuable works of art. Nothing about her son's life is withheld. The mythic importance of the heir starts here, and the Senator's sister, Lillie, is completely missing from the file. Her pride in her grandfather, George Cabot, is evident from the fact that she carefully kept his essays tucked into the scrapbook, notably, "Can the Suffering of Humanity Be Justified?"[46] The Senator would write his first of twenty-nine historical volumes about his great-grandfather and would dedicate the book to his mother.

Anna Cabot Lodge, although plain, sentimental, and of average intelligence, had taken the European tour required of educated Americans. She saw herself as the keeper of the flame and the guardian of the legend, and she would pass on the heroic deeds of her ancestors to her son. She helped to create the Mount Auburn Cemetery, originally built as an arboretum, where some of Boston's oldest families found their final resting place. She had her grandfather, George Cabot, and his wife, Elizabeth Higginson, unearthed and placed alongside her mother, the beautiful Anna Sophia Blake, and her father, Henry Cabot, in a brick Gothic shrine nestled in a romantic English-style garden. What was it about her mother, Anna Sophia Blake and her father, Henry Cabot, and her grandfather, George Cabot, that she passed on to her only son, the future Senator?

John Ellerton Lodge was tall and handsome with classical features and reddish brown hair. His portrait, painted when he was a young man, reveals him to be a fine-featured, sensitive person. No one could cross him and yet, "he was the kindest and most generous of men," the Senator writes of his father.

The Senator recalls:

> I never remember a harsh word from him except on one or two occa-

[44] See appendix for the letter.
[45] Aunt Elizabeth Cabot Kirkland's husband, a president of Harvard College.
[46] See appendix.

> sions when he spoke to me sternly because he thought I was not telling the truth or was exhibiting either physical or moral timidity. He was a man of great courage, entirely fearless and was said to have a high temper. Although I realized his courage, I never knew he had a temper until one night when as we were going to the theatre, at a dark place on the Common, two men pushed into us, there were words, I saw something glitter in one man's hand and then he was knocked down in the snow by my father who merely said as he passed on, "I think that fellow had a knife." He was a man of determined character whose word was law, and whose laws were promulgated in the most concise form and were subject to no debate....
>
> When the [Civil] war came and he was unable to go, for he was not only too old, which he would not admit, but he had injured his knee in a fall from his horse, could not walk freely and rode with difficulty. But he was an intensely loyal man and gave to the support of the war in every way. It was the habit to subscribe money to equip regiments. John Ropes, afterwards an eminent lawyer and a distinguished military historian, raised a great deal of money... and told me that when there was some especial need, my father handed him a check signed in blank and told him to fill it in as he pleased... the only blank check he ever received. My father enjoyed above all things the power of giving. He was overwhelmed, overburdened with business cares, which broke him down and caused his premature death. My mother begged him to retire, as he had an ample fortune for those days, but his reply was: "If I retire and live on a fixed income I shall not be able to give as I do now, and I want to be able to give without stopping to think about it.[47]

Anna gave birth to a daughter, Elizabeth (Lillie), but the family preference for sons meant that Lillie's birth and death dates went unrecorded. In a tiny family sketch, she appears about six years older than her brother Henry Cabot Lodge, the Senator, which would put her birth date sometime in 1844.

The Senator was born in Boston on May 12, 1850, "in a square stone house of smooth granite, facing south and open on all sides." Winthrop Place, as it was called, belonged to Henry Cabot (his maternal grandfather) for whom he was named. It had an ample garden with pear trees and a marble statue of a garden nymph, and extended to Summer Street, "lined with superb horse-chestnut trees beneath whose heavy shade the sober well-built houses took on in spring and summer

[47] Lodge, *Early Memories*, 27, 28.

an air of cool remoteness," an air which he himself attempted, not always successfully, to affect. To the east stood the New South Church with a broad green and a great English elm in front. The Senator's relationship to Boston was fundamental to his worldview as is revealed in the following passage, which displays as much his extraordinary grasp of history as it does his affinity for the eighteenth century character of Boston, "strong, manly and aggressive."

> It was long before I reasoned out the underlying meaning of all this, long after the old house and garden had been swept out of existence by the new street which was pushed through into the quiet court to make way for the roaring tides of business.... The year 1850 stood on the edge of a new time but the old time was still visible from it.... There was a wider difference between the men who fought at Waterloo and... Gettysburg or Sudan or Mukden than there was between the followers of Leonidas and the soldiers of Napoleon. This is merely one way of stating that the application of steam and electricity to transportation and communication made a greater change in human environment than had occurred since the earliest period of recorded history. The break between the old and the new came some time in the thirties, and 1850 was well within the new period. Yet at that date... the ideas of the earlier time—the habits, the modes of life, although mortally smitten and fast fading—were still felt, still dominant... the men and women... unconscious that their world was slipping from them. Hence the atmosphere of our old stone house with its lane, its pear trees, and its garden nymph, indeed of Boston itself, was still an eighteenth century atmosphere, if we accept Sir Walter Besant's statement that the eighteenth century ended in 1837....
>
> Two years before [1850], in 1848, the outbreak had come in Europe, and the movement which was to result in the consolidation of the United States and of Germany, in the unification of Italy, the liberation of the slaves, the emancipation of the Russian serfs, and the wide extension of democratic and representative government, was resuming its sweeping and victorious march, which had been checked at Waterloo [1815]. It was the day of the human-rights statesmen, just rising to power, of the men who believed that in political liberty was to be found the cure for every human ill, and that all the world needed in order to assure human happiness was to give every man a vote and set him free... But the Boston of 1850 had 133,000 inhabitants.... Whatever its merits or defects, however, Boston in the first decade of the second

> half of the nineteenth century had a meaning and a personality, and even a boy could feel them. It may have been austere, at times even harsh, this personality, but it was there, and it was strong, manly and aggressive. It would still have been possible to rally them as they were once rallied against the British soldiers on a certain cold March evening with the cry of "Town born, turn out!"[48]

The books the Senator and his contemporaries read from childhood onward were English, the fashions of dress were English, the long, generous, heavy dinners were English; the ladies left the men in the dining-room, as in England. His literary standards, his standards of statesmanship, and his modes of thought (apart from politics and diplomacy) were as English as the "trivial" custom of the dinner table and the ballroom. From his father, the Senator became fond of Cervantes, Scott's Waverley novels, Macaulay, Hawthorne, Dickens, R.L. Stevenson, Horace Walpole; from his mother, Byron, Shelley, and Browning. His traditional taste left him cool to the romantic and transcendental movement going on around him.[49]

In 1858, when the new street was being cut through the property, John Ellerton Lodge bought 31 Beacon Street for $50,000 from Samuel Eliot, father of Charles Eliot, who later became one of Harvard's most distinguished presidents. No. 31 was a large, solid, "swell-front" brick mansion with a spacious entryway, a wide staircase and large, cavernous rooms. From 1859 until his mother's death in 1900, whenever he was in Boston, the Senator resided there. It stood on the crest of the hill, not far from the State House and the Hancock House, home of the first signer of the Declaration of Independence, John Hancock.

East Point, with miles of ocean vistas on all sides, was the Lodges' summerhouse from 1862 until 1938. Nahant, only fourteen nautical miles from Boston harbor, was the Senator's true home, a narrow peninsula "thrust out into the open ocean, with nothing between it and Portugal, all rocks."[50] His grandfather, Henry Cabot, had a "villa" closer to the village where the family spent their summers, so it was Anna's association and childhood memories that led her husband to buy East Point:

---

[48] Ibid., 14-19.

[49] Ibid., 30, 39.

[50] Lodge to George Otto Trevelyan, August 30, 1918, Lodge papers. Unless otherwise indicated all the letters in this book are from the Lodge collection at the Massachusetts Historical Society.

Nahant in the fifties had already lost most of its original character as a fishing village and had developed a summer-resort economy. Located between Boston and Cape Ann, a mere fifteen miles from the Hub, it was one of the earliest of the fashionable resorts in New England. Thomas Handasyd Perkins, the "king" of the early nineteenth century Boston merchants, attracted to the region, according to legend, by the low tax rates, began the invasion in 1821. He bought East Point, then called "Ram Pasture" and organized a corporation to construct a substantial stone hotel, which was opened two years later.... In 1852 Paran Stevens, a promoter with grandiose ideas, got control of East Point and converted the hotel into a mammoth, multi-storied, four-hundred foot long monstrosity... [and] dreamed of making Nahant into a rival Newport... Prosperity disappeared with the panic of 1857 and bankruptcy came with the Civil War. On the night of September 11, 1861, with young Cabot Lodge as excited witness, the empty hotel "took fire" and burned to the ground. John Ellerton Lodge then purchased the property, and in 1868, after his death, the family constructed a summer residence there in which Cabot Lodge lived whenever he could for all the rest of his life.[51]

31 Beacon St.

The octagonal house on the rocky promontory was filled with friendship and airy laughter. The rocks off Nahant provided the ideal spot for (only) the men to dive, always naked, into the foaming sea. Across the lawn, ladies in white dresses came to tea. Groups of men gathered on porches, their cheeks brushed by the sea breeze. There were large open fires, nine bedrooms and nine bathrooms, lots of ser-

[51] John A. Garraty, *Henry Cabot Lodge: A Biography* (New York, Alfred A. Knopf, 1953), 6-7.

The octagonal house on East Point, Nahant.

One of the views of the sea from East Point.

vants, roses climbing on the wide veranda, and a porch for reading and talking in the summer breeze. On the bluff was "the Billiard Room," a small replica of the Parthenon. When Cabot was in the prime of life, Anna Cabot Lodge suggested that her son use the Billiard Room as an escape from the house at East Point.[52] Standing on the outer perimeter of Boston's harbor, East Point might have taken on the image of a castle or a fortress in the mind of a child. In the spring of 1862, twelve-year-old Cabot and his father, a few months before his death, enjoyed the carriage ride to East Point, the horses kicking up the dust, then changing horses in Lynn and proceeding on with a picnic in their laps. From there on the bluff, Cabot could watch the three-masted clipper ships in his father's fleet as they made their way to the harbor like ancient majestic animals. The Senator writes:

> The grace and beauty of the clipper ship as she spread her wings and set

[52] May 26, 1889

"My Darling Son,

...Why cannot you turn the Billiard Room into a retreat from office seekers? You could make it comfortable with books or writing materials and be there at certain hours when "men do congregate" and you would truly be "out"!

> out under full sail can never be approached by anything made of metal or powered by steam....
>
> My father was a China merchant... [and] had his office in the granite block which stretched down to the end of Commercial Wharf [Boston]. From his counting rooms, I could look out on the ships lying alongside the wharfs. They were beautiful vessels, American clipper ships in the days when our ships of that type were famous throughout the world for speed and staunchness. I wandered over their decks, making friends with the captains, the seamen and the ship-keepers.... They brought me firecrackers from China, strange fireworks, and bronzes and porcelain and pictures and carved ivories. Ginger and sweetmeats and lychees (then almost unknown here).... For the teas and silks which filled the holds I cared nothing but the history and adventures of the ships interested me greatly.... There was a fragrance of mingled spices in the air... ginger and nutmeg and dusty palm-leaf. The troops of small boys collecting foreign postage stamps were tolerated. On India Wharf, great vats were filled with molasses and a boy could draw forth the stick, run his finger along it and then to his mouth....

The wife of a China merchant became an adoring mother, a widow from the age of forty in 1862 until her death in 1900. His father's death when Cabot was only twelve affected him deeply; it explains why he took such pains with his grandchildren when his own son, Bay, died young. He knew what it was to be fatherless, and women became the dominant force in young Cabot's life. His mother was determined to instill in her son, the future Senator Henry Cabot Lodge, the sense that he was carrying on a legacy that began with her grandfather, George Cabot.

During Anna's early widowhood, Senator Charles Sumner was a de-

After John E Lodge died in 1862, when Anna was barely in her forties, Charles Sumner was a great friend to her, procuring valuable 'passe-partout' passports and often staying with her in Nahant, particularly after he was caned for his anti-slavery views. Toward the end of his life he gave her a silver dish used to hold flowers for her dining table centerpiece.

voted and admiring friend, providing her with valuable passports for travel abroad with her young son and heir.[53] Besides the scrapbook, there are a few journals in which she wrote out her favorite poetry of Tennyson and Keats by hand. In *Early Memories*, the Senator describes his mother as "clever, high-minded, high-spirited and well-educated according to the standards of Boston in the thirties." But Anna's character, best seen through her letters, reveals her to be none of these things. Anna glued a newspaper clipping entitled, "Woman's Deeds and Views" into her scrapbook; she probably agreed with the popular interpretation of the traditional woman's role, a role which was to change in her son's generation, and never again be entirely the same:

> The education of women in the 1820s never had a tendency to make them think or speak with any particular stress on the facts so long as their only object was to be entertaining, and what they were saying was not of any real importance. In those days they were prepared to make themselves agreeable in society. They were to be entertaining to men and one way of doing that was by telling them interesting stories. Common facts that would have had no point could be made worth talking about if they had the right twist or picturesque details that kept them from being commonplace. So exaggeration became an amiable habit with the women of that generation.[54]

The Senator's sister, Lillie, who seems to have been strong-headed and bossy with her younger brother, became engaged to George Abbot "Jabber" James, Henry James' cousin, in the summer of 1864, when she would have been about twenty, after a visit by George to Nahant. Young Cabot, then fourteen, wrote to George James that he finally received some attention from his older sister but complained of her aloofness. Clearly, her younger brother was the favorite in their mother's eyes.[55]

Cabot had curly brown hair, hazel eyes, small, regular features and a rather pointed chin. He appeared smaller than he was, wiry and slim enough to seem almost frail (which he wasn't). He went to Mrs. Parkman's school at the age of five when his father discovered he couldn't

---

[53] Their correspondence is archived at the Massachusetts Historical Society.

[54] Newspaper clipping, unattributed, Anna Cabot Lodge's scrapbook, 1860s.

[55] "This afternoon when we went to ride she did not take any interest in what I said and seemed displeased with me. I believe the only reason she cared for me was that you wanted her to. She likes me pretty well while you are on the spot but the minute you go she gets indifferent....I have done as you said I ought to about obeying Mother and now begin to think she is the best freind [sic]. I try to obey her and think it is the best way...." Garraty, 6.

read. From 1861 until 1866, he attended Mr. Dixwell's, "a private Latin school" where the boys were "picked" from a roster of Boston's first families—the Bigelows, Cabots, Lees, and Parkmans. Besides Latin and Greek, and Greek and Roman history, they took algebra and plane geometry and "a smattering" of French. His schoolmates named him "little Lodge," as the older boys considered him the school pet, and his contemporaries, at least in his first year, called him, "a miserable little dig." By the time he left Dixwell's, his efforts were consistently rewarded with the coveted "18" which for some reason represented the master's idea of perfection.[56] Before he was ten, his grandfather (Henry Cabot) had taken him to see *Julius Caesar* with Edwin Booth, E.L. Davenport, Lawrence Barrett and John McCullough in the leading roles; by the time the family moved to 31 Beacon, he was an experienced playgoer.

Anna Cabot, true to her husband's wishes, made Nahant into a watering hole for intellectuals, entertaining friends in summer like Emerson and Longfellow, Sumner and Motley. Having the "Olympians" as acquaintances gave the Senator an unusual upbringing. The octagonal house was his real home from the age of eighteen. Ralph Waldo Emerson, the guest of Longfellow at Nahant, gave it a stanza:

> All day the waves assailed the rock,
> I heard the church-bell chime,
> the sea-beat scorns the minister clock
> and breaks the glass of time.

Dr. Oliver Wendell Holmes spent his summers at Nahant and the Senator, in his memoirs, includes him on his list of the best after-dinner "talkers." The others were John Hay, Mr. Evarts, Lord Rosebery, Arthur James Balfour (later British Prime Minister), John Motley, Henry Adams, Mr. Speaker Reed, James Russell Lowell, and T.B. Aldrich.

> The art requires humor, wit, and seriousness and demands a wide knowledge of books and men. The anecdote used must be apt to the highest degree and sparingly employed. It must pierce deeply and yet touch lightly. In a word, it must have charm.... Dr. Holmes' wit and humor were boundless and always on the alert. His memory was extraordinary and his knowledge in all directions remarkable.... No one jested more or better than [Abraham] Lincoln; the joke was often his

[56] Garraty, 10. Dixwell's must have followed the French system, wherein 18 out of 20 is an A. Since the French never give a 20, 18 is the highest possible grade.

> armor of defense, and yet no man ever lived with a higher seriousness of purpose or who did a mightier work.[57]

The Senator's anecdotes indicate that he took an early interest in public speaking, and his recollections of certain New England "Olympians"—Sumner, Longfellow, Emerson, and Lowell—provide an intimate glimpse into the rarified circle of mid-nineteenth century Bostonians who formed young Lodge's upbringing and education. "When he [James Russell Lowell] had just arrived in England, Lord Coleridge, who was reputed to be the best after-dinner speaker in London, said to him: 'You will be asked very often to make an after-dinner speech and I wish to tell you how such a speech should be made. Select your anecdote beforehand. When you are called upon, lead up to your anecdote, tell it, go gently away from it and your speech is made.' It was excellent advice, as sound as it was witty."[58]

John Garraty, in his biography of the Senator, leaves a rich account of young Henry Cabot Lodge at the time of his father's death:

> During the [Civil] War Lodge lost his father, who died quite suddenly one September evening in 1862 of a heart attack.... The death of his father very much tightened the already close bond between the boy and his mother. Anna Lodge's daughter, Lilly, soon married and moved out of the household, and Mrs. Lodge and Cabot were left alone. He became the center of her life and she indulged his every desire. She had ample funds and intelligence capable of sympathizing with his talents, so she could be a great help to him, but at the same time she no doubt spoiled him. He had a selfishness in later life which many of his contemporaries noted.... [Lodge] confided to her his innermost thoughts and aspirations in letters that were much more than dutiful notes.... He was a product of upper-class 19th century Boston society.... They were a wealthy society, but lived simply and made almost a fetish of charity and public service. From their ranks, in numbers far out of proportion to their relatively small population, had come leaders in every branch of American life. But by the end of the Civil War this society was entering what Van Wyck Brooks has called its 'Indian Summer.' It was gradually becoming more interested in admiring its past accomplishments and reproducing itself unchanged than in moving forward with the times.With this complacency came a narrowness and stagna-

[57] Henry Cabot Lodge.
[58] See appendix for his other reminiscences.

> tion that was widely recognized.... In this society Henry Cabot Lodge grew up; he attended its schools, associated with its children, absorbed its standards, enjoyed its wealth, servants, and comforts. He was also a pampered only son, closely attached to an indulgent mother. But it would be unfair to say that at sixteen he was permanently marked with all the characteristics of the "typical" Bostonian.[59]

In the summer of 1866, before Cabot's entrance to Harvard in 1867, Mrs. Lodge took Constant Davis, Cabot's future wife's brother, and Cabot (along with her personal maid, Amelia) on a European tour. Constant wrote his father from Switzerland, that they led a very luxurious life, in the best hotels, without any regard to expense. "Breakfast at 10 if we please... and drive everywhere with the best carriages and horses."

Constant Davis left a formative mark on young Cabot who, at sixteen, needed Constant to tutor him for entrance to Harvard. "Under his guidance," Cabot wrote, "I began to get a little real education and to regard lessons as something other than an affliction devised for the torment of boys." They were all clever, all cultivated, all with a strong sense of humor and a wholesome liking for fun and nonsense.[60]

Anna Lodge was the kind of ethnocentric American who made nearly all of her visits abroad to Bostonians residing abroad. She was noted for her talent in developing close friendships.[61] Once during a visit to William Wetmore Story, the Boston sculptor living at the Palazzo Barberini in Rome, Cabot noticed that the name on one of his statues, "Lybian Sybil," was misspelled. While Mrs. Lodge was admiring it, the boy, fresh from his Greek lessons with Constant, whispered to her: "That inscription is not spelled right." An indignant Story demanded to know what was wrong. "Why it ought to be 'Libyan' and 'Sybyl' because the letters in Greek are Upsilons," Cabot retorted—an early hint of the boy's intellect and the uses to which he put it.

In October 1869, Cabot's use of "Mock Parts," an old Harvard custom, led to its abolition. The ceremony of the "Mock Parts" was intended to poke fun at the faults and quirks of the members of the junior class. Although a committee decided on the content, one person was chosen to deliver the speech. Cabot, seated in a windowsill opening out onto Harvard Yard, in an atmosphere of fun and affability, "rasped out

---

[59] Garraty, 13-15.
[60] From the Senator's tribute to Nannie.
[61] Cleveland Amory, *The Proper Bostonians* (New York: E.P. Dutton, 1947), 129.

barbed shafts with obvious relish. Gradually the mood of his audience began to change. The thrusts were too cruel, the speaker too savage, as he combined the gibe, 'God help the fool,' with the name of some unpopular and dull-witted classmate. A freshman recalled, 'The savageness repelled me utterly.' Then came the rude awakening: 'I soon had reason to regret my brief hour of triumph. Some of the men who were wounded never forgave me.'"[62]

[62] Garraty, 25; Lodge, *Early Memories*, 182-3; and Lawrence, *Henry Cabot Lodge* (Boston: Houghton Mifflin, 1925), 16-17.

Anna Cabot Mills Davis

Cabot found his match in Constant's sister, the brilliant and witty Anna Cabot Mills Davis (Jan. 16, 1851-Sept. 27, 1915), who was known as Nannie by her intimates; at her death, Theodore Roosevelt wrote that she was the closest woman America had to having a queen. She was the daughter of Admiral Davis, one of Lincoln's greatest friends and a hero of the Battle of Vicksburg (a mesmerizing photograph on the wall at the Big House in Beverly shows him at the foot of Lincoln's casket, one of Lincoln's pallbearers). The Admiral and Mrs. Davis lived in Cambridge, and their friends were Louis Agassiz, Longfellow, Lowell, President Felton and the ex-presidents of Harvard College James Walker and Jared Sparks. Cambridge, in those days more physically separated from Boston, had all the attributes and charm of a university town. These were the intellectual leaders of the country at that time. In that rarified world, though they knew they were socially superior, a high degree of social responsibility came along with that conviction.

Nannie's mother, Harriette Mills, was the youngest child of Harriette Blake and Elijah Mills. Anna Blake Cabot was only eight when her aunt, Harriette Blake Mills, twelve years her senior, married Elijah Mills, U.S. Senator in Northampton, Massachusetts. Since Harriette Blake Mills was Nannie's maternal grandmother and Anna Blake Cabot was the Senator's maternal grandmother, Nannie and the Senator were second cousins. Not only was Nannie's mother descended from John Howland of *The Mayflower*, but Nannie's father was descended from Robert Davis, who, as the Senator notes, "with his sons, Dolor[63] and Shubael, landed in Massachusetts with the first Puritan emigration in 1630. Robert Davis moved to the Plymouth colony and there his descendants intermarried with families of Pilgrim ancestry and in this way Nannie traced her descent from John Alden of *The Mayflower* and Priscilla Mullins, and from Constant Southworth whose mother became the second wife of Governor Bradford."[64]

---

[63] Bessy Davis Lodge, the Senator's daughter-in-law, was also descended from Dolor.

[64] Full text of the Senator's fine tribute to his wife is appendixed.

Nannie's grandmother, Harriette Blake Mills, had a much harder life than the one led by her niece in the drawing rooms of princes in Rome, and one probably typical of a prosperous American family. She wrote her husband, U.S. Senator Elijah Mills, of her management of their Northampton, Massachusetts farm—of the selling of wood and corn, of the various needs and qualities of their five children *and* the difficulties of finding good help. By all accounts she was exceedingly busy and Senator Mills wrote how disappointed he was in not receiving her letter:

> I have been disappointed again today in not hearing from you, dear Harriette; a few lines every evening, giving me a sort of journal of your life, would give you but little trouble and would afford me infinite satisfaction. Tell Helen [eldest daughter] she must write me. Give my love to all the dear things, kiss your little namesake a hundred times for me and do not let her forget me. Your ever affectionate and devoted husband.[65]

It is hardly surprising that Harriette had little time to write her husband since she was raising five children and running the farm. But she managed to write that she was waiting for money from him: she favored instruction of their son Elijah in Latin grammar; she was getting a tutor for William who needed discipline; Charles also needed "much vigilance" and prudence, "especially as to his manners and conversation, exposed as he is to such a host of rude and vulgar associates." She remarked favorably on the dispositions of their children. She wished Helen was with Aunt Helen where she could enjoy the advantages of education, and added that the "*cherub Harriette* has so completely entwined herself in my affections." The cherub was the future Harriette Mills Davis, Nannie's mother.

Miss. Harriette Mills, the youngest child on that Northampton farm, had beauty, wit, humor and charm. The Senator wrote in his memorial tribute to his wife that Nannie's mother had many admirers—among them Doctor Oliver Wendell Holmes and William Wetmore Story, the sculptor, who wrote poetry to her.[66] Harriette Mills mar-

---

[65] This valuable research from 1816 about life in Washington from Senator Mills is in the appendix.

[66] In his tribute to his wife, the Senator wrote of his wife's mother: "The beauty and fascination of a girl which never faded from the memory even at the close of a long life and which retained their hold on such men as Doctor Holmes and William Story were, you may be sure, of no ordinary quality. You will notice, too, how they recognized them as living again in your grandmother."

ried Admiral Charles Henry Davis. A generation later, in 1892, Doctor Holmes wrote to the Senator about Nannie's mother and Nannie when Nannie's daughter Constance, married Augustus (Gussie) Gardner at Nahant.

> June, 1892
> *Dear Cabot—*
> I had hoped that I might be able to attend the wedding of your daughter—the dear little girl whom I remember so well at Nahant; daughter of the sweet woman whom I recall so delightfully as maiden and as wife; granddaughter of the charming girl of an earlier date whose fascination I have never forgotten. If you could by any possibility think of an octogenarian's message at such a time, I would send through you my warmest felicitations to the bride and her husband, my kindest wishes to her mother and my tenderest remembrances to her grandmother.
> *Oliver Wendell Holmes*

The Senator admired Admiral Davis more than anyone; when he writes of his father-in-law, one feels that he himself would like to be remembered this way:

> His perfect simplicity, in his absolute courage, in his purity of mind and generosity of spirit, he always makes me think of Colonel Newcome. But, unlike Thackeray's hero, he was a man of the world in the best sense, of high professional ability and exceptional intellectual force. His manners were not only delightful but were quite perfect.[67]

Harriette and Admiral Davis' daughter, Anna Cabot Mills Davis, Nannie, was named after both her grandmother (Mills) and her grandmother's celebrated niece (Cabot) and Lodge's ancestor, Anna Blake Cabot. She always signed her name with both the Cabot and the Mills connection intact—Anna Cabot Mills Lodge. One of Mrs. Davis's sisters had married Benjamin Peirce, the great mathematician. Nannie was one of six children—as mentioned earlier, her sister Evelyn, nicknamed Daisy, married Brooks Adams, and so to her life-long friend Henry Adams, she would forever be "Sister." Henry Adams became so intimate with the Lodge family and he had various nicknames—to the children, "Dordy." If to Nannie, he was "Brother," he was of course also "Henry" to the Senator, Adams' former student at Harvard University, men-

[67] Lodge, "Tribute to Anna Cabot Mills Davis Lodge."

tor, and confidante. Another sister married Stephen Luce. The Senator writes:

> The successes and ambitions they saw about them had no connection with money-making but were far higher and nobler, for they concerned public service, science, literature, learning and art.... I cannot imagine surroundings more refining, more ennobling, or better calculated than these to infuse into children a high and fine conception of the meaning, the purposes and the conduct of life.[68]

From the time she entered Washington, D.C., at the age of thirty-six until her death at sixty-four, Nannie was the most important woman in government. She was often called on to receive at the White House, and she was also a kind of minister without portfolio whom Henry Adams would send to gather information for him. It is said that her greatest gift was her sympathetic warm-heartedness. But historians unanimously conclude she was brilliant—well-read in history and literature, gifted in languages and music. She particularly enjoyed poetry, and especially Shakespeare, which she could recite by heart. Her education consisted of intensive private tutoring and she graduated early from Wellesley College. When her father was in charge of the Naval Observatory in Washington, Nannie watched Lincoln's funeral bier passing under her window and from those days came a "passionate feeling about the Union."[69]

---

[68] See tribute in the appendix.

[69] Ibid.

Chapter 2

Young Love

In the summer of 1869, Nannie, eighteen, stepped off the train in Lynn, Massachusetts, to visit her Cousin Anna.[70] Her second cousin Cabot, who would become the Senator but was then nineteen, met her at the station. He describes the scene:

> She came to Nahant to stay with my mother. I had scarcely seen her since we were little children. I drove over to Lynn and met her at the station. The day is very vivid in my memory. I remember she had a book in her hand which she had been reading in the train. I asked what it was, and although I was fond of books, and had read more than most boys of my age, I was surprised at finding that a young girl had been casually reading Boswell's "Life of Johnson," one of the masterpieces of English Literature, instead of some obvious novel.... Before the summer of 1869, the most memorable of my life to me, had ended, we were engaged.[71]

By 1870, Cabot was composing love letters "to my own darling girlie." The match was judged a perfect one.

"Of course my maternal heart rejoiced," Cabot's sentimental mother (henceforth Anna) wrote Mrs. Bancroft, "for Heaven did indeed make the match. All our friends have looked upon the whole story as a love-poem in real life."

Nannie was slim and pretty, with dark blonde hair and what must have been extraordinarily arresting eyes. Contemporaries never agreed on their exact color; some said blue, others violet. Margaret Chanler, an old friend, wrote in her memoir, *Roman Spring*, "they were 'the color of the sky when stars begin to twinkle.'"

---

[70] Both Nannie and the Senator trace their ancestry to Anna Cabot. Nannie's grandmother, Mrs. Harriette Mills, was the great aunt of her mother-in-law, Anna Cabot Lodge. Nannie Lodge always called her mother-in-law "Cousin Anna."

[71] See tribute in the appendix.

"Years ago," John Singer Sargent told a friend in 1922, "I had the greatest desire to paint a portrait of Mrs. Henry Cabot Lodge. I still regret that I was not allowed to try, for I had such an unqualified regard for her that the odds were in favor of my succeeding in getting something of the kindness and intelligence of her expression and the unforgettable blue of her eyes."[72]

---

[72] Margaret Chanler, *Roman Spring* (Boston: Little, Brown, 1934), 192.; John Singer Sargent to William Endicott, Oct. 28, 1922, Lodge papers; Anna Lodge to Mrs. George Bancroft, Oct. 26, 1871. Garraty, 31.

Paris, 1871

Cabot and Nannie were very much in love and after Cabot's graduation from Harvard College, they were married on June 29, 1871, at Christ Church, across the street from Harvard Yard. In late July, the newlyweds set out for a two-year European honeymoon. By September, they were in Paris, three months after the Franco-Prussian War and the bitter street fighting that crushed the Commune. Order had just been restored and hatred of the Prussian conquerors dominated everything.[73] "The French are worse than ever," Cabot wrote to his father-in-law, Admiral Davis, "wanting in steadiness and strength" and dominated by "a wild desire for revenge and military glory."[74]

But Paris in ruins could not spoil their honeymoon and Cabot showed his bride the city. Nannie was much impressed by both the city and her guide: "Yesterday we went to the Louvre," she wrote her new mother-in-law. "Cabot greeted the Venus of Milo like an old friend, and I was fascinated.... It is delightful to see him. He enjoys everything to the utmost and I have never seen him in better health." Nannie went to the Paris dressmakers with her Boston friend Amelia Sargent, who was more concerned with the reception of her clothes back home than with the clothes themselves. But Nannie had strong convictions. "It seems to me," she commented, "if my dresses suited me, and were 'the thing' in Paris, I shouldn't much care how they were received in Boston."[75]

After a month in Paris, the couple went to Germany and in Leipzig, loaded up with furs at ridiculously low prices—coats for Nannie, carriage blankets, seal-skins, tiger-skin rugs, and bear blankets.[76] From there they went to Vienna and Rome where they passed the winter. In his autobiography, Cabot wrote that a change came over him that

---

[73] The cartoon engravings Nannie sent home to her mother are at the MHS.

[74] Lodge to C.H. Davis, Sept. 23, 1871, Lodge papers.

[75] Nannie Lodge to Anna Lodge, Sept. 27, 1871, Lodge papers. Garraty, 33.

[76] A tiger-skin rug with its (preserved) head, teeth bared, which greeted a small child who happened to wander into our grandfather's basement office in Beverly, might have come from this trip.

winter after meeting Michael Henry Simpson, a classmate who had also been wintering in Rome. The son of a well-to-do manufacturer, he had been brought up in the stern Congregationalist tradition of Puritan New England. He was interested in neither money nor business, preferring to make a career for himself in literature but he also believed, "every American, especially every educated American, ought to take part in politics and make himself effectively useful... working for what he believed to be right" through the Republican Party, "in the principles of which he had entire faith."[77]

On March 24, 1872, Mr. and Mrs. H.C. Lodge took a two-bedroom apartment in Paris on the Place Vendome, the corner of rue Castiglione and the rue St. Honoré. He wrote his mother of his wife in her ninth month of pregnancy: "She is just as cheerful and interested and bright as if the great event of her young life were not close at hand. It is her perfect self-control and determination to go on as if nothing were the matter that has kept her so well. As for myself my time passes uneventfully. In the morning I take a French lesson and in the afternoon I spend a couple of hours at the Louvre and then I stroll about the Latin Quarter in search of books and engravings, a pursuit which never tires to give me pleasure."

On April 5, 1872, Cabot returned shortly before dinner and found her just in from shopping and complaining of pains in her back. She insisted that her time had not come, however, and dressed for dinner in the usual fashion. After they had eaten, it became clear that the baby was on its way. Nannie, then nineteen, had a difficult time, for according to the doctor, "she was formed like a girl of sixteen." Just before one in the morning, Constance was born, named after Nannie's beloved brother and Cabot's former tutor, Constant Davis.[78] Cabot's pride in his wife is seen in this letter to his mother:

> I wish I could tell you how brave and plucky Nannie was, never a word or a murmur or an anxious thought for herself. After she was in bed with the pains at their height, she never uttered a cry and obeyed every word of the D[octo]r's and only a low half controlled groan and the perspiration of her face and the strong muscular action betrayed the anguish she was enduring.... She all through between the paroxysms of pain had a kind, loving word for me and a thought for

---

[77] Lodge, *Early Memories*, 236.

[78] Constant had died of tuberculosis while visiting his father in South America, where he was then in command of the Navy's South American squadron.

> Daisy [her sister Evelyn] and in that last fearful struggle in the very midst she said, 'Don't be frightened, Cabot.' I am not given to tears but I assure you I can hardly think or write of this without shedding them.

Nannie wrote her mother-in-law, on April 28, of her husband's dreadful disappointment that the baby was not a boy.

> *Dear Cousin Anna,*
> I must write you to tell you how well and happy I am and how I thank you for your kind note. I must tell you first, when you already know that Cabot is the best husband in the world. I can't tell you how splendidly and beautifully he has behaved all the time. I have been sick from the first. I only fear that he is far too good for me. **I am sorry for his sake the baby was not a boy to take his father's name** but she is such a dear little thing and little girls are so cunning and Cabot does hold her so beautifully.

The Senator dutifully corresponded with his mother, on a weekly basis, his entire life. On their return from their two-year honeymoon in Europe in 1873, the young couple and their baby girl lived in Boston at 31 Beacon. Mrs. Lodge (Anna) had welcomed them back to Boston, offering the couple her Beacon Street house, revealing her self-pity, sentimentality and effusiveness. She tried to lure them from Nannie's family in Cambridge by reminding her son that he would inherit her magnificent library:

> 31 Beacon St.
> Jan. 2 1873
> Your letter of the 31st of Dec., my darling son, reached me this morning and its contents would make any day a "Happy New Years Day" to me and therefore accept my hearty thanks for it as a gift of priceless value! [...] I had been happier this winter than ever dreamed it possible for me to be.... Since your good father's death and my friends tell me the tired look has gone from my eyes, so my darling, the close of the year must have brought you this one pleasant reflection at least—of having made your old mother very happy. I need not tell you that with my natural self-distrust, I hardly dared to hope I should succeed in rendering the home at 31 as attractive and comfortable as you had anticipated and with as few drawbacks to Nannie as under the circumstances was to

> be expected. I have tried very hard to make Nannie feel thoroughly at home and have as much undisturbed enjoyment of your society as if she was in a house of her own alone with you; —if I have failed to do this it has not been for wont of an earnest desire to make the pattern of life as smooth as I could, taking myself out of the way wherever possible—It rejoices my heart therefore to have you say you have been happy with the feeling of your perfect honesty in word and deed. I am so glad you feel about **the library** as you do, I shall enjoy it doubly *now that you have accepted it.* Give my love to the Admiral....

On Oct. 10, 1873, Lodge writes his mother from 31 Beacon St. of the birth of George Cabot Lodge, "Bay":

> The boy was ushered into the world at a quarter past seven. He is a fine boy weighing 10lbs. and if he lives and does well as seems likely now you know my intention is to have him christened George Cabot and **I can only pray that he may deserve that honored name.** Nannie is sleeping peacefully and could not be better. The milk came freely but not with a rush as in Paris and produced no pain and there was no fever. The boy took hold the instant he was put in the bed without the slightest assistance even as if he was 3 months old quite a contrast to Constance who fought and struggled.

In 1876, Nannie, at the age of twenty-five, gave birth to a second son, John Ellerton (1876-1942), making her the mother of three children. Through her lifelong correspondence with her son "Bay," it is apparent that he was the center of her life and favored by the Senator as well. When the Senator wrote his mother of his work in Massachusetts state politics, she, as previously mentioned, bequeathed George Cabot's, the Senator's great grandfather's, valuable paintings by Gilbert Stuart to her son instructing him that they should go to Bay. Betraying a modicum of guilt over her favoritism the Senator over her daughter Lillie and in spite of the intense and precious feeling between Lillie and her father, she nevertheless rationalized that the valuable Gilbert Stuart portraits should stay within the family. On May 12, 1880, she wrote, "My Dear Cabot, ...I give to you the two pictures of [Fisher] Ames and [Alexander] Hamilton which, of course, you will bequeath to your son, G.C. or one of them who still survives."

Henry Cabot Lodge was a complex person—vain and sympathetic, brilliant and insensitive, meticulous and patient, irascible and loving, a knowledgeable orator. In most ways he was a devoted son, husband, father and grandfather, though in other ways he was completely oblivious to his family. Cabot had been Henry Adams' student at Harvard, with a particular interest in Anglo-Saxon and Germanic law. Adams encouraged the young man to embark on a career of historian and man of letters. He was Adams' assistant on *The North American Review* between 1873 and 1876. In 1874, Cabot also earned a law degree from Harvard and in 1876, he went on to earn one of the first PhDs in History and Government at Harvard. Between 1876-1879 he was a lecturer in American history at Harvard College, but his classes were not well-attended. In 1880, he was elected to the Massachusetts House of Representatives.

Cabot wrote Adams for advice on his future and his revered teacher wrote back:

"Keep clear of mere sentiment whenever you have to decide a practical question. Sentiment is very attractive and I like it as well as most people, but nothing in the way of action is worth much which is not practically sound."[79]

Bay was four when Henry Cabot Lodge, his father, published his first book, *The Life and Letters of George Cabot*, his great grandfather. In 1884, Cabot's mother wrote to congratulate him on being nominated by acclamation to the Massachusetts Sixth District as its candidate for Congress.

> Sept. 21, 1884
> *My Dear Son,*
> ...My maternal heart rejoices—That sea of upturned, earnest faces following with eager interest every word uttered by so young a man was a scene never to be forgotten by an indifferent spectator and certainly an impressive one to a mother and wife! When you alluded to the state "Webster defended and Sumner led," I felt "a cloud of unseen witnesses held you in full survey and bade you onward, urge your way," in the words of the old hymn.... Ever, your grateful and devoted mother."

In 1884, Cabot backed James G. Blaine, the Republican presidential candidate, in spite of Blaine's presumed corruption, causing the "mugwumps" in the state, those who bolted the Republican party, to favor the Democrat Grover Cleveland and leaving him isolated in his

---

[79] Warren Zimmerman, *First Great Triumph: How Five Americans Made Their Country a World Power* (New York: Farrar, Straus & Giroux, 2004), 159.

constituency. "His Puritan heritage made him hide his feeling which only made matters worse. 'He was his own worst enemy,' wrote Bishop Lawrence forty years later. 'He held himself so aloof, was apparently so well satisfied that his decision was the only right one, that he seemed to assess us as ignorant and short-sighted in such matters.'"[80]

Not surprisingly, although he was the Republican candidate for Congress, Cabot was not elected to the U.S. Congress until 1887, where he served until 1893. At that point he was elected to the U.S. Senate, where he served until 1924. "Only God and his mother knows what that poor boy suffers," Anna Lodge wrote a friend. Only Theodore Roosevelt stood by him: "Now, pitch in for the party and leave the candidate severely alone. Go light on Blaine."[81] Cabot's speeches throughout his district concerned civil service reform, the tariff, and a sound currency, with occasional references to the need for a bigger Navy and an aggressive foreign policy.

The one thing he gained from his defeats was his new friendship with Theodore Roosevelt.

> Two more different personalities would be hard to find, but in 1884 they faced the same problems, and they solved them in the same way. The mugwump attack cemented their friendship with an enduring bond. By the time the campaign was over they had established a 'Cabot' and 'Theodore' relationship that was never broken, even when Roosevelt bolted the party in 1912.[82]

In a 1884 speech, Cabot's devotion to New England is evident: "'New England has a harsh climate, a barren soil, a rough and stormy coast and yet we love it, even with a love passing that of dwellers in more favored regions.' Harsh, barren, rough and stormy: these adjectives partly apply to Lodge in later years."[83] But in the early days, the young couple's life together was anything but harsh. Cabot and Nannie entertained often at 31 Beacon; they loved wit and clever talk. In April 1885, Nannie hosted a dinner at 31 Beacon for Senator William M. Evarts attended by Dr. Holmes, William Dean Howells and half a dozen others. Cabot reminded Evarts of the famous remark he had made when Lord Coleridge had questioned Washington over having thrown

---

[80] Garraty, 81.
[81] Ibid.
[82] Ibid., 86.
[83] Zimmerman, 162.

a silver dollar across the Rappahannock River. Evarts had accounted for this remarkable accomplishment, saying, "You know, of course, that a dollar went much further in those days than it does now." When Cabot mentioned this retort, Evarts immediately coined an even better one: "To throw a dollar across the Rappahannock was nothing to a man who had thrown a sovereign across the Atlantic." Cabot remarked, "His talk is phosphorescent, flashing all the time & with no more apparent effort than the waves," contending he outdid even Dr. Holmes, Boston's unchallenged master-talker.[84]

[84] Garraty, 89-90.

"Plus Ultra": Washington, 1887

There is a little of the student about him in appearance. He is tall and a well-knit man when he wears an overcoat. He wears a full brown beard, neatly trimmed. He has a deliberate manner, passive dignity, and a clear enunciation. He readily entered the field of debate and acquitted himself handsomely.

—Anonymous 1887 newspaper clipping,
scrapbook of Anna Cabot Lodge

When the 50th Congress convened in 1887, Henry Cabot Lodge, newly elected to the House of Representatives by a large majority, found himself in the back row with William McKinley.[85] Washington of that era was a small Southern town, but the ebullient new congressman wrote his mother from his desk in the House about Nannie's delight in their new life and gift for decoration, transforming their dreary rented new house at 19th Street and Jefferson Place into a showcase. The couple's small circle of friends included John Hay, a master-talker; Henry Adams' great friend Elizabeth Cameron, estranged from her husband Senator Donald Cameron of Pennsylvania, was another favorite.

Nov. 27, 1887
House of Representatives
Washington, D.C.
Dearest Mother,
This is not very pretty paper to write you on but it lies to my hand as I sit at my table and so in indolence I take it up. We are gradually settling into our place here. A furnished house, plenty of rooms, of good size

[85] Dec 7, 1887
Dearest Mother-
... I sit in a very bad place in the house way over to the left as I drew very near the last. I got a seat however next to McKinley of Ohio who is a first-rate man, one of the leaders of the House and a friend of mine.

and full of sun. The furniture is spare and in bad taste but Nannie has brought out her things and bought a few necessary articles and is giving it a look of comfort and refinement which follows her footsteps even in the most unpromising of hired houses. The children are going to school and the regular current of daily life is beginning to flow as usual. We went to a dance on Friday and last evening to the British Embassy to honor Chamberlain.[86] I was presented to Mr. C who closely resembles the Punch cartoons but looks clever and agreeable. Someone else was presented and I had no chance to talk with him but we are to meet him at dinner at John Hay's where we go on Wednesday and we dine with Mrs. Cameron on Tuesday. I went to Henry Adams's this morning....

In sentimental Victorian style, Anna Cabot Lodge wrote of her unreserved pride in her son and in Nannie; the heiress evidently pulled financial weight in the young Senator's life:

31 Beacon St.
Nov. 29, 1887
My Darling Son,
...I am sorry the house gave Nannie so much trouble but she has the Blake gift of making a refined home, wherever her lot is cast.... I like to follow you in my mind's eye.... I was amused... to see in large letters, "About Mr. Lodge" and dated Washington! [...] As I wish to enclose to you the cheque, you are to divide among the children as the present from me to them on Xmas day, I will not wait until Sunday to express my hearty thanks to you for your last letter....

In *The Five of Hearts*, Patricia O'Toole writes,

Henry Cabot Lodge had come to the capital in 1887, a freshman congressman from Massachusetts. Tall and spare, Lodge carried himself with the hauteur of the Cabots, who had grown rich trading rum and molasses in the early days of the Bay Colony. His patrician speech, his spike of beard, and his close-fitting suits with trouser pockets foppishly cut on the horizontal made an indelible impression on his House colleagues. They loathed "Lah-de-dah" Lodge on sight. Rigid and self-

[86] Joseph Chamberlain, prominent nineteenth century liberal British statesman, mayor of Birmingham, in Gladstone's government. Father of Sir Austen Chamberlain and Neville Chamberlain, who was Prime Minister until May 1940, when Winston Churchill assumed power when the Germans were at Dunkirk.

> righteous, Lodge believed himself ruled by no passion but the national good. But with his old history professor Henry Adams and other friends, Lodge was known as a genial host, and when political *bêtes noires* did not rear their fractious heads, he could work considerable charm on his guest.
>
> Intellectually, none of the women of Lafayette Square was a match for Nannie Lodge. Growing up in the erudition of Cambridge, Anna Cabot Mills Davis read voraciously and could toss off classical quotes with as much aplomb as a university man. The daughter of a rear admiral, she could also hold her own when the talk turned to naval affairs. Cabot, her distant cousin and childhood sweetheart, routinely asked her to pass judgment on his speeches. Whatever she thought inferior, he tossed into the fire and rewrote. Sensing— correctly—that the cure for Cabot's arrogance lay beyond her powers, Nannie settled for undercutting his ferocity at strategic moments by addressing him as "Pinky."[87]

The Lodges were invited out every day of the week, sometimes two or three times a day. Lodge became the new intellectual leader with a political philosophy aligned with the President's. The Harrison administration initiated America's imperialistic adventures for naval bases in the Caribbean, Canadian territory, the Samoan archipelago and the annexation of the Hawaiian Islands, vying with England and Germany for the control of the sea lanes in the Pacific. Hawaii was annexed in 1893, just before Harrison left office. Nannie was asked to receive at the White House, replacing Mrs. Benjamin Harrison in her official duties since the First Lady suffered from a nervous disorder. This is the earliest indication that Nannie had become a leader in Washington. Although the intellectual equal of presidents, senators and ambassadors, she was also self-effacing. She soothed wounded Secretaries of State, first James G. Blaine, in the Benjamin Harrison presidency of 1888 and then John Hay at the turn of the century. Her good friend Corinne Roosevelt Robinson, Theodore's sister, wrote this about Nannie:

> Born with a good taste that never seemed to err, she developed and refined her critical judgment, ever learning as the years with their increasing cares and many interests went by. She never would admit that she knew anything; she always with an extreme of modesty deplored her own ignorance, but it was that ignorance which is born of wide

[87] Patricia O'Toole, *The Five of Hearts: An Intimate Portrait of Henry Adams and His Friends, 1880-1918* (New York: Simon & Schuster, 2006), 208, 217.

> knowledge, of the sense of the petty done, the undone vast, which is the surest proof of knowledge of the highest and finest kind....[88]

Nannie approved of her husband's career. She read and criticized all of his political and historical writings; probably no one except Henry Adams was so influential as she in his literary development. Cabot was scheduled to speak at a local rally and had prepared a speech, which he then turned over to Nannie for criticism. She read it, and handed it back, saying with charming frankness that it was very inferior stuff, would not do at all, in short was quite impossible. Lodge ruefully tossed the manuscript into the fire and wrote another speech. This time Nannie's comment was: "Somewhat better than the other, yet far from satisfactory. Really you ought not to stand up before an audience to read that." Again Lodge started afresh, and produced a third effort. Nannie read it. "Better than either of the others," she conceded, "though not what it ought to be. However, I suppose it is as good as you can do, my poor boy."[89] Affectionate, deflating and motherly—that was the ideal woman for the Senator.

When Cabot's famous temper reared, Nannie was once heard to say, "I realize you are upset, Cabot, but **you don't have to kick me downstairs**," indicating that, for her, their marriage was a mixed blessing—and calling him Cabot meant she was furious. The Senator's intimates called him "Pinky," originating from his red hair and complexion, colored even deeper by his high temper. It served as an elegant put-down for his stuffiness and obsessions as much as a term of endearment. To Roosevelt, Lodge was just a "delightful, big-boyish personage." John Hay (1838-1905) remained faithful to the view he expressed in 1881 about reformers: "I have never met a reformer who had not the heart of a tyrant. Boundless conceit and moral selfishness seem the necessary baggage of the professional lover of liberty." Humor was a necessity and Nannie's letter thanking her mother-in-law for Christmas presents shows her style in this picture of happy family life; in the late nineteenth century, costume balls with powdered hair were the rage, it seems.

> Dec. 28, 1887
> 1211 Comm. Ave.
> Washington, D.C.

[88] Corinne Roosevelt Robinson, tribute to Nannie Lodge in *The Boston Evening Transcript*, September 30, 1915.
[89] Garraty, *Henry Cabot Lodge*, 101.

> *My Dear Cousin Anna,*
> I have left too long a time without thanking you for all your nice gifts, which were highly appreciated you may be sure. I believe Constance [15] and Bay [14] have already expressed their thorough satisfaction. Constance's furs are beautiful and just what she wanted, Bay is delighted to have money for his ammunition. John [9] has been perfectly happy with "Punch and Judy" and gave us an exhibition on Christmas night. The custard cups came safely and I know we shall find them most useful. I hope you had a pleasant Christmas, and am so glad you... dined with Lillie [Anna's daughter, the Senator's sister]. She writes so brightly now that I feel as if she must be quite herself again [implying her sister in law had emotional problems]. We had a very quiet pleasant day. It was as warm as summer and the children were out all the time that they were not opening their presents. We all had delightful things, and just what we wanted. We dined alone but for Willy Endicott[90] who came in as his parents had gone to Salem. After dinner, each child did something for the amusement of the family. Constance played a piece she had been practicing for a surprise. Bay spouted an extract from *Hiawatha*, and John played on the banjo and sang and then gave us the Punch and Judy... the children were too sweet and good and enjoyed everything so much. The children have been quite gay this week. I am waiting now for Constance and Bay to come from a party at Senator Hale's. Although Cabot and I have returned from a dinner and it is quite late, they have not yet appeared. Last night was a very pretty *bal poudré* at Mrs. Whitney's. It was so much better than expected. People generally looked very well and the party was gay all right with lots of pretty favors and a nice German [dance]. The trouble came today getting the powder out of the hair and generally resuming a natural appearance.... Cabot is enjoying his vacation very much and is taking the opportunity to do a great deal... He is remarkably well I think and gets a long ride every day, usually with Mr. Herbert, the English Secretary who is a great rider and hunter. I must say Goodnight, dear Cousin Anna; With much love and best wishes for a Happy New Year,
>
> Always Yr. Loving,
> *Nannie L.*

In that same winter, Cabot wrote his mother about having spotted a woman who would become his future in-law (when his son Bay married Mrs. John Davis' daughter, Bessy):

---

[90] Endicott College is adjacent to the Lodge compound in Beverly.

> 29 Jan 1888
> *Dearest Mother,*
> ...Tuesday we went to a little dance— I wiled away the evening with *Mrs. John Davis whom I had not seen for years but who is a very clever and amusing woman.* Nannie ended by dancing the German so that we made quite a night of it.... Love from all Ever yours, H.C.L.

In the fall of 1888, after Cabot's re-election to the House by a large majority, the effect of Nannie's exacting standard in his public utterances became apparent. He wrote a friend, counsel he later gave his son-in-law and U.S. Representative, Augustus "Gussy" Gardner, about his preferred style of oratory, "sticking closely to the point at issue and free from oratorical bombast, appeals to prejudice, and personalities. I have no faith in this hot air business."[91]

Nannie's success that first year in Washington was such that a new wardrobe was needed. Cabot, in thanking his mother for a Christmas present of $300, a large sum in those days, shows that Nannie never spent money on herself and he needed the money to invest in a new dress so that she could fulfill her new tasks at the White House as the surrogate First Lady in the Harrison administration.

> 13 January 1889
> *Dearest Mother,*
> Thank you for the handsome present you so kindly sent me and which I assure you was more than welcome. I am able now to get a present for Nannie. It is not of a very romantic order but she needs a dress more than anything else and so a dress it is...

In March 1889, Secretary of State Blaine wrote Nannie asking her who she would recommend as Assistant Secretary: "Do you happen to know a young gentleman—*gentleman* strongly accented—not over forty-five, well-educated, speaking French well, preferably German also (with an accomplished wife thoroughly accustomed to society) and able to spend ten to fifteen thousand—twenty still better, beyond the salary he might receive?" As a postscript, Blaine added that the candidate must also "believe in the 39 articles of Republican faith." Such a person could qualify for the post of Assistant Secretary of State (salary $4,500),

---

[91] Lodge to A.E. Cox, March 31, 1892; Lodge to Gardner, Oct. 8, 1908, Lodge papers. Garraty, 125.

"the most pleasant office in Washington."[92] Unfortunately for historians, she was too private a person to keep her response to Blaine, who "danced attention upon her like a young gallant. He was constantly sending her flowers, taking her riding, and writing poems for her."[93] He also consulted her on political and diplomatic matters. "I long for your good judgment & perfect prudence," he wrote once when she was not in Washington. "I have nobody to talk State Department secrets to." Such kindnesses could not help influencing Lodge, who was intensely proud of his wife.[94]

Nannie stands next to Secretary of State Blaine, the Senator, above left. President Harrison, lower right. Bar Harbor, Maine, 1889.

[92] Blaine to Nannie Lodge, March 19, 1889, Lodge papers.

[93] Garraty, 147. On the back of a calling card, April 18, 1889, Blaine wrote: "My Dear Lady of Boston,/I have once more lost on—/The hope of a fair afternoon!/I shall wait then in sorrow,/For the brighter tomorrow/Which cannot come for me too soon!"

[94] Lodge Journal, Jan. 21, 1892; Blaine to Nannie Lodge, Oct. 27, 1889, and *passim*, 1889-90, Lodge papers. Garraty, 147.

In the summer of 1889, Blaine invited the Lodges to Bar Harbor, Maine at the same time that the President was there. In a rare photograph of both Nannie and her husband, Cabot poses, neat gray derby in hand, while Nannie, in white, holding a white parasol, stands with that unforgettable combination—sure and demure, intelligent and kind.

John Milton Hay (1838-1905), Lincoln's personal secretary and future Secretary of State, had returned to Washington from Ohio, the year after the death of Henry Adams' wife, Clover (1843-1885), to comfort his close friend and get back into the center of things. The Roosevelts came to Washington in 1889 so that Theodore could assume his duties as head of the U.S. Civil Service Commission. Theodore and Cabot became as intimate friends as Hay and Adams and the Lodges; Hays, Roosevelts and Adams dined together several times a week.

On May 2, 1889 letter, Cabot wrote his mother that he would like to take Nannie to Europe for two months and on May 12, on the Senator's thirty-ninth birthday, Anna wrote back her birthday wishes that "since '64, ***you* have been *my* father and your own.**"[95]

Cabot wrote his mother that Nannie was so dear to "Brother" Henry Adams that theirs was the only house in which he would dine except for that of John Hay.[96] Adams was an aesthete who intellectually but not psychologically outgrew his New England heritage. He and Nannie were part of that generation of Americans who became instinctively closer to Europeans at a time when the American character became more international. Adams frequently used the expression, "se faire valoir" ("to make oneself worth something") because he was full of self-criticism and felt he had to justify himself. Nannie was, in spite of her brilliance, insecure; knowing so much,

---

[95] May 19

My Darling Son,

...We Cabots are not demonstrative as a rule but let our daily lives speak for us where we deeply love and I feared you might think me too "gushing" for so old a mother! Many years after my mother's death, your Father asked me one day if I had noticed the peculiar tone of my father's voice to me when I bade him goodnight and kissed him on the forehead? How I laughed when I replied, "My dear Ellerton," that quiet recognition of what I was to him has been food to a hungry soul and helped me to bear our many crosses with comparative ease. Since '64, ***you* have been *my* father and your own**; the 13 years we lived together, your morning and evening smile and word gave me strength for each day's battle and since our separation, your weekly visit, and lately your weekly letters, have been the source of my strength bodily and mentally up to the present time! I long for you to come to your native air..."

[96] May 12, 1889

Dearest Mother,

Wednesday night we had a few people to dinner... Henry Adams who has dined nowhere for the last five years outside his own house except at John Hay's. It is due to his liking for Nannie and he was certainly most genial and pleasant.

Henry Adams

she knew how much she didn't know. Over the years, Henry Adams grew to admire Sister Anne more than his student and protégé, as this letter from the Senator indicates. In this winter of 1889-90, Cabot wrote his mother of a stag dinner held to introduce Thomas P. Reed of Maine, the next Speaker of the House. On the back of the fantastic menu of gastronomic delights the likes of which no longer exist, he wrote the names of the guests.[97] There were "Blue Points on Shell, Consomme Financiére (with celery, radishes, anchovies and olives), Striped Bass, Joinville Sauce, Young Roast Lamb, Green peas, Terrapin, baked potatoes, Edmund's style, Lalla Rookh Punch, Canvas Back Ducks, lettuce salad, Fried Hominy, Savarin of rum, fruit sauce, fancy cakes, Ice cream tutti frutti, Fruits, crackers, cheese, coffee, cigars; wines: Chateau Y'Quem, Solero 1826, Chateau La Rose, Perrier Jouet, Clos de Vougeout, Liqueurs."

During the 1890s, diplomat Cecil Spring-Rice became an intimate of the Lodges. Cabot proudly talks of people falling under Nannie's spell and "Springy" was no exception. He was a tall, thin, young bachelor with a low English accent and a decided lisp—("I am Spwing Wice of the Bwitish Legation"). Intelligent, widely read, an accomplished amateur poet, brilliant conversationalist, he had a wry sense of humor. "Mad," commented Henry Adams, "but not more mad than an Englishman should be." He was a particular favorite of the ladies. He loved all kinds of social activity and, being unattached, was an ideal extra man. Washington hostesses knew they could count on him to chat urbanely over teacups and Springy described "teas" delightfully.[98] In his book about Spring-Rice, David Burton says: "He certainly

---

[97] J.G. Cannon, Geo E. Adams, John Sherman, Thomas Bayne, William McKinley Jr., Bery Butterworth, and J.B. Reed.

[98] "Now these teas are wondrous things. You call at a house on the lady's day together and a monstrous horde of persons from the uttermost parts of America. The lady says she is glad to see you and then asks your name. She then passes you on to another lady in a low dress who takes you to have tea at a table served by a young lady of her acquaintance from Buffalo or Little Rock, Arkansas. These ladies are often very pretty and charming; always rather amusing. I asked the one from Little Rock if it was a large town? She said, "Oh yes, there were two germans (Cotillion clubs) there." Quoted in Garraty, 88.

admired Edith Roosevelt but he said to Mrs. Lodge, 'I adore you, as you know.' This attraction was intense but not sensuous, mesmerized by Nanny Lodge, and enjoyed ready access to the Lodge homes in Washington and at Nahant."[99] Nannie became known for her tea-table, as a muse as well as a mother. This friendship blossomed in the 1880s and 90s and became even more intimate when Spring-Rice returned during World War I as British Ambassador to the United States.[100]

During his last two terms in the House—1888-1892—Cabot was a member of the Naval Affairs Committee. His interest in ships and the Navy, dating back to childhood, was advanced by his father-in-law and brother-in-law. Through connections at the Naval Observatory, he came into close contact with naval politics. One of Nannie's sisters married the son of Commodore Stephen B. Luce, the founder of the Naval War College at Newport and the patron of Captain Alfred T. Mahan, who in the late eighties was interested in the influence of sea power on history. Cabot was a quick convert to his point of view and pushed funding for the first three modern steel battleships through House appropriations, starting a revival of naval power culminating in the present fleet.[101]

Anna Lodge, neglected by her daughter, Lillie, and replaced in the Senator's affections by her daughter-in-law, Nannie, envied the role Nannie played in her adored son's life; she especially minded Nannie's intellect. The Senator's mother's letters show her hopes and dreams for him as a public figure and her anguish that she was liked only for her money:

> Sept. 13, 1889
> You have been the elixir of life to me—present or absent—from the year of my father's death and Lillie's marriage. From the 2nd year of my marriage, I gave up any individual life I might have had—the ***ugly duck*** became in a way essential to the comfort of the male circle. ***Life was very pale***—years rolled on, bringing with them private trials as well as joys. I never looked forward as long as I could make a home for each or all of the male circle nearest to me it did not enter my head or heart

[99] David Henry Burton, *Cecil Spring Rice: A Diplomat's Life* (Rutherford, London: Associated Universities Press, 1990), 58.
[100] Chanler, 204-8; Ford, Adams Letters, I, 383; Stephen Gwynn, *The Letters and Friendships of Cecil Spring Rice: A Record* (Boston: Houghton Mifflin, 1929), vol. I, 50, 54, 85; Spring-Rice to Lodge, July 5, 1891, Lodge papers.
[101] Garraty, 147.

> what it was to me or what the future might bring as long as my physical sufferings could be borne without annoying anybody.... ***I was told to think of my father***; it was as natural as to breathe and I now do not believe in forcing affection, which is not natural—I am by nature unselfish so there is no credit in one sense, in my finding my own happiness, in making that of others—but alas! The hour has now come when I can be nothing to anybody of my own blood and lineage and I am doomed to ***gilded solitude and servants.*** Please remember, my good son, that ***the brain does not take the place of the heart in a true woman***—mine especially if a mother and a widow! My three weeks in such a happy home as yours was like champagne to my hungry soul and the return to the empty house, produced a greater reaction than usual owing to the lowered condition of my whole system during the past year. It is needless to say that ***if my otherwise good daughter's eyes*** could be opened to the true state of the mother's condition both bodily and mental, all would be well.

The Senator wrote of his worries about Nannie's fatigue, her work at the White House, receiving visitors, renovating the house and worrying about her mother. Nannie was going with Anna Roosevelt to New York to get a week's change and rest.

> 5 Jan. 1890... Nannie went to the White House when she had been asked to receive and having assisted in that way, we came home.... Theodore and I drove about in the rain and made official calls.... Nannie has had callers all afternoon.

It is possible that Nannie's fatigue was not just in response to her demanding role as minister without portfolio. John Hay and Nannie Lodge had a crush on one another, according to the family, and her fatigue could refer to her divided loyalties between the two men she loved. Nannie called her husband "pretty cunning" to her friend Lizzie Cameron.[102] She worked hard and enjoyed being the wife of one of the most powerful men in the country, so if she was in love with Hay as well as Cabot, it might have made her ill. However much Hay and Nannie had a crush on each other, there was a code of honor in marriage and the Senator knew he had nothing to worry about. Contrary to the opinion of some historians, it is almost certain she did not have

---

[102] Elizabeth Cameron to Henry Adams, Oct. 29, 1890. "Cabot is speaking everywhere & is tired and nervous. Nannie calls him 'pretty cunning.'"

an affair with her friend Hay, though she enjoyed his "companionship." Hay was a man in love with love who flirted with Nannie Lodge and Lizzie Cameron, as his poetry indicates. Hay comes across as the more serious partner in the relationship and frustrated in his relationship with Nannie Lodge—he had a bad case of unrequited love.[103] John Hay rarely lost his temper with Cabot but when he did, jealousy may have played some part in it. The reverse was probably not true—Cabot's fits of temper with Hay had more to do with himself than with pique about his wife. Indeed, family members say that the Senator wouldn't have noticed if she had had an affair so much did he revere her, trust her sense of duty, discipline and loyalty.

It is difficult for us to conceive how differently men and women behaved at that time and it is easy to confuse romantic love and romantic friendship. Beautiful, brilliant women were goddesses—the fascination with them causing obsessions, and the fashion in the late nineteenth century was to place them on pedestals. This claim of a love affair between Nannie and Hay is a modern interpretation on the theme when the code of honor seems to have vanished. Adams' fascination with women, from the Venus de Milo to the twelfth century devotion to the Virgin, went beyond spirituality. To him, they were the "life force," making him a favorite with the Lodge women, both Nannie, and Bay's future wife, Bessy Davis, as well as any number of "nieces."[104] The chapter on the Virgin and the Dynamo in *The Education of Henry Adams* might have been written for the Lodge women—for Nannie as well as her daughter-in-law. Adams spoke of the power of women, not for their

---

[103] See April 22, 1891 letter from Elizabeth Cameron to HA regarding "unrequited love." The historians referred to are Patricia O'Toole, Warren Zimmerman and Kathleen Dalton.

[104] "The force of the Virgin was still felt at Lourdes, and seemed to be as potent as x-rays; but in America neither Venus nor Virgin ever had value as force—at most as sentiment. No American had ever been truly afraid of either... anyone brought up among Puritans knew that sex was sin. In any previous age, sex was strength. Neither art nor beauty was needed. Every one, even among Puritans, knew that Diana of the Ephesians nor any of the Oriental goddesses was worshipped for her beauty. She was a goddess because of her force; she was the animated dynamo; she was reproduction—the greatest and most mysterious of all energies; all she needed was to be fecund... the poet [Lucretius] invoked Venus exactly as Dante invoked the Virgin.... All this was to American thought as though it had never existed. The true American knew something of the facts, but nothing of the feelings; he read the letter, but he never felt the law. Before this historical chasm, a mind like that of Adams felt himself helpless; he turned from the Virgin to the Dynamo as if he were a Branly coherer. On one side, at the Louvre and at Chartres, as he knew by the record of work actually done and still before his eyes, was the highest energy ever known to man, the creator of four-fifths of his noblest art, exercising vastly more attraction over the human mind than all the steam engines and dynamos ever dreamed of; and yet this energy was unknown to the American mind. An American Virgin would never dare command; an American Venus would never dare exist." Henry Adams, *The Education of Henry Adams*, 375.

beauty but for their power to create, to give birth, and he deplored American men for not recognizing that force. "Women," he wrote, "are naturally neither daughters, sisters, lovers nor wives but mothers." "Boston's purpose in life," Henry Adams once said, in making exactly this point, "is to breed and to educate. The parent lives for his children; the child, when educated himself, becomes a parent or becomes an educator, or is both... when a society has reached this point, it acquires a self-complacency which is wildly exasperating. My fingers itch to puncture it—to do something which will sting it into impropriety."

Women throughout the ages have served to create and hold the family together and to inspire "man" to his higher self. Five thousand years before Christ, women were represented in art as possessed of magical powers. Sculptures with huge breasts and hips glorified their powers of procreation. From the Macedonian city of Thessaly to Mesopotamian Sumeria, early relics in clay or stone, sometimes with their arms crossed as if to protect the soul, invested women with a force; they were goddesses of fertility and the means of survival of the species. Suddenly in the third century in the Levantine, a place of passage, the fertility goddesses are replaced by another type. In Hellenistic times, the notion of the ideal woman took the form of a goddess—the Venus de Milo—no longer sensual and emotional with burgeoning fertility but embodied with majesty, with classical far-away beauty and virtue.

Nannie served both models—as mother and sage. Her famous charm extended to a select world of statesmen and historians in Washington and Boston at the time, but no doubt her favorite was John Hay, both of them being uncomfortable with fools, boors, and adversaries. In 1890, Nannie, a Washingtonian for three years, had come to appreciate Hay, the witty Midwesterner so different from her mercurial, spoiled Cabot. Hay's closeness to Adams no doubt drew Nannie closer to him. Hay had a made "a rich marriage" to Clara Stone, the daughter of a vastly wealthy railroad entrepreneur from Cleveland. Certainly, Hay's marriage to Clara Stone enhanced both his financial security and his place in Ohio politics, notably under President McKinley. He was a good husband, no doubt, and loved his plump wife.

Nevertheless, John Hay had a fastidious nature and was inclined to caution in both public and private life. Brilliant, accomplished, prone to depression and self-doubt, he was also a great wit. "There are three species of creatures," he once wrote, "that when they seem going are coming, when they seem coming, they go: diplomats, women and crabs." Nannie appreciated Cabot's literary cultivation but enjoyed Hay's gift for wordplay. Hay, Cabot, and possibly Nannie as well, were bigots with a taste for imperial diplomacy. She admired Cabot's tenacious pursuit of his goals in the Senate as much as Hay's equilibrium under fire as a diplomat. Although Hay had been in diplomatic service under Secretary of State Seward in Paris and Vienna, he did not achieve the rank of ambassador until his appointment to the Court of St. James's in 1897, followed by Secretary of State soon thereafter. Hay was versatile, reliable, trust-worthy, and charming. Physically a small man, 5-foot-2, he no doubt preferred a woman closer to his own size.

Henry Adams described Hay this way: "Always unselfish, generous, easy, patient, and loyal, Hay had treated the world as something to be taken in block without pulling it to pieces to get rid of its defects; he liked it all: he laughed and accepted; he had never known unhappiness and would have gladly lived his entire life over again exactly as it had happened."[105]

Nannie made her role as the mother of Constance, Bay, and John her first priority but clearly enjoyed her role in government as wife of the powerful Senator. Nannie's love and strong sense of duty and admiration for her husband outweighed any romantic attachment. Still, family sources confirm that Hay's admiration and love for Nannie was reciprocated—"he had a crush on her and *she* on him." Their strong lifelong friendship was probably similar to that of Henry Adams and Lizzie Cameron.

Nannie Lodge, whom Warren Zimmerman has called "an effervescent beauty," had everything—an exciting life as the wife of a powerful Senator who was devoted and adoring, a Secretary of State in love with her, and three beautiful and talented children. Historians have written of Nannie's vivid conversation, her brilliance, her generosity and her sense of values. So it is wrong to confuse those qualities with the more sordid claim that she had an affair with Hay, as Zimmermann, Patricia O'Toole, and other historians have done. "They fell in love and went to great lengths to arrange trysts that would not provoke gossip."[106] While there is no doubt about their keen devotion to one another as friends, there is no indication of any romance, at least from Nannie's side. Her husband adored her and paid a great deal of attention to her in contrast to what historians claim.[107]

Patricia O'Toole's marvelous description slightly overstates the

---

[105] Ibid., 375.

[106] Zimmermann, *First Great Triumph*, 78.

[107] "Whether Lodge's curious failure to mention his own wife can be put down to a Bostonian sense of privacy or whether, as seems likelier, he simply took her for granted, one can begin to understand why in later years Nannie took up with John Hay, who was prepared to pay more attention to her." Ibid., 157. This is nonsense. Zimmermann's first hypothesis as to family privacy is the correct one as is obvious from the Senator's exquisite commemoration of his wife at her death, in the appendix.

relationship:

> By the summer of 1890, John Hay often found his thoughts drifting to the Lodges' cavernous wooden house on the crags of Nahant. Only Henry Adams and Lizzie Cameron knew it, but John Hay and Nannie Lodge had fallen in love. In 1887, when Cabot took his seat in Congress, Hay needed only a glimpse to see that Nannie at thirty-seven was easily the peer of Henry Adams' beloved Lizzie Cameron. Her dark hair was swept up into a loose knot at the back of her head, her skin was pale pure ivory, and her eyes, according to John Singer Sargent, were "an unforgettable blue"—verging on violet.... With her elegant silk gowns, perfect carriage, and aquiline nose, Nannie looked as queens ought to look but never did, said Theodore Roosevelt.[108]

When Nannie was in Washington, as has been said before, she assisted at the White House in receiving guests and afterwards for the Secretary of State as is evident from the correspondence between Senator Lodge and his mother. This correspondence reveals that the Lodges dined with the Hays frequently and sometimes Cabot had private dinners with John Hay. Mrs. Lodge also took a break in a foursome; the quartet of friends—Nannie and Hay, Adams and Lizzie—unmarried to each other, went out, mostly to concerts, museums and operas. After their outings, the quartet frequently retired to Adams' house. Hay's letter to Mrs. Cameron shows that he begged her to accompany them—evidently Mrs. Lodge refused to see him alone. They wanted to avoid scandal at all costs and that was why they made such an effort to arrange to see one another with friends.

The story of Hay and Nanny's muted friendship is told through his poems, some of which have never been published.[109] Indeed it was a great discovery for me to come across the poems by accident at the Brown University library where John Hay's papers are located. On May 1, 1890, Hay attended a concert of quartettes by Beethoven, Schubert and Grieg which inspired him to write *Love and Music.*[110]

Eleven days later Hay sent Cabot a fortieth birthday present. Hay's esteem for Cabot was demonstrated in his giving him a Rubens sketch. Hay, fifteen years older, saw in Cabot an up-and-coming young man, and his wit with a touch of irony was demonstrated by

---

[108] O'Toole, 217. Nannie was thirty-four in 1887.
[109] See appendix.
[110] See appendix.

the motto he assigned to Cabot; but the picture may have been meant for Nannie.

May 12, 1890
My Dear Lodge,
I want to associate myself a little with this fertile day and to send you this sketch by Rubens. I got it at the sale of Russell's collection at Christie's three years ago. Mrs. Hay tells me you liked it when she showed it to you. I congratulate you on your position, your talents, your time of life. You have a right to adopt the motto Charles V assumed in his young manhood, "*Plus Ultra.*"

Yours Sincerely,
John Hay.

Lodge returned the irony in his reply:

House of Representatives
May 13, 1890
Dear Hay,
Taking this note and the gift together, I do not think I have ever read a note or gift which pleased me so very deeply as your note and gift have done. I found them both on my return this evening from New York and they have quite relieved the gloom which overspread me yesterday on turning another decennial corner. What puzzles me more is what I have done to deserve note and picture and next in intricacy is the perplexing question of how any man owning such a drawing would develop the generosity to part with it. I noted the drawing well when Mrs. Hay showed it to me and to see it was to love it. "I long have loved it from afar." Now it is mine and I cannot find words to thank you and Mrs. Hay for I please myself by thinking that I am indebted to her as well as to yourself. The drawing is superb. That you know. What you cannot know is the extent of pleasure which the words of your note gave on my forty years.

Yrs. Ever Sincerely,
H.C. Lodge

Mrs. Lodge is as much pleased as I am if that be possible.

Clover and Henry Adams' "breakfast" table—an early lunch—drew together a small circle of friends, also attended by a sprinkling of French and English dignitaries—French Ambassador Jusserand and Cecil Spring-Rice—to add spice. After Clover Adams' suicide, Adams headed off to the South Seas to soothe his grief. He wrote to a friend, "Our little family of Hays, Lodges, Camerons and Roosevelts, has been absolutely devoted to each other, and as I was the one to be lost, I came in for most of the baa-lamb treatment."[111]

In August when Adams left for the South Pacific, the Hays visited the Lodges and Roosevelts in Nahant. In the dining room, facing south to the Atlantic, the table had just been cleared. Mrs. Lodge rose first, being the lady of the house, and strolled on the lawn with John Hay while Lodge and the young Theodore Roosevelt wandered out to the porch with their cigars. Nannie's carriage was impeccable—for a small woman she seemed tall. All women wore white in summer and her dresses were made of lace with high collars. Mrs. Winthrop Chanler, whom Nannie first met in Washington, recalled her "as the most charming woman I have ever known; an exquisite presence in this workaday world."[112] Nannie's brother-in-law, Brooks Adams, also remembered her as "one of the most sympathetic and appreciative natures that ever lived."[113] If annoyed however, Nannie was capable of a "spiced, even somewhat acid, turn of phrase."[114] Mrs. Chanler admired Nannie's combination of "the usually contrasting qualities of keen intelligence and warm-heartedness."[115]

In the autumn, Hay wrote "An Idle Question," an unpublished poem (October 1, 1890) on Hotel Brunswick, NYC, stationery.[116] In the same month, Elizabeth Cameron wrote Henry Adams from Ohio that although there was gossip, the story of an affair amounted to nothing: "...Mr. Hay was here yesterday. Cheerful and brisk. I find that the story of Nanny has crept even here. There was a good deal of Washington comment. I know but I did not think it amounted to anything. And I hate to hear it in Mrs. Hay's home."

Hay, in an unpublished light-hearted rumination, *Enough of Thunderous Passion*, revealed that he was a ladies man, a romantic, and in love with love more than with his wife, Nannie, and Elsie (Mrs. Cameron).[117] In a December 30, 1890, letter to Henry Adams in the South Seas, he

---

[111] O'Toole, 213.
[112] Chanler, 192.
[113] Garraty, 100.
[114] Harold Dean Carter, *Henry Adams and His Friends* (Boston: Houghton Mifflin, 1947), lxvii.
[115] Chanler, 193.
[116] See appendix.
[117] See appendix.

complained he was a failed lover:

Hay as a young man.

> I remember [Clarence] King's saying in one of his exquisite tirades against women as a climax of contempt, "Sex is such a modern affair, after all." You seem to have come upon it at a moment when it is purely a matter of structure.... What a paradox... seeing it as a wholesome fact in Polynesia, as an instrument of mere perversity in Paris, as a sentimental reminiscence in the etiolated society of Washington... Washington is as dry as a remainder biscuit.... Helen (Hay's daughter) has to keep the peace between some half dozen appreciative youths. Cabot Lodge [Bay] is the biggest.... Mrs. Lodge and Constance have fled from Washington in disgust & gone to Boston for three weeks of gaiety which is denied us here.

Although Hay, in his failed attempts with women, could be bitter and contemptuous, there is no doubt he tried. Interestingly, Hay paid homage to Mrs. Cameron as well as to Mrs. Lodge as it was the fashion for men to pay homage to the women they admired, much as in the court of love of Eleanor of Aquitaine. "Goodnight my tantalizing goddess," Hay wrote to Mrs. Cameron in 1891. "A dozen times this day I have been on the point of believing that you are not really so complicated as you seem, but that last half hour threw me into the wildest confusion again."[118] Obviously, Hay was sexually attracted to Lizzie Cameron to whom he also wrote the poem, "Obedience," which she wrote out in her own hand and in which clearly, Hay's excessive ardor was discouraged.[119] In an 1892 letter to Mrs. Cameron, whose nickname was "Elsie" as well as "Lizzie," Hay wrote:

> Don't you see, you darling, why I love to grovel before you. It is such a pleasure to worship one so absolutely adorable. There is no one in sight of you in beauty, or grace, or cleverness, or substance of character. You

[118] See appendix.
[119] See appendix.

> sweet Elsie, you dear, beautiful love, with a thousand miles between us I can say things I would not dare to say under the clear cold light of your lovely eyes. You are all precious and divine.

But Hay's true love seems to have been for Nannie—enough to cause in him the pain of unrequited love, enough to affect his health. It is unclear if Nannie's lifelong friendship with Hay affected her own health. What is clear is that John Hay loved having fun with women who were not his wife.

On Jan. 27, 1891, Mrs. Cameron wrote Adams:

> John Hay managed to say to me discreetly that Mrs. Hay is going to Cleveland on Thursday & he should like to lunch quietly at the Country Club and go to the theater... so Friday we go to the play... but we cannot decide upon the fourth man and Mr. Hay and Nanny seem to think it very stupid of me not to like anyone well enough to want to spend long hours with him alone. Oh how I miss you... Cabot has to be the fourth man in all these little parties & it is fatiguing for me.

In April and May both Nannie and Mrs. Cameron had been ill and nursed each other back to health. April 22, 1891, Elizabeth wrote to Henry Adams:

> Nanny is recovering from the flu; she looks like a lily. I wish that I could see some chance for a change and a rest for her. The children are very Cabot-y in their selfishness and she must go on as usual.... When are you coming home? John Hay sailed yesterday. His love for Nanny does not wane. I am awfully sorry for him...

On May 7, 1891, Mrs. Cameron wrote to Henry Adams that she had had a violent attack of the grippe and that Nannie had called on her and given her a valuable present.

> I had a sharp but violent attack of grippe which left me weak & heady so even the journey (to Europe) was hard to bear. Nanny bent over to kiss me goodbye and when she was gone I found a little parcel in my lap containing a tiny silver heart full of scents—or salts—to hang to my watch. The card with it said, "Cordoncita para mi corazon." Wasn't it like her?[120]

---

[120] Translation: "A pendant for my dear heart."

In another anecdote about Hay's amorous adventures with Mrs. Cameron in Paris, she also mentions Bay's future mother-in-law, Sally Davis, and gives clues about her racy character.

> May 26, 1891
> *Elizabeth Cameron to Henry Adams:*
> John Hay and I have had a real Parisian spree. I hope that you are jealous? Please don't tell him I told you but we dined in a cabinet "particulier" & went in a lower loge to the ballet. I actually felt wicked and improper! He did too for he felt obliged to follow up the precedent and tell me how much he loved me! I feel as if we'll always have this delicious secret between us—only I have to take you in.... Sally Davis' talk is more daring than ever... how thoroughly Sally suits Paris and Paris suits her.... She hates little Frenchmen—says they all look like "fausses couches"—but they buzz about her all the same.

> June 7, 1891
> *Elizabeth Cameron to Henry Adams:*
> John Hay has been very ill & still looks badly. It seems that he had an attack of heart one night and actually came near dying.... He told me yesterday that he felt that this was the last year of his life. I think he is awfully down about himself—and he certainly looks badly.

In this letter to Adams, Mrs. Cameron explains that Hay wrote her a sonnet about a kiss which she insists was poetic license;[121] but that she felt she was losing Hay's affection to Mrs. Lodge.

> Sept. 26, 1891
> *Elizabeth Cameron to Henry Adams:*
> ...John Hay's sonnet amused me immensely. He wrote it almost immediately for I saw it at Beverly (Farms) and he never saw yours unless someone robbed me of it for I like best to have that & other things just between you & me alone. The kiss must be poetic license. Indeed it must! John Hay writes me now and then. He pretends that he likes me since our London season together but I know better. Nanny is the first.

Cameron's letter proves that Hay took poetic license whether with

[121] See "Through the Veil", in the appendix.

her or with Nannie; sadly for him, Hay's ardor for Nannie never waned. In 1893, he wrote this unpublished poem to Nannie; it speaks to the unique color of her eyes, her beautiful figure and her royal soul:

"Sapphires and Violets"

I.
The violet is shyly bright
(So are my Lady's eyes)
Filled with the June sky's azure light
(So are my Lady's eyes.)

So gracious, fresh and debonair,
Like slim girl-queen's serenely fair,
It holds all charms of earth and air.
(So do my Lady's eyes.)

II.
The sapphire shows a royal soul,
(So do my Lady's eyes)
It rules by beauty's sweet control
(So do my Lady's eyes.)

It sheds abroad its regal rays
upon the noble and the base,
Unmoved itself, all hearts it sways,
(So do my Lady's eyes.)

III.
The violet shines with heaven's own dew
(So do my Lady's eyes)
The sapphire gleams with heaven's own hue,
(So do my Lady's eyes.)

There all their charms together thrown,
The dainty flower, the wondrous stone,
Still my dear Lady's smile alone
Could match my Lady's eyes.

Although Nannie was more than a conventional wife and mother, her chief interest in life was her family. The principal person in her life was her son Bay and there is no question that the principal person in Bay's life was his mother. Being sensitive and prone to fatigue with her duties as the wife of the powerful Senator, the link with her son, the poet, was more potent.

The Senator's mother warned him to be more attentive to Nannie, to the strain of her daughter-in-law's duties as a public person. She also spoke of Bay, Nannie and the Senator's oldest son—the center of their hopes. Bay was not a good student, probably due to psychological problems. Besides comparing himself to his father, he may also have suffered subconsciously from Oedipal guilt, being so close to his mother. Consider that "they shared their youth": she was twenty when she gave birth to Bay. He grew into a tall, handsome, well-built young man, sensitive, zestful and exuberant. But he neglected his studies. Actually his intellectual development was over-stimulated by his environment. Indeed, Edith Wharton called him a "genius." "He grew up in a hot-house of intensive culture," Wharton wrote in 1910. "He was one of the most complete examples I have ever known of the young genius before whom an adoring family united in smoothing the way."

Nannie in 1893 at thirty-seven.

Nannie Lodge served to enlarge and refine the Senator's character and tame his temperamental outbursts. Self-disciplined and unassuming, she exerted a powerful influence on both her husband's and her son's careers. The Senator wrote his mother that Bay had failed badly at school. influence on both her husband's and her son's careers. The Senator wrote his mother that Bay had failed badly at school.

July 10, 1889
Dearest Mother,
I am sorry to say that Bay has failed and failed badly. The hard work at the end could not make up for lack of work in the winter. I am of course, much disappointed but I contemplated this result and hope that it will teach him a lesson that will have better results.

In her response, Anna Lodge shows she was ambitious for her grandson: "I consider him to be one of the most promising statesmen of the day and I feel sure that his patriotism is as great as his talents."[122]

Evidently, Theodore Roosevelt had become a good enough friend to Bay to warn him about the implications of his actions. Bay's son (my grandfather, Henry Cabot Lodge, Jr.) wrote in his autobiography:

Constance at 20 with Bay, 19.

> Theodore Roosevelt was a lifelong friend of both my grandfather's and my father's. When my father had disastrous examinations at Harvard, Theodore Roosevelt wrote him, "A dropped man is in a most unenviable position; and he is always looked down on by the very men who have encouraged him to

[122] May 25, 1890 (40th birthday)
My Darling Son,
Your noble son Cabot, passed an hour with me in my old study, and gave me more pleasure in that one hour than I have known for many a day. He spoke of many of the great questions of the day, a correct understanding of which is so important not only to the people of our own country but to all mankind. His intellectual force enables him to look into the nature of all these questions and to understand their essence, more readily and fully than most people are able to do. He is very clear, and comprehensive in his statements and exhibits a good deal of what I call "common sense." I was delighted as well as surprised to hear him express so many opinions that are in exact accordance with my own. I consider him to be one of the most promising statesmen of the day and I feel sure that his patriotism is as great as his talents. I may well congratulate you as might anyone upon the possession of such a noble son as he is. I rejoice to think that he lives and moves in our midst and I sincerely hope that he will live long, to be a blessing to his country and his friends.

> get into that position." He wrote an introduction to my father's collected works of poetry after my father died.... In what he was, did, and said he exemplified to me Aristotle's belief that a man's worth is not measured by his wealth, nor by his position in society; but by the amount of himself that he has given to his people. To him, public service was an incomparable challenge.[123]

In 1891, Lodge had his eye on Henry L. Dawes seat in the Senate, the seat of Webster and Sumner, and he spent a lot of time perfecting his organization to win the necessary votes: "'To win a campaign the first thing is to know where you are' [he told Robert A Southworth]."[124] John Hay's comment to Henry Adams that same year shows how closely he kept track of the Lodge family—that he ran into Nannie on the street, that Constance Lodge was making her "debut" and that the Senator rather liked a good fight:

> Aug. 20, 1891
> The Fells
> Newbury, N.H.
> ...I have been down to Boston once or twice shopping. On one occasion I found Bill Bigelow and Mrs. Lodge in the street. They took me to the Somerset Club to lunch where I saw Lodge. He feels pretty gay being in full control of the state organization & rather enjoys the furious kicking of his enemies. Mrs. Lodge was in high spirits having just heard of your intended return. My little Helen has just got back from a short visit to Nahant—Constance was starting for a brief campaign at Newport.

The summers were full of wit and good cheer. As David Butler has written, Cecil Spring-Rice spent happy times at Washington and Nahant. "[The Lodge's] style of living became his ideal—its pleasures, its diversions, its conversations, as well as in the deeper meaning Spring-Rice attached to marriage."[125] John Garraty quotes Spring-Rice, whose typically British wit makes a lively and subtle portrait of the Lodge family during the summer of 1891, when he stayed in the Lodge house

---

[123] Henry Cabot Lodge, Jr., *The Storm Has Many Eyes*, 21-22.
[124] Garraty, 130.
[125] Butler, *Cecil Spring Rice: A Diplomat's Life*, 58. When Springy [Cecil Spring-Rice] told Nannie that he and his friends sunbathed in the buff on the rocks when the British legation moved to the North Shore from Washington in the summers, she replied, "Carrion for the gods!" The story is located in O'Toole, 58.

on Massachusetts Avenue while the family was in Nahant:

> It was about 12 o'clock at night when I saw the first [ghost] who entered the room on the ground floor where I am writing a report on the copyright law of England. He was a tall dark majestic and rather terrible man, arrayed in an American flag and a russet beard. He asked me what I was doing; and on being told grew six inches taller, much to my astonishment, and was going to speak further when we were interrupted by a vision of exquisite loveliness in the person of a sylph-like form surmounted by the most brilliant pair of purple eyes and a fascinating smile. I was about to enter into conversation with this charming apparition (who addressed the previous phantom in terms of endearment which reduced him to his previous dimensions) when I heard a noise which made me believe that the judgement day had come.... I suggested to the phantoms that it was time to look for their bodies but the shorter and more affectionate of the two informed me that it was only her black-eyed darlings. I don't know what that meant as the taller phantom gave an explanation in which there was no reference to "darlings" at all.

In winter, Cabot and Nannie were dining with the British Ambassador Sir Julian and Lady Pauncefote, the British attaché Spring-Rice, the Blaines and the Hays. Cabot rode every day in the mornings with Theodore before going to the Capitol. Evidently the winter of 1891-92 was tiring but by the spring, Nannie's health had improved. In late February, Cabot and Nannie had been to see Anna Cabot Lodge, then broke up the trip in New York and came on to Washington the following day. The next night was a dinner for twenty-four at the Vice-President's [Levi Morton] for the Blaines. By May, Cabot wrote his mother that "...Nannie to my great delight seems *decidedly better* & like her old self—the talk was almost entirely confined to Bay after she told me of your illness on arrival and other news of family life."

In the summer of 1892, Constance, the Senator and Nannie's daughter, was married. Mrs. Cameron did not approve of the match and had written Henry Adams from London the previous October that "Nannie has written to announce Constance's engagement to Gus Gardner! Isn't that disgusting? Constance—so bright, clever, & young and he such a boor [sic]! I am furious. I am off to Paris in an hour & since Paris means you, I am glad to go...."

Constance Lodge and Congressman Augustus "Gussie" Gardner were wed at Nahant. The Nahant church overflowed with family and friends. Easter lilies, rhododendrons and orchids along with the gold-hearted field daisy were knotted together with ferns and tropical greenery. The clusters of bridal knots were attached to the pews with white satin. The bride wore white satin upon which a *mousseline de soie* formed a basque and girdle. The veil of tulle was held by the bridegroom's gift of a diamond tiara and the soft folds of chiffon on the bodice were held by a crescent-shaped broach of diamonds. She carried a few white roses. The bridesmaids wore white muslin with blue satin sashes and large garden hats of creamy Leghorn. Nannie wore a demi-trained gown of white crepe, striped with smoke, made with a Watteau back of beautiful old lace, a pointed girdle of smoke-grey velvet and a vest of blue chiffon with a small bonnet to match and carried a spray of pink sweet peas. The newly-weds took up residence in Washington where the spoiled and assertive bride of the young congressman could be near her father.

Lodge was elected to the Senate in 1892 and must have been invested on the 4th of March, 1893. For the first time, he wrote his mother from the Senate Chamber. Mrs. Lodge congratulated her son on winning a seat in the Senate as the highest possible ambition for him and complained about the fact she hadn't been invited. Her ambitious, anxious, lonely and jealous nature is heightened, comparing herself to the fascinating Nannie. It's a wonderful Victorian story—nowadays if a mother wanted to see her son, she would announce she was coming.

> March 12, 1893
>
> *God Bless You, My Darling Son,*
>
> ...I sympathized with you heartily on every path of your noble life and tried never to be a hindrance and if possible only a help in your course onward and upward to the desired goal when you said to John in my presence "in regard to the Senatorship, it was the only office you should ever care to have." My anxiety for your mental and physical condition during that fearful struggle was naturally increased tenfold so that when the verdict came and [William] Sturgis [Bigelow] appeared to announce it, I heartily acquiesced in his sentiment, "Mrs. Lodge, there is nothing left us but the grave!" The widower mother of an only son had never been a stumbling block in his career, from any doting fondness and this was her success. It doubtless was one of my Cabot inheritances—I never was ambitious for you but with you as our tastes were similar doubtless this made the labor music for both. I do not know why you think "it may seem vain to wish me to see the visible sign of your

> success." You have worked hard and honestly for a prize and you have won—you ought to be proud of having won it. Oh! How I longed to be in that Senate Chamber in that hour! **No one ever suggested my going to Washington at that especial time** and... it was too late for me to ask permission to go either to a Hotel or to your home. I must confess that I was with you in spirit at that hour.... Why was I not permitted to be in that Senate Chamber when I had been so much in earlier days, seeing my only and idolized son, receiving the outward sign of an honor achieved—beyond the wildest dreams of his dear father? ...I looked eagerly for your seat and if the journal was right in my mind's eye, I see the place in the Senate Chamber—How joyful dear Father and good, simple old Sumner would have been—With loads of love to dearest Nannie and the one lamb [John] at home, as ever,
>
> Your grateful and loving mother,
> *A.C.L.*

The Senator's first move after his election was to buy a proper house in Washington. On April 2, 1893, he announced buying a mansion on Massachusetts Avenue and asked for his mother's financial help. The heiress easily dispensed with (the equivalent of at least) $5,000,000 to her beloved son.

> We have bought the Aldi's house on Massachusetts Ave. and the vacant lot next to it. It is in the out part of the city and faces south, having sun all day in the front and the two lots give 75 feet front on the avenue—on the vacant lot I can put my stable—there is a big library in the front.... We get the house for $40,000—a reasonable price—the lot of $19,000 and $12,000 will make the improvements.... I do not want you to give away any part of your money and especially now when it would look as if the gift to both was made because I was after you for money for my house. I must beg you not to think of it. But you can help me very much if you will. I want you to lend me $50,000 [$5,000,000 in today's dollars] on a mortgage on the whole property at 4 and 1/2 percent....

Five years later when, with Lodge's help, Theodore Roosevelt became Assistant Secretary of the Navy, the Senator had a special door created on the ground floor of the house for Theodore with direct access to the Senator's study, family legend has it. Not only would Theodore ride with Lodge in the morning but he would also come to the house for

John Singer Sargent of Henry Cabot Lodge in 1890. Donated to the National Portrait Gallery.

private talks at night; if it was during a dinner, Nannie simply took over as host and skillfully guided the conversation to a successful conclusion.[126] Such was the Senator's influence that John Singer Sargent wanted to paint him; Nannie desired a full-length portrait[127] but in the end it was three-quarters, cut just above the Senator's knees but showing a strikingly strong turn of the face, with level eyes, a powerful jaw and beautiful hands.

In the correspondence of late spring, Anna expressed concern about Nannie's popularity and appearances; the Senator assured his mother that Bay acted as his mother's escort if he himself was not available. In February, the Senator wrote that Nannie had gone for a week to New York but "Bay, of course, went with her." The proper Victorian, Mrs. Lodge wrote her son to pardon her for saying how improper it would be for Nannie to go from Boston to Washington unaccompanied. Historians here have an inkling of how much Nannie was admired and interestingly, how much freedom she had to do as she pleased though her son Bay acted as his mother's escort and guardian. Anna Lodge seems to be warning her son that Nannie was putting her reputation on the line by traveling alone.

> May 6, 1893
> 31 Beacon St.
> *My Darling Cabot,*
> I hope you will pardon me for the liberty I have taken in persuading Nannie not to go alone by night to [Washington]—**She has been moving anywhere, without children, servants, as a rule, without you and in addition, a group of friends and beaux!** For *your wife* also

[126] As Ernest Samuels wrote, "Indeed, Lodge's influence became proverbial. The boy, Quentin Roosevelt [Theordore Roosevelt's son], once blurted out to a White House guard, 'I'm going to see Lodge; that what Father tells everybody when he wants to have anything done.'"

[127] Anna Cabot Lodge to Henry Cabot Lodge, April 6, 1893: "I am so glad Nannie desires a full-length portrait."

to take that journey, for no sense—illness or death the cause, without anyone to appeal to in case of any unforeseen trouble, it struck me so painfully that I could not help speaking so strongly as I did. It is the first time I ever took a liberty with you as a husband! Her one desire was to do what you expected but she thoroughly appreciates my view of the position. Hoping she will reach you in health and not too tired for all the complications and labors. Ever yr devoted mother God knows her first offence will be her last!

Private
Dear Cabot,
Your darling wife has just left **with Bay as escort** and I know you will pardon me for the liberty I took with keeping her overnight—As usual she came in that first evening very hot and tired from a day of work then opened the windows tight and left in her bedroom for the cove wind to come in not east but west and cold, she left the door ajar by accident all night and slept in a draft—Yesterday she had that trouble in her throat and last evening came on the cough and today it is incessant. She has been an angel of peace and joy to your mother.

The Senator's mother wrote her son on October 17, 1893, of Nannie's visit, revealing that Nannie's mother had died. Anna spoke mysteriously of "the truth," which may refer to Nannie and Hay's friendship, and perhaps she had sympathy for it, pretending to have had an admirer possibly Senator Charles Sumner who kept up a lengthy correspondence with her upon the death of her husband, John Ellerton Lodge, when she was only forty-one.[128]

My Very Dear Son,
It is curious that your most unexpected and welcome letter of the 15th was brought to me just after your good wife had appeared at 31.... She was consoling me with the knowledge that she too had had no news; so [we] both were made doubly happy by companionship. She was very well and in better spirits than at any time since her mother's death. Of course, we talked of "the truth" of which my experience was unique—seeing by the transcript the wires had broken down between W[ashington] and [here], I knew you couldn't telegraph.

On December 21 and 30, 1894, the Senator wrote his mother of

[128] Their correspondence is part of the Lodge Collection at the Massachusetts Historical Society.

another of Nannie's conquests: they had attended a dinner for Anna Roosevelt at the Cochran's with Reed, the Storers, the Hays, Theodore and Edith, Professor Langley, British Ambassador Pauncefote and his wife, and Secretary of the Treasury Carlisle and his wife, saying he was "stupidly placed and coldly placed by the window and had a dull time. Nannie however went in with Carlisle—he is an interesting man and she enjoyed drawing him out and from the way he talked to her, I gathered that he had fallen a victim."

In the winter of 1894-95, a boundary dispute between British Guiana and Venezuela exploded when gold was discovered and the Senate passed a resolution that the parties should arbitrate. It was a test of the Monroe Doctrine, first initiated in 1823 by U.S. President James Monroe, whose primary objective was to free newly independent Latin American countries from European control. The doctrine stated that efforts by European powers to colonize land or interfere with the states in the Americas would be viewed as acts of aggression by the United States requiring U.S. intervention. It asserted that the Western Hemisphere was not to be further colonized and that the U.S. would not interfere with existing European colonies nor meddle in the internal concerns of European countries. Both the U.S. and Great Britain hoped to avoid having any other country become involved in Spain's colonies.

On January 15, Arthur Balfour, Lord Salisbury's nephew, whom Lodge had met the previous summer in London, and who had quickly become one of his closest English friends, said that no one in the British Isles, not even "the crotcheteers or the lunatics" wanted any more South American territory. The thought of fighting the United States, "our own flesh and blood, speaking our own language, sharing our own civilization," Balfour declared, "carries with it something of the unnatural horror of a civil war."

Lodge replied by sending him his speech on the Monroe Doctrine, and in a long letter on February 1, told Balfour:

> I feel as you do about a war between the two great English speaking peoples. I readily accept your statement that you do not desire to extend your possessions in the Americas, but other nations are less scrupulous. There is no nation on earth which England could so easily make her fast friend as the United States... yet from 1776 English policy has been one of almost studied unfriendliness....

"Thereafter, both at home and abroad, the wider implications of the Monroe Doctrine were understood and generally accepted," writes

Garraty. "Lodge was gratified by the outcome of the Venezuelan affair. An early advocate of American intervention, he had seen that policy adopted and carried through to a successful conclusion. At the height of the crisis, and at least partially because of the prominent role he had played, he finally won a seat on the Foreign Relations Committee of the Senate, a place that he desired above all others.... From a broader viewpoint, the incident marked a gigantic step forward for the expansionist ideas Lodge promoted so strongly. It led directly to the strengthening of the Navy as well as of Monroe-ism, and greatly awakened public interest in hemispheric defense and aggressive imperialism. Finally, it enabled Lodge to practice his theory that politics should stop at the water's edge...."[129]

Only four years later, however, Senator Lodge was one of a small group in power who used the Monroe Doctrine as a means to attack and take possession of the Philippines and Cuba, Spain's former colonies—assuredly not the original intent of the doctrine. However, they did so at a time when the Germans and the British were going to take them as their coaling stations. The Navy was important to the Senator not only for his own family history but because the best friend of his father-in-law Admiral Davis was Admiral Mahan, historian (notably, *The Influence of Sea Power upon History, 1660-1783*, published in 1890) and chief strategist of the plan for American control of the sea lanes to the Pacific. As my Uncle Harry told me, characteristically tongue in cheek, "You know you could inflict a lot of harm, never get hurt and be back in time for dinner. We were liberating Cuba and the Philippines from Spain, after all." When asked about the many hundreds of thousands killed in the process, he replied, "They were yellow and everyone was racist in those days. No one cared about the indigenous peoples."

In January, 1895, the Senator's mother, referring to England and the boundary dispute between British Guinea and Venezuela, wrote her son, the Senator: "Three cheers and a tiger for the secret twist you gave to the lion's tail! Dear Bay came in very unexpectedly to ask for a bed—I am, I never saw him look so handsome and distinguished—his eyes were luminous and in that fur coat especially." That winter, the Lodges gave a party for Bay, in his senior year at Harvard, attended by a young lady who would become Bay's wife. Senator Lodge also reassured his mother that he was attending to his wife:

---

[129] Garraty, 164-165.

Jan. 6 and 16, 1895
...Your interest and pleasure in my work are among the greatest pleasures of life to me.... We had another young dinner for [Bay]—Him, Bonaparte, **Bessy Davis**, the daughter of John Davis' just out—a very pretty and attractive girl and various others.... Two long walks in Rock Creek park—vigorous exercise and I do not know when I have enjoyed two days more. Theodore and I got out for a ride again this morning.... I am getting along well and I assure you, I shall look after Nannie and try never to let her overdo or get too tired.

Historian John Crowley has written that "Nannie Lodge was so self-effacing that scarcely any details of her personal life survive."[130] Henry Adams wrote Elizabeth Cameron: "Curiously enough, I have come to think that the clue to her character is timidity and want of self-confidence. She is easily scared."[131] This could explain Nannie's family nickname, "Oops." The Senator set high standards for everyone and she set high standards for herself. "Oops" is what one says when one is careful not to make a mistake. Bay enlarged the nickname—Oops, Oopity, Oopa, Huppity—and lightened it, teasing her into refraining from worrying. No doubt that the Lodge household was a tiring one.

In another letter to Lizzie Cameron, Adams refers to her unselfishness and extreme modesty and also to her friendship with Hay:

Sister Anne came to dinner last night, quite alone with me.... We had more or less gossip about everything but herself. She has much to say about Wolcott and Hay and Root and so on but is silent about what she cares about.... Meanwhile the true type of successful cant, which rests in no belief at all, is Cabot, who grabs everything and talks pure rot to order.

Devoted to her family, Nannie Lodge during the Washington years preferred the relaxed company of a few friends to the role of society hostess. She was, above all, a private person. The Senator's adoration of her demanded her presence almost all the time. Bay's letter to his mother from college asking why the Senator wouldn't allow her to come to Boston makes this selfish insistence evident.

Jan 17, 1895
Dearest Wüps,

---

[130] Crowley, 3.
[131] *Letters of Henry Adams*, Sept. 1, 1901.

I meant to write you long before but I have been very busy for you know the mid-years will be here next week. I was so sorry you couldn't come to Boston—**I don't see why Pa wouldn't let you**. It's too bad because I know how anxious you were to see sister.... I have a scheme of writing essays on Schopenhauer, Swift, Moliere, Poe, Lecomte de Lisle, Carlyle, Alfred de Vigny, Thackeray (perhaps) and any others I may think of and entitling the collection "Studies in Pessimism".... I wish you would ask Pa what he thinks of this idea....

Nannie had gone to visit her family in Cambridge and dropped in to see her mother in law.

Feb. 3 1895
Dearest Mother,
Nannie's absence has made the last week seem rather a long one... I have been busy...I have had no letter from you, an event I always look forward to but I hear of you from Nannie and count on hearing a great deal more when she returns on Tuesday. Dined with Theodore, Senator Davis, Wolcott, John Hay, Harry White—men's dinner. Dined en famille with the Camerons and Edith and Theodore.

Feb. 4, 1895
A Thousand thanks, My Darling Son, for your most delightful letter, brought by the mail today, to give me strength for the present sorrow—I went last night to Sturges' to see Constance and Nannie in ball costume for Constance's dance! It is needless to say that Nannie looked handsome but what was more to me, she looked so much stronger and like her old self than when she left Boston that my heart rejoiced. Constance never looked so lovely and beautiful and G.C. [Bay] too with "those eyes"—Nannie has telegraphed to know whether she shall stay for the services tomorrow—If you say yes please tell her to go to NY for the night. It will let her reach home refreshed—Let me pay the extra expense!

Evidently the Senator and Nannie's daughter Constance had a baby that winter, probably a girl since it was not deemed important enough for the Senator to mention, although he did write his mother of his pride in Nannie—a forty-two-year-old grandmother—being attractive to other men, indicating that he had complete faith in her fidelity.

> March 6, 1895
> *Dearest Mother,*
> You will readily understand why I did not write as usual on Sunday. Last week, the Senate sat day and night.... We went to a musical party at the Hearts. It was a costume 18th c. party. The musicians were all in the dress of the last century led by Seidl. The music was charming and all Haydn and Mozart. The women were powdered and in costume. **I came home after the music but Nannie stayed on and danced and had a delightful time. Harry White with whom she danced said she was the belle of the ball & so did others—Pretty well for a grandmother.**[132] She was taken all the time—What a lasting charm to have at forty. What a gift. We have been to various dinners. Night before last we dined at the Hays to meet Rudyard Kipling. I had heard such unpleasant stories of his bad manners. I enjoyed seeing him. He is obviously clever.

In 1895, the Senator was occupied with the problem of Hawaii. At the start of the American nation, the sea was the highway to the world, and Lodge intended that both the Atlantic and Pacific Oceans remain free and open to international commerce. Nannie, as the daughter of an admiral, would probably have agreed with him. These islands were seen as essential to securing American control over the sea lanes in the Pacific. The Senator was not an isolationist, as he is generally considered; on the contrary, being fanatically anti-slavery did not mean the Senator was anti-imperialist.

Warren Zimmerman explains that the American imperialists were expansionists:

> [Lodge's] own sense of superiority, reinforced by social Darwinism, made him a natural candidate for the imperialist philosophy, though he avoided using the word "imperialism," preferring expansion. More profoundly, his imperialism had twin roots in romanticism and technology. Lodge had a romantic belief in America's destiny which he saw foreshadowed by the great figures of its past, like his biographical subjects, Washington, Hamilton, and Webster.... He believed in the importance of individuals in history.... "The personal qualities and individual abilities of public men...make the history and determine the fate of nations." Nations have lives of their own. "We are a great nation and **intend to take a nation's part in the family of nations**," he said

---

[132] Henry White was later Ambassador to France and the Republican representative at the League of Nations talks.

> in a speech in 1896.... In his speeches of 1895, he spoke of a "large policy," which meant control of the Caribbean and parts of the Pacific; seizure of the strategic islands like Cuba, Hawaii and the Philippines; and even the incorporation of Canada. Lodge's large policy was greatly influenced by the writings of [Alfred] Mahan and later by personal contact. He considered Mahan "the greatest authority living or dead on naval warfare."[133]

The chief concern of the 1896 presidential campaign between William Jennings Bryan and William McKinley was sound currency. Bryan galvanized the silver forces in the primaries to defeat those who supported the Democratic incumbent, President Grover Cleveland. His famous "Cross of Gold" speech advocating bimetallism lambasted the monied classes for supporting the gold standard at the expense of the average worker.[134] The Democratic Party wanted to set the value of the dollar to silver and opposed pegging the value of the dollar to the gold standard. The inflation that would result from the silver standard would make it easier for farmers and other debtors to pay off their debts by increasing their revenue dollars. Bryan, thirty-six, the youngest presidential nominee ever, whose stance directly opposed the conservative Cleveland and united the agrarian and silver factions, won the Democratic nomination.

Lodge felt that international bimetallism was a defense against "the free silver craze." He was not in sympathy with a straight gold standard because "you throw the whole strength of the bimetallic argument and all theoretical bimetallism over to the silver people." Still, true to his Republicanism, he felt the platform should be uncompromising and the party was against free silver. The Senator loved conventions and never let pass the opportunity of going to one. As part of the Massachusetts delegation, he went to the St. Louis convention determined to fight for the gold standard on principle, hoping to work in a plank on bimetallism in practice. On June 15, he met with "Boss" Platt of New York in the latter's hotel room where Platt pledged his support for a strong gold plank in the platform and guaranteed that the powerful New York delegation would back the

[133] Zimmerman, 184-185.

[134] "Having behind us the producing masses of this nation and the world, supported by the commercial interests, the laboring interests and the toilers everywhere, we will answer their demand for a gold standard by saying to them: You shall not press down upon the brow of labor this crown of thorns, you shall not crucify mankind upon a cross of gold."

plank should it come to a vote on the convention floor.[135]

"No more brilliant summary of the campaign has been written than that penned by Nannie Lodge," writes Garraty. Fully sharing the political preconceptions of her husband, Nannie still had to pay tribute to William Jennings Bryan and the battle he had waged.

> The great fight is won... a fight conducted by trained and experienced and organized forces, with both hands full of money, with the power of the press—and of prestige—on one side: on the other, a disorganized mob at first, out of which burst into sight, hearing, and force—one man, but such a man! Alone, penniless, without backing, without money, with scarce a paper, without speakers, that man fought such a fight that even those in the East can call him a Crusader, an inspired fanatic—a prophet! It has been marvelous. Hampered by such a following, such a platform... he almost won. We acknowledge to 7 millions campaign fund, against his 300,000. We had during the last week of the campaign 18,000 speakers on the stump. He alone spoke for his party, but speeches which spoke to the intelligence and hearts of the people, and with a capital P. It is over now, but the vote is 7 millions to 6 millions and a half.[136]

Nannie.

Lodge returned from St. Louis "on top of the wave."[137] A few days later he addressed the alumni dinner at the Harvard Commencement ceremonies. It was the twenty-fifth anniversary of his graduation and the citadel of mugwumpery. Blaine, Hawaii, and Venezuela were (for the moment) forgotten. When Lodge rose to speak he was greeted with real

[135] Garraty, 169; H.H. Kohlsaat, *From McKinley to Harding: Personal Recollections of Our Presidents* (New York: Charles Scribners, 1923), 37.
[136] Garraty, 176; Gwynn, II, 197-8.
[137] Henry Cabot Lodge to Margaret Chanler, May 27, 1901.

enthusiasm. "Praise and blame often come to a public man from the same quarter at not remote intervals.... There are many evils, many shortcomings in our politics.... Let us go down into the dust and heat and try to cure them.... This great democracy is moving onward to its great destiny. Woe to the men or to the nations who try to bar its imperial march."[138]

By the mid-1890s the Senator's "imperial march" was his chief concern and it came in the form of "readiness"—both his and Theodore Roosevelt's great interest.

> The United States had a mission and through technology and wealth, possessed the means to fulfill it. But the country had to be prepared. [Lodge] and Roosevelt wrote in *Hero Tales*: "The only peace worth having is obtained by instant readiness to fight when wronged." Preparedness meant a large navy, a natural objective for a man whose own, and whose wife's, families had maritime backgrounds. Lodge ridiculed those who proposed "to meet the encroachments of a foreign power by a diplomat on a ferryboat."[139]

Later that summer, Henry Adams joined the Lodges on a trip to England and France. The Senator wrote his mother of the trip. Nannie wrote that touring Europe with Adams was "a liberal education" for Bay and John, then twenty-two and twenty. The Senator and Bay shopped at Charvet and visited the Venus at the Louvre who was "as lovely and perfect as ever," then strolled to the Pont Neuf. The fivesome visited Saint Chapelle and Notre Dame—"the coolest spot in Paris"—and dined outdoors under the arcade of the Palais Royale. The Senator told how Nannie helped Adams choose linens for his Paris house, how they lunched at Le Grand Vefours and visited the Pantheon, "whose simple, severe and fine proportion were the best example of modern classical that I know." At the house of Jacques Coeur at Bourges, the merchant who furnished Charles VII the money to fight the English, the Senator took note of a coat of arms that could have been his own—a scallop for his patron saint (Jacques) with the gallant motto, "Aux vaillants coeurs rien n'est impossible."[140]

Adams wrote of Nannie in *The Education*, comparing her to other American women, during the famous trip to Europe which inspired the writing of *Chartres* and *Mont St. Michel*:

---

[138] Garraty, 172.
[139] Zimmerman, 131.
[140] "For valiant hearts, nothing is impossible."

> Towards midsummer, 1895, Mrs. Cabot Lodge bade him follow her to Europe with the Senator and her two sons. The study of history is useful to the historian by teaching him his ignorance of women; and the mass of this ignorance crushes one who is familiar enough with what are called historical sources to realize how few women have ever been known. The woman who is known only through a man is known wrong, and excepting one or two like Mme. De Sevigné, no woman has pictured herself. The American woman of the nineteenth century will live only as the man saw her; probably she will be less known than the woman of the eighteenth; none of the female descendants of Abigail Adams can ever be nearly so familiar as her letters have made her; and **all this is pure loss to history for the American woman of the nineteenth century was much better company than the American man**; she was probably much better company than her grandmothers. With Mrs. Lodge and her husband, Senator since 1893, Adams's relations had been those of elder brother or uncle since 1871 when Cabot Lodge had left his examination papers on Assistant Professor Adams' desk, and crossed the street to Christ Church in Cambridge to get married. With Lodge himself, as scholar, fellow instructor, co-editor of the *North American Review*, and political reformer from 1873 to 1878, he had worked intimately, but with him afterwards as politician he had not much relation; and since Lodge had suffered what Adams thought the misfortune of becoming not only a Senator but a Senator from Massachusetts—a singular social relation which Adams had known as fatal to friends—a superstitious student, intimate with the laws of historical fatality, would rather have recognized him only as an enemy; but apart from this accident he valued Lodge highly, and in the waste places of average humanity had been greatly dependent on his house. Senators can never be approached with safety, but **a Senator who has a very superior wife** and several superior children who feel no deference for Senators as such, may be approached at times with relative impunity while they keep him under restraint. **Where Mrs. Lodge summoned, one followed with gratitude....**[141]

When Adams decries the tendency in history of the United States to fail to give American women their due, he would no doubt be appalled by the many histories who have failed to understand Nannie. Adams agreed with the Senator's own admission that he reached the

[141] Adams, *The Education*, 353-354.

seat he coveted most of all on the Senate Foreign Relations Committee in 1894 thanks to the love and immense talent of his wife and her ability to temper and inspire her husband. Adams' belief that a study of history shows an immense ignorance of women shows he was ahead of his time. By implying that he knew Nannie better than her own husband did and considered her to be superior to her husband is certainly a good reason to attempt to piece together her life, though one could argue, as Adams says, "women known through a man are known wrong."

Chapter 3

The American Queen

Nannie

I can see her now, her cameo face and her port like that of a slender queen. She looked as queens ought to look, but as no queen I have ever seen does look; the carriage of her head, her eyes under their level brows, the erect, graceful figure—all conveyed instantly the impression of something fine and elusive and utterly dauntless, utterly fearless. And she had so many sides! And she always rang true, she was always mistress of any moment, no matter what that moment might bring.

—Theodore Roosevelt

Nahant became a political meeting place in summers. Henry Adams visited when he was at Beverly Farms, the Theodore Roosevelts came up from Sagamore Hill, the John Hays from New Hampshire, Edith Wharton from The Mount, and Henry James while he was visiting his cousin, George Abbot "Jabber" James, and George's wife Lillie, the Senator's sister. Henry James wrote a friend about Beverly, words which could just as well be applied to Nahant: "I envy you—for I see you in the mind's eye at Beverly—the element of the wide verandahs, cut peaches—I mean peaches and cream, you know—white frocks & Atlantic airs. You make me... in these high lights, quite incredibly homesick."[142]

When McKinley became president in 1897, the Senator worked hard to get his best friend Roosevelt named Assistant Secretary of the Navy; and Roosevelt received the appointment. "To the younger and more brilliant man, [Lodge] was unfailingly solicitous, selfless and sensitive."[143]

Theodore, as he was known in the family, loved Lodge and both

---

[142] Henry James to Miss. Frances Morse, June 1897. Percy Lubbock, ed. *Letters of Henry James*, Vol. I, 265. Peaches and cream, like fresh corn and lobster, is one of the culinary delights of New England.

[143] Zimmerman, 177.

Nannie

were professional historians. Roosevelt wrote thirty-five books to the Senator's twenty-nine. The Roosevelt collection includes works on outdoor life, natural history, the American frontier, political history, naval history, and his autobiography. Roosevelt was also a naturalist and explorer of the Amazon Basin. He was also, like Lodge, a lawyer. Both Lodge and Roosevelt were active in the Spanish-American war in 1898 but Roosevelt organized and helped command the 1st U.S. Volunteer Cavalry Regiment, the Rough Riders, in that war. Returning to New York as a war hero, Roosevelt was elected Republican governor in 1899.

Roosevelt, in turn, envied the Senator's happy marriage and enjoyed sparring with Nannie; because he was the Senator's best friend, he was perhaps the only person who called her Nannie:

> Anna Cabot Mills Davis Lodge… enjoyed quoting Dickens and Shakespeare to confound him. Lodge's frank spouse showed Theodore that he preferred women who were not the long-suffering and docile Patient Griselda type, and when Nannie teased about an intellectual gaffe, he merely joked back: "My youth was an unlettered one."[144] […] "When the Lodges visited him at Leeholm, Theodore tried to get Nannie to run with him down Cooper's Bluff. She flatly refused. Afterward he said admiringly: "Nobody who heard her would ever again have accused her of possessing a timid or irresolute character." Nannie's forthrightness impressed him as well as her worldly concerns: she would join the Women's Educational and Industrial Union to help working women in Boston, and she sponsored the good works of the Visiting Nurses Association in Washington, D.C. He had animal skins he gathered from his western hunts turned into footmuffs for Nannie and confessed to her: "Indeed I would be almost ashamed to say how much I prize yours and Cabot's good will and friendship. You see I never make friends at all easily; **outside of my own family you two are really the only people for whom I genuinely care.**"[145]

Theodore Roosevelt's affectionate letters to Nannie reflect the level of her intellect, coupled with her mysterious gift of charm:

> *Dear Nannie,*
>
> I return Gissing's book on Dickens and also, "The Greek View of Life."

[144] Theodore Roosevelt to Henry Cabot Lodge, vol. 1, 45.

[145] Kathleen Dalton, *Theodore Roosevelt: A Strenuous Life* (New York: Alfred A. Knopf, 2002), 95.

Isn't it curious how much resemblance there is between the Japanese spirit and the Greek spirit of the Periclean age? The Japanese, unlike the Greeks, were able to transform their spirit of intense but particularistic patriotism into a brand of national patriotism and so they have been formidable as a nationality in a way in which it was wholly impossible for the Greeks to ever be. It is curious that one of the worst of the Greek attitudes, that toward women, should be reproduced in the Japan of today.[146]

Grover Cleveland was president until March 1897. The president's wife, Mrs. Grover Cleveland, was unable to receive and Nannie was again called into service, the Senator wrote his mother. He described Nannie, resplendent in purple velvet, a color which no doubt drew attention to her extraordinary eyes.

Jan. 2, 1897
The President invited Nannie who was obliged to go to the White House to receive. She wore purple velvet and looked very well but it was hot and crowded so that I went and made my bow and took her away early. In the evening was a great dinner at the Brice's and a dance afterwards—180 people at dinner at small tables—Nannie and I left before the German. It was a brilliant and successful affair and very well-managed. I took in Mrs. John Davis[147] and had Mrs. Cameron on my other side.

In 1897, when Hay was named Ambassador to the Court of St. James's, Henry Cabot Lodge wrote his mother on April 4 that Nannie and Constance would be going to New York on the 8th and that the Senator would join them three days later.

March 7, 1897
I dined with John Hay to meet the President elect [McKinley]. It was a dinner of 25, rather an interesting crowd of men. John Hay goes to London—an admirable appointment.

April 4, 1897
Constance leaves on the 8th and Nannie is coming on with her to

[146] Theodore Roosevelt to Anna Cabot Lodge, Jan. 11, 1907.
[147] The Senator's future in-law.

stay a few days in New York so you will see them and the baby (Constance's).... I am very glad you are coming to NY.

Secretary of State John Hay.

On April 11, there was a farewell dinner in New York for John Hay attended by Senator and Nannie Lodge that left the new ambassador feeling that he had had "gallons of melted butter" poured over his head.[148] Hay took a suite at the Hotel Brunswick, with several bedrooms to house his large family. Hay and Nannie's relationship seemed to have reached a climax during this visit as is revealed in this ambiguous unpublished poem—on the eve of the Hays' departure for England. Hay could be taking poetic license since he often fantasized about both Nannie Lodge and Lizzie Cameron. He liked his infatuations and cultivated them, for they allowed him to remain in a perpetually erotic state, the eternal "soupirant," sighing and aspiring for someone unattainable.

April 1897.[149]
"Last Night"

Was it a beautiful dream
Sent down from the bowers above
To flood my soul with its tender gleam
Of rapture and of love—

To fire the dark with fleeting gleam
Of the purpling heaven of love?

For now it glimmers afar
As in a hazy magical beam,
Like the trembling light of a dying star
Dim seen in a poet's dream

[148] O'Toole, 289.
[149] John Hay, unpublished poem, April 1897, Brown University Library. On the back of the same sheet of Hotel Brunswick stationery, "A Night Fancy."

She stood in the light of a dying star
More lovely far than a dream.

Ah! Never the starlight shone
On a vision half as fair
The mystical light slept tranced upon
The curls of her shadowy hair

And the low south wind made musical moan
In the bliss of her floating hair.
Then fainted the low south breeze
And lay hushed in the heaven of her sight,
And the happy stars died in a dream of peace
For the love of her violet eyes.

But her sweet voice died away
Vanished her eyes dear light
And my heart grew withered and old and gray
as I wandered into the night

And shadows of evil, wild and gray
Walked dim in the haunted night.

Gone the fair light of my dream
It will never come back to me.
The spectral glare of the morning beam
Flits grimly over the sea

And the shadows dim in the cruel gleam
That streams o'er the dreary sea.

"A Night Fancy"

Night glooms o'er the slumbering world
And over the waste of the sea
And the dim waving shadows are hurled
Vast mysteries over the sea.

But they fly when the sweet -swirling morn

Flings afar the full treasures of light
That she gained from the opulent sun--
Fair all mover-queen of the night.

In the glimmering kingdom of woe
On a plane demon-haunted, I lie
And the spectres that glide to and fro,
With their wings blot of joy of the sky.

Let thy spirit shed o'er me the light
That it gained from the Father above,
And my soul shall come out of the night
To the sunshine of Infinite Love.

A few days later, on April 12, Hay and Henry Adams sailed on *The St. Paul* to London and stayed first at the Brown Hotel then at Holland House. On May 3, Hay took up residence at the stately Curzon Mansion at 5 Carlton House Terrace, and presented his credentials. Mrs. Cameron, from 21 Lafayette Square in Washington, D.C., announced her forthcoming arrival May 7 to see doctors in London and Paris. In the year that followed, relations between Hay and the Senator became increasingly tense.

In 1898, when John Hay became U.S. Secretary of State, he skillfully guided the diplomacy of his country during the critical period of its emergence as a great power. Hay and Henry Adams expressed doubts about the U.S. move to take the Philippines. But in the Paris peace negotiations to end the Spanish-American War, Hay actively promoted the momentous decision for the U.S. to retain the entire Philippine archipelago as one of the spoils of war, thus marking the U.S. as a major imperialist power. He is probably best remembered as the promoter of the Open Door Policy designed to counter the trend toward divisive spheres of influence in the Orient. In 1899, he sent diplomatic notes to six interested nations proposing equal trading rights in China for all nations. A second circular the following year proposed all nations cooperate in preserving that country's territorial integrity.

Adams writes of the immense talents of his best friend:

> Hay had become the most imposing figure ever known in the office. He had an influence that no other Secretary of State possessed, as he had a nation behind him such as history never imagined. He needed to write

> no state papers; he wanted no help, and he stood far above counsel or advice; but he could instruct an attentive scholar as no other teacher in the world could do; and Adams sought only instruction—wanted only to chart the international channel for fifty years to come; to triangulate the future; to obtain his dimension, and fix the acceleration of movement in politics since the year 1200, as he had been trying to fix it in philosophy and physics; in finance and force. Hay had been so long at the head of foreign affairs that at last the stream of events favored him.[150]

The spring after Hay became Secretary of State, Nannie and the Senator traveled to Europe. Uncle Henry went with Hay to London and then on to Paris to see his adored Lizzie Cameron. That winter, Adams delighted Lizzie with this humorous account of the grand ladies of Washington life in 1898-99, Mrs. McKinley, Mrs. Hay and Nannie:

> *Henry Adams to Elizabeth Cameron*
> January 8, 1899
> My Sister Anne gives me all the perspective I want, and you know that if Sister Anne happened to care to play Mme de Montespan or any other part, it is not the role that would dash her, but only the want of a competent audience. So last Thursday or Friday evening, when the [Grover Cleveland's] Vice President [Adlai E. Stevenson] gave a cabinet dinner, he invited Sister Anne, with some other of the court ladies, to come in later, and Sister Anne went there and was ushered up into your great Louis Quatorze Pompadour Regence Marie Antoinette gilded drawing room, where she found all the court ladies seated about in solid splendor, and in the middle, Mrs. Faulkner, her senatorial colleague from West Virginia, in a dark street walking dress, with a hat and veil, not in the least embarrassed by the singularity of her costume. Mrs. McKinley was lecturing Mrs. Hay on her favorite topic, that of husbands. Hay was at home, having gone to bed with a headache. "I don't understand these wives," quavered poor Mrs. McKinley, "who put their husbands to bed, and then go out to dinners. When I put Mr. McKinley to bed, I go to bed with him." Sister Anne told this to me at the opera yesterday afternoon in the intervals of Melba and I fear that our ribald laughter was indecent, as, indeed, were some of the poet Bay's comments. Certainly Mrs. McKinley's suggestion that Mrs. Hay was going to bed somewhere else was poetic and even lyric.... Between

---

[150] Adams, *The Education*, 422-423.

> grippe, dinners, Lord Abinger, and Mrs. Warder who insisted on an improper arrangement of the chairs, Pinkie lost such mental balance as he ever has and became more and more obnoxious in his behavior and remarks, until, after all was over and he was taking his leave, he said to Mrs. Warder that she had ruined her party, and that he would never enter her house again. Upon that, Ward Thoron, who was looking, mildly took him by the arm and walked him downstairs and out doors and bade him good night with a civil request that it should be the last… all this was confirmed the next day and added to by Sister Anne. Pinkie the next day crawled. Apologies fell like snowflakes. Pinkie fled to New York… I wept while the others shouted with laughter….

Sister Anne was the dominant power in the marriage, ambassador without portfolio and envoy between various political groups and perhaps particularly between the Senate and the Department of State. In a December 18, 1898, letter from Henry Adams to Elizabeth Cameron:

> …the Senator, while agreeing in general approval of the Secretary of State's health, expresses an earnest wish that he would not look so exceedingly tired when approached on business at the department; while the Secretary with sobs in his voice assures me that the Senator gives him more trouble, about less matter, than all the governments of Europe, Asia and the Sulu Islands, and all the Senators from the wild west and the Congressmen from the rebel confederacy. Tell me, does patriotism pay me to act as buffer-state? **Does patriotism pay Sister Anne to act as a buffer state?**

Hay confided in Nannie the way Adams did in Lizzie Cameron, but Nannie, who saw Adams daily or at least weekly, was the key player. The Lodges kept a frantic pace. In 1899, Nannie was diagnosed with valvular heart trouble although earlier reports of fatigue indicate that the trouble started in the preceding decade. The duties of her office, the complexities of diplomacy, her loyalty to her love, Cabot, and to her friend, Hay, her divided loyalties, and her children leaving home, made this a particularly stressful time. On Jan. 8, the Senator wrote his mother:

> …Nannie went to receive at the White House, there I escorted her to the Diplomatic breakfast at the Hays and thence to the Vice-President's when she received with Mrs. Hobart. In the evening we all went with Henry Adams and the Hays to see Francis Adams.

In the winter of 1899, Henry Adams wrote Elizabeth Cameron of the necessity of staying and fighting in the Philippines but only to a point. Adams complained that the Senate had made war inevitable and that the terms of the war were "madness," complaining in early March about what a "plunger" Roosevelt was.

> January 29, 1899
> ...We can thrash the Philippines and kill them by the hundred thousand but it will cost us in one season at least 50,000 men, fifty millions of money, and indefinite loss of reputation.... **To dinner came Sister Anne and John... I cannot do like Hay who soothes his smarts by confiding his odd and unnoticed moments to Sister Anne's sympathies**; I can only write to you. Perhaps two old fools of sexagenarians might do better than imitate themselves as boys in their teens; but at least Sister Anne and you keep your tongues and your tempers.

> February 12, 1899
> ...Hay drops in of an afternoon. Cabot sometimes of an evening... I've little to say to them, and they might but twaddle.... Though... we could not escape the war, and though we have already killed or captured more Philippines than we ever want to hear of again, I am uneasy to see that as yet none of them have made submission.... Sister Anne wearies of her boys' love-affairs and writing notes to their girls and asking them to dinner.

> March 5, 1899
> *Henry Adams to Elizabeth Cameron*
> Of all the new phenomena, however, Teddy Roosevelt is the queerest, for he has become a serious fact... Teddy is ready to fight anybody and anything. Teddy is too much of a plunger and too little serious to suit my taste, but he helps to muddle... I think the Lodges will go to London. Probably Bay and I will cross directly to Paris.

In February of 1899, John Hay confided to Elizabeth Cameron about the "evil life" he was living, aware of the imperialistic tendencies of his countrymen and presumably, himself: "I think no race on earth is so keenly alive to its own interests and so shameless in pursuit of them.... I see the blessed Adams every day for a few minutes—otherwise I should perish. And even he is preparing to abandon me. He and the Lodges sail the latter part of this month for sunshine and a sight of you—which is tautology. How I envy them! The winter has been abominable, morally and materially. There has never been so much snow nor so little fun."

Before the Lodges sailed for Europe, the Senator worried about the health of his seventy-eight-year-old mother. In the winter of 1899, Anna Lodge's doctor, Dr. Morton Prince, wrote the Senator about his mother's controlling, strong-willed nature, which only elicited a sympathetic response from the Senator, who was aware that he had no control over his mother whatsoever.[151]

In spite of the deteriorating health of his mother, the Lodges took another European tour from April through November 1899, perhaps largely due to the Senator's concern about Nannie's health. In London there was a garden party at Lambeth Palace, dinner with the Archbishop of Canterbury and Lord Balfour. In April the Senator wrote his mother from the Hotel Brighton, Rue de Rivoli, Paris, that he, Nannie and son John and Bay, had gone to the Louvre, and had dined with Mrs. Cameron. From Cannes the same month, he wrote that Mrs. Wharton and Nannie met at the hotel and that other friends visited them from Sienna to Nice and Monte Carlo. In late April, they were in Palermo and Naples, and in early May, Rome and Sicily. The Senator wrote his mother: "Nannie looked remarkably well and handsome in a very becoming dress which she had just got in Paris."[152]

During their return from Europe, on November 19, 1899, the Senator wrote his mother: "We came comfortably on from New York the day after I wrote and found Bay waiting for us at the station and endless

---

[151] February 18, 1899: Dear Cabot,

I found it absolutely impossible to do anything for her medically as she refused to take any advice or to follow any treatment excepting that which she herself thought best, although I urged her very strongly to have proper treatment.... It is impossible for an outsider to contend against her peculiarities. Fortunately she was not so ill that it made much matter.... I don't think she is strong enough to cope with the daily demands upon her strength that comes with the management of a large house. If she had someone who could act as housekeeper through whom she could manage the house it would save her strength.... She is not a well woman: she does have a great many uncomfortable feelings and mental and physical discomforts which are more or less distressing. Her symptoms which are numerous are partly due to long continued habits of mind and partly to degeneration of the arteries commonly known as "arterio sclerosis."

"Dear Morton," Lodge wrote back, "The difficulty is very great unless I am to treat her as a patient not fit to have any opinion and this I shirk from doing nor do I feel justified in doing it—it makes me very anxious and unhappy. I am in great perplexity as to reaching what we all desire—better slowly to care for her."

[152] They also visited Florence, Nuremberg, Munich, Lausanne, Interlaken, and Lucerne.

boxes and trunks.... The next morning I went to see the President with whom I had a long and interesting talk about the election.

At the turn of the century, Lodge sent a New Years greeting:

> Jan. 7, 1900
> *Dearest Mother,*
> The New Year began with the usual official performances. Nannie received at the White House and afterwards at the Hays' diplomatic breakfast. I went to the White House and made my bow and took away [son-in-law Gussie] Gardner with me. He was much amused and interested and it was an unusually good show. The diplomats turned out in full force and in very gorgeous uniforms... Nannie and Bay send a great deal of love.

In her last letter to her son, January 11, 1900, Mrs. Lodge wrote, "May strength be given you for your high office." A month later, on February 18, the Senator wrote that he dined at the Hays in commemoration of the twenty-fifth anniversary of the Hays' wedding. She never saw this letter; she died on the 19th of February.

***

In early February 1900, the friendship between Hay and Lodge began to deteriorate and the storm which had been gathering finally broke. On February 5, after a year of discussion, Hay and Pauncefote, the English Ambassador, met to sign their agreement giving the United States the right to build and operate, though not control, the Panama Canal. Hay signed with Pauncefote *but failed to consult with the Senate*, thus incurring the wrath of Lodge who, with Roosevelt at his side, engineered the rejection of the Clayton-Bulwer Treaty. In the treaty, England conceded the essential—America's right to build an isthmian canal—but the principle of neutrality was maintained. Lodge objected to this because in case of war an enemy fleet could not be prevented from using the canal within the three-mile limit. Lodge made two consultations with Hay before a report was made to the full Senate and they must have been heated, for Lodge wrote in his Journal: "Our second discussion was so earnest that I saw no good purpose could be served by repeating it." The Secretary [Hay] insisted upon interpreting Lodge's original approval of the *idea* of modifying the Clayton-Bulwer pact as an inflexible commitment to support the particular convention he had worked out with Lord Pauncefote. [Hay] now complained that Lodge had "suddenly lost his nerve," that he was one of the "weak sisters" in the Senate who abandoned their principles at the first sign of newspaper criticism. This pained Lodge, for Hay was one of his close personal friends.[153]

Historian Patricia O'Toole and I have discussed the probability that envy was the reason for the dramatic change in Hay's temperament: the consistently steady, even-tempered Secretary of State became incensed with the Senator out of his intense envy of the Senator for his wife. In *The Five of Hearts*, O'Toole writes,

> ...Watching the hostilities from the safety of the sidelines, Adams... listened in silence while Hay excoriated Cabot, and once a week, when Adams called on the Lodges, he suffered through Cabot's philippics against Hay. Roosevelt's gratuitous intrusion only added to the merriment. "You can imagine to what extent the fat is in the fire!" Henry told Lizzie. Hay vowed to resign if the Senate defeated his treaty, and if Hay didn't quit, Henry predicted, "he will certainly hamstring Teddy. Won't it be fun?" After considering the likely personal consequences of the brawl, however, Henry grew alarmed, "I foresee the bitterest kind of breach between Hay and Cabot," Henry told Lizzie. For Cabot he cared little, "but Sister Anne will feel a quarrel, and if Hay is forced out of office by Cabot's act, as seems to be rather expected, you can judge better than I whether sister Anne will feel it." While Adams had come to loathe the sanctimonious Cabot, he treasured Nannie.[154]

Adams called Sister Anne (Nannie) and Elizabeth Cameron "gentle diplomats"—arbiters of political disputes who set the standard. Sister Anne defended her husband's (and Roosevelt's) reasonable objections to the treaty with the Secretary of State but in her subtle way, proved to be a better diplomat than her husband.

In a February, letter to Elizabeth Cameron, Adams makes his devotion to Sister Anne clearer than ever in the fight between Lodge and Hay:

> Every day I receive Hay's comments on Cabot and once a week I receive Cabot's comments on Hay and what is much worse, I know that the brunt of it falls on Sister Anne and that she is, as usual at her wit's end

[153] Garraty, 212; Henry Cabot Lodge, journal, December 21, 1900.
[154] O'Toole, 315.

> to make her husband out not to be what he is. You have seen this show so often and you know it so thoroughly by heart that you will understand all my embarrassments as well as hers. As usual the Senate makes trouble and you know that to me the Senate means practically Cabot: and you know that Cabot is ten times more *cabotain* [doggy] than ever. The word was made to describe him and it fits as though it were a Sargent portrait.... It is quite useless for me to play pretend about Cabot. He knows by instinct my contempt; and Sister Anne and Bay know it still better; in fact, our little family knew each other pretty well from the start.... I take refuge in silence but this time, silence is rather more expressive than words. I shall have to run or fight unless a miracle happens; and I can't run yet, and I can't fight, on account of Sister Anne; and Lord! Lord! How often have I said that in the course of a life at times accidental, I never knew a woman to go back on me and I never knew a man who didn't. All this is of course, profoundly secret.

Sister Anne helped to negotiate a compromise and soothe the troubled waters. In the second draft treaty, the United States would own the land around the canal and have the right to defend it (the U.S. controlled the canal and the canal zone until 1977). Even though it may have made Hay angry, this time he submitted the draft to the Senate *first* before going back to Pauncefote. Naturally, the treaty passed the Senate. Would that Woodrow Wilson had later borrowed a page from John Hay's diplomatic handbook and brought in Lodge prior to presenting the plan for the League of Nations for debate.

> February 5 and 12, 1900
> *Henry Adams to Elizabeth Cabot:*
> My sister Anne is absolutely rose-colored... John Hay negotiates a treaty a day or thereabouts and sends it over to the Senate to sleep forever. By some incomprehensible oversight, the Senate has accidentally approved one of his Treaties, which happens to be the most important and naturally in my view the most likely to be opposed.... Sister Anne flourishes. Cabot is more important than ever.... Hay is about as furious as you can imagine and threatens to resign if they defeat more of his treaties.

In 1901, Theodore Roosevelt, the forty-two-year-old Vice-President, succeeded President William McKinley after McKinley's assassination. Roosevelt, the youngest person to become President (John F. Kennedy was the youngest elected President), became a reformer who sought to move the Republican Party into the Progressive camp. He distrusted wealthy businessmen and as a trustbuster, dissolved forty monopolistic corporations. He carefully explained that it was only when trusts and capitalism became corrupt and illegal that his hand was forced. The famous "Square Deal" promised a fair shake for both the average citizen (through regulation of railroad rates and pure food and drugs) and the businessman. He was an avid conservationist and outdoorsman, and an early advocate of the efficient use of natural resources. Roosevelt's physical courage and personality ran counter to Adams' subtle character, not to speak of Adams' stymied presidential ambitions. Given his family history, some degree of envy inspired Uncle Henry to call Roosevelt, "Theodore Rex." When the President risked his health, Adams thought him "one of the brainless cephalopods who is not afraid." Every choice story of Roosevelt's naïveté came flying to Adams's breakfast table. Few bettered one of Hay's morsels: "Teddy said the other day, 'I am not going to be a slave of the tradition that forbids Presidents from seeing their friends. I am going to dine with you and Henry Adams and Cabot whenever I like.' But (here the shadow of crown sobered him a little) 'of course I must preserve the prerogative of the initiative.'" Studying his victim at such close range and blinded by personal feelings, Adams could see nothing good in Roosevelt's program. In private

Theodore Roosevelt.

anguish he could only cry out, "Stupid blundering, bolting, bull-calf!" He felt sure that Lodge and Roosevelt would never get on together. "The most dangerous rock on Theodore's coast is Cabot," he said. Yet it turned out that Lodge was far closer in spirit to Roosevelt than Adams realized. Lodge was content with the enormous influence he wielded in the Senate, desired no cabinet office, and their friendship withstood Roosevelt's elevation without a jar. Indeed, Lodge's influence became proverbial.[155]

Alaska had been acquired from Russia in 1867. In the 1890s, gold was discovered in the Klondike region, and in the years that followed, the boundary with Canada, part of the British Empire, was increasingly disputed. The Senator was asked to go to London to find a compromise. Late in October 1903, on his return from this diplomatic mission, one wit composed this political doggerel in the *Boston Post*, announcing the return of "boss" Henry Cabot Lodge.

> Why do Republican manufacturers Now begin to cut up pranks?
> Why do they shriek "Reciprocity!"
> When they mention platform planks?
> When do they think they'll get that board
> Even if Lodge has captured Nome?
> Sure, the wireless has tipped them that
> The "boss" is coming home.

Between 1900 and 1905, when Hay was Secretary of State, the tense relationship between Hay and the Senator continued, and Hay's health declined. He complained to his go-between, Lizzie Cameron, about not being able to see Mrs. Lodge.

> March 17, 1901
> *John Hay to Elizabeth Cameron*
> 800 16th St.
> I have not seen Mrs. Lodge for nearly a year except once accidentally at Adams! Cabot sends me word by Theodore that all he has done against me has been from the loftiest motives; the loftiest motive with him being a not too intelligent selfishness.

Henry James wrote to Edith Wharton on January 16, 1905, during

[155] Ernest Samuels, *Henry Adams: The Major Phase* (Cambridge, MA: Belknap Press of Harvard University, 1964), 252.

his return to the U.S. after twenty years, to say he had been placed at the President's table at the White House and described "Theodore I" as "the mere monstrous embodiment of unprecedented and resounding noise." The city of Washington, D.C., was "vacant"—a vast wasteland with only a tiny exclusive cultured world in which the Lodges figured. He also refers to Nannie ,who was fifty-two in 1905, as being marked by her inability to see her friend, Hay.

> *Dear Mrs. Wharton,*
> If I have delayed writing to you it is in order not to resemble too much certain friends of ours who *don't*, in similar situations, delay—who send back Parthian shots, after leaving you, from the very next *étape*.... And the same a little with this so oddly ambiguous little Washington, which sits here saying, forever, to your private ear, from every door and window, as you pass, "I am nothing, I am nothing, nothing!" and whose charm, interest, amiability, irresistibility, you are yet perceptibly making calls to commemorate and insist upon. One must hold at one's end of the plank, for heaven only knows where the other rests! But withal, it's a very pleasant, soft, mild, spacious vacuum—peopled immediately about me here, by Henry Adams, La Farge, and St. Gaudens—and then, as to the middle distance, by Miss. Tuckerman, Mrs. Lodge and Mrs. Kuhn, with the dome of the capitol, the Corcoran Art Gallery and the presence of Theodore—Theodore I—as indispensable *fond*! I went to Court [the White House] the other night, for the Diplomatic Reception, and he did me the honour to put me at his table and almost beside him—whereby I got a rich impression of him and of his being, verily, a wonderful little machine: destined to be overstrained perhaps, but not as yet, truly, betraying the least creak. It functions astoundingly, and is quite exciting to see. But it's really *like* something behind a great plate-glass window "on" Broadway. I lunch today with the Lodges, I dine with the Jusserands tomorrow—he is really delightful and **she much better, a little "marked" but perfectly adequate....**[156]

Henry Adams, first on James' list of American aristocrats, was in a kind of self-exile from politics and identified strongly with Bay. Adams, no longer the Senator's mentor, shows a combination of disdain and jealousy for his protegé, who was after all, a doer, who enjoyed imposing his will and who unlike Adams, chose a more active life. Lodge

---

[156] Henry James, *The Letters of Henry James,* Vol. IV (1875-1916), Leon Edel, ed. (Cambridge, MA; London, England: Belknap Press of Harvard University, 1984), 339.

did not actually or even figuratively poison Hay's life. Still, even considering Uncle Henry's penchant for exaggeration, jealousy could have been a motive for Hay's uncharacteristic belligerence with the Senator. Not long before Hay died, he wrote this published poem, "A Challenge," in which he seems to be admitting that he envied Lodge for his wife:

> The luminous pages of all story prove
> High love hath ending in heroic woe:
> Sharpfanged and fell, dark death doth ever go
> In waiting for the wandering feet of love.
> And if that fate be shunned, love's footsteps move
> Down the dull slope that leads to regions low
> Where the thick pulse of ease and wont beats slow
> As in some dusk and poppy-haunted grove.
> Shall we accept, or shall we not defy
> Entrenched in our fast love, this augury?
> Never shall I less than adore thee, Sweet!
> No use, my queen, shall dim thy radiant crown!
> And if, in envy, death shall strike me down
> Let his dart find me here, kissing thy feet.

When Hay died in 1905, Adams hypothesized, with bitter irony, that it was the Senator who had "killed" him.

> July 9, 1905
> *Henry Adams to Elizabeth Cameron:*
> The Senate killed Hay. Our friend Cabot helped to murder him, consciously as possible, precisely as though he put strychnine in his drink; but I always insisted to Hay that it was his own fault. He kept himself there, knowing he was being killed, because he was afraid of being bored. So am I afraid of being bored, and God knows how reasonably, seeing that I've endured more of it than Hay ever dreamed of—for he was never bored in his life—but, bored or bore, I have sight enough to protect myself from political bravos like Cabot and Theodore. I don't hold out my glass and ask for the arsenic.

Adams' following letter to Mrs. Cameron shows that Nannie Lodge and John Hay had an extremely rare kind of friendship—they were soulmates who cherished one another throughout their lives.

July 16, 1905
Sister Anne wanted me to go to Chartres with them [Nannie and the Senator] on Friday. As it happened, I was not in a state to go, but in any case, I cannot venture myself any longer with Cabot. He has become physically repulsive to me. It is very hard. Of course, one is perfectly transparent. **She sees every shade of my feelings. We keep up a sort of mask-play together, each knowing the other to the ground. She kept it up with Hay to the end**. It has gone on for years, and may go on for more, but only on condition that I do not let my irritability show itself. At my age, one cannot be cautious enough. If I told Cabot that he is personally and physically loathsome to me, like [Constance Lodge's husband, Congressman] Gussie Gardner, he would not understand what I meant, but she would; and that is certainly what I should tell him if my temper for a single instant gave way to the senile irritability of sixty-eight years.

In November 1905, Adams indicated that Nannie had written to ask if he would make the opening remarks at the new Senate. Adams, while proclaiming his devotion to her, made a veiled reference to Hay's death and to his annoyance with the Senator:

My adored Sister,
You are infinitely kind to write sweet letters on every sort of subject except those on our minds, but this is our little play in the world, where one is best off when dumb, and if possible deaf. Yes! I suppose I shall open Congress as usual. Why not! If anyone were to come and take me by the ear, and lead me off to statesmen in the moon, I should go more readily, but lunatic for lunatic, the Washington type has to me the merit that I have known him drunk and have known him sober, for fifty years, and drunk or sober there was never anything in him—but himself. One can exist, more or less, in the atmosphere by violently holding one's tongue, and I suppose you and I can go on doing it, as we have done so long; but if you could manage to unearth one human companion of the male sex, more than three years old, you would save imminent risk of asphyxiation to yourself and others.

Dr. William Sturgis Bigelow (1850-1926), a close friend of the Lodges who had a lifelong infatuation with Nannie, became a Buddhist monk in Japan where he is buried, near Kyoto. He contributed

40,000 pieces of his fabulous collection of Japanese art to the Boston Museum of Fine Arts.[157] Adams' ironic letter to his niece by marriage, Mary Hooper, speaks of Nannie's exceptional multi-faceted character. He believed she needed more than one man to satisfy all her different sides but in referring to "husbands," Adams displays his penchant for exaggeration. She was fifty-two in 1905.

> July 17, 1905
> I was weeping all last week; Sturgis' pains began yesterday; Cabot's are due next. It gives Mrs. Lodge something to do. She hasn't husbands enough. No woman of her age can do with less than six.

In the winter of 1906-07, in the aftermath of Hay's death, Henry Adams showed his autobiographical masterpiece, *The Education of Henry Adams*, to a few close friends. Early on in his life, Adams' allegiance was to Cabot then to Nannie and gradually, over the years, more exclusively to Nannie, Bay, and Bay's wife, Bessy.[158] Speaking of himself in the third person, Adams gives a vivid though acerbic description of Henry Cabot Lodge:

> Education... is a matter of psychology which lies far down in the depths of history and science; it will recur in other forms... Roosevelt was lost but this seemed no reason why Hay and Lodge should be lost yet the result was mathematically certain. With Hay, it was only the steady decline of strength and the necessary economy of force; but with Lodge it was the law of politics. He could not help himself for his position as the President's friend and independent statesman at once was false and he must be unsure in both relations. To a student, the importance of Cabot Lodge was great—much greater than that of the usual Senator—but it hung on his position in Massachusetts rather than on his control of Executive patronage; and his standing in Massachusetts was highly insecure. Nowhere in America was society so complex or change so rapid. No doubt the Bostonian had always been noted for a

---

[157] Bigelow's collection formed the nucleus of the Asian art collection at the Museum of Fine Art, Boston. The MFA ran a Ukiyo-e exhibition until the end of 2007 entitled, "Drama and Desire: Japanese Painting From the Floating World 1690-1850," where most of the works displayed were from Bigelow. The museum curator, John Ellerton Lodge, elder brother of Bay, started the Freer Gallery in Washington at Freer's request; it also contains many Bigelow pieces.

[158] "Your honored father," Adams once confided to Bay, "is a companion to dragons and John Hay is a brother to owl," a word play on Job 30:29: "A brother to dragons and a companion to owls."

certain chronic irritability—a sort of Bostonitis—which, in its primitive Puritan forms, seemed due to knowing too much of his neighbors and thinking too much of himself.... The trait led to good ends—such as admiration of Abraham Lincoln and George Washington—but the virtue was exacting; for New England standards were various, scarcely reconcilable with each other and constantly multiplying in number until balance between them threatened to become impossible. The old ones were quite difficult enough—State Street and the banks exacted one stamp; the old Congregational clergy another; Harvard College, poor in votes, but rich in social influence, a third; the foreign element, especially the Irish, held aloof, and seldom consented to approve any one; the new socialist class, rapidly growing, promised to become more exclusive than the Irish. New Power was disintegrating society, and setting independent centres of force to work, until money had all it could do to hold the machine together. No one could represent it faithfully as a whole.

Naturally, Adams's sympathies lay strongly with Lodge, but the task of appreciation was much more difficult in his case than in that of his chief friend and scholar, the President. As a type for study or a standard for education, Lodge was the more interesting of the two. Roosevelts are born and can never be taught; but Lodge was a creature of teaching—Boston incarnate—the child of his local parentage; and while his ambition led him to be more, the intent, though virtuous, was—as Adams admitted in his own case—restless. An excellent talker, a voracious reader, a ready wit, an accomplished orator, with a clear mind and a powerful memory, he could never feel perfectly at ease whatever leg he stood on, but shifted, sometimes with painful strains of temper, from one sensitive muscle to another, uncertain whether to pose as an uncompromising Yankee; or a pure American; or a patriot in the still purer atmosphere of Irish, Germans or Jews; or a scholar and historian of Harvard College, English to the last fibre of his thought—saturated with English literature, English tradition, English taste—revolted by every vice and by most virtues of Frenchmen and Germans, or any other Continental standards, but at home and happy among the vices and extravagances of Shakespeare—standing first on the social, then on the political foot; now worshipping, now banning; shocked by the wanton display of immorality, but practicing the license of political usage; sometimes bitter, often genial, always intelligent—Lodge had the singular merit of being interesting. The usual statesmen flocked in swarms like crows, black and monotonous. Lodge's plumage was varied, and

> like his flight, harked back to race. He betrayed the consciousness that he and his people had a past, if they dared but avow it, and might have a future, if they could but divine it.[159]

In response, Nannie asked Adams, "Why were you so hard on poor Pinky? You didn't mean all you said, did you? And of course you are going to change it and leave out all those remarks?" Henry Adams replied, "Only husbands can make such a request. Wives don't count." Lodge had the chance to change it but he changed nothing.[160] Such was the trust between them that Lodge signed the preface at Adams's request but Adams actually wrote the preface.[161]

The last years of Roosevelt's reign in Washington were marked by growing signs of a split between conservative Old Guard Republicans and the liberal progressive element with Roosevelt (and to a lesser extent, Lodge) straddled somewhere in between. After 1906, Roosevelt attacked big business and suggested the courts were biased against labor unions.

> ...Theodore was a brilliant politician who usually managed to be all things to all men; satisfying the liberals with promises and aggressively reformist speeches, and at the same time, craftily playing politics with the Old Guard in a manner calculated to prevent a conservative revolt.... Lodge, who really belonged to neither camp, was subject to many conflicting pressures. His chief criticism of the progressive Republicans was that they were becoming Progressives—that is, that they were undermining the party, to him the cardinal crime of any politician.... After the election of 1904, Roosevelt had announced his intention of retiring on March 4, 1909. Later, he wavered. As late as November, 1907 he told Lodge: "If the party voluntarily comes to me & demands my nomination I owe the party too much to refuse." Lodge was upset by this and wrote in his Journal, "For his own sake, for his future fame, his present health and happiness, I hope that he will not have the nomination forced on him." The prestige of being the closest friend of the most powerful man in the United States, the convenience of having "dear Theodore" in Washington, struggled with the desire to see Roosevelt step down while at the height of his fame before he be-

---

[159] Adams, *The Education*, 418-419.

[160] Henry Adams to Elizabeth Cameron, March 1, 1915.

[161] A decade and a half later, in September 1918, *The Education* became public. See Lodge's preface in appendix.

came irretrievably entangled in the growing party squabbles of the day and before his never too robust health was undermined by the cares of his fatiguing position. In this conflict, Lodge's better nature won out, and when the President finally decided against running again, he was greatly relieved....[162]

Roosevelt chose William Howard Taft as the Republican Party candidate and at the 1908 National Convention. Lodge, a key figure as permanent chairman of the Republican Convention, and Roosevelt's personal representative, had a large hand in writing a platform that would bridge the Old Guard and the Progressives. The Senator's task was both to prevent a popular stampede for Roosevelt, and to act as mediator.[163] The speech was a success, Lodge's management style perfection, and on the next day, Taft swept the convention on the first ballot. Theodore Roosevelt, in an extraordinary letter from the White House, wrote Nannie in Nahant of the fateful events of the 1908 Chicago Convention:

June 19, 1908
Dearest Nannie,
Sturgis Bigelow wrote us the other day giving us all the news and telling us all about you. We were so glad to hear from him. Now I wish to send you just a line, primarily to say how admirably I think Cabot handled the peculiarly delicate and difficult work at Chicago. In point of judgment, taste and power, it would be literally impossible to better either his words or his actions. He was in a peculiar sense the guardian not only of the national interest but of my own personal honor; and to do his full duty as guardian it was necessary for him to effectively thwart the movements not merely of my foes but of the multitude of my well-meaning friends who did not think deeply or who were not of very sensitive fibre. **It was absolutely necessary that any stampede for me should be prevented**, and that I should not be nominated; for now that it is over we can confess to one another that it would have been well nigh impossible for me to refuse the nomination, and perhaps ruin the party thereby, if the nomination had actually been made; and yet if I had accepted, my power for useful service would have forever been lessened, because nothing could have prevented the wide diffusion of the suspicion that I had not really meant what I had said, that my actions

[162] Garraty, 257-258; Henry Cabot Lodge, journal, November 19, December 10, 1907.
[163] See the appendix for more about the Senator's talent at that convention.

did not really square with the highest and finest code of ethics—and if there is any value whatever in my career, as far as my countrymen are concerned, it consists in their belief that I have been both an efficient public man, and at the same time, a disinterested public servant.

We loved having all of you with us at dinner, and sitting out on the portico afterwards in the summer evening, the last night you were in Washington... I have never known the grounds to be more beautiful, nor the flowers and the flower-bearing trees more lovely. Massachusetts Avenue is now fragrant with the scent of lindens. Edith and I breakfast and lunch on the south portico and dine on the west terrace; and after breakfast and lunch we usually stroll around the grounds. I do not believe any one else has ever enjoyed the White House as we have enjoyed it and now we are ready to leave it without a pang, with plenty of interest and pleasure ahead of us.*

Have you read Murray's book on the History of the Greek Epic? If not, it is well worth your reading. You probably know some of his poetic translations of the old Greek dramatists.

Goodbye dear Nannie.

Ever lovingly yours,
Theodore Roosevelt
Mrs. H.C. Lodge
Nahant, Mass.

*Of all persons that cheerful small pagan [Roosevelt's son] Quentin remarked thoughtfully today "there is a little hole in my heart when I think of leaving the White House!"

The actions of the 1908 Convention proved fateful for the Republican Party since Roosevelt ran in the 1912 election on his own "Bull Moose" ticket. Roosevelt beat Taft in the popular vote and pulled so many Progressives out of the Republican Party that Democrat Woodrow Wilson won in 1912, causing the Senator no end of trouble.

The Lodges were among fifty relatives and close friends who gathered at the White House for a midday Christmas dinner in December, 1908.[164] Nannie and the Senator continued to be the "power couple" of the early twentieth century but after the Roosevelts left the White House on March 4, 1909, a chapter closed in the life of the Lodge family (that had begun September 14, 1901). In the midst of their most

[164] Edmund Morris, *Theodore Rex* (New York: Random House, 2001), 545.

active time in the history of America, Nannie stood above the fray, at the side of her powerful husband. She was a devoted wife of strong opinions who made her husband's life more successful. Peacemaker, spellbinder, and muse, she enjoyed the admiration and close friendship of men in positions of power as much as she did the challenge of being married to Cabot Lodge.

In the spring of 1912, three years before her death, long after her years with Hay, Nannie wrote her friend Corinne Roosevelt Robinson, to congratulate her on the publication of her poems in *Scribners Magazine*. In this important letter, Nannie wrote with wisdom and detachment about the happiness of her relationships, commenting on how she felt about **companionship**. She seems also to be comforting her friend when she said of those bittersweet memories—"**we have all passed that way**."

> Your "By-Ways"... seems to me to express such a beautiful side of life. This right we all feel born to, of finding happiness unexpectedly & by chance—spontaneously to give ourselves to the passing mood & moment & to the companionships which spring to meet us. We have all passed that way, as the French say, & it is a comfort to have it put into words and then to be reminded of that simple sort of happiness (very complex too, sometimes!) when all that side of life has so completely disappeared & everything must henceforth be very *grim*, is a consolation. To remember that one has been young & gay & desirable & mysterious & all the rest of it![165]

[165] See appendix.

George Cabot Lodge (Bay).

Chapter 4

Bay and His Mother

Everybody loved Bay and everybody from any walk of life. Even a road was named after him—Bay Road leading from Beverly to Ipswich. He had enormous charm.

—Uncle Harry

...that great and abundant social luxury...

—Henry James

Across the lawn at Nahant, George Cabot Lodge, "Bay," the second child, eldest son of Nannie and the Senator, sauntered jauntily back from the Billiard Room, a small Greek temple perched out closer to the sea at East Point. His dark looks and exuberant charm were evident as he saluted the gardener and laughs at the sight of old Gerdy, one of the townspeople, who searched for fossils in the rocks. "Find anything interesting?" he called, his eyes twinkling.

Bay was born October 10, 1873, at 31 Beacon Street. Until the age of fourteen, he spent his childhood in Boston and then in Washington in winters and Nahant in summers—the source of his lifelong fascination with the sea. After being privately educated, he went to Harvard in the autumn of 1891. His only friend at Harvard was a fellow poet, Joseph Trumbull Stickney (nicknamed "Joe") with whom he planned to spend a year in Paris. Stickney characterized his friend as prosperous and polemical.

Everyone loved Bay yet he was strangely friendless among people his own age. Dr. William Sturgis Bigelow, henceforth "Dokko" (the family nickname), was one of the Senator and Nannie's closest childhood friends and part of their extended family, living with them at Nahant, or they with him at his Beacon Hill mansion. Dokko owned a place on Tuckanuck, a smaller island off the larger island of Nantucket. The vacation spot for men only where the Senator, Bay and fellow poets like Bay's future friend, Langdon Mitchell, bathed in the nude, devoted their lives entirely to literature, attended to by servants, and surrounded by the beauties of nature. My grandfather, Bay's son, wrote of his beloved Dokko in his autobiography:

> My grandfather's friend from boyhood days, William Sturgis Bigelow, after becoming a doctor of medicine, left his federal house on Beacon Street in Boston to go to Japan where he lived sixteen years and became a convert to Buddhism, then a Buddhist priest, and a friend of the emperor of Japan. He was awarded the Order of the Rising Sun, and acquired the reputedly most beautiful and largest collection of Japanese artifacts outside of Japan. My grandparents had two houses—one on Massachusetts Avenue and the other at East Point, Nahant, that rocky promontory sticking out into the Atlantic where I was born. The house at Nahant would be opened in June, with staff, even though my grandfather could usually not leave Washington until mid-summer. Dr. Bigelow would come from Boston and live there until late in October when the house was closed for the winter. He had a bald head, a white beard which, parted in the middle of his chin, went off in southeasterly and southwesterly directions, and a prodigious sense of humor. He was like a beloved uncle to my sister, my brother and me.[166]

This rare letter from Dokko to the Senator about Bay in his college years reveals Bay's quizzical nature:

> Bay seems decidedly more "dans son assiette" now than a few days ago and his cold has slacked up.... He says "there isn't a d_____ soul in Cambridge he can talk to," or who would understand what he meant if he talked about anything that interested him and he seems to like discussing questions of life with somebody, in a general way. He has very good stuff in him and it is interesting to watch his mind develop in very unexpected directions. When alone with his fellows, the sense of solitude seems to weigh on him and I have been telling him that a feeling that he is different from the crowd does not necessarily mean he is worse than the crowd as he seems to tend to think but which is, blues and all, a safer belief for him now than the opposite. He has a curious interest in religious and philosophical matters (where did he get it?) which I try to steer as well as may be, without encouraging or

---

[166] Henry Cabot Lodge, Jr., *The Storm Has Many Eyes*, 18, 19.

> stimulating too much as he has time for that later and he should be working off his steam now in other ways.

Bay was self-centered but not conceited. His fascination with his own thoughts and feelings over those of the people around him made him a curiosity. He was full of self-doubt, an introvert in the body of an extrovert. Undeniably charming, he was handsome in a rugged sort of way—vigorous, enthusiastic, gifted with "immediate responsiveness," as Edith Wharton described it. He was exceptionally cultured and rich in attractive powers. Henry James on meeting him described him as "that great and abundant social luxury."

After college, while his contemporaries were becoming millionaires, he grew increasingly guilty about living off an allowance from the Senator. A Puritan by blood, he disdained the nouveau riche and spurned them. At the same time, he was anguished by "my crying inability to adapt myself to my time and become a money-maker." A romantic, he would have liked to have been a mystic. He was a believer and a pessimist—in Christ not the church—a spiritual warrior in rebellion against society. A sexual creature, he reveled in natural beauties, particularly the sea. The division he felt over the active versus the meditative life was to plague him his whole life and it was never really resolved. There is no question but that his mother, Nannie, was the principal person in his life and he the principal person in hers. Such is evident from his letters. Certainly, Bay gave his mother the solace she desperately needed. He was guided to a literary life, the life of the aesthete—the study of beauty—by his mother; he was also as virile and robustly masculine as his father, heavily influenced by the cult of manliness in the Theodore Roosevelt tradition. John Crowley writes eloquently of the ties between mother and son in the Lodge family:

> Traditionally in the Lodge family, mothers and sons have established deep and lasting ties of affection. Until her death in 1900, Henry Cabot Lodge [1850-1924], faithfully wrote his mother every week when they were separated; and her pride in his accomplishments was one of the motivating forces in his career. Henry Cabot Lodge, Jr. [1902-1985] and his brother John Davis Lodge have both said that their mother, even in her old age, never hesitated to disagree with them; and they always respectfully considered her opinions. Of George Cabot Lodge's extant letters, the overwhelming majority were written to his mother. His un-self-conscious expressions of love for his mother, possible per-

> haps only in a pre-Freudian time, testify to the intimacy of their relationship. The intensity of emotion in Lodge's [Bay's] letters to Nannie contrasted sharply with the reserve and formality he observed in letters to his father, even those written in states of mental crisis.[167]

Bay's private feelings about not living up to his father's worldly ambitions haunted him. At the age of twenty-two, he decided to devote all his energies to becoming a poet. It was a career which his father, himself a literary figure, could understand and one for which he would have his mother's complete and devoted sympathy.

Referring to Louis XIV's mistress, Madame de Montespan, her two sisters and her brother, Bay wrote his mother from college. "Ces quatre personnes plaisaient universellement par un ton singulier de conversation melée de plaisanteries, de naiveté, et de finesse qu'on appelait l'esprit des Lodges."[168] Bay's reading list tended toward the philosophical. In May of 1893, he wrote his mother that he was making a study of the religious and philosophical side of Carlyle with a view to writing a book. He read "attentively" almost everything Carlyle wrote and took notes on the more philosophical works like *Sartor Resartus.* He also studied Plato, Descartes, Malebranches, Spinoza, Schopenhauer, and Fichte. Referring to Carlyle's *Life of Cromwell,* Bay enthusiastically wrote his mother:

> Cambridge, January 20, 1894
> Ask Mr. Roosevelt if he has read the preface to *Cromwell.*[169] If he says he hasn't, tell him that until he has, he cannot be said to understand in any measure the belles-lettres of the 19th century. This preface was the foundation—the expression—the rubric of the French Romantic School which was beyond question, the greatest literary movement of this century.

In 1893, the French writer Paul Bourget went to Newport and impressed Edith Wharton. But Bourget's *Mensonges* [*Lies*] and other works, decadent psychodramas about the middle class, did not impress the high-minded Bay who told his mother, "I felt as if I had been living in the mire. Never have I read books whose atmosphere was so unhealthy

---

[167] John W. Crowley, *The Education of George Cabot Lodge: A Literary Biography.* Submitted to the Faculty of the Graduate School for the degree Doctor of Philosophy in the Department of English, Indiana University, September, 1970.

[168] "These four people universally pleased by a unique conversational tone mingled with chiding, naïvité, and finesse that one called the Lodge spirit."

[169] Referring to Carlyle's *Life of Cromwell.*

and fetid." It is curious that this extremely privileged attractive young man who saw no one but the best people was so deeply alienated by his generation. One wonders what he means by the following diatribe. Perhaps he was affected by his father's cynicism. All of the letters from Bay to his mother show that for him, she was his most precious refuge. Bay may have detested cynicism, but he also admired pessimists.

> Cambridge, February 28, 1894
> It is a constant struggle for me to prevent myself from becoming cynical and when I feel blue and depressed, the dykes break and it all comes to the surface. I suppose I have seen more of the evil and mean side of men and things than most men of my age which accounts for my having naturally a pessimistic turn. Really though, I hate cynicism—it is a compilation of cheap aphorisms that any fool can learn to repeat and yet, the world does seem a bad place.

In 1894, in the early spring of their junior year at Harvard, Trumbull Stickney and Bay met and became inseparable soulmates. Bay's intellectual curiosity was fantastic. His letters became more positive and intense. He read widely—Balzac, Flaubert, Alfred de Vigny, Leconte de Lisle, Musset, Hugo, Renan, and the Upanishads. "Next time, French literature is discussed, ask them what living poet equals Sully Prudhomme."[170] Overly sensitive to powerful influences, he wrote personal confessions. He found it difficult to fulfill all his many ideas; although the letters shows how his mind was working, he never wrote the book on St. François de Sales.

> Cambridge, November 16, 1894
> I am beginning to read preparatory to writing on St. François de Sales. Considering the favor with which Sabatier's book and that life of St. Theresa were received, I think it probable that... I may make a book that would not fall absolutely flat.... If I were living in the Gobi Desert or Sahara with the British Museum next door and the Louvre around the corner, I think I could do almost anything. When I work, I have to fill myself full of the subject and then write everything down without referring to any books....

[170] Prudhomme, 1839-1907. His lyrics are gentle, sentimental, and faintly melancholy. He was awarded the 1901 Nobel Prize for Literature, and was recognized for turning abstract, scientific and philosophical systems into epic verse.

In the winter of 1895, he told his mother he would write essays on Schopenhauer, Swift, Poe, Leconte de Lisle, Carlyle, Alfred de Vigny, Balzac, Thackeray (perhaps) and to entitle the collection *Studies in Pessimism.* He admired the sonnet form more than any other (particularly Petrarchan) and especially Shelley. In the spring of 1895, from Cambridge, he wrote Nannie, "I am devoured by ambition and I long to do something that will last." In the May, 1895, edition of the *Harvard Monthly*, Bay anonymously published his first poem, later entitled "Nirvana." Founded by George Santayana and his friends a decade earlier, the monthly had become a testing ground for aspiring Harvard poets on whose editorial board figured William Vaughan Moody, Norman Hapgood, Hugh McCulloch, Philip Savage, Charles Macomb Flandrau and Joseph Trumbull Stickney.

> And shall we find thee? Shall the tired soul
> Toiling in gross dull clay, doomed to abide
> In blurred oblivion, condemned to hide
> Its eager wings impatient of control,
> And God-lit eyes that yearn to view the whole
> Of that divinest splendour glorified
> In earth's rare visions—shall it feel the tide
> Of thy calm love in endless pity roll?
> Oh, let the inward vision drink the light
> Of thine effulgent countenance! Then might
> This immaterial dream of Thee and Me
> Dissolve away like moon-mists in the morn,
> And we could lapse in silence from the scorn
> Of Destiny to thy great unity.

George Santayana's character Oliver in his 1936 novel, *The Last Puritan*, was by his own admission a composite of the young New England poets:

> An important element in the tragedy of Oliver (not in his personality, for he was no poet) is drawn from the fate of a whole string of Harvard poets in the 1880s and 1890s—Sanborn, Philip Savage, Hugh McCulloch, Trumbull Stickney, and Cabot Lodge: also Moody.... Now, all of these friends of mine, Stickney especially... were visibly killed by the lack of air to breathe. People individually were kind to them, as they were to me but the system was deadly, and they hadn't any alternative

> tradition (as I had) to fall back upon; and of course, as I believe I said of Oliver in my letter, they hadn't the strength of a great intellectual hero to stand alone.[171]

In an letter explaining the plight of the Boston poets, Santayana writes to Mrs. George Sturgis:

> [Oliver] was not only austere to the natural man but he was austere to all the conventions: to his mother, the Harvard philosophers, and even the Vicar's religion. And the dynamite was actually applied to him by Jim and Mario, and he failed to become human. Why was that? Just because he was tied up? But he wasn't tied up intellectually: he was absolutely without deliberate prejudices. The real reason—and I am afraid I have failed to make this plain in the novel—was that he was a mystic, touched with divine consecration and *couldn't* give way to the world of the flesh, or the devil. He ought to have been a saint. But here comes the deepest tragedy in his lot: that he [Oliver] lived in a spiritual vacuum. American breeding can be perfect in form but it is woefully thin in substance; so that if a man is born a poet or a mystic in America he simply starves, because what social life offers and presses upon him is offensive to him, and there is nothing else. He evaporates, he peters out. The trouble was that he wouldn't be commonplace: there are plenty of people to be commonplace: the trouble was that *he couldn't be exceptional, and yet be positive*. There was no tradition worthy of him for him to join on to.

The summer of 1895, after Bay's graduation from Harvard, the Senator and Nannie took their first European trip since their honeymoon in 1871-72. They arrived in England in July with their two sons—George Cabot and John Ellerton—and Henry Adams. They traveled through Normandy—Amien, Caen, Coutances, Bayeux, Saint-Lo, Mont-St. Michel—that part of France to which Adams felt he belonged by natural right—then on to Rouen, Paris, Lemans and Chartres. Adams' letter to Elizabeth Cameron dated August 30, 1895, from Normandy, reveals the intimacy of Adams' relationship to the Lodges as much as his passion for French religious architecture. Adams' book *Mont St. Michel and Chartres* wasn't published until 1910, but this is clearly when he

---

[171] George Santayana, *The Letters of George Santayana*, Daniel Cory, ed. (New York: Scribners, 1955), 306.

became inspired—captivated and pregnant with the subject. He discovered the beauty of veneration amid a deep sense of the vacuity of life. The ten-day journey with the Lodges was a kind of spiritual rejuvenation as well as a complete course on Norman architecture for John and Bay Lodge. Adams wrote Cameron:

> ...the Abbey is marvelous, and our two days were worth remembering, in spite of legs, backs and stomachs. We passed our time wholly in enjoying it from all sorts of points, and passed hours studying the details of the church, and the perfection of its taste. The boys dragged me up and down walls, moats, cliffs and beaches, and Cabot beamed with satisfaction. He ought to have been professor in history at Harvard College, as I meant him to be when I educated him. He showed it at Mont St. Michel where the Church is not so religious as military. Then we came across country to Vitré, and called on Madame de Sevigné, who was quite entertaining.[172] Then we slept at Le Mans, and so to Chartres where we passed two hours yesterday afternoon, and after thirty-five years of postponed intentions, I worshipped at last before the splendor of the great glass Gods. Chartres is a beautiful gate by which to leave the Norman paradise, as Amiens is a beautiful gate to enter.
>
> Bay Lodge is a very good fellow with illusions and ambitions and an exaggerated idea of Parisian standards. John is less sympathetic and more commonplace and much too old for his years. Their father is a sort of elder brother to them and all three are so young that the weary world stops in its orbit to wonder at them. John alone approaches 19. They are pleasant companions—fresh, intelligent and good-natured.

While the Lodges were still in Europe, the Senator wrote his mother of Bay's plans to stay and study in Paris. A devoted father, he lamented John's returning to America and loyally supported Bay's ambition:

> September 23, 1895
> John's departure made Nannie and I feel very low all day and I confess I had many pangs of homesickness and longed to go with him.... It was not made more cheerful by devoting the rest of the day to looking

[172] Les Rochers, near Vitré, was the country estate of Mme de Sévigné (1626-1696). Hardly a writer of the age escaped the enchantment of the far-off dimly beautiful "old order" in which life had dignity and a spiritual purpose. Tennyson's "Idylls of the King" did more than any other work to fix the highly romantic image of the Middle Ages as one of sanctity and heroic dedication.

about with Bay for rooms for him next winter. We have finally decided very slowly and reluctantly to let him stay here next winter and study modern language at the Sorbonne. It is a great personal sacrifice to us both to be separated from him and a pretty heavy pecuniary strain is involved also. But a year at the Sorbonne strongly advised by Prof. Bucher who has been here and approved by Henry Adams would be of great value to the boy if he is to follow a literary life as he wants to. He is anxious to remain here himself and will I believe take advantage of his opportunity.

In the fall of 1895, Joe and Bay Lodge, both aspiring poets pursuing their literary studies at the Sorbonne, found an apartment at 55 ave Marceau. It was the beginning of Bay's first real excitement about his future. Joe wrote his sister Lucy:

Paris is just the same as five years ago. Just as delightful. The lamps at late afternoon; carriages rolling by and away; people walking quickly past; the shining windows, the affiches, the ladies, the cafes with their devotees sitting at their absinthes with the lump of sugar melting on the perforated spoon; the perfume, flowers, rustling—etc.—it's all the same! And quite the same too is the sensation of sadness that comes over you at being somehow so far from it all and drinking as little of the world's beverage. Welt-trank!

At the end of the nineteenth century, when Baudelaire's *Flowers of Evil* was the vogue and Flaubert's "Bovaryism" caught the romantic imagination, the atmosphere annoyed Adams but affected Bay and Joe and their natural pessimism and disenchantment. Bay's vitality and enthusiasm was complemented by Joe's cultivated cynicism. For Joe, a life of pure intellectual pursuit wasn't as dangerous as it seemed to Bay. Though a terrible pessimist, Bay again speaks of his hatred of cynicism:

"Poor Joe," Bay wrote his mother, "is becoming dreadfully depressed. His father may be intelligent but he is about as cheerful and enlivening as a skeleton.... I have taken a good many meals with them lately and I tell you it requires all my robustness to preserve me from utter gloom. There is an atmosphere of inanition and utter unenthusiasm and lifelessness about the whole family.... They are quite forlorn. I am a pessimist unfortunately but also I am a living human being and my

> pessimism is an active thing, I revolt, I do not dwindle into positive dreariness. It is indescribable and I don't see how Joe bears it. It would kill me.

In a letter from Paris in December, Bay wrote his mother of his struggle:

> We have progressed (one must use the word, I suppose) away from what seems to me beautiful and ideal and spiritual. We are, for example, débile in our religious faith. I love aspiration and I love the men who painted on their knees. I abhor my incapacity for faith, my utter scepticism, all that makes of me a man of this end of the 19th century. In fact, I might write fifty pages why I dislike the spirit of my time. To ask me not to be a pessimist is like asking me to change the color of my eyes. Personally, I can live a very happy life, I dare say. I have my poets and cathedrals, etc. to make me happy, and fortunately I want very little money. To earn that very little and to write down my thoughts and publish them—voilà all I ask to do....

In the afternoon he went to his courses and about five o'clock, played billiards with Joe and in the evening, he worked on romance philology. He admitted to being powerfully affected by Joe to the point of madness. Bay became a good friend of Joe's sister, Lucy, "an ardent American" who hated being in Paris and longed for home. On December 30, Bay wrote his mother about Joe's decision to stay three years, take a doctorate, and go back to Cambridge. But Bay did not have to earn a living and his choice of becoming of poet clashed with family commitment to public service. "I suppose this agony of soul comes from the sudden realization that I am a man grown and that the world is very large."

Thomas Riggs, a Princeton University doctoral candidate, wrote about Trumbull Stickney with references to Bay:

> For Bay Lodge, the adjustment [to the Paris venture] was painful, the situation obscure. Paris for him became an arena of a sharp and desperate struggle which throws into bold relief the hostilities latent in the polarities of Paris and Boston, Europe and America. How, as an American in Paris, was he to retain his identity as his father's son? How, as his father's son, was he to establish his identity as a poet?[173]

---

[173] Thomas Riggs, Trumbull Stickney, unpublished thesis presented to Princeton University, May 1949, 95.

"Lodge," wrote Joe:

> is prosperous as ever and if he were not so polemic that he leaves no suggestion of an idea unchallenged, would be a perfect companion. But my temper is so tried by him at times that I break out into the most lurid apostrophes to the spirit of peace and intellectual modesty. The fact is all human relations are temporary; and the better you and your friends realize that a split is inevitable, the better. I always—it's the remarkable feature in the friendship!—refer to the epoch of dissolution and the grand smash-up of affection.[174]

But the friendship survived and Bay made his peace with the choice of career as poet. Toward the end of January, Joe wrote Lucy:

> Yesterday a spree at a cafe with Bay and some excellent champagne and music have set me up and made me feel young and witty and disgraceful. Lodge after changing his mind about ten times has yielded to the temptation of Paris. It's curious how nothing but falls prey to the great French metropolis and the stubborn patriotism of Massachusetts has softened to putty under the influence of the Parisian gaslight... He has signed his name to a contract for a Parisian sojourn and this puts off for another year, the becoming a machine and a dictionary... under his guidance I grow happy and human like the premature chicken of twenty-one I am. He's a good man, a good man, and our troth, plighted with two gold rings, has bound us before the altar of eternity. I must end this epistle to play billiards. I am tied down to this habit like a drunkard to drink.

Bay's letters grew brighter in the spring: "Here it is Easter Sunday and I haven't had a happier day in a long time. The sky has been bright blue and the sun pure gold and the trees all 'uttering leaves' everywhere.... Early this morning Joe and I rode horses in the Bois." Nannie drove Bay's ambition for becoming a poet though his father supported the decision. How was he to fulfill her aspirations for him to find for her that "piece of pure gold"?[175] That's what inspired and drove his ambition! But war fever struck Bay in Paris over the Senator's speech and

---

[174] Joseph Trumbull Stickney, *The Poems of Trumbull Stickney,* (Boston: Houghton Mifflin, 1905), 79. See poem about Bay in the appendix.

[175] Reference to one of the things she forever strove to find; from Henry Cabot Lodge's tribute to his wife.

President Cleveland's actions regarding the Monroe Doctrine and the boundary dispute between England and Venezuela. Bay wrote his father about how guilty he felt studying French poetry in exile.

> Yesterday I read Cleveland's message to Congress, and today I read that Congress has supported him and that the whole nation is behind Congress. My state of mind is almost apoplectic.... The Stickney family are mugwumps of the old school, anti-war, anti-everything except to let England do what she damn wants to. And here I am with my heart and mind going like a trip-hammer, hardly able to sleep or eat for thinking about war and what is going on at home and no one who has any sympathy with my point of view within reach. Joe tried to be sympathetic but it's not very warm or genuine....

Bay found an outlet for his natural pessimism in Adams' cynicism. Bay Lodge was more than Henry Adams' spiritual heir; he was the son Adams always wanted. Bay followed the meditative life to the very end—something Adams could not entirely bring himself to do. Adams wrote of the dilemma between the active and meditative life in his poem "Buddha and Brahma." He deeply admired Bay's courage or madness—his particular brand of individualism. He saw Bay as a standard bearer against the times, a romantic in search of his soul in an age when men devoted themselves to making war or making money.

The Conservative Christian Anarchists (C.C.A.) was a club formed by Adams, Lodge, and his friend Stickney, cementing a partnership which, the game required, could only be played by two. The C.C.A. was more a way of thinking than a party of any sort. Essentially they were the ultimate moralists, rooted in the philosophy of Hegel and Schopenhauer and the Upanishads, "to restore true poetry to the Götterdammerung."[176] C.C.A. conversational jousting usually took

---

[176] Götterdammerung: light of the gods. From Chapter XXVII of *The Education of Henry Adams*, "Teufelsdröckh" ("Devil's temptation"),"...the world contains no other spot than Paris where education can be pursued from every side. Even more vigorously than in the twelfth century, Paris taught in the twentieth, with no other school approaching it for variety of direction and energy of mind... one could... totter about with Joe Stickney, talking Greek philosophy or recent poetry... or discussing the charm of youth and the Seine with Bay Lodge and his exquisite young wife.... Still something remained to be done for education beyond the chaos, and as usual the woman helped. For thirty years or thereabouts, he had been repeating that he really must go to Baireuth. Suddenly Mrs. Lodge appeared on the horizon and bade him come... Bay Lodge and Joe Stickney had given birth to the wholly new and original party of Conservative Christian Anarchists, to restore true to poetry under the inspiration of the 'Götterdämmerung.' Such a party saw no inspiration in Baireuth where landscape, history and audience were—relatively—stodgy, and where the only emotion was a musical dilettantism that the master had abhorred." Adams, 178.

place in Paris where Adams lived every winter including that of 1895-96. The enemy was convention, society, and religion, as opposed to self-reliance, free spiritedness and spirituality. These conservatives espoused liberation from suffocation by the status quo without being libertine. They were anarchists against the unquestioning mediocrity they saw taking hold not only in America but throughout history. They railed against anyone and anything which curbed, quantified, or emasculated the human spirit. Christ's message of love and compassion was, in their view, distorted by even as great an artist as Michelangelo in the Sistine Chapel where Christ is seen to banish evildoers. Emersonian neo-Platonists, they believed that the search for pure truth ennobled the Will, the very essence of our being and in detachment as a means to obtain enlightenment, as oriental thought championed. The Will is God, nature, all that is, and knowable only through ourselves.

> Lodge, as a Conservative Christian Anarchist, reacted against the assumptions of Social Darwinism; he rejected the identification of evolution with progress and the rationalization of ruthless business practices as the inevitable working out of "natural selection." Lodge believed that Western culture had degenerated from a primitive state in which the individual intuited his potential for transcendence into a corrupt, commercial culture in which man's individuality and his sense of indwelling divinity had been lost. Since financial success, not mere survival, had become in modern culture the purpose of life, the "fittest," Lodge argued, were determined by economic and not natural criteria—by what he called "artificial selection." Artificial selection favored vulgarity over refinement, greed over charity, shrewdness over intelligence, and deceit over honesty. In short, artificial selection bred a "mediocracy".... Because he was fully "human," the anarchist sensed his transcendent potential; he felt compelled to... the role of "Truth seer and Teller;" and the cost of speaking the "Truth" was alienation.[177]

Besides the fun of jousting with Stickney and Adams, Bay felt the crush of society. There was a lot of snobbishness in the air—Roosevelt's snobbishness toward expatriate émigrés as well as toward the Gilded Age billionaires—old aristocrats versus the new money. There was a snobbism about the American colony abroad to which even Henry James fell victim. Roosevelt was macho and saw American expats as

[177] Crowley, 52-53.

effeminate. The clash between Roosevelt and James is vividly described by the latter. When visiting the Roosevelts,he was heard to say, "When I visit the White House, I am reminded of my reason for leaving this country."[178]

Bay's dilemma was worsened by a letter from his friend, Theodore Roosevelt: "Don't let the worthless society of emigré Americans in Paris and London influence you to harm.... I do not think they could persuade you that life was not strife." Bay misunderstood Roosevelt's letter—that it concerned a different society—and had the unintended effect of making Bay's friendship with Stickney stronger. In February Bay wrote his mother:

> I got a letter from Theodore Roosevelt... he said "don't let the worthless society of emigré Americans in Paris and London influence you to harm.... I do not think they could persuade you that life was not strife." When I remember what I have written to you and Pa and that he has been staying in Washington I know he must mean the Stickneys and by the last phrase Joe. I am very very sorry because the Stickneys have been tremendously kind to me and though I don't approve of the way they live or their point of view I didn't mean anyone to know but you and Pa. As for Joe, he is about the best friend I have... Joe has a plot for a romantic tragedy and if I can get him home with me next summer I am sure he will write it.... I work pretty hard and enjoy life as much as possible, though there are times when it seems as if there were "nothing but dry, grey air."[179]

Only his mother understood Bay's creative effort that he otherwise thought a failure—the failure of a man unable to support himself. His letter of January 6, 1896, summed up the terms in which he had seen the rending choices presented to him during weeks of crisis:

> The thing which tore me most in all this mental struggle I have been through is the thought of money and my crying in ability to adapt myself to my time and become a money-maker... I said to myself that I ought to go home in order to get into the tide of American life if for nothing else that I oughtn't to be dreaming and shrieking inside and

[178] Letters, 1905; James, *The American Scene* (New York; Penguin Classics, 1995), 579.

[179] According to historian Stuart Preston, Roosevelt was not referring to Bay or the Stickneys but the whole class of millionaires who built the American Cathedral in Paris' 8th arrondisement and the American Hospital in Neuilly-sur-Seine—that society, Roosevelt felt, was nouveau riche.

> poetizing and laboring on literature here in Paris, supported by my father, and that I ought to go home and live very hard making money. I said to myself that I know I could not be very quick at money-making, but that at any rate in the eyes of men I should lead a self-respecting life; my hideous, utter failure would only be for myself and you, who understand. But somehow all the while my soul refused to believe the plain facts and illogically clung to the belief that I might do some good in creative work in the world after all, and so I struggled with the facts and my faiths and loves and there was the Devil of a row inside me and I most wretched.

Interestingly, the Senator had nothing but pride in Bay's choice of career; it is unlikely that he made him feel guilty. Throughout the winter of 1896, Bay wrote prolifically and his spirits were raised by the publication of one sonnet each by *Scribner's* and *Harper's*. On February 9, 1896, the Senator wrote his mother of his pride in his son's accomplishment:

> ...Bay has had one sonnet accepted by *Scribner's* and another by *Harper's*. They were taken at once and paid for at full regular rates. This is quite remarkable for the first time of asking. Burlingame of Scribner's wrote a handsome letter and said he would like more. For a boy not a year out of college this is doing well. Rather startling success—put to the test of a cold-blooded editor. You can imagine the pride and pleasure it has given me. I think you have rather a remarkable and promising grandson and I know this start and success will please you as much as it does me.

In the early summer of 1896, Bay left Paris and returned to Nahant. With the romantic hero's intense worship of nature, a passionate commitment to "the just cause," and a deep and abiding appreciation for living life to the fullest, Bay was a dazzling talker. That summer, he was pursued socially in nouveau riche Newport. He was rather high-handed—though the new money repelled him, he realized he wasn't going to make it himself and he was jealous of it—a snobbishness he shared with his father. Henry James once famously said that he knew Newport "before that little fist of land was crammed with gold."

> Newport, August 20, 1896
> I am here engaged in being pursued by society. I avoid it skillfully.

> Monday I came and tomorrow I go. I hate the philistine-plutocrat atmosphere of this place and it tends not to diminish my views on modern civilization and the money power.

In December 1896, the Senator wrote his mother that Bay was to sail to Europe again, making a terrible gap in their lives. "It is rather depressing as the time draws near but I think it wise that he should go." In early January 1897, Bay settled into a rigorous life at the University of Berlin, where in pursuing Germanic Studies, he was following much the same pattern as his father. Meanwhile the incessant pace of social life in Washington continued. The letters show that the Senator's mother subsidized Bay's lifestyle but that he also tried working as a journalist. The Senator wrote to thank his mother for having paid his expenses: "You have helped him to make his start in the great world of letters."

> March 14, 1897
> Bay had another piece in the *Sun* about socialism in Europe. I told you that I did not want you to do anything about his allowance—that I would take care of that for you have done and are doing always enough for him and me—But if you feel like sending him a present, it would be very welcome to him.

That winter, when Bay was in Berlin studying German philosophy, particularly Schopenhauer, Adams gave Bay some important advice—advice he didn't take. He seemed not to have much of a sense of humor about himself nor was he versatile. Indeed, quite the opposite:

> Your duties are probably absorbing, if they require the study of Latin and German... intelligent men have been obliged to use those tongues.... Who knows the future? Perhaps these writings may be useful... shall I not be better and wiser if you teach me more? [...] Let this teach you, *my son*, to hold your tongue and send me all the literature which is likely to be of use at the next election. If you have a grain of common-sense, you will work hard and write a play, with comic songs and dances, and a Cleveland comic character, as for instance, Hanna, to beat Francis Wilson (an American comedy musical star).... **Cultivate a sense of humor and be versatile**. If you could see your elders here laugh and jest, you would learn how... Society is raging here as usual but your mamma probably tells you all you want to know about that. I

> saw her last night at the opera, looking bright and fascinating as ever.

In the winter of 1897 letters to Nannie refer to articles Bay was attempting to write for *The Baltimore Sun* about socialism in Europe. Journalism didn't suit him but the "New England conscience part of him" made him think that he ought to write prose and no verse. Nevertheless, he explained that since the previous April, he had been going over his poems forcing the events into sequence and building a sort of "soul-territory, fibrous and coherent." He was "clearing out the refuse" and feeling strong and self-reliant as never before. Then suddenly, he sensed the shock of the artistic void of the period, and feelings of self-doubt reoccured.

> The article for the *Sun* nearly kills me as I can't write prose and try as I will the sentence comes out wrong and the whole thing becomes cramped and sort of muscle-bound 'til I quite despair.... I shall then send it to Pa.... I entirely mistrust my own judgment on all my own things but especially on prose.... It's strange that when I'm working or writing with verse I am quite happy and quite the reverse when I am trying to write prose. The soul sort of clears itself up in this solitude—picks up all the raveled threads and weaves them carefully together again and gradually simplifies and straightens itself out. Dieu sait![...] Philosophy is dead and despised, art is not and music dies with Brahms.... In perfectly lucid moments I see with a ghastly distinctness how far short all my work falls of what I seem sometimes to know as an Ideal.

From his letter we learn that Bay was more interested in opera than society and was leaving for Bayreuth. Nannie urged him to attend Queen Victoria's Diamond Jubilee in London, where John Hay was then Ambassador to the Court of St. James.

> June 1897.
> I want to come home Oopity despite your letters to the contrary. I feel very lazy and sort of "do nothing" over here and don't want to wait any longer. I dare say I'm foolish but I can't help it. As for the Jubilee, I don't take the smallest interest in it and though I should love to hear an opera at Bayreuth... I'm getting rather desirous of settling down. Even weighing all you say, I find the impulse stronger than anything to come back to you and my own native land.

But Bay Lodge *did* go to London for the Queen's Diamond Jubilee as his mother wanted him to. On June 7, 1897, Henry James, in a letter to Fanny (Frances Rollins Morse), recounted meeting Bay for the first time; it is one of the few descriptions of Bay as a young man, one valuable description of him from an outsider and from "the master" whose temperament couldn't have differed more from the Senator's: "Cabot Lodge's big, ugly, pleasant son whom I dined with at the Hays.... I can't swallow Cabot Lodge (though I am afraid he *is* cousin) but I much liked his clever and civilized, and withal modest and manly, young son."[180]

If Bay's opinions of society were lukewarm, his future mother-in-law, Mrs. Davis, cared for little else. Bessy made her debut in both

Elizabeth Frelinghuysen Davis

[180] James, *Letters*, IV, 46.

Bessy Davis and Helen Hay, 1899.

Washington and New York in 1897. The white dress with the diamond bodice[181] was undoubtedly destined for her presentation at Court on the occasion of Queen Victoria's Diamond Jubilee. Mrs. Davis certainly would have encouraged a visit to the Hays at Carlton House Terrace (rented from Lord Curzon) and it helped that Helen Hay was one of Bessy's best friends. Referring to their presentation at Court, Adams wrote: "Helen Hay and Bessy Davis were pretty yesterday in their trains and feathers, wearing the required head-dress of three feathers, symbolic of the fleur-de-lis, the ancient British claim to the French throne."[182] Bessy Davis also made a sensation when she appeared as Cleopatra at the famous Devonshire House Ball in 1897.[183] As the Hays were intimate friends of the Lodges, it was inevitable in that close circle of friends in Washington that Bessy and Bay would meet. Evidently Bay was also interested in Helen Hay (and John in Alice Hay) as this letter from Adams to Elizabeth indicates; he also makes a damning remark of

---

[181] See cover.

[182] Adams to Mabel Hooper, May 12, 1897.

[183] Photographs exist of her as Cleopatra. Uncle: "There is a picture of her as Cleopatra at a fancy dress ball which is just extraordinary." Lady Randolph Churchill (Jenny Jerome), Sally's great friend, two years a widow, was not bereaved and went to the Devonshire House Ball in 1897 as the Empress Theodora.

Bay's early poetry:

> December, 1898
> You who know the fiendish jealousy which tears the vitals of Sister Anne when her two boys look at a woman, can partly guess her emotions when John [Lodge] wickedly professes to stand to Alice [Hay] in the same relation of plaything which his brother Bay assumes to Helen [Hay]. Meanwhile Bay, being "accouché" of his volume of poems, also in imitation of Helen, has gone to bed with grippe or grief or something consequent of catching love and cold... [Alice] had better (imaginative poetry) to Bay's, in whose poetry I find much of everything except imagination—but I mean to search again.

In the spring of 1898, Scribner's published Bay's first book, *The Song of the Wave*, dedicated to Giacomo Leopardi, the early eighteenth century Italian poet.[184] Howard Mumford Jones has called *The Song of the Wave* an example of "The Genteel Tradition" in American poetry[185] —meaning that Bay failed to escape the conventions of English Romantic poetry which by the end of the century, was no longer stimulating and fruitful. While in the beginning, traces of Whitman's influence are evident, it is only later that Bay Lodge passed to larger philosophical ideas and dramatic form. "The most distinctive thing about *The Song of the Wave*," Edith Wharton said, "is its title!"

> The sea was no mere symbol to him, nor his love of it a literary attitude... the sea is a great inspirer of song, but she may be pardoned for sometimes repeating the old refrain in the ears of her new lovers. It was inevitable that George Cabot Lodge, like other young poets, should pass through the imitative stage of which his first three volumes give occasional proof, and equally inevitable that the voices of Whitman and Swinburne should be those oftenest heard in them.[186]

Sometimes the sea is master and sometimes it is feminine. "It is both womb and tomb, both the substratum from which masculine force is born, and the dissolving death into which all force returns.... The poem as prayer [attempts] to resolve personal conflicts by incantation,

---

[184] Bay's great grandmother, Anna Cabot, as mentioned in Chapter Two, was invited into a society from which Leopardi was excluded.

[185] Howard Mumford Jones, *Guide to American Literature and Its Backgrounds Since 1890*, 2nd ed. (Cambridge, MA: Harvard University Press, 1959), 113-14.

[186] Edith Wharton, "George Cabot Lodge," *Scribner's Magazine*, 1910, 236-238.

to create strength by the magic of saying so, by producing images of the unified personality to put an end to the heart's quarrel with itself."[187] The poet envisioned himself transcendent within a decadent society, isolated and silent. If society ignores him, the poet's eerily prescient reward is not "a fillet of morning stars," but death. One wonders why life in all its splendor was something to be endured.

> Come, said the Ocean, if thy soul is fit
> To bear my mastery, thy words shall flow
> Simple and adequate as human tears,
> And all thy discord fall in great accords....
> This is the song of the wave, that died in the fullness of life.
> The prodigal this, that lavished its largess of strength
> In the lust of attainment.
> Aiming at things for Heaven too high
> Sure in the pride of life, in the richness of strength.
> So tried it the impossible height, till the end was found:
> Where ends the soul that yearns for the fillet of morning stars,
> The soul in the toils of the journeying worlds,
> Whose eye is filled with the Image of God,
> And the end is Death...
> Can we pass to the perfect cessation where life
> Is a dream unrecurring?...
> Oh, Heart!—could the flesh but endure the full
> splendor of life and enduring
> Dissolve in the quiet, perfection of death,
> Without hope, without pain?

From 31 Beacon Street, Bay's grandmother, Anna, wrote the Senator congratulating her grandson on the publication of *The Song of the Wave*, referring to the influence of the sea on both sides and especially to the idea that if her grandfather and husband were sea captains, Bay *was* the sea! The Senator confides to his mother his and Nannie's agony over Bay's decision to enlist in the Navy and join the Spanish-American War:

April 4, 1898
...When John [Bay's brother] came in with a long paper clipping, "I

---

[187] Thomas Riggs, *Trumbell Stickney, 1874-1904,* doctoral dissertation, Princeton University, 1949.

> think you may not have seen this Mrs. Lodge," [...] you can hardly imagine my contending feelings when I read alone in that parlour house what George Cabot Lodge had done! It was a blessing that it came on the lowest night and I could leave the tomb and be among human beings and listen to beautiful music! [...] In my lonely vigils, I thought after all how natural it all was—my George Cabot for whom he is named, was captain of a vessel at 21, left wife and home for sea—Bay was the ocean—then he comes of fighting stock—Father was in the war of 1812—of course Nannie's father was a very enthusiastic navy man which his namesake inherits... Bay is going under the most favorable auspices—we must think of that. I live in you and for you and wish I could help you.

Almost simultaneously with the publication of *The Song of the Wave*, Bay had succumbed to his conscience to do his duty as a patriot. The thought of being left out of a struggle in which his identity as his father's son was so strongly involved created a great upheaval and confusion of mind which lasted as long as the crisis itself. Bay, who had little interest in another summer of Newport "sassaety," as he liked to joke with his mother, preferred to return and join the Spanish-American War where he could finally fall in with the WASP cult of manliness. He returned from Germany to America to enlist and on June 30, 1898, and boarded the ship *Dixie* in the U.S. Navy with the rank of naval cadet. The Senator confided to his mother that "there was no stopping him," and that the Massachusetts governor had given him a small commission on Nannie's brother's ship to take part in active service in Cuban waters. "I will not dwell upon it but he comes of fighting stock—It must be I suppose and we bow our heads."

Bay begged his mother to do what she could to get him to the front lines. His Captain, Mahan, along with the Senator, Roosevelt, Elihu Root and John Hay, was credited with bringing about what Warren Zimmerman has called America's "first great triumph." Bay enjoyed raising the flag at the Cuban port of Guantanamo Bay; but even in the throes of active duty, his consciousness of his own lack of spirituality bothered him as intensely as did his perceived ignorance of the average American. He wrote that it seemed as if his imaginative side was under lock and key and that the practical things occupied him entirely. He displays a good deal of personal vanity and impetuosity, wanting another pair of white gloves, five hundred cigarettes, and more collars.

> [Captain Mahan] intends to keep us here indefinitely. It's very disheartening. It's not what I on this ship came for. I guess it was done purely by the use of influence.... I ask you to bring all your influence to bear to have us sent to Cuba or to the coast of Spain or somewhere where there is fighting. To make a man in time of war serve his country in place of profound peace is to make him absent....
>
> It is difficult to conceive of the wealth of stupidity and ignorance that these naval reserves display.... They have only one virtue and that is that they are enthusiastic about guns [that] seem to have the right spin... densely ignorant.... It seems to me that the real purpose of this war should be to teach all Europe a lesson and that can be done effectively only from the Mediterranean.... In Guantanamo Bay, we landed under a flag of truce.... I had the honor to raise the flag over the office of the captain of the Port amid immense enthusiasm of the populace.... Crowds appeared cheering and crying, "Vivan les conquistadors Americanes," "Viva el Puerto Rico libre"...liberated 16 political prisoners... then with great solemnity the Mayor and I raised the flag over city hall... as the flag went up they cheered—such noise as I never heard....

By August, he wrote his father that it was all over and "from the terms that the Spaniards agreed to... McKinley has let the Philippines go." Implying the Senator had the pull to do it, Bay told his father, "what I want to write you about is getting home myself. I wish to goodness the ship could be ordered right home...." Only a month later, he left for home and wrote his mother of his plan to resign the Navy "without waiting for the ship to leave." When he speaks of weakness, one wonders if he is referring to a naval career, to life in general, or to himself. Through his experience in the active life, he seems to have turned more decidedly towards the spiritual and he wrote his mother of the darkness of his quest. He told her he needed time in the wilderness to contemplate.

> September 2, 1898
> *My darling Oops,*
> [...] One marvels at the sheer weakness of it all. One falls and has to pick oneself up so many times and the light grows very little stronger and sometimes one wonders, firstly, what the good of the incessant struggle to keep decent and clean is and what the compensation for the bitter self-reproach and pain—It isn't that one does anything very bad but it's the muddy state of mind. **My mind is like a constant**

nightmare to me. I think the pain of life must increase in direct proportion to the strength of the spiritual desire and aspirations in a man: for constant tearing of the human earthy longings in him must grow more acute and more agonizing. I think it is only on this theory one can perceive the awful martyrdom of a life like Christ's or St. Francis or Buddha's and for the rest of us with our scant visions and weak faiths, we suffer in proportion as we desire and love the little we have seen and the much we have wanted to believe [in] spiritual things. We suffer because we are constantly thrust back by the irresistible force of our own lives. Constantly blinded and choked and must begin laboriously again our poor edifice of beauty and light....

I am nauseated with the incessant noise that has so cheapened and obscured the great silent dead deeds which were done in those three or four months [possibly speaking of the August, 1895 trip to the French cathedrals.] Anyway my part is played. I must get away for six weeks or two months then if war comes again, I shall be fit to go again. I want to go abroad in the first part of October—go around and see some Cathedrals and get some peace and order and quiet into the noisy chaos that is inside me.

Bay was honorably discharged from the Navy September 16, 1898. In October, Bay went to Tuckanuck with Dokko (William Sturgis Bigelow) and wrote his father a short note about his refusal to return to the Navy. "I won't go. I can't see the thing as you do now. Perhaps I shall in time. Anyway I won't go...."

Tuckanuck Island, two miles long and a mile wide, lies about a mile west of Nantucket and five miles east of Martha's Vineyard's Chappaquiddick. To the north is Nantucket Sound, to the south, the Atlantic Ocean. Purchased in the mid-17th century by the Coffin family from Indian owners, Tuckanuck was for more than 200 years a small fishing, farming, and sheep-raising community. Once cultivation stopped, the fields reverted to a heath, the fertility of the land eroded by the winds whose scything effect also served to keep bushes low and scrubby. The first recorded summer visitor was Dr. Henry Jacob Bigelow of Boston and later his son, William Sturgis Bigelow, and subsequently of the LaFarge family. The encroaching Atlantic long since eroded the land where the Bigelow house stood on Tuckanuck's west end overlooking East Pond which, with North Pond provided anchorages to small boats even though wave action heavily silted the approaches to these little bodies of water. At one time, Smith's Point, the long sandy arm which forms the western tip of Nantucket, stretched all along the southern shore of Tuckanuck, providing a protective barrier reef for the smaller island. In the first decades of the 20th century, this reef curved in to join Tuckanuck's southeast corner, forming a third pond. This bit of sheltered water, called South Pond, is now broken into scattered sandbars.[188]

Despite his sympathy with Roosevelt's strenuous life, Bay finally cast his lot with Bigelow (who was later to become a Buddhist monk) and his withdrawal from modern life. He became what Martin Green has called a Boston aesthete, one who "renounced responsibility for social and political reality—resigned it to the philistines,"and embraced "high culture" as an alternative.[189] Dokko wrote Nannie from Tuckanuck about Bay's health—he had evidently contracted a case of malaria—and his uncertainty about Bay's choices, his health, his infatuation with Bessy and need for his emotional support.

Tuckanuck
Dear Mrs. Lodge,[190]
...Bay is contented, stringing decoys—The afternoon he got here, he sat down and wrote three letters—to his father, to the S.S. Co. and to *her*.... Bay wants you to mail him vol. I of "Epistolario di Giacomo Leopardi." He has given it [the Navy] up and is tranquil—I think relieved at bottom—it was a hard wrench for him—he had got inclination and duty and noblesse oblige all mixed up—made me say that I thought he was acting like a gentleman and that I would do the same in his place—Then came the question of reasons to be given—he puts it on the grounds of health—malaria in system, accumulated fatigue and is satisfied. All's well that ends well. He is a little below par physically. Chilly with a tendency to warm up in the late afternoon—sleeps a good deal.

In November, 1898, Bay returned to Washington, working days as the Senator's secretary and at night, writing poetry. Walter Van Rensse-

[188] Unattributed essay, Massachusetts Historical Society.
[189] Crowley, 24, and Martin Green, *The Problem of Boston* (New York, London: W.W. Norton & Company, 1967), 11-12, 14.
[190] No matter how intimate friends were, they never called their lady friends by their first names.

laer Berry brought Bay to lunch to meet Edith Wharton at the Gordon Hotel. The entrance of Edith Wharton into Bay's life was to remain one of its great strengths and one of his great comforts. At her departure, she sent him a nonsense poem she had read at a farewell banquet in Washington; one wonders if she was slyly imitating Bay's impudent style:

> And let us, O my soul, a way discover,
> A way, my militant soul, forth out of K Street,
> Forth from the bondage of accepted dinners,
> Of lying lunches, of tyrannic teas,
> Spurning the servile and degrading dues
> Of gratitude for hospitality
> And cringing mean politeness, as the man
> Blest with a new Pole coat casts off the old,
> And flings it to his butler (if he has one)[191]—Soul,
> Thus, let us rise, & lightly flinging off
> The warders of convention, wing our way
> To that remote high-pinnacled pure lodge
> That at the uttermost far-vistaed verge
> Of Massachusetts Avenue, awaits
> The bold free spirits of the Impolite.

---

[191] "The authoress is indebted to her husband for this beautiful simile."

Part 2

Bessy at the time of her debut.

Chapter 5

Love and Marriage

The garment of your love was about me like a light.

—Bay

Bessy was an extraordinarily beautiful woman—and not a phony bone in her. She was the opposite of the Lodges—good, kind, and sweet. She didn't have sex appeal but structurally—her bones—she was a beautiful woman.

—My Uncle Harry

Bessy's mother, Sally Frelinghuysen Davis (1860-1936), was "not a good woman," or so the family said. She was a woman of such questionable morals that even in the 1950s, a taxi driver in Washington, D.C., once pointed out to my grandmother (to her dismay) the house of Sally Frelinghuysen Davis as being that of the mistress of President Chester Arthur. Bessy was nine and her mother twenty-five when her lover, President Arthur, a widower, wrote the following letter indicating they had met when Mrs. Davis was only twenty-one, not long after her wedding day and a year after his wife's death in 1880. It is hard to equal this letter as a specimen of hypocrisy and banality:

Sunday, May 17, 1885
Mrs. John Davis
1211 Commonwealth Ave.
My Dear Mrs. Davis,
It is a bright and beautiful day, this anniversary (four years earlier) of that most fortunate day on which it was our fate to first meet each other in this world. I hope you feel some of the things I am thinking and saying to myself about it all. If I were with you this blessed Sunday, I would tell you how full my heart is of thankfulness for all that has been given to me during the last four years, in having the constant and unwavering friendship of a good and true and brave woman, always

> staunch and loyal to her friends, who has done so much for my happiness, who has given me rest from care, comfort in time of trouble, and a refuge from worry and annoyance—Yes, this you have been, this you have done. You and all your household have been so good to me. Your husband and your children—and you are all very dear to me. May God bless and keep you all safely. Always Faithfully,
>
> Yours,
>
> *Chester A. Arthur*[192]

In the photograph below, Bessy is standing, center, near her mother, Sally, who, typical of her rebellious character, is the only one who looks to the side; her father, Secretary of State Frederick Frelinguhuysen, holds her brother, Bancroft, while Mrs. Frelinghuysen (Matilda Elizabeth Griswold) looks at the camera. Their straight mouths, neither frowning nor smiling, reveal their strict Protestant North Dutch Reform roots. In Bessy's mother's generation, the Frelinghuysens became Episcopalian.

Left to right: Frederick Frelinghuysen; Bancroft; Bessy; Sally Davis; Mrs. Matilda Elizabeth Griswold Frelinghuysen.

[192] The plain black lacquer pen used by President Arthur to sign his name the last time as president, March 4, 1885, just before Cleveland's inauguration, is in the Lodge collection.

Mrs. Davis had placed Bessy in a French boarding school in Versailles at the age of thirteen in order to afford herself more time with Lady Randolph Churchill who, historians say, had literally hundreds of lovers (294, according to one source). Sally's father's side was old New York, "tiresome" strait-laced clergymen. Frivolous Sally was the opposite of her serious daughter who took after her North Dutch Reform great-grandfather—with his iron constitution and practicality.

The first Frelinghuysen to come to America was Theodorus Jacobus Frelinghuysen, a Dutch Reform Minister who came in 1720 to lead the Dutch Reform Congregation at Raritan, New Jersey, now called New Brunswick. Family legend has it that one of the first Frelinghuysens found a walking stick and a pair of shoes outside his door. He took the hint and went back to Holland. But one of his North Dutch Reform sons remained in the new world.

Sally Frelinguhuysen Davis.

Sally's mother was born a Griswold. She grew up in one of the Greek Revival style houses in white stone of the newly created Washington Square (1826), at the end of Fifth Avenue, a posh suburb far from the center of town, and now perhaps the most sought after neighborhood in the center of New York City's Greenwich Village.[193] Legend has it that her maternal grandfather, George Griswold, went to his office on Wall Street on horseback, knotted the reins, and gave a kick to his horse who then returned on the same dirt footpath.

[193] The famous marble arch, modeled after the Arc de Triomphe in Paris, was built by Stanford White in 1888 to celebrate the centennial of George Washington's inauguration as president, on the grounds of the park in the center of the square which in earlier days had been a cemetery for 20,000 people, mostly the poor and indigent. The cemetery was closed in 1825 in order to build the square.

Bessy once wrote:

> My great-grandfather, Frederick Frelinghuysen, was born in New Jersey in 1753 and graduated from Princeton in 1770. At the age of twenty-two, he was elected to the Continental Congress where, as part of the New Jersey delegation, he annoyed the family by disapproving of the Declaration of Independence and refusing to sign it, and was thus deprived of the coveted Order of Cincinnatus. Later, as Captain of a Volunteer Corps of Artillery, he fought at the battles of Trenton and Monmouth and it is said that he killed Colonel Rahl, the Hessian Commander. In 1793, he became a U.S. Senator. His son, Theodore Frelinghuysen, was elected to the Senate in 1829 and in 1850, became President of Rutgers College in New Brunswick, New Jersey. He also served as President of the American Temperance Union and the American Bible Society. Theodore's nephew and adopted son, Frederick Theodore Frelinghuysen, born in 1817, served as U.S. Senator from 1866 to 1877. He was appointed Minister to the Court of St. James's in 1870 to replace John Lothrop Motley, historian and statesman, but declined and became Secretary of State under President Arthur from 1881-85.

His daughter, Sally, on the other hand, turned out to be "a regular selfish Edwardian mondaine," according to my Aunt Helena. Sally, unlike her forebears, was not a leader in any moral movements—quite the opposite.

My Uncle Harry paints a vivid picture of Sally and of that time, someone one would today describe as a "cougar"—certainly of strong New Jersey stock:

> She was snappy—big black eyes, high color, pink cheeks, white skin, animated, vivacious, outrageous, enormous sense of fun, always went one step too far. You wanted to be with her. She had several love affairs but that with President Arthur while her father was serving as his Secretary of State was the most well-known. If you were really chic, you wouldn't do it with the milkman but with a Prime Minister. Add a few scalps to your belt. That's how women exerted power. You didn't go groveling. You took them off for a heady romance. There were class distinctions. Women of that class were not bound by the same rules. All that egalitarian crap came in after the first war. No one thought they had to behave as the common people did. You hire governesses to bring up the children and see to the baby bottles. Their job was to use their God-given talents as they saw fit. Some of it was to make your husband successful, some of it was for fun. Sally Frelinghuysen Davis didn't give

a damn for her husbands. She loathed Judge Davis, Bessie's father, and the second, General MacCauley, was merely decorative.

Sally's husband, Judge John Davis (1851-1902), Bessy's father, was named Assistant Secretary of State in 1882 under President Arthur a year after Arthur started having an affair with Davis' wife, Sally. In 1885, the same year Arthur was writing love letters to Davis' wife, Davis was nominated to the U.S. Court of Claims where he wrote the opinion in Gray versus the United States settling claims during the quasi-war between the United States and France.[194] Educated at the University of Heidelberg, the University of Berlin and the University of Paris, he was, according to the family, a "club man"—one of founders of the Metropolitan Club in Washington—as opposed to a family man (no wonder). Like Nannie Lodge, he could trace his lineage to John and Priscilla Alden of *The Mayflower* but, most interestingly, also to Isaac Davis (1745-1775), who was among the first killed—the first American officer to die at that "rude bridge" in Concord that began the American Revolutionary War.[195]

Isaac Davis occupies a place of singular honor in the American nation. The battle on April 19, 1775, at "that rude bridge" at Concord, Massachusetts, memorialized by Daniel Chester French in his sculpture, *The Minute Man*, was elevated by Ralph Waldo Emerson in his "Concord Hymn" as the spiritual beginning of the new country:

By the rude bridge that arched the flood,
Their flag to April's breeze unfurled,
Here once the embattled farmers stood,
And fired the shot heard round the world.

The foe long since in silence slept;
Alike the conqueror silent sleeps;

[194] In 1798, the U.S. refused to pay back the debt it owed to France saying it was owed to the king not to the revolutionaries; this lead to a brief naval war and privateering.

[195] A gunsmith and commander of a company of Minutemen from Acton, Davis set unusually high standards for preparedness; his unit was chosen to lead the advance in the Battle of Concord against British Regulars because his company was entirely outfitted with bayonets. Davis is memorialized through the Isaac Davis monument at the Acton Town Common and was the inspiration behind *The Minute Man*, the sculpture at the Old North Bridge by Daniel Chester French, modeled after Davis, which is now an iconic national symbol.

And Time the ruined bridge has swept
Down the dark stream which seaward creeps.

On this green bank, by this soft stream,
We set to-day a votive stone;
That memory may their deed redeem,
When, like our sires, our sons are gone.

Spirit, that made those heroes dare,
To die, and leave their children free,
Bid Time and Nature gently spare
The shaft we raise to them and thee.

John Davis' grandfather, also John Davis (1787-1854), was Governor of Massachusetts and served in the U.S. House of Representatives, where he became a leading anti-Jacksonian figure, and in the U.S. Senate with Daniel Webster and Charles Sumner. He married Eliza Bancroft, daughter of a prominent Unitarian clergyman and sister of George Bancroft, the distinguished American historian and statesman who was prominent in supporting secondary education.

Governor Davis' son, Judge Davis' father, Hasbrook Davis, started out life as a Congregational Minister in Worcester, where he was married with children. He left them and went west "out of boredom" and became an influential lawyer and politician in Indiana. General Davis became a professional soldier, commissioned by Prussia to fight in the war with Austria but he drowned off the coast of Ireland on his way to join the fight, "unable to continue his slaughter."[196]

Bessy, a studious young woman who read "by the mile," was close to her father; but her mother did not want Bessy to be "a literary bore"[197] and took her out of day school. The two years with Madame Passat in Versailles represented the first rigorous education she ever had. She learned to read and write in French and Latin faultlessly. When she visited her Aunts Tilly and Lucy Frelinghuysen in New

[196] My uncle, Harry Lodge.
[197] Aunt Helena.

York, any number of tutors were hired for her. Bessy took to education like wildfire. At the age of sixteen, when she returned from France to Washington, Bessy insisted on her mother hiring a governess for her, to which her mother replied, "alright but you'll have to find her yourself" which Bessy did. "Later in life you couldn't mention education without a shadow going across her face. She never got over it. That was why she was so insecure, why she cared so about her children, and why her interests were almost totally intellectual," her daughter, Helena, explained. Her famous "slow smile" had great magnetism and underneath, a beguiling insecurity. She was easy prey largely because her mother's lack of sympathy deprived her of a proper education.

Sally, Bessy's mother, ran the wittiest salon in Washington. Daughter of a Secretary of State, she was clever and terrifyingly powerful, but neither good nor kind. "Sally had no maternal instincts whatsoever," family sources concluded. Her son, Bancroft, a few years younger than Bessy, died in 1910 of typhoid fever; his mother, fearing to catch the disease, didn't bother to visit him on his deathbed.

Was Sally a rebel against her North Dutch Reform roots? Was she a spoiled child, the prettiest of three girls in a stifling old New York family? Or was she a libertine who used her world as a woman of a certain class and background to her complete advantage? Aunt Helena explained, "There were some *nice* people too but there is no question that some of them were horrid. Judge Davis was weak with his wife but popular with men." In New York at that time, with its emphasis on wealth, the older aristocrats—the so-called "nice people"—snobbishly looked down on the nouveau riche and on their ostentatious use of wealth.

In January 1895, when the Senator gave an intimate dinner for his eldest son, Bay, in their Washington mansion, eighteen-year-old Elizabeth Mathilda Frelinghuysen Davis (1876-1960), "Bessy," was making her debut. She was exquisite. Adams compared her to the Madonna. She had a special force of light about her with a kind of purity and goodness that merged the real and the unreal. From the first moment he met her, Bay adored her innocence, honesty and lack of personal vanity. In spite of childhood hardships, her father encouraged her to read history and literature which she did "by the yard," as Helena told me, and learned German and Italian in addition to Latin and French; she was also a gifted pianist. Bay, a man of great intellectual gifts, had what Bessy wanted for herself—an education, a quintessential literary life. But she was also a great humanitarian, and self-sacrificing to an unusual degree. During the Spanish-American war, she wished to become an army nurse and it grieved her that her parents prevailed upon her not to take up the hardships of such a life.

Bay was very romantic; but there couldn't have been anyone among the more than two hundred eligible bachelors at the time who would irritate Bessy's mother more. Sally Davis had her sights set on big money. In upper class society, money was extremely important, especially for women, who were unable to work independently. Their only success in life came from making a good marriage. Consequently, Sally Davis, ambitious for her daughter took a violent dislike to Bay; he was not "a catch" in her eyes and he was deeply conscious of her dissatisfaction with him. It was an uncomfortable situation. It was in his changeable nature to be both genial—pathetically dear to other writers sympathetic to his work—and resentful, particularly of the Newport world.

Ten months later, when the twenty-two-year-old Bay was writing poetry in Paris, he saw eighteen-year-old Bessy at a dinner party there. He was wildly attracted to her and she seems to have taken more of an interest in him but Bay was disappointed by her conversation:

> Paris
> November 27, 1895
> [...] She [Miss. Davis] looked very handsome and was more awake than when I last saw her but I fear she is principally physical in her attractions. Her mind is going the way of all flesh into a sort of blurred and confused youthful innocence which is the inevitable fate of any intellectual or moral value when left to its purposeless and forceless self in such an atmosphere as she lives in. She hasn't the strength to keep up and it is so easy to slide gently an inappreciably slowly backwards to the regulation vacuity of the girl in New York and other even less attractive societies. The dinner was rather dull, not even improper for me because Mrs. Davis and her sister sat at the other end of the table and Bessy was not supposed to hear. Thus whenever there was a silence at our end of the table, the conversation stopped as if it had been cut off with a knife.... I think of you a great great deal and love you very much,
>
> Ever your loving son,
> *George Cabot Lodge*[198]

From the fall of 1898 through the winter of 1899, after his brief naval career, Bay returned to Europe but if in his September, 1898, let-

[198] Strangely, Bay signed all his letters to his mother in this way.

ter to his mother he had claimed to want to see cathedrals, all he could think of was Bessy. In *George Cabot Lodge*, Henry Adams remarked: "If poets may be judged by the excellence of the women they are attached to, young Lodge would take rank among the strongest." Adams believed Bay's love letters to Bessy were among Bay's best poetry and an important part of history, and therefore should be published.

In his biography of Bay, Henry Adams included these love letters. Bessy had at first given them to Adams for his biography of Bay, then later, her modesty won out over her common sense and she cut them.[199] Through these letters, we catch a glimpse of what Edith Wharton meant when she said that Bay was "a climate"—he gave voice to the natural world. Through them we learn that Bessy thought herself "commonplace," that she was full of despair, and that Bay sought to give her confidence in herself. How lucky she was to have lived even briefly such a passionate love.

Bay wrote her from Paris in April 1899:

> You hold me between your hands. I am on my knees before you. Think of me so. You are like a sanctuary, a pure fabric of an unuttered song. As I have struck the first note, so let me have each semitone, each whisper. Save everything. If I were not sure that you would send for me at the slightest need, I would not go. Do not forget this! Use me as a thing more yours than mine. I believe in you more than in God. Forgive me for writing to you so wildly but the pain of going is very keen, and yet it is better.

And from Rome, April 20, 1899:

> You are so much better than I, what does it matter that I have written a few verses! You are more music than I would ever find in my soul. Can't you see that? You make me ashamed when you write to me so. God knows I see difficulties enough to overcome, before we can bring it all out right. Love is the greatest of all tests. Can we bear it? I feel so much strength for it! It seems sometimes sure that we can. But I have to consider all the strain that so splendid a passion must put upon us. For you and I must hold the greatest love, or none at all. We cannot accept the wing-clipped tame love of the world's making. Is it not so? Therefore

[199] Discovering them in the Adams rather than the Lodge papers was very exciting; they have never been published. Exceedingly private, Bessy would not have liked it; indeed, as I discussed these discoveries over dinner with my husband, the candle flickered and went out.

for us in particular is the test enormous.... Think often of the sacrifices this thing means for you! Do not pass them over lightly! Think into the future! Be surer than sure before you hold out your hand to me! I write thus to you calmly, with God knows what expense of self-caring....

In a letter to his mother, July 1899, he confides his feelings about meeting Bessy again, as well as his desperate worries over his continued financial dependence on the Senator.

My Darling Oops,
Who do you think asked me to Bar Harbour? Bessy Davis. I went for a few days and had a bully[200] time. Isn't it a wonderful place, as beautiful as Sicily and more so for there are trees.... Bessy was very beautiful and marvelous—it made a pleasant change. I'm almost crazed with the desire **to be independent** and yet, I won't do anything that I don't approve and I won't give up my writing, God willing. I must keep at it and accomplish what I can in my own way. I feel sure it's the only way for me and I know my intention is not low whatever my performance may be. I feel desperate that it all comes so slowly and that I do no better but I grit my teeth and keep at it. The agony of getting a thought into adequate expression is enormous. However I feel so much resolution, that I take heart and now too I see my path clear ahead of me. I believe my purposes are good. Dear Oops, I can say all these things to you and you will understand. It is a great comfort to me. *I only wish I might do something to get Pa's respect* but I can't leave my own God's and continue to be anybody.

If Bay agonized over his words and was desperate to gain the respect of his elders, he was also deeply in love.

From Nahant, August, 1899:

Please don't tell me again that you are commonplace. I don't believe it, and I don't want... all my senses, for the low chord of your voice, and the enduring marvel of your beauty. I wonder if, when you read this, all the heat of my heart as I write will have gone;—if the words will seem dead and extravagant and silly. And now I live them—these words—intensely. I suffer too much without you. How long... oh Lord! How long! You are like all the grace and power and marvel of old romance interpreted in a woman. Divinity, be pitiful to me: I love you too much!

---

[200] Slang for "great." Roosevelt's word for "bravo."

> I come near to you and kiss your feet, my dear, my dear!... In the ceaseless strumming, empty noise and hurry of this modern life. I wonder if all this revolt in me is because I'm weary. I can't believe it! I can't! I can't! But in good truth, if I didn't have the hope of you to live on, I believe I'd chuck the whole business of living one way or another. You are all to me—all! This is so very simply true.

Later, in November of 1899, on his way to Washington, he apparently stopped in New York to see Bessy Davis, as he wrote his mother from the Waldorf Astoria hotel, "I came to NY partly on Doc's [Dokko's] account, partly to see Miss Davis, and partly because I was going to Washington. I didn't tell you because I didn't see much use." He wrote Bessy for the first time of their future together:

> New York, November 1899
> I have thought tonight of our future together—you and I against the world. Please never take an interest in the mean necessary details of my life, let me be to you a passion answering yours—a force to compel you, a man to love you. You are to me something too marvelous and too elemental to even suffer the confinement of a name. I wonder if, after all, Dante's whole heaven was not merely a frame for Beatrice!... I wonder if you would starve with me happily. Could you? I can't imagine it. I'd better stop before I scream. I want you so very achingly much.

The courtship continued from spring and summer through the fall and winter. For the first time, Bay revealed his wild, violent side—someone caught in a labyrinth of despair, a despair that later would contribute to his early demise. Even his love letters to his future wife were all about him and Bessy, his redeemer, life-giver, and the embodiment of truth and source of peace.

> Washington, January, 1900
> I was very happy when I left you yesterday, my dearest girl. *The garment of your love was about me like a light.* Even now the certain cruelty of lacking you is not realized. Indeed, can anything, even your absence be intolerable pain when I hold the certitude of your love, and the ineffable peace of having reached my inevitable goal. I have wandered wildly and so violently that it seems I should never have come out of the labyrinth; and indeed I did not come out, —only the walls fell prone about me, as the shadows fall westward at dawn—it was you. And

> now they can never be builded [sic] up. Through the whole measure of my day of life I must live in the revelation of your body and heart that brought sunlight amid my candles and made the flame of them dark. I accepted you from the first; you were truth, breaking upon me briefly and emphatically; and as I've said to you so often, *the greatest thing I have ever done or shall do was that I knew you for my love. It showed, I believe, that there was some metal fine enough to tell the loadstone [sic], amid all my dross...* over all, my dear, the thought of you, like a caress and an interpretation. Through you I climb in moments to that peace of the soul where all are embraced and loved and comprehended. Your beauty merely the completeness!...

Bar Harbor, a chic summer resort on Mount Desert Island, Maine, is about one hundred and fifty nautical miles from the peninsula of East Point, which, in turn is only twelve nautical miles from Beverly. George Vanderbilt summered in Bar Harbor not far from the Davises who summered in Northeast Harbor. He had taste—enough to own a house at 58 rue de Varenne in Paris and the immense mansion-chateau, Biltmore, in North Carolina. Vanderbilt had attempted to interest Bessy in games of badminton and archery and boating on the fabulous family yacht; he was mad for her. But George Vanderbilt, the suitor that Mrs. Davis favored, was of no personal interest to Bessy who wanted a different life than the one she would have had at Biltmore. In 1900, the last thing Sally Davis wanted was for her daughter to marry a poet when she could have New York Central!

By marrying Bay, Bessy rejected her mother's values, a rejection of the "Gilded Age." He freed her from the world of the nouveau riche. But in return, she shouldered a heavy burden, struggling financially and dependent on the Lodges almost all her life. Ironically, rejecting her mother's values sealed her doom. Bay tried his best to be friendly with the Frelinghuysens. In the winter of 1900, he wrote that he had just visited Bessy at her aunts' Lucy Frelinghuysen and Matilda ("Tilly") Gray,[201] and hoped he had "cemented a durable friendship." In March Bay wrote his mother of his continued effort to make money on his literary efforts. In the years 1899-1900, Bay, under pressure from the Davises, tried to write plays and novels that might bring commercial success.

Bay wrote Nannie, March 1900:

---

[201] One of Sally Frelinghuysen's maternal grandfather's daughters married Mr. Winthrop Gray, who then remarried Matilda Frelinghuysen, Sally's sister. Thus, Bessy's beloved Aunt Tilley, who enters the story later, married her half-first cousin.

If I squeeze my brain as dry as a withered lemon, I will get another play on the stage by next year. Voilà mon bilan est fait.

Henry Adams wrote Elizabeth Cameron January 22, 1900:

Sister Anne is looking young and rosy.[202] The Davises were not enchanted by the prospect of a poet son-in-law. Bay is reduced for the moment to slavery by his sultaness and labors to work and live.

In Bay's unpublished novel *Mediocracy* (1900), the wife, Alice, never understands the poet's quest, and the hero feels it as a betrayal. Here is a fictionalized illumination of Bay's C.C.A. philosophy, a society whose sense of Christianity had been lost. The portrait of Alice, a woman of the Gilded Age who fails to escape her upbringing and ends up having an affair with a Senator, brings Sally Davis to mind. Alice's disappointment over her poet husband's inflexibility concerning his career is a precursor of what Bessy became years later; and how eerie that in this work, Bay hint at his "brutality" and presages his own death:

In the first blush of his youth, he had gone his own road with a carelessness of what stood in his path amounting to almost brutality. As life passed, he grew insensibly much gentler though now as always since that long ago springtime, he had lived entirely and confidently on his own judgments, he had relied essentially not at all on the opinions of others or the atmosphere of the world's opinions. Indeed this became a necessity. If he went into the world he was like a man with a voice in a place where no sound-transferring medium existed. The world of this stock-market civilization was deaf to him, or was he mute for it—at any rate, they had no common speech. From the first moment of his waking, [...] he was conscious of a mute intangible opposition, of something which discouraged his impulses, ridiculed his dreams and his aspirations, thwarted his desires.... As he sat there in the dark room with the threads of his existence tangled in his hands, he felt chilly. Gradually he was learning how vast a price the world expected from its mutineers, for the privilege of putting in practice the ideas of beauty and truth vaguely professed by so many in their churches and parliaments. He had resigned ambition, for the world's success meant compromise; he had resigned companionship, for among men he found no sympathy, and he

[202] Nannie was forty-seven in 1900.

well-nigh resigned love, for in his wife he seemed to recognize the spirit of the world that opposed him and wherever this spirit appeared he knew with an intimate sadness, that he must fight. Her times were stronger than her love and she was going from him.... Someone once said: "There is in every man, a poet who dies young." In him the poet lived and its point of view became the only one he could accept. He expected the impossible, he judged by ideal standards, he saw the truth with a feminine swiftness of intuition and he condemned ruthlessly with the decision, almost brutality, of youth.... The light fell on her pure, fine profile and he savored her beauty with his eyes and noticed indignantly the lines of disappointment and desire and bitterness that made little shadows about her mouth. In the silence, her mind went on with the familiar argument. Success! How she had striven with her husband in the early days, striven from the victory of his natural ambitions over the teaching of his inner light and how she had failed! She had said that life was presented as a thing not to be changed, an accomplished fact, that the world was as it was and must be accepted and that he had deliberately refused life, made himself a thing apart [for] the price to be paid was a compromise which would have taken from him the very capacity for joy. It seemed to her mere cowardice and she turned to him as though they were alone.

On July 4, 1900, Edith Wharton wrote a letter of reference to Bessy approving the match. She had known Bay for two years and expressed her real affection for him.

Dear Miss. Davis,

Though I have not known Mr. Lodge very long I have had over you the melancholy advantage of surveying him from the standpoint of a good many more years of experience, and when I tell you that *I think him one of the best fellows I ever knew, as well as one of the cleverest,* you will know that this is a very emphatic way of expressing my approval of your choice. I am so glad that he is to have the good fortune he deserves, and I hope you will let me include you in the friendship I feel for him, in expressing my affectionate good wishes for your happiness. My husband joins me in messages of sympathy and I am,

Very Cordially Yours,
Edith Wharton[203]

"**It was Romeo and Juliet all over again**," my Uncle Harry com-

[203] Letter to Elizabeth Davis on July 4, 1900, from Lenox, MA.

ments. Senator Lodge was a touchy man and it did not amuse him that Sally Frelinghuysen Davis considered the Lodges upstarts.[204] The Senator did not think highly of Sally's morals any more than Mrs. Davis considered the Senator moralistic. Senator Lodge thought Mrs. Davis unprincipled, high-handed, and difficult, while she found the Senator was a boring, pompous, self-righteous Puritan. Bay was caught between his powerful father and Bessy her nasty mother. In this July 5, 1900, letter from Bar Harbor, Bay, a hyper-sensitive and madly self-centered person, confided in his mother:

> *Darling Oops,*
> I got here dirty and glad on Fri. morning. Miss. Frelinghuysen is very kind and no serious conversations yet. Bessy is the same. She says she will come to Nahant probably toward the end of July. Darling Oops, I think I am only now beginning to fully appreciate how sweet and good you have been to me and to Bessy ever since I was engaged. If anything could make me love you more, my dearest Oops, your loveliness now to me would do so. I feel it all the time and I miss you very much indeed. At least Bessie and I have a scheme for next winter which I think may smooth things out and obviate rows. It's bitter cold here though beautiful, God's green woods and blue sea and green round islands and tides of air—still it's too arctic for me.
>
> It has all gone smoothly but this is not the time in my career when I want Bar Harbour and society. I am horribly enervé and depressed. I think I have never been more so. Everything and everybody—the gossip, the taking for granted that marriage has the same definition in my dictionary as everyone else's, the ghastly *embourgeoisant* atmosphere—oh how the whole thing weighs on me 'til I could almost scream. I am impatient and horribly nervous and have a keen sensation of not adding to Bessy's comfort. What a vile creature one becomes when one's nerves jangle. I've had half a dozen minds to clear out alone and get some peace from you but it would be childish and it's not for long.... Lord, how I hate to fight and how much I've got to do before I can save Bessy from her family and her conscience. Really I think the two most immoral inventions in all the history of man are science and duty. For the sake of conscience one is supposed to sacrifice one's dearest friend if they sin and for the sake of duty one feels obliged to sacrifice one's love and happiness. O respectable ethics. Can anything be conceived more inhuman, more unreal, and more horribly destructive.

[204] My grandmother, a Sears, agreed.

> Thank God none of the great passions, love, poetry, music have any moral value—they are too large. I wonder why people even thought there was any connection between the Ten Commandments and real value. They are rules of conduct—socially admirable doubtless—but Good God how can an act have a moral value, how can anything be good or evil except a motive or an intuition and they only in so far as they are large or mean, how can any sin, any good thing be done anywhere except in the depths of the human soul. How well Christ felt this when he gave his two commandments which are really spiritual and the direct opposite of the ten precursors, how well Buddha felt it when he said, "Except thou lose the desire for heaven too thou shalt not escape from the chain of death and birth."—How they have all felt it—the ugly folly of duty-conscience-duty-respectability, love of ethics, of acts. Oh Lord what a dreary mess.

Bay's mood suddenly lifted and he apologized for his outburst and announced they had decided to elope:

> Please don't worry about the letter I wrote you. I am ashamed I sent it. I am happy again. Bessy and I are coming to you for Sunday. We shall get off at Lynn Saturday night and go to town Monday because Bessy wants to buy things and to Tuckanuck Tuesday. Doc writes he is going to Dr. Shattuck's so we shall be alone.

In this age, marriage was the supreme social event. The wedding invitations had gone out and the presents were arriving. Although it was an elopement, it was done in the most formal possible way. Bessy came down from Bar Harbor, a few weeks before her wedding, with her fantastic wedding dress and her French maid, and stayed with the Lodges at Nahant.

From Bessy to Mrs. Lodge:

> *Dearest Mrs. Lodge,*
> Thank you so much for your kind note. Bay has written to say that we would like very much to go to you Saturday night, to spend Sunday. The train arrives about 8:30. I hope you will be as glad to see us, as we shall be to see you. John came to see us yesterday with that perfect breeding that always distinguishes him. He was already swamped with invitations and had a bored attitude towards popularity. Looking forward much to our visit.

Always Affecly [sic]
Bessy

For the Davises, the elopement was a social catastrophe. Once in Nahant, Bessy sent an affectionate letter, carefully crafted in Bar Harbor prior to her departure, to her Aunt Lucy, explaining her actions. It is a rare example of Bessy's character and her humor—her honesty, her spurning of society, her intense spirituality about the institution of marriage and, of course, her sadness over her mother's boredom.

August 16
Dearest Aunt Lucy,
I shall mail this in Boston to tell you in detail why I decided to marry in this way. It looks ungrateful, unnecessary, unkind, and unfriendly. I know it looks this way and it grieves me immeasurably to think that I may have hurt you. It has made me think and think and in spite of the appearances I decided to go and this is why. Love is the most beautiful thing in the world—love and marriage, the most gloriously happy day. The wedding day is always remembered in after life and there are but two ways to marry—either surrounded by joy or solemnly and alone. The family—Mama[205] has made no secret of the fact that the whole affair bores her to death. She has said consistently ever since I came here that the trouble and waste seemed quite unnecessary up here as there were only people for whom she cared nothing bar the family. Aunt Tilly [sic], on the other hand, cares a great deal and there has consequently been much friction. Joy and poetry have of course fled long ago but I thought I had no right to go away to my lonely wedding as in spite of the frustration would be miserable if I did go. Bay and I felt so deeply the inadequacy of such a wedding that we had decided to get married a second time the next day quietly in Boston. The wedding here was to show that we loved our families and wanted to see them. The second wedding was so that we could really feel the beauty of it all, for surrounded by all the Bar Harborites [sic] (as we should have been for they would all have been there) it would have ended by being merely a social gathering with all the sacred beauty gone. Say we are cranks but don't, don't, my darling Aunt Lucy, say we are heartless cranks, for we hated the thought of wounding you all and that was why we were having the

[205] "Mama" is pronounced "Mamaw" with the English accent.

first wedding as you all wished.

Lately Mama has grown more and more bored with the whole thing and frequently said she wished we would elope. As that is what we have been restraining ourselves from doing ever since we were engaged, as we hate all the paraphernalia of receptions etc., we came to the rapid conclusion that this tempting invitation said in absolute sincerity and perfect good faith should not be scorned. The *only thing* that held us back was the thought of you and Aunt Tilly [sic] for we were afraid you would care. Finally we decided that after the first shock, you would not care whereas Bay and I feel it deeply and Mama is sick and utterly disgusted, exhausted, and bored with the whole thing. You see the joy would not have been there so we have chosen the solemnity. Dear Aunt Lucy, disapprove of us, call us idiots and exaggerators but never never never think it was because we had not thought of you and did not love you dearly dearly. These few days before the wedding I have time to think over all your love to me and it goes to my heart more than ever. Say you understand at least this—that I never loved you more. My dear love to darling Frederick and Alice Murray.

Always your loving,
Bessy
Bar Harbour, Maine

Please understand that on the whole I am grateful to Mama for feeling this way and certainly for being explicit for it makes us realize the dream of our lives.

P.S. 2nd In fact what it all amounts to is: that we got bored and eloped.

On the appointed day, Bessy went with her French maid to Dr. Bigelow's at 51 Beacon Street to change into her white taffeta silk wedding dress. A young lady of a certain class never traveled without her maid; the maid fastened and unfastened the dresses—countless changes of clothes during the day—and kept track of the required jewelry and the aspirin. Their wedding at the Church of the Advent in Cambridge (not at Christ Church where the Senator and Nannie had been married) was "unattended." John, Bay's brother, was hidden in the organ loft. A bystander on the street was taken as a witness and the minister declared it the most beautiful wedding he'd ever seen.

Bessy reached the church accompanied only by her maid. Her gown, a magnificent bridal dress of lustrous white taffeta silk, was richly and profusely trimmed with lace and made with a longer train than other brides of the day wore. Her veil of rare old lace, beautiful in design, reached to the waist, and was thrown back from the head, after the Spanish effect, and fastened with orange blossoms. The bride carried a bouquet of tuberose, her favorite flower. Quantities of tuberose and red American Beauty roses were strewn about the altar. Bay had sent the flowers to the church and under his direction, they had been arranged prior to the arrival of the bride.

Bay dressed in the conventional way with a long frock coat, dark-striped trousers and light cravat and carrying the usual high hat. He wore no boutonnière however, and in this small matter differed from most bridegrooms. There was no maid of honor and Mr. Lodge had no one with him to serve in the capacity of best man. He met Miss Davis at her arrival and escorted her to the altar where the ceremony was performed by Rev. Harold E. Addison, curate. Father Addison had a friend visiting him at the time, Mr. Moore, and by invitation of the curate, he served as crossbearer.

The candles were all lit and the altar, strewn with many flowers gave a fervently romantic effect, a fervently sacred event, completely different from the typically festive wedding with guests. Bay's brother, John, arrived with Bay's friend, Wallace Goodrich, an organist who played selections from Wagner's "Meistersingers" after the couple had been pronounced man and wife. Mr. and Mrs. Lodge sat quietly, heedless of the fact that a few others were present. Although John witnessed the ceremony, he kept it secret so as not to offend the Senator and Sally Davis. Mr. Goodrich and the bride's French maid signed their names as witnesses.

Personal news concerning the prominent Senator—even an elopement—was closely followed. On August 18, 1900, *The Springfield Republican*[206] published "Quietly Married At The Advent."

Miss. Matilda Davis, Daughter of Judge Davis of Washington, Becomes the Bride of George Cabot Lodge, Son of Henry Cabot Lodge

Announcement of the marriage on Saturday Aug. 18, 1900 at the noon hour comes as a surprise to their wide circle of friends, who had ex-

[206] It is unusual for an elopement to be in the paper, showing that the Senator was the most important man in Massachusetts.

pected this event to take place at Bar Harbor early next month. The report not long since of the engagement of the young people was coupled with the announcement that their marriage would be at Bar Harbor. The ceremony on Saturday was quietly celebrated with only a few present to witness it. Miss. Davis is known to be of quiet tastes and opposed to undue prominence socially. Her mother, so it is understood, had desired the wedding to take place in the winter in Washington, where Mrs. Davis is a leader in social circles. Mr. Lodge also preferred his marriage to be a quiet affair, in part probably because his own family is still in mourning because of the death not long ago of his grandmother, Mrs. John E. Lodge. Even the compromise on the arrangement to have the wedding at Bar Harbor, however, was set aside by the young people themselves, in order to carry out their preference for a ceremony lacking publicity. The bridegroom is a Harvard man and since his college days has acted more or less as a private secretary for his father either in Washington or Nahant. The bride, who a fortnight ago was a guest at East Point, the Lodge's summer home at Nahant, never has seemed to care for the social life which surrounded her in Washington.

In this firm letter to his new mother-in-law, Bay wished her a kind of farewell, a formal rejection with no talk of seeing her again.

60 Beacon Street
"On our wedding day":
My dear Mrs. Davis,
I want to write now and thank you with all my heart for your continued kindness to me ever since I have been engaged to Bessy. Believe me I shall always remember it; and I hope you will believe also that Bessy and I would never have been married as we have if we had not felt sure from what you said that you would not be seriously annoyed—as it is we have had a very happy day—more so than I can tell you and I know you will be glad of this on Bessy's account.

Believe me, dear Mrs. Davis,
Ever Yours,
George Cabot Lodge

I hope you will explain the matter to Judge Davis so that he will not feel that I have acted otherwise than rightly.[207]

---

[207] Family papers.

The aunts—Tilly and Lucy—were terribly fond of Bessy, and this letter shows how deeply the elopement affected them. Bessy was like their own only child and they doted on her.

Bar Harbour, Maine
5:40pm
Monday
My Dearest Bessy,
I have stayed out in the rain as late as I could rather than come to this desolate house. I try to be thankful for this lovely summer that you have given me and not to feel badly treated because the joy and delight of my life had to go away.

There is not one smile to be found in the household. How I miss you and how glad Mrs. Lodge must be to have you all! Be sure to send me your telephone number. The reason we had no *Springfield Republican* was that the subscription expired Sept. 1!

It is pouring here, you left just in time!

Good Night and God bless you my beloved child.

Yours Ever,
Aunt Tilly

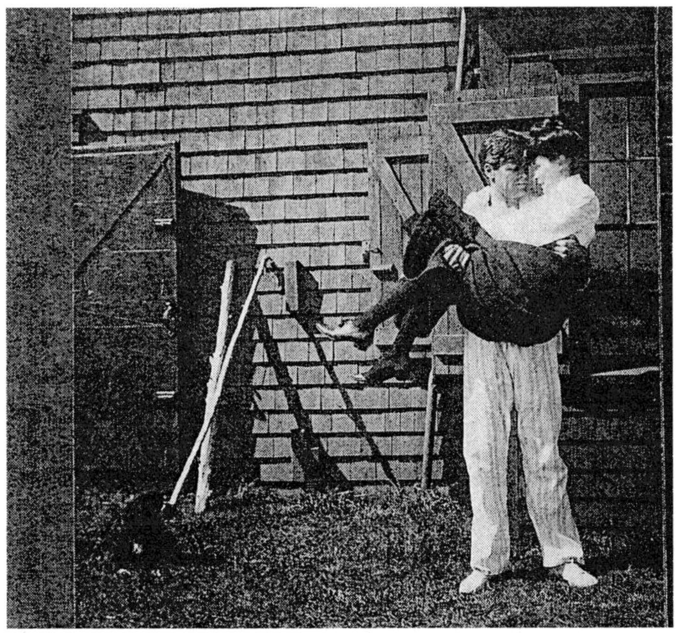

From a viewer slide, the sole photograph of the honeymoon couple.

In 1900, Tuckanuck Island was almost uninhabited, and reaching it was difficult. Dokko's house had a lonely perch among the low-lying deep green bushes, the air startlingly fresh from the salt of the sea. What had always been a bachelor's retreat was exceptional; a family photo shows Bay carrying Bessy in his strong arms in his nightclothes around the deserted island. Dokko had even rented a piano, knowing that music was essential to her. Bessy's birthday was in late August and Nannie had given her a photograph frame of rhinestones and pearls. A month later, Bessy thanked her for the ring saying, "but I have never half told you how much I love you."

Because Tuckanuck was essentially a men's club, it was the only time Bessy ever went there, where Bay wrote that "everything was tranquil and beautiful; I am writing every day." In this extraordinary letter to his mother, dated August 21,1900, Bay reassured her that he was not deserting her and pleaded with her to remain the central person in his life. Nannie was intelligent but not enough that she ever eased the connection with her son:

> *My Darling Oops!*
> Thank you for your sweet letter. My only regret in the whole business is that you were not at my wedding. I have thought of this many times. Otherwise the whole affair was splendid. What I had always dreamed of, only even more beautiful. Everything was perfect, there was not a detail to change. We are completely happy here. The whole thing comes to me as a revelation. In this beautiful country, we dine and read verse and nothing is wanting now that I have your letter and Pa's. If we had been married in the usual way, I should look back on the whole thing as a dreary farce whereas now it is the most beautiful memory in my life. I have tried to tell Pa how deeply I appreciate his kindness. He has behaved so splendidly. I hope you will tell him how very touched I feel.
>
> My darling Oops, I hope you will never stand aside out of my life. I feel as near to you and I need you as much now as I ever did and I always shall to the end. Bessy loves you very dearly I know and you two are both so wonderful that I know you will be always close together.
>
> Oh my darling Oops, I love you and think of you constantly. Please tell Pa that Bessy has written to her mother saying that we will go there in September if she wants us. I doubt if she does and we only hope not.
>
> Ever your loving son,
> *George Cabot Lodge*

> Bessy feels sure her father will not care. He could probably not have given her away as he is too weak and Mrs. Davis said that in that event he would not have come to the church.[18]

Mrs. Davis was furious and despised Bay Lodge. A letter from a consoling friend is very revealing. Edward Wolcott, a Colorado politician, a shrewd observer, and a friend of both hers and Bay's, consoled her.

> Mrs. Davis
> Foster Cottage
> Bar Harbour, Maine
> Aug. 24, 1900
> It was most kind of you to write me, dear Mrs. Davis, about Bessy's marriage. Ever since I read the announcement in the paper, I've wanted to write you, but close as is our friendship, I hesitated to intrude in so personal a matter.
>
> I sincerely hope you won't permit yourself to be troubled over it. The whole proceeding was unusual but most natural. Bay Lodge is a man of many fine qualities. He has power and abilities of high order and I believe he will someday reach distinction. He happens now to be passing through a mental period when all convention seems folly to him, and forms and precedents a nuisance. It is the slouch hat period. He is also vehement and perhaps ill balanced. He was tremendously in love and he didn't want to wait. He was, of course, inconsiderate and selfish but he didn't fully realize how he was hurting others. Bessy evidently loves him devotedly. Such love is always unselfish and always counts sacrifice a pleasure. He urged it and she yielded, and in the bottom of her heart, she knew she could count on the love of her mother and her Aunts to forgive her. It's all so natural! It's just what I should have done when I was a young fellow. Oh! How many years ago! If I could have persuaded the girl I loved, if I had loved one. The only person to suffer is Bessy, and her regret will grow and not lessen. And so I hope you'll make it easy for her. Your pride is wounded: but that is really of so little importance where her happiness is concerned. I trust I haven't written you too freely, but I am really greatly concerned about anything that touches you.
>
> We are having a very busy campaign. I am over the state a good deal and am working hard. My best regards to the Judge. I hope his journey helped him and that he will be fit this winter.

I think often of you and am always gratified when a letter comes from you.

With affectionate regards,
Yours Sincerely,
Edward Wolcott

P.S. If you don't find in this letter the note of deep and affectionate sympathy that our friendship demands, it isn't because I don't feel deeply and sympathetically for you and with you; but because I do want you to forget all about yourself and to think only of her. After all, it was such a human thing to do—Suppose it had been the daughter of some dear friend of yours. You would have seen the droll side of it, and it wouldn't have seemed a catastrophe!

Always Yours,
EW

Bessy did not play the part that Consuelo Vanderbilt played for Mrs. Belmont, her mother, in marrying the Duke of Marlborough. Bay was so disliked by Mrs. Davis that it annoyed the Senator, who was a good and loyal father. Rightly, he felt that his son was a catch. In this stern but handsome, loving, and understanding letter, the Senator answered Bessy regarding their elopement. He disliked drama within the family and resigned himself to do his best with his new in-laws.

August 29, 1900
East Point
Nahant
My Dear Bessy,
Thank you for your note which has given me great pleasure—I realize fully that you did not act without thought and much thought—I know you had reasons which seemed to you and Bay fully adequate. So far as I am concerned my regrets were almost wholly on account of others—For them I felt strongly but my own personal feelings were not wounded. The thing is all over as I wrote Bay and I have not a reproval to utter. Even if I had, I should refrain for I am far too fond of you already and much too happy in having you for a daughter to say a word that could cloud your happiness for an instant—My best regards to your father and mother. Love to Bay.

Affectionately Yours,
H.C.L.

Theodore Roosevelt was like a second father to Bay and he also admired Bessy. Indeed, a few years earlier in 1897, Theodore humorously had invited himself to dinner at the Lodges, and his letter underscores Nannie's powerful intellect and also his regard for Bay and Bessy. "Dear Nannie," he began, "I write to you because I feel more confidence in my ability to exert a favorable response from you than from Cabot. Can you have me to dinner either Wednesday or Friday? Would you be willing to have Bay and Bessie [Lodge] also? Then we could discuss the Hittite empire, the Pithecanthropus, and Magyar love songs and the exact relations of the Atli of the Volsunga Saga to the Etzel of the Nibelungenlied, and of both to Attila—with interludes by Cabot about the rate bill."[208] But when Bay asked Roosevelt to help him find "a small job in a consulate abroad" to give him work, he didn't get what he wanted. Naïvely, he wished a diplomatic post but not a social one; he wanted to be a diplomat but not act like one. A consulate job would do fine, he said, for the purpose of getting away from Bessy's family.

September 1900
My dear Father,
I am told Mr. Hay told you of the effort I am making to get appointed to some small consulate abroad. I had not meant to tell you of this until I had got the place as I thought it would please you better if you knew nothing of the matter until it was settled. I did not want to ask your help as I thought you might be unwilling to ask for a place of that kind for a member of your family. **Now that I am married I do not want to live in Washington.** Bessy has all her life had far too much family and she needs a change. I do not want to begin by being next door to Mrs. Davis and within walk of the aunts for they, with the best intentions in the world, could not help interfering somewhat. I think in marriage a good deal depends on the start and as I neither want nor expect to live on the opinions or judgments of other people, I think it is much better, if it is possible, to begin by living on one's own and away from possible complications. I hope you will agree with me. Bessie feels exactly as I do and in fact, the idea for the foreign post was originally hers.

I wrote first to Theodore, he wrote to Mr. Hay. Mr. Hay is very kind and evidently willing to help me but I should far rather have a small consulate than a Secretary of Legation. From what I have seen of the diplomatic person does not make me anxious to be like one.

---

[208] Louis Auchincloss, *Theodore Roosevelt* (New York: Times Books; Henry Holt & Co., 2001); H. W. Brands, *T.R. The Last Romantic* (New York: Basic Books, 1997).

I don't want a social position but some post where I shall have some leisure to write and no social obligation. Therefore I should much prefer a consulate. Of course I fully realize the difficulties and if it should not be possible to get an appointment this year, we could go to Washington and do very well there for the few months before the session ends. I hope you will be sympathetic and will understand the reasons which make me wish to get away from Bessy's large and very affectionate family.

Your devoted son,
GCL

To his mother, Bay confided the nastiness of his first encounter after the wedding with the aunts while Sally Davis at that point seemed resigned, perhaps oblivious. Mrs. Davis was "as nice as possible," sympathetic to their going abroad, while Judge Davis was "very weak." Aunt Lucy Frelinghuysen and Mrs. Gray (Aunt Tilly) called Bay a liar for pretending to go along with the wedding then publicly humiliating them by eloping with their cherished niece. Bay also objected to the politics of Frederick Frelinghuysen, Bessy's maternal grandfather, Secretary of State under President Chester Arthur, who opposed Theodore Roosevelt's trust-busting efforts and admired "boss" Mark Hanna. Bessy, revealing her thrifty Dutch roots and being typically sweet and humble, thanked Nannie for her Christmas present before leaving for Paris where they would spend the first year of their marriage.

December, 1900
Dearest Oops,

We are going in a few minutes and I must tell you before leaving how I hope you will not miss Bay too much and how I love you. You have given me the most perfectly beautiful jewel-box which I should never have chosen as it is far too handsome but Bay insisted upon it. It should be the last Christmas present for several years for it is a most extravagant gift and will last till I resign my position in this world.

Bessy

Honeymoon: Paris, 1901

In January 1901, Bay returned to Paris for a prolonged honeymoon to show his young bride the city he had so loved as a student. There is description of Bessy's beauty in a letter from Mrs. Cameron to Bessy's aunt consoling the family about the elopement:

50 Avenue du Bois du Boulogne
Paris
To Miss. Lucy Frelinghuysen
7 West 35th St.
New York:
Jan 23, 1901
Dearest Lucy,
We haunted the steamship office from Tuesday morning last but no news was heard from our couple 'til Friday afternoon when a telegram from Plymouth to Dr. Bigelow from Bay told us that they were at least on this slope of the globe. As Dr. Bigelow and Mr. Adams had waited a fortnight—deferred their passage, I mean—to see that mad young couple, it was hard luck to have to pass right by them on their way to Cherbourg without even a chance to touch their hands. I went down to the hotel on Sunday morning—they reached Paris Saturday night—and **found Bessy still in bed, though for other reasons she protested than those of fatigue and the pounding of their long rough voyage. She was lovely. I think I was**

never more impressed by the quality of her beauty than that morning seeing her in bed, tired and not well and just off a 15 days voyage on a winter sea. There is something luminous, gay, fawn-like, shining in her eyes. She is very unusual indeed. I was commissioned by Mr. Adams to offer her his apartment and man servant—as a gift, of course,—and I think she means to take it. It is not far from me—just by the Etoile—and I am looking forward to having them so close by. Bay is in adoration before her, of course. And really, Lucy, when I see their youth and love and enjoyment of things, I forgive—and envy—their folly. Was there ever anything like it? Everyone shakes their heads over them,—but dear me! I came away from them so impressed that I could believe that it is they who are wise to live and love and enjoy without a thought of that awful tomorrow. Don't shake your head. Neither you nor I have ever tasted what they are now living on,—don't you regret it? Well, now I must leave that willful and attractive pair and come to other things....

The couple took Adams up on his offer and stayed in his apartment near the Etoile favored by rich Americans; but they disliked the society of the quarter and soon found an apartment of their own. On January 28, 1901, Bessy wrote Nannie with charming frankness, about her and Bay's domestic arrangement and amusements. Bessy found a cook named Jean and had a maid for the table service:

Dearest Oopa,
We are getting on so nicely that I am sure you would be glad if you could see us. By some miracle, I seem to have hit on a cook who is not a cheat (I pay her $3 day).... Privately Mr. Adams' man is rather an objection as he evidently has a profound contempt for us but my two servants that I discovered all by myself are perfect. Bay is so anxious to show me that my cuisine is good that he eats really quite a respectable amount and seems well. The continued smoking always worries me because I know what harm it can do. He is just as darling as ever which means more than anyone that was yet created and I often feel sorry for you that you can't see him. Your jewel-box is a perfect joy to me. I'm afraid I wrote you rather a horrid letter about it but a dozen people were chattering all about me. It is perfectly beautiful and so useful. I ordered a beautiful black brocade cloak with some money Aunt Tilley [sic]

gave me and as soon as it arrives I shall sail over and say carelessly that I have just ordered it in order to see her look of horror, for people who **eat beans because they are cheaper than peas....** That's what I love about us—our utter contempt for [avarice]. I loved your letter that you wrote on the boat and

I love you,
Bessy

In this important early 1901 letter from Elizabeth Cameron to Henry Adams, we catch a glimpse of the dynamic of Bay and Bessy's relationship and how they complimented one another. Lizzie writes Adams:

> Friday, when Bay and Bessy and Mr. Stickney dined, I wish you could have heard the conversation after dinner, it seemed to me very characteristic. Bay bashed himself into noisy enthusiasm and was all over the place in his argument, illogical, contradictory and fiery. Stickney, quieter and quieter, as the argument went on, never leaving the main road and keeping the point always in sight. **Bessy only spoke once or twice and then very well—far more wisely than fiery Bay** whose noise was like Teddy's without its genuineness. **Bessy was singularly beautiful, tall, languorous, mysterious with her Egyptian profile.** They moved into your apartment Friday and they expect to remain here until autumn. Bay is writing but God knows what and Bessy is admiring which makes the same query rise to my mind. However, they are proudly happy and self-satisfied. All these nights I have dined alone, with a book propped up in quite your fashion, and the experience is so pleasant that I am wondering if I can make the effort to go out again.

After a brief stay in the 8th arrondisement, they rented an apartment at 46 rue du Bac which became their home for a year, a seventeenth century palace of the days when the rue du Bac was a fashionable street, built on three sides of an enormous court, airy without sidewalls.[209] At the back of the court were the large greenhouses of a florist. Their second-floor apartment was above the entre-sol, at the top

[209] The house was built by Samuel Bernard, a Jewish banker under Louis XIV, who was received at Versailles after one of the king's more expensive campaigns to the apparent horror of Saint-Simon who wrote about the encroaching bourgeoisie. Bernard sold the boiseries to the Rothschilds who installed them in their house on the Faubourg St. Honoré. The U.S. government bought the house for the American Embassy residence in the 1950s, the Rothschilds moved the boiseries to the Israel Museum in Jerusalem.

of the house, on the court, on the southwest corner, and filled with sun. The mansion had a splendid wide staircase with slight slivers of steps, with three great windows on every landing and a fine wrought iron railing, the first flight in stone, and the other two in brick. Bay wrote his mother that the apartment was "the funniest, nicest place you ever saw, a sort of vie de bohême poetry about it." The walls were very thick so that the place was full of closets and the windows in deep recesses. Some of the floors were stone; the others were wood. There was a small entryway and coat closet, a well-proportioned dining room, a grand salon big enough to hold the piano comfortably and two small bedrooms in the back. Bay appreciated Bessy's thrift and gift of housekeeping, writing from their temporary quarters in the 8th:

> The rue du Bac runs up from the Pont Royal, you remember, and 46 is near the river and in fact within striking distance of everywhere. Mr. Cambon has been kindness itself lending us things to cover the walls etc etc. Bessy is a miracle. The Frelinghuysen capacity of housekeeping she has inherited *en plein* and she makes one dollar go further than I ever could 5. She is as good as a Frenchwoman at getting her money's worth and talks to concierges and shopkeepers and all sorts of people who frighten me to death with an aplomb which is terrifying. Really the intelligence she shows with all the practical details is marvelous.[210]

In February 1901, while he continued playwriting, Bay became a journalist involved in the turn of the century political scene. Bay and Bessy, so perfectly happy alone that they didn't care about other people, returned to their own solitude with relief. They were not part of the American colony in Paris at the time—indeed, strenuously against it—insulated in their "old" American and French literary group. Paul Bourget, the late nineteenth century poet and his wife, Minnie, and a limited number of Americans led by Edith Wharton and Henry Adams, formed their circle. Paul and Minnie Bourget lived at 20 rue Barbet de Jouy, a quiet street in the Faubourg Saint Germain, and a five-minute walk to the rue du Bac. Minnie, in Percy Lubbock's words, was the "Tanagra Madonna," "so curiously did that little head combine the gravity of a medieval Virgin with the miniature elegance of a Greek figurine… shy, elusive, and somehow personal to herself… but I find no words delicate

---

[210] "We are delighted with it and are happy, happy, happy to get out of this beastly quarter [the 8th.] Apartment: 200, food: 400, servants: 140, coal, wood and extras: 300 = 1040 francs per month."

and imponderable enough to describe the Psyche-like tremor of those folded but never quiet wings of hers." Bay wrote his mother that he had "got into the harness" and was working all the time when he was not "playing" with Bessy. Bay also indulged in a bit of gossip about Mrs. Cameron who had a crush on Joe Stickney.

> *Darling Oops,*
> ...Bessie has developed marvelous faculties for practical things and she has great taste in making the place pretty. I am more than happy to be in my own place away from that beastly quartier of the Etoile.... It appears that Uncle Henry was distinctly uneasy and several times at dinners at Mrs. C's (present J. Stickney, the Lady and U.H.) and was, at it were, quite rude to Stickney from no motives more obvious than the above-mentioned uneasiness. This strikes me as rather pathetic. What it all actually amounts to I can't tell. I know Mrs. C takes a large interest in J.T.S. and second, conceals things which is rather stupid because one can suppose. I think one thing—that she is much more interested than *he*. Certainly they are very intimate. I doubt however—and I say this with genuine regret—if there is anything to bring a blush to the cheek of innocence. She and he both conceal their movements especially from us out of fear of Mrs. Davis (very justly) and conjecture is all I have. Joseph has changed a good deal. He seems to me like a man who has been spoilt by women and taken it seriously which is unpardonnable [sic] in a man of his intelligence. [We went to the] Theater and Café de Paris with J. and Mrs. C. Certainly, Mrs. C spoils him and flatters him absurdly. He has grown more prudent and with less élan. I enjoy immensely talks with him; he has got a marvelous understanding of the ways and methods of intellectual work in this country. He has unbounded contempt for the way he has spent the last five years and said he has wasted his youth on gamesmen. I feel a difference which does not seem to me the natural result of my marriage. Bessie has been extremely sweet to him and of course he seems to admire her immensely.

Mrs. Cameron's affair with Trumbull Stickney saddened and angered Henry Adams and sickened Bay and Bessy. Not much is known about how physical Henry Adams and Mrs. Cameron were; this passage hints that the relationship might have been more than platonic.

> *To Oops,*
> This is for you alone... that in my opinion there's more under this ex-

citement of HA's than meets the casual eye. Here's my idea and rather tragic it is. HA before he left here in January got pretty unhappy about Mrs. C because he was conscious of her interest in Joe. His being rude and other small details at Mrs. Cs, in short he went away rather sad in his mind and with the full sensation of having a rival who was young, etc. I think Mrs. C took small pain to conceal the fact that she liked the attention of a young man and the whole thing made HA pretty sick. If Mrs. C wanted him to come back, he would fast enough but when I spoke to her on the subject of how sorry I was etc. she was brutally cheerful about the whole thing. She speaks of UH without any kindness—for example she told me he was losing his mind and little lapses of memory which strike me as hardly fair play. This idea may be all wrong of course and I haven't an idea how much she cares for Joe or he for her. I am sure however that she cares more than he....

Bay confided to his mother that he had written a good deal, had sent his work to Dokko; he asked her get it from him and read it as Bessy thought it was the best thing he ever wrote. In April, Bay planned to get a room to himself "to write a play and a novel or both." Bay, perhaps influenced by his brother, John, a linguistic scholar,[211] had taken an interest in Middle Eastern languages and was learning hieroglyphics, working in the salon which he shared with Bessy who took music lessons.

"Mi-Carême has come and gone and Joe and Mrs. C and Bessy and I went on to the Boulevards to throw confetti with the other children and enjoyed it immensely. We are always hugely happy and wander about together, both well and very young.... I'm full of ideas and hope lingers strong in me. We want so much to show you our apartment. Bessie loves you like a mother really truly and I adore you." Bay's letter to his father shows how they shunned the nouveau riche "American colony," insulated within their tiny old American and French group.

Dearest Pa,

Bessy saw some American colonist lady the other day who told her that Porter was a very bad ambassador. Bessy: "Why?" American Colonist Lady: "Because he is pro-Boer" Bessy: "But I thought that was popular in France." AC Lady: "Oh no! All the Americans here are

---

[211] See chapter beginning on page 252.

Trumbull Stickney.

> pro-English." This strikes me as a very characteristic exhibition of the American colonist point of view. Bessy and I see very few people and no "sassiety" and less than no American colony and we are very happy indeed. We are looking forward very much to your advent on the scene.

In the same month, Bessy and Bay declined going to Sicily and Florence with Joe and Lucy Stickney, Mrs. Cameron, the Canfields, Miss. Marbury, and Miss. De Wolfe, among others. They wanted to work and be by themselves. He may have been beginning his play, *Cain*, in which he speaks of the "incalculable damage" done to man by "orthodox Christianity." Bay's skepticism about the church's foundations extended into the lives of his future children, whom he wanted to go to Middlesex boarding school rather than Groton "where they could choose which religion they wanted to belong to rather than be forced into the Episcopalian faith." Bay used the established church of Protestantism as a symbol of the division in life between true spirituality and the rule-bound restraining influence that often accompanies its opposition. He saw the right-wing establishment church as a symbol for the Bostonians' effacement of their spiritual life. This letter reveals that Nannie was Bay's literary agent and that Bay was jealous of John Hay—Hay's attention to his mother and his success in literature:

> I find myself less and less desirous of taking the necessary trouble to know people who are not my real friends. I suppose it is one of the reasons I don't get on in the world. But in truth, I have such an intensely real life between Bessy and my work that to put on the masque becomes more and more of an effort. I have begun another novel. The plot is very good, the difficulty of getting it on paper very great. If I get this finished in time, I want to write another tragedy—this time for the stage. I can't ask for things with any conviction and I find one doesn't get what one doesn't ask for. To be perfectly honest with you, there are remains of ambition for worldly success in me, which makes this thought trouble me a little. Nevertheless, I am genuinely convinced that if one writes for others one writes badly—that art for art's sake is the condition of good art. As you have written me nothing concerning my novel, I suppose it's been refused. If I could get a novel finished it might bring me sufficient reputation to enable me to get a tragedy

on the stage. But I confess the vista seems a long one. However I still believe in myself, which is the main thing for me certainly, and I've written some poems which I am tolerably pleased with. I am very happy and had rather have this winter and spring with Bessy than all the fame going—solid truth... I don't care if Mr. Hay stops by my apartment. I think he's pretty small but then I always did... not pushing it without saying that I don't want the appointment, which might annoy him. If this letter seems a little depressed it's because my novel has gone slowly today and my nerves are in consequence irritated. Bessy is very well. She's lying on a chaise longue in front of me as I write. It's wonderful to watch her and feel her here. What does anything else matter? Not having your presence....

An April letter shows the Bay Lodges accepting an invitation to go to the music festival at Bayreuth and demonstrates the political nature of Bay's relationship with his father. The socialist French premier Emile Combes had put through laws dispersing religious orders; Bay laughingly said that after confiscating the religious orders, the next move would be confiscating the Rothschild Bank. He praised Paris' new bridge, Pont Alexandre III.[212] He asked if his father could send his "Villon" by post. Bay enjoyed making wild remarks at a conventional American dinner party. "Most everyone seems empty and dead. It's so disgusting to see the young smoke the old smoke. Fortunately such an experience is rare for us. For that reason it makes a greater impression."

This teasing letter from Bessy to Oops shows she had a funny side, ingratiating herself to her powerful mother-in-law who would son be making a visit.

May 4, 1901
Dearest Oops,

---

[212] The Great Exposition of 1900, during which the magnificent Pont Alexandre III was built, alarmed Adams. Writing to John Hay in September of that year, he stood watching in the machine gallery of the Champs de Mars, "by the hour over the great dynamos, watching them run noiselessly and smoothly as the planets, and asking them—with infinite courtesy—where the Hell they were going.... It is a new century and what we used to call electricity is its God.... The curious mustiness of decay is already over our youth, and all the period from 1840 to 1870. The period from 1870 to 1900 is closed. I see that much in the machine gallery at the Champs de Mars. All I can see is the compression, concentration and consequent development of terrific energy, represented not by souls but by coal, iron and steam."

> Bay writes so often that it hardly seems worthwhile for me to do so too but still I want to tell you how very glad I am that you are both coming over even if we must wait two months to see you. I am looking forward to having a "real good time." You might have rather a hard time keeping UH and me in order for I foresee a violent flirtation. We have been corresponding in a most compromising manner and I trust it will not end there.... I have grown to love you and feel as if you cared for me. I hope you have not been disappointed in me but that seems a rather audacious thing to say. With much love to you and Constance when you write,
>
> Lovingly,
> Bessy.

Bay, who wrote six hours a day, expressed his uncertainty about his choice of livelihood to his mother and his unhappiness with not being able to fulfill his great gifts. His spirits sink and then rise minutes later.

> I have written quite a number of short poems and one act of tragedy (*Lorenzaccio*[213]) after infinite labor. The second act is begun and by the help of heaven I shall produce something that can be acted. I met George Gissing, an English novelist, the other day and had a very sympathetic talk with him. We have also dined with Mrs. Raoul Duval (she is a cousin of Mrs. James Brown Potter[214]) and there met the Comte de Mun who is a Royalist clerical leader at the Chamber, also another député (very nice) and Paul Adam (novelist) all with their wives... [Regarding] Whitman—and my own search for truth—I have learned that **one cannot be a real man by the wishing, nor find truth by the seeking, but that life and much labor are the price one must pay and perhaps then the reward cometh not. The terrible irony of life is the finding out too late that one has made a mistake.** I feel filled full of ideas and Oh Lord, Life is short and art is long.... Paris is warm and full of millionaires from New York.... Mrs. C is going home I imagine with a glittering realization that she better had and talks of not coming back. If she should not come back, I merely indicate that Stickney will be at home next winter also. The crash—if one there be—is, I'm sure, principally on her side. This scandal is of course, for you alone. The experience of happiness becomes more and more absorbing.

---

[213] Alfred de Musset wrote about this lively Renaissance Florentine, a Medici who had a dramatic life.
[214] She had been the mistress of Edward VII, King of England, and had children by him.

In May and June 1901, Bay, already having delved into Egyptian history and languages, wrote his mother that he was considering writing an article for a scientific magazine on Chaldea, Syria, and Babylonia. "I have a pretty good idea of the classic orient. It's a point of departure I've always lacked." He told her his tragedy was moving and that he had laid the groundwork for another novel "which ought certainly to be better than my last," while also working as a journalist, writing his father he received checks from *The Century* and *The Atlantic*. He and Bessy met the Lodges in Salzburg, where the Lodges gave their son and daughter in law a handsome sum of money so that she could afford a new dress. Bessie wrote an amusing thank you letter:

> Yesterday I ordered a most beautiful dress at Jeanne Hallie's with your present. It's a Louis XV evening dress—**light blue chiffon skirt and brocade top**. It's a reserve force to be used only as a great emergency when Bay's love seems on the wane. Then I appear in the lovely gown and make an easy conquest. As long as I feel that dress in the background, I shan't give up hope.... I did not have a chance to tell you and Mr. Lodge how very very much I enjoyed the whole trip, the lovely music, the Danube and all the rest to say nothing of the pleasure of being with you. At Trouville, I found lovely big black hats. I do wish you would get a big black hat this winter. You did look perfectly sweet in the one you had this summer. We have found a book on the rue du Bac which says that our house was the prettiest one there in the 17th and 18th c. When you are here, do walk by and notice the door. Of course the boiseries are sold to Rothschild and the garden where there used to be a status of Louis XIV is inhabited by a florist. I am so looking forward to Nahant...
>
> Lovingly Yrs,
> *Bessy*

Later that August, Bessy wrote of their search for a summer house on the Normandy beaches, an existence she would repeat eight years later under very different conditions. The intellectual excitement of living in the Paris of 1901 and Bay's personal quest to constantly advance his literary life is described in *The Education of Henry Adams*.[215] In August, the Senator and Nannie returned to Nahant while the young couple remained in Paris, and this letter from Bay to his mother shows their particular closeness, such that he may have been unable to lead a happy life.

---

[215] See Adams, 172.

Bay, to Nannie:

> *My Darling Oops,*
> I had a sad journey away from you.... There is some vice in my character that prevents me from getting all the love and tenderness and intimacy that life might give me. However, it is, I felt desperately sad at leaving you.... I wish I could put my head in your lap at this moment as I've done so often at the twilight in Nahant for I feel horribly discouraged about myself—character, work, everything—it will pass however and you will think me as happy and hopeful for I shall be by then. My darling Oops, I adore you...
> *George Cabot Lodge*

Adams described Nannie as "a super-annuated mother" in this delightful letter to Elizabeth while Bay was honeymooning in Paris:

> Cabot is more Cabotain ["dog-like" in French] than ever, or would so if he could, for human nature has limits even in selfishness and humbug. Sister Anne is a little like me in one respect: she has seen too much and her birds have flown too far. The world has grown vague and a shade impossibly absurd. She shows a little that the game is much played out. These super-annuated mothers feel that way till they start fresh as old women.[216]

By September 1901, a year after the wedding, Bay and Bessy had returned to Boston. In a letter to Elizabeth a month before their return, Adams spoke of Bessy's emotional intelligence and common sense. "[Bessy] will end, I suppose, by ruling it [the family]. To me, she has been very natural and good. Bessie, without being clever, has more sense than Bay. But Bay is growing rapidly conventional and urbane."[217]

Imagine having a mother-in-law like Nannie—no woman could ever measure up. But the intellectual Nannie did not have Bessy's emotional intelligence for she spoiled Bay; and spoiled children are always unhappy, attaching importance to the least whim.

My grandfather wrote about his mother and grandfather,

> My mother [Bessy] was the greatest influence in my childhood. After her came my grandfather [the Senator] and my father's brother, my uncle John—an orientalist of great originality, brilliance and charm. In the sum-

[216] Adams to Elizabeth Cameron, February 3, 1901.
[217] Adams, *Letters*, August 10, 1901.

> mer at Nahant, my grandfather, Doctor Bigelow, Uncle John, my brother, and I would meet, equipped with bath towels, at an inlet on the rocky shore. A flight of wooden steps, fastened to the rocks, led into deep water. Small platforms from which to dive were affixed to natural rocky shelves. The rocks were so steep that they formed a pool completely cut off from human view. Thus we all swam in the nude—with the result that I have never since been able truly to enjoy swimming while wearing a bathing suit.

On Sundays, after the swim, we would lunch at my grandfather's house (wearing a coat and tie at my mother's direction) where we always had cold lobster, from the then unpolluted waters, with mayonnaise. This was followed by roast beef! What gastronomic orgies![218] The letters from Bay to his mother between1901 and 1909 show a happy life.

Nannie with Bay at home in Washington.

[218] Lodge, *The Storm Has Many Eyes*, 25-26.

Between 1902 and 1905, Bessy and Bay had three children—Cabot, John and Helena. Cabot, the eldest, was my grandfather, Henry Cabot Lodge, Jr., born in July of 1902. He was working for his father as secretary, while burning the midnight oil writing poetry. If the rejection slips from his literary contributions were a disappointment, his magnificent children were a happy recompense.

The correspondence about Bay and Bessy's married life shows Bay's double allegiance to wife and mother. His spiritual and intellectual life was much more evident in the letters to his mother which show his moody disposition even in a heaven of marital bliss. Nannie emerges as a greater confidante of Bay. He didn't share his intellectual life with his wife to the extent he did with his mother. Rather, he sets himself apart, admired Bessy's beauty, housekeeping and child-rearing skills, like any conventional nineteenth century male, while running to his mother for literary advice. Bessy was aware of the dissimilarity in their relationship. But she was too good and had too much dignity to ever let it affect her connection with Nannie. On the contrary, she loved and admired Nannie and wanted to please her.

On their return from Paris, Bay and Bessy went directly to Dr. Bigelow's house in Boston and from there to reconcile with Bessy's mother, followed by Nahant. Bay wrote Nannie about his reconciliation with Mrs. Davis: "Went to Newport to see Mrs. Davis—very kind and nice—**we buried the hatchet and are on the best of terms....**"

From Nahant two days later, Bessy thanked Nannie for the house and made clear that Americans in this period bought their clothes in Europe, where Nannie and the Senator were vacationing until the congressional session began in the winter. "We enjoyed Nahant more than I can say, the place so fresh, green and the weather delicious. Agnes proved a delicious cook, Georgette managed to do the housework and seems very happy wherever she goes. If I keep getting happier every year, there will be an explosion. We went over to see Mama at Newport. Absorbed by Mr. Lodge's *Life of Washington.*[219] Would you get Bay some gray suede gloves and pick up some Charvet ties?"

In a letter from Washington, Bay described his complicated life working for a busy man like the Senator while his poetic works were constantly rejected. In this light, his depression seems normal. In a Christmas Eve letter to Dokko, Bay wrote that he had refused a White House job for in his present job, he was free from three in the after-

[219] The Senator's biography.

noon for his own work. He was at the Capitol through the morning, and was at work on his poetry from three p.m. to three a.m., with brief intermissions for refreshment. At first, Cameron, Blake & Co. of New York City agreed to publish Bay's poems, but the publisher "turned out to be a fraud." In May of 1902, Bay wrote Nannie that he had lunched with Mrs. Wharton and given her his manuscript, that Dokko was trying to decide if he was going to Japan. Dr. Sturges Bigelow never liked being a doctor and became a Buddhist priest. At the end of the letter, Bay wrote that Bessy was pregnant with their first child and the baby expected on July 14.

Two months later, they were back again with Bay's muse, Edith Wharton. On September 2, Bay wrote his mother a vivid description of the beauty and harmony of her Lenox, Massachusetts house, The Mount:

> We got our train alright and arrived without accident. Bessy was not too tired and she wants me to thank you for your sweet thought of her. This is a really beautiful house—as a whole—in every detail. The sort of house one longs to live in because of its exquisite harmony throughout and its real luxury and distinction. It's the best house in every way I've seen for a great while as it shows that intimate care and precise sense of power which is so satisfying. Mrs. Wharton most kind and delightful and I'm enjoying myself enormously as I think Bessy is also. However it's always pleasant to go back to you and Nahant. Walter seems pretty wretched but I hope he will pick up here.

From the Frelinghuysens' at 4 West 49th Street, that same month, Bay wrote his mother that he found the Frelinghuysens' company imprisoning and that he missed Mrs. Wharton. "New York... depresses me to the urge of suicide and I look forward with a sinking of the heart to being here any time at all.... Mrs. Wharton is not here so there's no one I can talk with.... Everybody is kind, very kind indeed, but no Frelinghuysen ever lived, I have discovered, who didn't have at least three grievances in the space of 24 hours. Bessy and lamb-baby had broad smiles for his dear Grandma."

"Lamb-baby" (my grandfather) hardly slept, hardly cried and ate considerably.

In the fall of 1902, Bay wrote his Pa that he had moved into a new house at 1925 F. Street Garden (F and 20th Street), full of honeysuckle, morning glory, rose trees and bushes, box, hydrangeas, two magnolia trees. Lamb-baby, Senator from Massachusetts and a diplomat, wrote in his autobiography:

> [My father's] great interest was poetry, but he also worked in my grandfather's office in the Senate. At first we lived in a beautiful old house with a big garden at 1925 F. Street, which is now the "1925 F. St. Club." My parents then built [in 1907] a house on Massachusetts Avenue, near Sheridan Circle, backing on Rock Creek Park. Washington in those days was a sleepy Southern town. The streets were quiet. The streetcars on their rails made little noise and the sound of their bells was pleasant. The clip clop of the horse-drawn taxis (known as herdics) and the almost inaudible hum of the "electrics"—the automobiles moved by storage batteries in which ladies traveled about the town—would never even drown a whisper. Gasoline autos were infrequent and the air underneath all the leafy archways lining the streets was clean. There were many large private houses, mostly of red-brick Federal style, with white columns and trim.... As a child I was surrounded by some remarkable people, to whom the statement of the French philosopher Montaigne applied: "It is an absolute perfection, and as it were divine, to know how, in all sincerity, to get the very most out of one's own individuality." The adults in my childhood certainly knew how to do that.[220]

In August of 1903, Bay wrote from Tuckanuck to Nannie at the Hotel Brighton in Paris that he had been with Langdon Mitchell, a fellow poet, while Bessy was in Northeast with the children. The week at Tuckanuck had been "full of good talk and good work—glorious week." He and brother John continued on the Northeast Harbor to see Bessy and "Boo" (Henry Cabot Lodge, Jr.), "my inexpressible happiness." Bessy, who was in the final months of her second pregnancy, was "in tolerable spirits, considering all things." It was evident after a time that their being there made things more difficult. Meanwhile, Mrs. Wharton had written to ask the brothers to Lenox for a few days but John did not enjoy it. They returned to Nahant when Bessy and Boo came down from Maine. One wonders about the guilty letter to Nannie: "Terribly lonely I am and sometimes my mind reaches dreadful excursions into the past and I see what a fool and worse I've often been and I count all the mistakes of my life and suffer—a dreary business. Don't be worried by this because by the time you read this, my spirits will be again on the top of the wave...."

In *The Education*, written in 1905, Adams made a contribution to

[220] Lodge, *The Storm Has Many Eyes*, 17, 18.

the annals of women's history when he identified Nannie and Bessy Lodge as examples of women's superiority, referring to a May 1903 dinner and to a woman's dilemma:

> The woman seldom knows her own thought; she is as curious to understand herself as the man to understand her, and responds far more quickly than the man to a sudden idea... Adams owed more to the American woman than to all the American men he ever heard of... This spring, just before sailing for Europe in May, 1903, he had a message from his sister-in-law, Mrs. Brooks Adams [Evelyn], to say that she and her sister, Mrs. [Nannie] Lodge, and the Senator were coming to dinner by way of farewell; Bay Lodge and his lovely young wife [Bessy] sent word to the same effect; Mrs. Roosevelt joined the party; and Michael Herbert shyly slipped down to escape the solitude of his wife's absence. The party were too intimate for reserve, and they soon fell on Adams's hobby with derision which stung him to pungent rejoinder: "The American man is a failure! You are all failures!" he said. "**Has not my sister here more sense than my brother Brooks? Is not Bessie [sic] worth two of Bay? Wouldn't we all elect Mrs. [Nannie] Lodge Senator against Cabot?** Would the President have a ghost of a chance if Mrs. Roosevelt ran against him? Do you want to stop at the Embassy, on your way home, and ask which would run it best—Herbert or his wife?" The men laughed a little—not much! Each probably made allowance for his own wife as an unusually superior woman... **The cleverer the woman, the less she denied the failure. She was bitter at heart about it. She had failed even to hold the family together, and her children ran away like chickens with their first feathers; the family was extinct like chivalry. She had failed not only to create a new society that satisfied her, but even to hold her own in the old society of Church or State; and was left, for the most part, with no place but the theatre or streets to decorate. She might glitter with historical diamonds and sparkle with wit as brilliant as the gems, in rooms as splendid as any in Rome at its best; but she saw no one except her own sex who knew enough to be worth dazzling, or was competent to pay her intelligent homage. She might have her own way, without restraint or limit, but she knew not what to do with herself when free. Never had the world known a more capable or devoted mother, but at forty her task was over, and she was left with no stage except that of her old duties, or of Washington society where she had enjoyed for a hundred years every advantage, but had created only a medley where**

nine men out of ten refused her request to be civilized, and the tenth bored her.[221]

In a November 4, 1903, letter to Bay, Adams spoke again about his isolation, his contempt for politics and, again, his belief in the superiority of women, congratulating Bay and Bessy on the birth of their new baby boy, John Davis Lodge (the future Governor of Connecticut and Ambassador to Spain), named for Bessy's father.

23 Avenue du Bois de Boulogne
To Bay
1925 F. St.
Thanks for your letter, oh Père Eternel! And I am just furious to see St. Thomas Secundus. Your mamma and I will have a gorge this winter. She shall have the baby and I'll take Thomas [Saint Thomas Aquinas was Adams nickname for my grandfather].[222] If she is meek, I'll lend her Thomas now and then. Bessy ought to be made President. I am ready to nominate her, and she would rattle all the men off the course. You who are saturated with old conventions will never feel the joy in politics which we should show if two beautiful women ran against each other for the Presidency. It is our only hope for art. Within three months we should revive Greece. We should return to a sense of beauty, sex and decoration. It can never be. We are dead to joys like this. Our eyes are blind and our minds are sodden. Our model of beauty is Roosevelt—or is it Hanna. Is it possible that, under such conditions, one can care for elections! This morning I can see that George McClellan has whacked the wise and good. This gives us another Presidential candidate. I suppose, and a still better candidate, for I am told that Mrs. G.B.M. is virtuous and soothing. A campaign between Roosevelt and McClellan[223] would be fun, but on the whole they should swap parties.

As for me, I know nought; I am St. Simeon Stylites on the Arc d'Etoile; I pray to my Ming vases and lead W.S.B.[224] to meals on a string.

Bless you, my children! I am coming home soon, after settling the La Farges.

Ever *hers*,
H.A.

---

[221] Adams, Chapter XXX, "Vis Inertiae."
[222] My one-year-old grandfather.
[223] McClellan was a candidate for President and Mark Hanna, an Ohio politician, "created" McKinley, who was assassinated in 1901. Roosevelt, Vice-President, became President and was elected in 1904.
[224] William Sturges Bigelow.

After reading Bay's second novel about New York society, *The Genius of the Commonplace*,[225] Adams put his finger, most elegantly and generously, on what was wrong with Bay's work. Adams who wrote two highly successful novels—*Democracy* (1880) and *Esther* (the first published anonymously and the second under the name of Frances Snow Compton)—counseled Bay against moralizing. He was essentially saying Bay wasn't subtle enough and that an autobiographical and sarcastic novel was of no use.

> 22 April, 1903
> *My Dear Bay,*
> I return the manuscript. The mere fact that it is far better than anything I would do, and that it has some of that freshness which is worth all the finish that time is sometimes supposed to give, would not prevent my trying to offer suggestions, if I saw any that were likely to be of use. Practically I know but two, and have practiced these with so much success that at last, I have ceased to practice at all… As a matter of course, you go over your work, as you would go over anybody's work, with a comb, combing out all the inevitable knots, and straightening the crooked angles, and filling the defective lines. The point is, not so much to do, as to see; once seen, a defect is easily handled. Anyone who means to be an artist has got to study his defects, and the only way of studying one's own defects is to lay one's work aside until it is forgotten, and then to go over it again with no other thought than to see where it is wrong. As a rule one finds that it is mostly wrong. A man is generally artistic in proportion as he sees what is wrong, and most work is good in proportion not so much to what one leaves in it as to what one strikes out. […] Please lock up the volume for a year. Then read it over—carefully—and tell me your conclusion.
>
> Ever Yrs,
> *Henry Adams*[226]

Obediently, Bay locked up the novel and never published it. Later that year, Adams wrote Henry James an important letter about both Bay and his own sentiment about Boston. Congratulating James on his recently published biography of William Wetmore Story, the sculptor who spent most of the late nineteenth century in Rome, Adams revealed his views on the thinness of that Bostonian culture that couldn't

---

225 First published in 1976. John W. Crowley, ed.
226 More of Adams' letter on the art of fiction writing is appendixed.

nourish genius. In this letter, justifying his own existence and claiming not to have achieved greatness, he exaggerates the dilemma. In what is an autobiographical text, Adams lends insight into the Boston against which they both had struggled from 23 ave du Bois de Boulogne, November, 18, 1903.[227]

Whatever else can be said of Bay's artistic aspirations and the extent to which both Bay and Adams shared the Bostonian's "nervous self-consciousness," his greatest success seems to have been fatherhood. Nannie, Bay's greatest confidante, was in London at the time when Bessy was about to give birth to their second child. Bay was at Tuckanuck with Walter Berry but he returned for the birth. Bay wrote his mother that his father had sent him money even though financially Bay admitted to being "in a good way." Of the new baby they were expecting, Bay proclaimed, "If it's a girl, we shall call it Helena because it's beautiful; if it's a boy Bessy wants to name it for me." But they didn't name the baby after Bay; they named him after Bessy's father, John Davis.

Nahant
Sept. 13, 1903
Bay to Nannie, Thomas' Hotel, Berkeley Square[228]
Oops,
Your dear letter brought the greatest comfort—the utmost joy to me—

---

[227] "It is a tour de force, of course, but that you knew from the first.... Verily, I believe I wrote it. Except your specialty of style, it is me.... The painful truth is that all of my New England generation, counting the half-century, 1820-70, were in actual fact only one mind and nature; the individual was a facet of Boston. We knew each other to the last nervous center, and feared each other's knowledge. We looked through each other like microscopes. There was absolutely nothing in us that we did not understand merely by looking in the eye. There was hardly a difference even in depth, for Harvard College and Unitarianism kept us all shallow. We knew nothing—no! but really nothing of the world! One cannot exaggerate the profundity of ignorance of Story in becoming a sculptor, or Sumner in becoming a statesman, or Emerson in becoming a philosopher. Story and Sumner, Emerson and Alcott, Lowell and Longfellow, Hillard, Winthrop, Motley, Prescott, and all the rest were the same mind,—and so, poor worm!—was I!

Type bourgeois-bostonien! [...] God knows that we knew our want of knowledge! The self-distrust became introspection—nervous self-consciousness—irritable dislike of America, and antipathy to Boston.... Improvised Europeans, we were, and—Lord God—how thin! No, but it is too cruel! Long ago—at least thirty years ago—I discovered it, and have painfully held my tongue about it. You strip us, gently and kindly, like a surgeon, and I feel your knife in my ribs. No one else will ever know it. You have been extremely tactful. The essential superficiality of Story and all the rest, you have made painfully clear to us, but not, I think, to the family or the public. After all, the greatest men are weak...." Henry James' biography of William Wetmore Story sheds light on the artist's life as it applies to Bay. See appendix.

[228] Bay asked, "Get a dog collar for Mike in London 3 inches wide, very strong leather or yellow or tan, studded with nickel-plated spikes for a big bulldog." The Senator's dog was a black Labrador named Veto.

please forgive my correspondence—*unstable, wandering, and rather cheerless life* explains my neglect, not any lack of tender thinking of you constantly. Bessy, the babe, John and I at Nahant with some noble but cold autumn weather.... Bessy is well but thin. Doctor put her on a diet—fish and meat and no fruit, no vegetables, no water, no milk, one starvation meal a day etc. The babe resembles a fat pigeon.[229]

Bay to Oops:

October 20, 1903
Boys, both well. The new baby is mighty soft and cunning.[230] Sometimes he looks like a fat squirrel and sometimes like the picture of Egyptian babes. Bessie had a remarkably easy labor—no anesthetics and no instruments. The new Boo is mighty nice. Cabot is magnificent and as charming as ever. So you see all's well. He only weighed 8lbs at birth but he is strong and active and well. I think he is going to be dark and look more like Bessie, thank God. Cabot—Ideal baby.

In this November 18, 1903, letter to Nannie, Bessy couldn't resist making a sarcastic remark about Mrs. Hay:

This is just to tell you how glad I am that you have arrived and how much I am looking forward to showing you the new boy. Am in the hope that you will be able to solve the name difficulty which Bay and I are unable to do. He has been gaining a pound a month but is terribly hampered by the mature beauty of the big baby. I feel so sorry for him, poor little lamb! For everyone draws unfavorable comparisons though he is really quite as good-looking... seems to have a gentle nature but all the traits of character are not yet perfectly developed. Bay is so pleased with his shirts from Charvet. The nurse (who could easily receive in Mrs. Hay's place without anyone knowing the difference) is disappointed not to see you. Uncle George and Aunt Lily [James] seem to be enjoying their honeymoon.

Adams, in this January 10, 1904, letter to Lizzie, reveals how ever-present he was in the Lodges' life and how Bessy was the star of the family:

---

229 One of the dangers women ran in pregnancy was Bright's disease—abstinence from liquids.
230 My Great Uncle, John Davis Lodge.

> St. Thomas is changed into an Eros, a regular little Cupid, and pretty as paint when he has his bath, and runs about the nursery with fat legs and a huge stomach and no neck at all. The new one is dark and different, we think going to be like his mother. Bessy and Bay dined here last night in a snow-storm and I devoured her with eyes. **She fascinates me more every year and I don't know why except that she is fascinating which is not a reason. She is a type Madonna.**

My grandfather wrote of Adams in his autobiography:

> Another important figure of my childhood was Henry Adams, author of *Mont St. Michel* and *Chartres* and *The Education of Henry Adams*. In Nov. 1904 (when I was two and my brother was one) he wrote Martha Cameron, the child of one of his closest friends, that my mother had "sent the babies in their giant baby carriage for inspection, the prettiest little show you ever saw." Both of us had long curls.... Henry Adams had a way with children. He invented fanciful nicknames for himself, which he wanted small children to use. One of these was "Dordy." He was also very short in stature and my brother John received a maternal reprimand for once having asked him why he was so short. In an effort to make amends brother John said, at his next meeting with Henry Adams, "Dordy, I think you've grown."

Evidently Nannie was also the muse of Bay's friend, fellow poet and playwright, Langdon Mitchell. He shared Nannie's gift for languages and sent a translation of Persian poetry to her! Bay implored Mitchell to stop on his way to Hot Springs. The letter reveals that Bay believed wives should be relegated to the nursery and the kitchen at a time when women were suddenly beginning to emerge with more power in the world. Women, he wrote in a letter to his friend, when they held power, could no longer be placed on the exalted, rarified (but not powerless) pedestal that WASPs prepared for them except when it came to family management. Bay expressed his powerlessness and scorn for the dying race of the "well-to-do" class of American men who had been "dethroned" by their wives. Bay argued that American women were refusing to bear children and only wanted a "money-getter" because they hadn't fallen in love and didn't want to risk their lives in childbirth. "And who could blame them?"

Neither Bay's nor Mitchell's plays were published and Bay expressed his powerlessness and scorn for the American male, for he took it as a sign of the intellectual, moral and spiritual childishness of the audience. He also complained deeply about the way women were taking over as the head of households because the American man was no longer able to exert authority over them:[231]

> Fifty yrs ago he was the unquestioned head of his family, the master of his house, the father of as many children as he wanted to have. His wife's business was to rear his children and manage his household to suit him and she never questioned it. **Today he is absolutely dethroned—women rule in his stead.** His wife finds him so sexually inept that she refuses to bear him children and so driveling in every way except as a money-getter that she compels him to expend his energies solely in that direction while she leads a discontented, sterile, stunted life not because she genuinely prefers it but because she cannot find a first-rate man to make her desire to be the mother of his children and to live happily. I speak only of the well to do classes which as a matter of fact comprises most real Americans and of which the average number of children per family is under two. We are, dear Mitchell, a dying race.

In October 1903, Bay, as the Senator's secretary, set himself apart from the imperialistic American foreign policy of his father and Roosevelt in Panama where the latter was determined to build the canal. "Venezuela owned Panama and Roosevelt simply thrust his way through. Washington stretches about me, a human void.... Even in the church it is necessary to sift truth from falsehood. Panama—when one considers how the chariot of empire has been broken down by slaves and greased with blood, this Panama business seems pretty wan."

Bay wrote Mitchell his poems had "an innocence and quiet dignity," and how much he admired Baudelaire, who was "like Villon, like Verlaine, a city poet." Bay reveals how central Christ's truth was to his personal philosophy and vision. Was Bay a demon or a saint? He delighted in his role as spoiler, as exemplified in this amusing story of how when he was in the middle of *Cain*, a bishop came to visit and thought so

[231] "...The American theater is exclusively either for importations or the worthless manufacture of illiterate Americans who view plays merely as merchandise and who would manufacture boots with equal engagement and success. Indeed it's most depressing and what's to be done? ...Indeed was there ever such an anomaly as the American man? In practical affairs his cynicism, energy and capacity are stupefying and in every other aspect he is a sentimental idiot, possessing neither the interest, the capacity, nor the desire for even the most elementary processes of independent thought.... he is the most astonishingly efficient creature the world has ever seen and in everything else he is a windy, blatant, shallow, canting poltroon."

much more highly of Bessy.[232]

In the spring of 1904, Bay wrote Mitchell how he despised his social equals and the vacuity of Washington's social scene just as Henry James was to do the following year—in the "dreadful, blank, wild nothingness of this nice, agreeable, easy spatial vacuity and here I am again alone beyond belief." He admired men who, unlike him, had the "peculiar" faculty of remaining, "au fond," quite detached from his own circumstances and experience. In June, Bessy, thin and tired, went to Northeast Harbor while Mrs. Wharton "happened to turn up in Nahant," he wrote his friend. Ominously, Bay wrote his mother of bad health and financial difficulty and in July he wrote his father from the Mount asking for an advance on his allowance. On his return to Nahant, he asked his mother to join him in Tuckanuck, though he admitted, "I hate to leave Pussy alone again." Bessy wanted him to go because it seemed to him "the only way of combining everything." To Mitchell, urging him to come to Tuckanuck, Bay revealed that his friendship meant more to him "than is easily said in words."

> 1925 F St. Mitchell,
> I've got hold of such a splendid thing to write—immense. I'm shutting down on society in which we've been wandering this winter to the detriment of all that I value in life and I'm getting to work—God be praised. One gets glimpses, such glimpses of incredible, tremendous things... To feel yourself once again in the saddle after enduring the grievous sensation of insecurity is surely a happiness.

Houghton Mifflin published Bay's plays *Cain* and *The Great Adventure* in 1905, *Herakles* in 1908, and a volume of verse, *The Soul's Inheritance*, in 1909. In this previously unpublished important letter from Edith Whar-

---

[232] From 1925 Street, Washington, to Langdon Elwyn Mitchell, Esq., "Apples," Penllyn, Pennsylvania. "The civilization of an old society is I'm certain the fair material of poems... I feel you have appreciated as I do that Baudelaire is, in his best moments, really a great poet, one of the torch-bearers. At least we can follow on 'the great roads of the universe.' I'm glad your fourth act is finished. I wish I could say the same for Cain. I have talked with an engaging and amiable Bishop who told me the path of virtue which he cordially advised me to follow... I replied with a discretion that Christ, like all Orientals, clearly believed and taught that the kingdom of heaven was not good deeds but in a vision. Bessy, he loves, being so virtuous... You, sir, are a good churchman and I am not... The supreme and unique importance of Christ was that he saw and spoke truth and exemplified truth in his life and that his death was caused by the rich, respectable, orthodox, decent society of Jerusalem who with the insight of the timid, very justly confounded truth and anarchy. By the way, before I leave the Bishop in final oblivion, I was in the act of describing for the mouth of Cain. Meanwhile, the earthly ambassador of an almighty and sovereign God was waiting for me in the next room."

ton to Bay regarding *Cain*, she encouraged and instructed him as an artist; she was clearly searching for things she liked. Eve in *Cain* was obviously inspired by his mother and even Edith noticed they "pet each other too much." He was fascinating enough for such an artist as Edith Wharton; in any case, she took a lot of trouble helping him to correct the text.

> Nov. 30, 1904, The Mount, Lenox, MA
> *Dear Bay,*
> Bravo Cain—Prometheus—Job! The Zeus-defier is always good company, and in this case, there is great originality in his attitude toward poor little Bertie-Abel, (who, I am sure, was "going on" to the Ambassador's after leaving his card on God). As for Adam, I sympathize with him for having had to leave the steam-heat and sanitary plumbing of Paradise for that visual western prairie where there was nothing to do but sit in a stuffy tent, or have his head taken off by Eve every time he

Edith Wharton at the Mount.

put it out.—Seriously, *cher maître*, I think your idea a very fine one, and the drama culminates splendidly and cumulates too, for the poetry and the action both progress with it—by action, of course, I mean the shock of ideas. All the last act is good, and some of Cain's big tirades are fine—i.e. p.135-138, and the splendid "God is like one who by the wayside stands," which seems to me the most striking thing in the book—Then I like very much Eve's "Abel, most young and loveliest child of earth—" Then there are plenty of lines all through that I meant to mark and didn't—no pencil, of course! Fine things in Cain's opening tirade, Act II, for instance—and so on. Why aren't you here to talk it all over?—When it comes to picking holes—I think perhaps Cain and Eve *pet* each other a little too much: my dear and my heart each other—I have an idea that large utterance of the early man would have been rougher, and terms of endearment not among the first things invented. Least of all, I think I like Eve's calling God's thundering denunciation on p.124 a "vile slander." That is what she might have said if Cain's wife, for instance, had questioned the legitimacy of Seth; but when it came to talking to God, with only a cloud between, surely she would have found a bigger word?—To go back to Abel—another is: "Ask no more of life than life, for life has nothing more to give"—That is a splendid idea finely put.—Oh, but—since I seem to be praising and picking alternately: I take issue on one more point; p.127, where I think you missed an opportunity—when Eve says: Where is thy brother Abel? Cain answers—"He is where all is dumb, deserted, dead—"and I thought it was meant metaphorically and would go on in the sense of—"He is gone where all must go—*che visser senz' infamia y senza lode*—where the negations and the ineffectuals go—&etc.—"so that it was rather a shock to find that Cain—& at such a moment!—was only describing the scenery. Do you see what I mean? I think the néant might have been splendidly done in these lines—As for the *moral* of your play, my dear sir, I cannot but fear that Cain was brought up by his injudicious mother on that revolutionary song: "When Jay and Willie came to play, you should have seen that horrid Bay—But, happily for posterity, Abel had evidently time to found a family… before Cain fetched him that knock over the head—So all is for the best in the garden where the blue flowers blow—We were very sorry you could not come to us for Thanksgiving—It would have been great fun, as Walter would elegantly say, to "gut" Cain over the pinewood fire. Be sure to let me know when you and Bessy are in N.Y. again (we go on Dec. 12) and believe me,

Affly Yrs,
Edith Wharton

P.S. I don't think Adam's tent was half as rude as Eve.—
P.S. no. 2 Awful thought! How do you know *my* story wasn't one of the 22 incredibly bad 'uns that you and your father disposed of at a gulp? Answer me that, please![233]

In late November 1904, Henry Adams wrote a niece, Mabel Hooper LaFarge: "Mrs. Lodges (2) [Nannie and Bessy] I depend on. Bay's *Cain* is very strong." For once Uncle Henry was pleased.

December, 1904
Adams to George Cabot Lodge
Dear Bay,
Cain is good. I refer not so much to its moral orthodoxy, although as I read it, you have taken the exact attitude of the Conservative Christian Church in your conception of *Cain*; but rather to its dramatic force. Unlike most dramas and all poems, it interests. Distinctly, one wants to know why Cain killed Abel and what Eve said about it.

In the summer of 1904, Bay, who must have been either living apart or traveling without his wife, wrote Bessy of brother John's news that Joe Stickney, Bay's closest friend, was seriously ill with a brain tumor. Bay tried to see him but with Joe's almost constant pains a visit was forbidden by the doctor, and Bay was completely unnerved: "I feel at present utterly prostrated. Somehow I have never conceived of Joe's dying... I had hoped to take Joe to Tuckanuck with us."[234]

When Joe seemed to improve, Bay, John, and Bessy took turns coming from Nahant to Boston to see him. But he was going blind and visits became more difficult. When asked by a friend what he was doing, he responded, "Some of us are doing this, some that and some of us are dying." He managed to walk to the jewelers one day and bought Bay a little gold matchbox to carry on the gold chain Bay always wore. In this letter of October 7, Bay turns to Langdon for support.

In the presence of Stickney's danger, I have incessantly and intensely

---

233 Family papers.
234 Thomas Riggs, Jr., Trumbell Stickney, 1874-1904 (unpublished dissertation, Princeton University, 1949), 269.

> felt a gaunt sensation of immense solitude whose vague menace we both know so well and in the pain of its immediate presence I have very often and very keenly missed you and our talks which are among the permanent realities of life. Stickney's condition is improved but his recovery is in doubt.

At Dokko's for tea in October, Stickney suddenly felt cold and put his head in his hands. When they walked home, the pressure in his head affected his sense of direction; the next day, October 11, he went into a coma and never regained consciousness.

Bay's passage through this period marks the first time that he evolved from being impossibly abstract toward being more personal. For Edith Wharton:

> The first opportunity to test himself,... came to Cabot Lodge as it comes to so many, through a private grief—the death of his friend Stickney; and in the sonnets commemorating this loss his verse sounds a distinctly personal note. The one beginning: "At least," he said, "we spent with Socrates / Some memorable days, and in our youth / Were curious and respectful of the Truth," has a gallant ring of young defiance, but a more sustained level of beauty is reached in "Days." "Still on his grave, relentless, one by one, / They fall, as fell the mystic, Sibylline / Sad leaves, and still the Meaning's secret signs / Dies undeciphered with each dying sun."
>
> To wrest from life the secret of that meaning was the problem that haunted Cabot Lodge; and the insistency with which his verse reverts to it is saved from sameness only by the varied notes it wrung from him.[235]

Stickney had assigned three friends to edit his poems for publication. George Cabot Lodge, William Vaughn Moody, a friend and fellow poet, and John Ellerton Lodge, Bay's brother, wrote the short preface.[236] In a January 26, 1905, letter, Burlingame, the famed Charles Scribners publisher, writes: "Are the sonnets which you have sent me separable?

[235] Wharton, *George Cabot Lodge*, 237.

[236] "Stickney said to us just before he died, 'Here are my manuscripts; you will do as you please with them.' We were, he explained, with no further word of advice or guidance, to use only our own judgment: free to publish or suppress, in whole or in part, exactly as seemed best to us. Therefore it happens that, in the particulars of selection and editing, we are responsible for this present volume, which, in our intention, offers to the public, in definitive form, all of Stickney's work that is for any reason valuable."

We should like very much to publish three of them, the first, third and fourth which seem to us not only admirable but to make a complete whole perhaps even better than all the four would do it.... I have not known Stickney's work—sorry because it makes me realize more than ever how easy it is to fall out of knowledge of the younger men who are carrying on the succession." In June of 1905, Houghton Mifflin expressed an interest in publishing Stickney's poems and asked for a short description of the man and his poems from Bay.

Stickney's death must have been as much a blow to Nannie for the force of the loss to her son, and the only clue of her feelings comes to us from Adams. This May 16, 1905, letter from her "Brother" to Nannie, a model of dignity and reserve, lectures her about allowing herself to show her feelings: "My dear Sister, You always hide your annoyances and anxieties as though they were kittens and you the mother cat nursing them; but I love to scream about mine and insist on their being admitted by everybody. Grievances are no fun except when worn like hats at Easter."

Bessy, then in her third pregnancy (she was seven months pregnant while baby John was barely toddling), wrote Nannie of the saving grace of Nahant:

> May 27, 1905
> I can't even begin to tell you how grateful I am to you for everything—for the lovely, huge, cool house, the good cook and the steady sleep which I found for the first time in weeks. You can never know how I feel about you and your kindness unless you took an x-ray and looked into my heart. When I think of your running two separate establishments entirely on my account, makes me terribly ashamed. Bay looks pale—probably the effect of the strain I have been through. Cabot had climbed into the baby's bed [John] and they were both beaming with joy. It was such a delicious sight.

In July, Bay wrote his mother about the birth of his daughter, Helena, at Northeast Harbor. The next month, we learn from a letter to Langdon, that he was starting his second play, *Herakles*, which he would finish three years later. Adams wrote Bessy from Paris that he was already planning Helena's education, that he had looked into a country place for let,[237] indicating that Bessy might have wanted to get away from America again and go to France where she and Bay had been so

[237] "Mabel... has now gone to her country place at Villers-sur-something where she has a six-foot cottage with a three foot garden. I don't know exactly how much she sends, but I guess it's about a thousand a year a head, say six thousand dollars for the let."

In this 1905 photograph, Bessy stands holding baby Helena. Bay sitting holds Henry Cabot Lodge, Jr., left, three, and John Davis Lodge, right, two, with long hair, the custom until three-years-old.

happy. Or was she tiring of Bay's absences, depression, violent tendencies? More and more after Joe's death, Bay relied on Langdon and Edith for intellectual companionship. Bay wrote his mother:

> Helena born. Bessy had only a whiff of chloroform. She is a dear lamb and I am overjoyed to have a girl. The relief of having the whole thing over is intense. Bessy is convalescing and the baby is fat and well and mighty cunning. Cabot in a mature style is charming and both he and John covered the baby with kisses. Mrs. Davis and Aunt Tilley [sic] have, I regret to say, arrived at Bar Harbor and are coming over tomorrow to see Bessy.

Only a month after Helena's birth Bay wrote to "dear" Langdon;

> Where are you? How are you? I long to see you. My sonnets will be out early in November and I shall begin *Herakles* while I'm here. I wish you were here to fill your eyes with unspeakable spaces of sea and sky. Friendship is so precious a possession.... I was refreshed and stimulated and delighted to hear from you. I was much distressed by your letter of farewell, and I prayerfully hope that your journey was not injurious.... I was so occupied with the delight of being with you again....

There is no doubt that Bessy was Bay's muse. "She is the soul and tragic heart of youth; she is the dreams and raptures... She is the touch that sets the door ajar. She is the peace, she is the passionless chill wonder of the Night's infinite breath. She is the nameless light, the mystic star." But the lovely lines of "For E.L." below have a slight chill, like the disenchantment evident from the photograph of Bessy on the previous page.

"For E.L."[238]
by George Cabot Lodge

She stands before me till the space grows void,
And round her form the desert's sterile heat
Throbs with the tread of strong, impassive feet
And song in fanes She builded and destroyed...
She moves in the dusk of my mind like a bell with
The sweetness of singing

[238] Elizabeth Lodge (Bessy).

> In the twilight of summer fulfilled with the joy of the sadness of tears,
> And the calm of her face and the splendid, slow smile
> are as memories clinging
> Of songs and of silences filling the distance of passionate years.
> She moves in the twilight of life like a prayer
> in a Heart that is grieving,
> And her youth is essential and old as the spring
> and the freshness of spring;
> And her eyes watch the world and the little, low
> ways of the sons of the living
> As the seraph might watch from the golden, grave
> height of his heaven-spread wings.

Here, Bessy is an "angel" watching the "little low ways" of man. Bay is writing with distance of the passionate years, of a new phase in their marriage, of poems (songs) Bessy built and destroyed, and of a grieving heart, rather than a joyous one. Even her youth was "essential and old," although she was as pure as the spring and as mighty and superior as a seraph. Implicitly one senses a widening gap between the cultivated, self-centered youth and the woman who was bearing his children. Both Bessy and Nannie were their husband's center, their strength, their partner, their love and inspiration. Here are two extraordinary women from different generations, whose choice of husbands was so antithetical that their story is almost like a fairytale.

> July 12 1905
> 23 Avenue du Bois de Boulogne
> *My Dear Bessy,*
> The niece [Helena] pleases me greatly, though I am almost puzzled to know what sort of an education to give her. With the serious views of the C.C.A., it is very unsafe to look ahead twenty years for girls. I will do my best especially as I have several other nieces more or les asking the same questions. I have also a large number of nephews of a suitable age to marry her. I will send you a list to pick from.
>
> You should first see my four LaFarge nephews, pretty boys, all eligible, with Paris educations… I would take the baby out en auto, like my other nieces, but I bust it up the other day, and it is in the shop for a month. No happy home should be without two *autos*; one is worse than none. Saint Anne will have to wait. She has time. Give

her my love.

Ever Affly
Henry Adams[239]

The letters from Bay to his mother in this period between 1901 and 1905, when Bessy was having babies, show that Bay's health was declining. Perhaps with each new brilliant addition to the family, he felt the pressure to succeed more keenly and spread himself too thin, working for his father as secretary while burning the midnight oil writing poetry. And he would occasionally throw fits brought on by stress, followed by guilt that may have weakened his heart. Like Lily Bart in Wharton's *The House of Mirth*, Bessy, with her high moral principles, chose not to marry for money. Had she not found Bay and happiness in love and marriage, it is possible that Bessy would have been similarly exposed. Bay naturally gravitated to friends with whom he could have intellectual companionship. Mrs. Wharton satisfied that longing, as is evident from his letters. In a 1905 letter from the Mount, Bay described to his mother a laughter that was a little too giddy when the subject of *The House of Mirth* came up. One wonders if Bessy, through her financial situation, wasn't part of a composite character Mrs. Wharton drew of Lily Bart. Mrs. Wharton found the Senator, Bessy's father in law, tyrannous and perhaps more selfish than the son, which is why Bessy turned to Henry Adams for friendship and support.

In December, Bay and Bessy visited Mrs. Wharton at the Mount and Bay wrote this telling letter to his mother.

> December 1, 1905
> When conversation turns to *The House of Mirth*, which it often does, **I detect a laugh of willingness a little too free, a gaiety a little too genial, I cannot accurately determine.** The question is one I ask nobody except myself and now, you. However, it may be there is much kindness and friendliness and a subtle and substantial interest and enthusiasm too of a kind I happily share and too often, feel alone. It will therefore be with real regret that I shall leave tomorrow for Boston whereto a telegram of Dokko's summons me....

In early 1906, from 1925 F. Street, Bay wrote Langdon that he foresaw "with sorrow" a chaotic and perturbing couple of months ahead,

---

[239] Saint Anne is Nannie.

and he puts into words the artist's universe:

> I become increasingly convinced that precisely as perfection of being consists in a perfectly triumphant reality, so artistic perfection depends upon the degree to which the artist speaks his own verses in his own voice and is unhampered by the vocabulary of convention and the influence of oratory—which exists and would exist only on the theory of an omni-present multitude. The core of the struggle for ourselves and for art is to enlarge from the envelopes of thoughts and deeds which are not our own but the laws and conventions and tradition found of a kind of composite of other men's ideas and emotions and prejudices.

In the fall of 1907 the Bay Lodges moved to their new house at 2346 Massachusetts Avenue near Sheridan Circle, generously bought and paid for by the Senator. "It was a house a Vanderbilt would be proud of," my Uncle Harry commented, "a double house with a huge staircase in the middle and two wings on either side. From there, he wrote Nannie how much it annoyed Bessy that Mrs. Davis would remarry (General MacCauley), confiding to his mother that Bessy didn't look well and that it was "no doubt partly due to her mother":

> Bessie says she will keep up appearances but her personal and intimate relations with her mother will come to an end. She will be civil to Mr. MacCauley but nothing more. Not a real grief but an outrage to her feeling for her father, a humiliation to her pride and an extraordinary inconvenience and she is taking it extremely well. The whole situation will adjust itself in the course of time without any great difficulty. It has been and is now a sickening sort of experience and what with it and one or two other minor worries my poor Pussy is not looking as well as I could wish. She is thin and pale.[240]

In this complex November 6 letter from her new house, Bessy sympathized with Nannie's suffering:

> *Dearest Oops,*
> Aunt Lucy agrees with me that you have everything—as she puts it—beauty, heart, mind and wit—but unlike me, she does not know how dearly you have to pay for it. The capacity for seeing without the power

---

[240] Judge John Davis had died.

Bay, Bessy and Teddy Wharton at the Mount.

The Mount in winter.

of remedying and the gift of loving and suffering which you possess to such an unusual extent though they add pain to your life, help to make the remarkable personality which so many people love—this counts after the worst pain subsides as you must have found out before. I know how paltry and second-rate they often seem at the time. I am sure you must know how keenly alive I am to all your thoughtfulness and it is useless for me to repress what you must know that I feel about your willingness to work and delve for our comfort. The Boos are well though rather queer in this funny new place. Helena was good last night and did not cry but murmured firmly, "I want to go home to Gamuzzy."[241] My aunts were both much amused at your anecdote about the lawyers and the pen when you signed away your dower and said how killing your pose of being old was. Please thank Dokko for his lovely flowers when you see him.

Much Love from Bessy

The same month Bay wrote to Langdon about his "second-rate heart" weakened by malaria:

I've been knocked out by malaria of which my rather second-rate heart went singularly queer, a fact which I've told no one but you. I don't want my mother and Bessy to be worried more than is necessary. So don't mention it. I've been a little fussed about my heart—taken in connection with the fact that my "Herakles"—which signifies such endless things to me—is only just three-quarters done. For the first time in my life I think and on account of my **passionate anxiety to finish the poem for all I was worth, I have been a little nervous and anxious**.... There are few things in my life which mean so much to me as your friendship and companionship. I believe I shall be in first-rate shape again and after that if you say New York, I'm with enthusiasm your man. Forgive me this dreadful, dull, all about myself letter. I hate to have bothered you with the dreary details of ill-health and I beg you to forget them.

Thomas Riggs, Jr. wrote that Bay's need to identify himself publicly as a poet was greater than his patience with the development of an idiom. He concluded that men who destroy what they love was a theme in both of Lodge's plays, *Cain* and *Herakles*, approaching "forms of

[241] Grandchildren's name for Nannie.

> psychomachia." He suggested that Bay had a wicked side, a theory that has resonance for some members of the family. "The heroes are indeed damned. All they touch in human love, they must in time wither and destroy; they are trapped in the cold loneliness of an ego which knows nothing outside of its own remorseless needs."[242]

In the summers of 1906 and 1907, it seems that the tradition of Bessy visiting her relatives in Northeast while Bay visited Mrs. Wharton was kept up—and neither author with their spouse, though Bay gave a passing reference to his family.

> Tuckanuck
> July 1907
> *Darling Oops,*
> Thank you for your sweet letter. I saw much, much more of Mrs. Wharton and in a more satisfactory way than I should have if he [Teddy Wharton] had been there. I had some very interesting times with her. The days and country were beautiful. Pussy and the babes are well.

Edith Wharton struck a refined critical pose when she carefully ana-

[242] "Like Prometheus' vultures they return over and over again to the theme for rebirth: the great need for it, the overpowering sense of guilt which accompanies the assassination of the shapes that tie the poet to his paternity. The heroes are indeed damned. All they touch in human love, they must in time wither and destroy; they are trapped in the cold loneliness of an ego which knows nothing outside of its own remorseless needs. Like Ethan Brand or Ahab, they have committed the Unpardonable Sin. But unlike Ethan Brand or Ahab, they do not possess the full consciousness of their acts. Cain and Herakles are like infants in the cradle, who reach out to possess some glittering object at the limit of their reach and who, in touching it, shatter it into a thousand pieces: they are left crying helplessly in the darkness of their guilt, their loneliness, their frustration and their fear.... It is at the points at which the poems present a consciousness of the ferocity of the inner war that they are most powerful—as in Herakles' images of the soul struggling to find itself among bestial shapes. At the points at which the heroes are depicted as having achieved their release, their perfect self-discoveries and self-knowledge, the poems are empty. The moment of apotheosis which Cain and Herakles approach through disciplines of destruction turns out to be little after all: their souls are infinite and God is dead. In the slaughter of the deity, they are left alone and bleak against a stark Promethean scenery, for there is no dramatic equivalent for a goal which eludes Lodge's language and swims off into the vagueness of "the light," "the life," "the secret," "the soul's inheritance," the Great Idea.... Despite the symbolic rituals of rebirth the moment is exhausted in the attempt to compel it, the bush burns but no voice comes from it, and the secret remains a secret still. One begins to be a little abashed in the face of these compulsive images, these Titanic aspirations, these Senecan slaughters, their rejected fathers, broken mothers and heroes who are the Resurrection and the Life and to shift a little uneasily, as if the characters had left the world of citations and had come to lean over your shoulder and whisper too many confidences.... In Lodge's tortured heroes we have perhaps the most direct perception or projection of the agonies of change in space and time: the old identities are destroyed by murder and the new ones are assumed in renunciation and guilt." Riggs, 200-202.

lyzed the slight improvement in Bay's work. "Intellectually and imaginatively," Wharton wrote, Bay had traversed a great distance in the year interval between *Cain* and *The Great Adventure*. Three years after the latter book, he brought out another dramatic poem, *Herakles*.

> [...] It is well that a young poet should measure himself with a long task. Cabot Lodge, in *Herakles*, certainly proved the value of the effort. It freed him from the tendency to draw all his effects from his inner experience, and roused him to a perception of dramatic values.
>
> As regards the growth of Cabot Lodge's art, perhaps the most interesting thing in the volume—aside from the more complex harmony of the verse—is the drawing of Creon's character. Hitherto, the poet's personages had been mouth-pieces, but in the Theban King, he created a man, and the ease with which he "exteriorized" Creon's good-humored disenchantment and tolerant worldly wisdom gave promise of a growing power to deal with his themes objectively. This promise is reaffirmed in "The Noctambulist"....

In *Herakles*, which some consider his finest work, Lodge wrote:

> So I am dead—
> I, who was once the man you loved and knew!
> It is not I—it is the Soul, the Truth—
> It is the God who dwells and reigns within me—
> for man shall lose his life to gain his life—and more than all was found?
> Found was the sense and source and strength of life;
> Found was the way, the light, the truth—the soul!

Bessy, abandoned by her mother, her education neglected, was also neglected by Bay as years passed. But in marriage, she became wise through experience. Strict and traditional in her severe reaction to her flamboyant mother, Bessy seems to have been on a different wavelength from her artist husband and mother-in-law. She had the temperament of a reformer and humanitarian and some stubbornness or authority in her nature failed to satisfy his imagination, leaving a vacuum between.

Although Bessy was (also) intensely spiritual, she was more of a realist than the dreamy romantic Bay. As his work was met with rejection slips, she wanted him to have some active pursuit in the real world that would complement his literary and philosophical work. She thought that he might thus be happier and his work richer. Bessy's views about her husband were probably closer to those of Senator Lodge and of Theodore Roosevelt. But Bay was willful and self-absorbed—too given to loving that part of others which reflected himself. He was Narcissus eternally in search of Eros.

Henry Adams feigned not to know what change, physical and moral, explained the darkness of *Herakles* but he was well aware of Lodge's deteriorating health and morale after 1907. In the year before he died Bay did not live with his wife and children. He also went abroad with his parents, according to the family; he stayed with friends, seeking seclusion and quiet. He may have sensed he was dying. In the beginning of the marriage, Bay was loyal to Bessy but he had a lover in the year before he died.[243] Bessy discovered the letters after his death and burned them, never revealing the woman's identity to anyone. In this love letter to Bessy at his departure for Europe, Bay appears to be expressing guilt (if you love someone you don't have to say it over and again) at leaving her at the Mount to go abroad with his mother. Perhaps Bessy had refused to come with him.

> June 30, 1908
> From The Waldorf-Astoria
> *To Bessy, The Mount:*
> In the haste of tomorrow's departure I may not find time to write you, my darling Beloved, so I seize the moments now to send you a word to tell you with what an anxious and absorbing love I have thought of you & longed for you ever since I left Lenox. You have been, my darling, so beautifully good & dear to me for so many days, so flawlessly gentle and loving that I am very near to tears when I think that tomorrow I shall be going away so far from you. My love, I am pretty homesick for you and my dear young lambs this day! I got an Indian wigwam which I guess Duncan can set up on the lawn for Cabot & also a rubber duck for his bath. For Helena, I got a big Dollie & a little rubber one—for the bath. And I got for poor fat pumpkin a rubber duck like Cabot's as a consolation prize. If for any reason you go to Boston, telegraph to Kenny and Clark's, Charles St. Boston for a cab to meet you at the station. Dokko's house is 56 Beacon St. The [Somerset] club is 45 Beacon. Mumford's, Haddon Hall, 29 Commonwealth Ave.
>
> Goodbye, goodbye, my dear beautiful darling. I love you, love you with all my strength. Take care of your sweet self.
>
> *G.C.L.*

---

[243] According to family sources. See appendix for one of his love letters.

Bay's childhood friend Marjorie Nott responded in this 1910 letter to Henry Adams, who, while researching for Bay's biography, was seeking to determine who Bay's lover had been. He had asked her if her relationship with Bay had been intimate. I place this correspondence with Uncle Henry out of the chronology because it sheds light on Bay's life, not after his death where they would normally belong.

Dear Uncle Henry,
I once read that the more polished, finished and recherché manner of acknowledging a letter was to gracefully quote from it instead of crudely announcing "it has come." This I did in a more artful manner showing you how your sentences had sunk into my thought. But this flattery you brush aside and say "did you get my letter?" To which I reply, "I did." I shall be more anxious to know how you are.... Yes, as my intimacy with Bay began when I was 12, I think that "a friend from childhood" combines vagueness and accuracy in desirable proportions. But "a confidant" *never*. Call me grandchild or grandaunt rather. A confidant as I understand it, knows concrete facts and personal problems and predicaments and, while leading themselves well-reputated lives, bestows admonition. But I never knew one such about him nor, I rejoice to remember, gave advice ever. Imagine that only unselfish and unegotistical beings can fit into the role of confidante. At any rate it never has been mine. I will show you all the letters generated to convince in a minute and a half. Indeed all these assorted letters you have from everyone are calculated to give quite generally smooth and false impressions.

Marjorie Nott

Pavillon des Bains
Dear Uncle Henry,
One of the last times we were together, **Bay said the church was devised as a protection against the direct rays of Christ's spirit** which undimmed would compel to action and transmutation of character. Like black goggles. I liked the idea immensely. "Little plentiful mannequins skipping about in collars and tailcoats" was a favorite description of the world by Whitman!

When we meet here as you suggest one thousand years from today and compile a real life of Bay with nothing left out "for respect of fools, I think I shall suggest citations and appreciations. I am just very glad that you have to find them and I don't. Bay once told me his favorite line in poetry was Swinburne, "Far in the garden remote mild muse where the sea millions share is..."[244] And I thought the Anis of Coleridge that some one sent Mrs. Lodge as suggestion of him very beautiful:

"He stood beside me like my youth / Transformed for me the real to a dream / Clothing the palpable and familiar / With golden exhalations of the dawn."

Marjorie Nott
Grand Hotel Astoria
De L'Arc Romain
Aix-Les-Bains

P.S. This place is so beautiful that you must see it some time in May before the 33,000 Americans (literally) arrive.

In contrast to the letters of Edith and Marjorie, full of references to people and events, Bay, in his vivid poetry and his life and daily correspondence, dwells entirely on himself and on his decreasing energies.

Winter 1908
From Washington
To Langdon Mitchell
Your letter, what it means to me, the encouragement, the life, the hope... I am now amazingly well and my heart functioning as decently as can be. Good Heavens, I know what it is to wait, how intolerable it may become sometimes, just holding on. But the muscles of patience and that daily courage which patience implies are fine muscles to have developed even at some loss—isn't that so, my dear man? The key of the gate of paradise is not purchased in any single payment; the travail of God's nativity within us, gradual and slow and laborious. It is the sustained courage, the long patience, the incessant daily labor, the dear perpetual vigilance of thought, the great order, tranquil and pitiless in its strength—It is these things, it is the work, the wonderful slow work of man about the soul's business which accomplishes constantly some real thing; which reaches us however gradually, nobler and greater we are because it makes us more than we are. For the temptation to think that the reward, the advance is tomorrow and that paradise is in the

[244] From "Atlanta and Calidan." She misquotes it; the correct verse is: "Out of the golden remote wild west where the sea without shore is / Full of the sunset, and sad, if at all, with the fullness of joy."

next country and that it can be got by some adventurous extravagance, some single deed of excellence is very great to us all. We realize that only patience can see us thro'....

Bay wrote to Langdon a joking but nevertheless contemptuous apology for his wife who had mixed up the dates of his visit with another visitor and asks about another time. "Beautiful," Bay said, "but in some respects deficient in mind." Contempt seems to have been part of his nature. He certainly wouldn't have said this about his mother. Bay wrote to Langdon of his admiration for Nietzsche's *Thus Spoke Zarathustra*: "important and profound, prose spontaneous. First-rate." Meanwhile, in summer 1908, Bay wrote, "Oops, My heart is growing with anxiety when I see you looking tired and feel you are taxing yourself beyond your strength. I would like to go abroad or to Lenox with Bessy. Without your endless love and sympathy, I could not get along in life...."

The following letters about Bay's poem, *Herakles*, published by Houghton Mifflin on June 21, 1908, show it received mixed reviews—puzzlement and flattery. This unpublished December 12, 1908, letter from Henry James to Bay about *Herakles* was full of love but was essentially an elegantly crafted put-down, saying he preferred "the real dramatic form"—a play written with stage directions.

Lamb House
Rye
Sussex
Letter from Henry James to Bay
My Dear Bay Lodge,
...I have deciphered more or less the one & very gratefully, and have had the second at my elbow only a couple of days, & had only time, amid many complications, to dip into it. It looks very distinguished ___ [underlined], which is the right way for a work of art to look & I shall attack it absorbently as soon as I shall have been able to make my peace with **two little lions that sit growling in my path**—my general path of approach, always, to Dramatic Poems. One of these is **my chronic constitutional jealousy of all verse** (except the quite irrepressible lyric cry). The jealousy of our trying to write pretty prose that shall usurp the prize for form too—which the successful swagger of such effectually presents, making my dear purpose recoil upon myself & to my confusion. The other is a great love of the real Dra-

matic Form & economy, the (ideally) representable thing which the "mere" dialogued Poem passes to one side of. But why do I dip into such depths? —saying not what I mean & only betraying my vain wish that you weren't so far away & my desolate sense that we might, under better stars,—as for instance just here, tonight, in this little ancient oak parlour where I sit alone,—delightfully converse—I quite always sit alone—& Mrs. Wharton has lately sat with me, most benevolently,—so that in default of talking with you I've talked—as more particularly asked—"considerable" about you. That lady is still in England—in London—everywhere going out & about immensely & everywhere welcomed and admired. I think **she really likes it** and so should I if I had **a frame of steel, a chariot of fire, the curiosity of youth**. Come and see me my dear, Bay Lodge while these helpful attributes are still yours. I take great pleasure in the gentillesse of your letter. I wrote your mother the other day & I renew my earnest assurances—both to her & to your Father. I commend myself to your wife's kind remembrance & am all faithfully Yours,

Henry James

This letter from Henry Adams' brother, Brooks, expressed the sum total of disapproval of the older generation—they didn't understand the language of the young:

25 Dec 1908

My dear Bay,

I have not written before because I have been reading your poem slowly.... To us of the older generation, the form in which young men express their thought is a new language. It is a great attempt you have made and time alone can test your success. Your idea is fine. I have very little doubt that you are making articulate an instinct of the age. For good or for bad it is our modern civilization. You must like others stand or fall by that. It is the future you must look to not the past. Frankly I must admit I have doubts as to your philosophy but the literary excellence of a book has nothing to do with philosophy. There can be no doubt of the power of your conception and some of the songs have very great tenderness and charm. Give my love to your wife.

Affectionately Yours,
Brooks Adams

By contrast, Bay was pathetically proud of Alfred Brown's intoxicated enthusiasm for his work.

> 687 Boyston St.
> Jan 4, 1909
> I find you have therein expressed in most exalted verse, the deepest truths of life and have striven to express them both in speech and in life...your majestic diction, your exquisite lyrics and your perfectly fitting verse; and let me speak of your thought for which your literary powers have provided a worthy vehicle. Your soul lives and has stood like Herakles upon the crag of the Caucasus above the human Prometheus, bound in the chains of convention, ignorance and fear. You have sounded the new (old) gospel of redemption, the one great truth, I am, willing to bear the burden of the world; living now and forever for self and for humanity, for the world and for the cosmos. *Herakles* is the greatest spiritual poem I have read in American literature. It is tremendously true.

In this unpublished letter, Edith Wharton, who clearly went over the poetry carefully, wrote to say she liked the first few verses:

> Hyeres
> On March 2 1909:
> *Dear Bay,*
> I have waited a long time to write you about *Herakles*, for the best yet most improbable of reasons—that I've only just read it! [...] There is some splendid poetry in it. You know what great things I think of your rhythms—they are all here and abundantly confirmed. My pencil has been busy too, with a few single lines such as "the harsh dominion of the inconstant gods" which seems to me one of your best; "sepulchred living under dreams and dust" and lots in the poet's talk with Creon (p. 110), "the huge and haunted night" (p. 162) But I wish you were here and I could cite de vive voix!—I love Creon all through; I think the frightfully difficult scene of the killing of the children remarkably swift and dramatic; and I exult in the scene in the temple of Delphi where Herakles finds that he and the gods are one. My chief criticism, on a first reading, is that *Herakles* perhaps repeats himself, not in words, of course, but in thought; and that this gives, here and there, a static quality to the poem. But I may be wrong—All my congratulations on the strength and perseverance with which you have carried through

so large and serious a work and one last word of admiration for "the huge and haunted night" and its context, p.162...Dearest Bay, this is a very unsatisfactory word, but I am tired and harassed and almost inarticulate; though nonetheless tenderly attached to you and Bessy, whom I embrace.

Ever Yr Affte
Edith W.

Write to 58 rue de Varenne till May—Excuse this untidy letter. I've had a lot of writing to do.

In this long last letter to his mother, Bay described a harrowing trip from Washington to Nahant in which he lost his manuscripts on arrival in the station, had to send his family—his wife, the children, the maids and governesses—on to Nahant by boat while he returned to the station to recuperate the verse. Henry Adams also used the vivid description in his biography, *The Life of George Cabot Lodge.*

Nahant
June 13, 1909
Our train was seven hours late to Boston.... I had retired to rest reconciled, or at least steeled to the thought of a two hours' delay in our journey; when, on waking (abysmal moment!) in the squalor of my berth I found that the fog had changed the two hours delay to seven, [...] entitled, a "fifteen minutes for refreshments" at New Haven; and there, dingy dreadfulness of the waiting room, we—that is the passengers of that luckless train—thronged four deep round a vastly rectangular barrier like a shop-counter, girdled, for the public, by high, greasy, "fixed" stools, covered with inedible, pseudo-foods [...] at last our interminable journey did end at Boston, we found, of course, no porters! And with a heavy microscope, book, coat and cane, my three poor unceasingly good, weary and toy-laden children, and my two weary and child-laden nurses, were, perforce, obliged to leave our four bags on the platform, in charge of the well-fed train porter, to be immediately "called for" by Moore's man. Which man, young Moore himself, I duly found and straitly charged about the four bags, as well as about my seven pieces in the "van".... I drove off to the North Station, stopping en route merely to rewards my lambs for their exemplary conduct by a rubber toy apiece... in the North Station waiting room, our bedraggled, dirty, worn-out company waited a full hour for

Moore and the trunks, …And then Moore arrived—arrived, having just merely forgotten the four bags—having in short left them—one of them containing Uncle Henry's manuscript and all of mine, both irreplaceable—just there on the platform where I couldn't have not left them. Well! For a moment I didn't "keep up" a bit and addressed to Moore a few—how inadequate!—"feeling words." I then dispatched him back to recover the bags, packed my poor babes into the 3:20 for Lynn,—trusting, as I had to, to Fraülein's ability to get them out at Lynn,—and remained myself at the North Station, where I waited for Moore for exactly one hour and fifteen minutes. My state of mind I won't describe. At the end of that vigil, however, I mounted—always with microscope, book, coat and cane—in a taxicab, went to the South Station, found Moore, and after an interval of almost panic, when I thought all the manuscripts were lost for good, did, by dint of energy at last—find the bags… and got, at last, to Nahant at about seven o'clock…. The children are none the worse for the journey and are already benefited by the good air. The house is incredibly clean and charming and we are delighted with it.

Bay wrote from the Billiard Room at the tip of East Point:

Nahant
June 15, 1909.
Oops,
Thankful for your letter today. I am having the most beautiful days, darling Oops, endless air, and sea and sky and beauty and best of all, with Langdon's splendid companionship. I've shown Langdon my latest work, "The Noctambulist." He is most splendidly encouraging…. **I have a note from Pa who, dear man, in Dokko's absence apparently relies on me for his visit in Aug.**[245] I don't want to spend my whole summer away from Bessie, and you and my lamb-children. However that is a bridge obviously to cross when we come to it…. I feel so anxious that you should improve the shining hours of solitude by getting into really good condition.

Adams wrote in an excised part of *George Cabot Lodge*, that to his confidante, Marjorie Nott, "He [Bay] could say what he was too proud to say even in his own family, that his endurance and courage were beginning to yield." In truth, he probably knew, or suspected, that it was his physical

[245] The Senator's planned visit with Bay to Tuckanuck.

strength that had yielded, thus affecting his powers of endurance. But he would not submit to invalidism, and rebelled against facts. This late letter suggests that he had a consciousness of having come to the end of the first phase of his poetry, and of standing on the threshold of some other. He seems to have reached the pinnacle of vanity and egotism; but he is right that facts are not necessarily the truest reality for an artist. It is unusual that he invited Marjorie to go to Tuckanuck as the only other woman who had been invited were his wife and mother.

> Nahant
> July 8
> *From Bay to Marjorie Nott*
> I hate facts—they are always so damnably and needlessly interfering with the truth, and with everything else worth having and doing. Facts are the disabling and senseless things,—like poverty, conventions, illness, etc. Facts are what's the matter with the world. People believe in facts and that's what prevents them from doing or being or believing anything worthwhile. It's the last lowest and worst superstition, the faith in facts. In proportion as we yield to that arrant credulity we are weak and helpless. You would go with me to Tuckanuck at once except that the fact is you won't.
>
> Meanwhile I write—not much, but well. It seems to me that, for the first time I really long for some encouragement. It would save me so much, so much! I get tired with having to whistle constantly to keep up my courage, when as never before, I need all my voice to sing with. I sometimes feel as though the isolation and the effort were secretly **"taking it out of me"** more than I know. I discover at last what an immense reservoir of strength is any aggregation, so to speak, of human consciousness. Only I discover it by having so completely to do without it. But how long do you suppose would most people keep going at all, if they were not fostered and fed, supported and sustained by the ambient human atmosphere? It's that indefinite general consciousness,—that aggregate consciousness—which does all their work for them; not well, of course, for it can't do anything well, or even decently, but still, for the general gross purposes, sufficiently. And, of course, a collective consciousness, small in numbers, is quite imaginable, which would do the best things in the best way, which would be just the human reservoir of strength on which I would draw. But as it is, there is just nothing done for me, and I've no strength but my own, which will doubt-

less suffice, as it always has sufficed, to pull me through somehow. Only I know that I could certainly do more and better if I didn't constantly have to spend such vast sums on maintenance, so to speak. I complain, as you notice,—perhaps you'll think childishly, and certainly selfishly and self-indulgently, because I suppose I know you'll stand it, my dear. However, you mustn't think of me, of course, as being really or specially, as things go, badly off. I complain merely of the usual, and, I suppose, for a man like me, inevitable situation for which I glory to acknowledge my entire and sole responsibility. And of course I wouldn't change anything essential if I could. Persons living on the frontier have always, I imagine, been obliged to do all their own work. But they may be excused, I think, for longing for their friends—as I long often for you—to be with them.

Do write to me again! It really means so much to me to hear from you. And forgive this long and perhaps not very lovely essay on egotism.

In *George Cabot Lodge*, Adams implied that the new poem written just before he died, "The Noctambulist," one of the long poems of *The Soul's Inheritance*, Bay's last book and considered by Wharton to be his best work, was entirely out of key with the earlier poems. On June 13, 1909, regarding a poem from the volume which Bay delivered at Harvard's Phi Beta Kappa ceremony, Edith wrote her friend Sara Norton that Bay's problem was his failure to use imagery: "I agree with all you say about Bay's poem. Alas but it is not Europe or opportunity of any kind he lacks; it is the real intrinsic higher sense of beauty—visible beauty especially. He doesn't see things in images. Still, it was well done."

On July 11, Edith Wharton wrote Bay from Swinford Old Manor, Kent at Tuckanuck, a month before his death.

Dearest Bay,

I wish for you often these days, but I never wished harder than when, the other evening at Howard Sturgis's, the only Henry (James) gueulé-d [mouthed] "Cor Cordium" to us, & after rolling it meditatively under his tongue, said with emphasis: "That's a fine sonnet—yes, that's a fine sonnet."[246]

I was so sure it was that I had made him read it—a risk to which

[246] From "Cor Cordium": "Then, as it were against the inward ear, / We held, in silence, like a chambered shell, / The dazed one human heart—and seem to hear / Forever and forever rise and swell / And fail and fall on Death's eventual shore, / Tragic and vast, Life's inarticulate roar."

> I seldom expose my friends' works! *Tous mes compliments* on the admirable new turn—the last turn of the spiral—that you've given to the shell metaphor!—It's a real thing.
>
> I have been meaning this long time to thank you for your good letter & to assure you that the missing isn't all on your side—*loin de là!*—but I have had a furious attack of hay fever, that has raged ever since I came to England over a month ago. You know, alas, the lourdeur of the head that accompanies this damnable disease, & the difficulty of making any mental movement. I am still groaning with it, but it's on the wane, & I have got as far as pushing my pen over the paper, though not to much purpose.
>
> But for this curse, I should have had a good month here chiefly with __ and Henry. I tried London for a few days, but found it abhorrent & fled to the country. It's so much nicer in winter! Now I am on my way back to Paris, & there in the neighborhood—I shall "wait round" till Teddy turns up next month.
>
> All England... I saw a good deal of Uncle Henry in Paris, & we talked of you by the yard. I am so impatient to know where you and Bessy are to be this summer. Do throw light on your plans.... Give my best love to Bessy, & tell her I wish we could repeat some of our good hours of last summer. Even the rivalry for Richard's favor had its charm, apre as the contest was!
>
> Yr Affte Friends,
> *E.W.*
>
> Henry James is more beautiful & complete & beyond everyone else than ever—but not very well, alas![247]

Bertie Otis, a Nahant resident, gave an interesting description of Bay and Nahant a few months before Bay's thirty-sixth birthday. Otis' delight in coming out to East Point to explore for fossils clearly amused Bay. It is another vivid description of his charm and astonishing that this encounter took place only a month before his death.

> I drove up to the Senator's inwardly trembling lest the Lodge-keeper should order out such a plebian outfit in a shabby old trap. We got safely by and breathed a little easier on reaching the mansion-house. The maid said, "Mr. Bay was at the billiard hall" and to wait at the gate and as I feared for the success of a second

[247] Henry James had a slight stroke that summer.

intrusion, I grabbed my little leather bag (full of geological tools) giving the impression of a doctor's kit and started up that delightful "Cambrian floor." The grass was slippery and I was weary with toil since sunrise and proceeded after once getting my bearings, with bowed head. A **cheerful greeting call and whistle** caused me to look up and there came old Bay. The sky, blue with the East Wind, made a glorious setting for the two classic figures, Bay and the old Doric Hall (the Billiard Room)—so full of memories to me! ...Bay's boyish face and welcoming smile forbade all but happiness and pleasurable anticipation. **His old panama was jauntily locked on the back of his leonine head, his tie streamed out in the wind like a homeward bound pennant, his left hand was thrust into his belt, like a middy conscious of his exquisite waist. He seemed not to walk nor run, so lightly he balanced. He merely got nearer, like a sunlit cloud drifting over a green sea.** His lips were parted with a chuckle, his eyes, half closed, twinkled with good humor and amusement at my comical appearance, purpose and enthusiasm. And I could see him saying to himself, "well, well, look at fat old Bertie Otis coming to hunt for fossils."

Chapter 6

Tuckanuck

And out of the bronze of the image of
'the Sorrow that endureth for Ever,'
he fashioned an image of "the Pleasure
that abideth for a moment.

—Oscar Wilde

"And they shall say to thee: 'He died distraught,
His mind was crazed by dreaming on things past…'"

— George Cabot Lodge

Tuckanuck, an almost deserted island in the Elizabeth chain in Buzzards Bay off Nantucket, was a place of unimaginable beauty—sparkling sea, summer air, swallows winging over ocean grasses and sand dunes in apricot sunsets. There were so many fish—bluefish, striped bass, scup and quahogs—that gulls followed boats, and fishermen bringing up lobster pots caused feeding frenzies. Bay's Tuckanuck was a replenishing well and at Dokko's island sanctuary for men, Bay recovered his strength. It was an intellectual retreat, not a social center; outside of Bessy on her honeymoon, Nannie was the only woman invited there (she never went).

Bay wrote:

Dear Langdon,
It isn't nice and it isn't natural to be here without you. The sun and sea and sand, the sky and stars, the everlasting air and warm fields are all the same, but your absence rob them of half their delight. It would be easy to tell you how variously and deeply both Bessie and I enjoyed (your) brief visit at Nahant. Could you afford to write your plays and publish them without production; if we enjoy them, they would not only be an

> enduring contribution to dramatic literature but they would also be and probably very shortly produced everywhere.... I know that its life-offering strength to a giant to offer encouragement to you. Yet I cannot refrain from saying to you what is often in my mind and what you yourself well know, namely that for you the real victory is handsomely won already.
>
> *George Cabot Lodge*

The aforementioned difficulty of reaching Dokko's island made it a somewhat tricky venture for anyone in bad health. His house, a lonely perch among the low-lying deep green bushes, was a refuge of natural and spiritual loveliness, the air startlingly fresh from the salt of the sea. We learn from a September 1909 letter from Wharton to Bessy that Langdon spent ten days at Tuckanuck with Bay in early August, when the Senator, happy to have a break from the madness of Washington politics, returned there with Bay, after a "long tariff siege." He longed for quiet and isolation. Bay had had a little cold and Dr. Winslow had come up to Nahant, looked him over and said that it was all right for him to go to Tuckanuck, and that it would probably do him good, so off they went. He got rid of his cold, slept well, ate well, went to bed early, worked in his evenings, was never more delightful, nor, as it seemed to him, happier, or more cheerful, although he was always happy at Tuckanuck.

The Senator noticed, however, with anxiety and with pain, that Bay was more careful of himself, limited himself in exertion much more than the year before; and that worried him because he thought it meant that Bay felt his heart more, and in this the Senator was right. But his anxiety was general, in no sense immediate, and Bay otherwise seemed extraordinarily well. In the same week, Mr. Brown who had lectured on Bay's *Herakles* to his classes that winter, came down from Nantucket to lunch. They had a delightful day. "Brown is a very intelligent and interesting man," the Senator wrote Dokko later, "full of affection for Bay." But the isolation of the island, it turned out, did not render the expected solace. Indeed, the heaven became a kind of hell.

On August 18, both Bay at Tuckanuck and Bessy at Nahant wrote the other a love letter to honor what was their ninth wedding anniversary. Bay's loving doggerel/baby-talk (a family tradition) and Bessy's ("Puzzy's") wishes crossed paths. "Shag" wrote what amounted to an apology, even though self-serving, as if he took pleasure in the guilt he attempted to induce in others. When he referred to Puzzy hating her Shag, of being cold, lofty, and scornful, one can hypothesize that the reason rested squarely on Bay's unfaithful shoulders—on the time spent away from his young family:

O Puzzy hates her Shag so foul
No word to him writes she;
But Shag he loves his Puzzy-Moal,
So good and pure is he!

Poor Shag! Poor lonely Shag! He Writes
And weeps sad tears the while;
But Fur with cold and lofty mien,
She smiles a scornful smile!

Poor Shag! He hopes at least his Boos[248]
Still love him fond & true;
For if their gents are foul like Moal's[249]
He knows not what to do.

Shag

But Bessy didn't hate Bay. Neither would she appease his guilt. This is clear from her note full of dignity and love, that his health cure at Tuckanuck meant more to her than being together on their wedding anniversary.

Here's my love to you,
Shaggy Darling on this day & so many thanks to you for being well & happy in your work—The Boos are very plump & prosperous & your room all ready & anxious for you, only I advise you not to come back yet as you are always better at T. than anywhere & seem to store up more health.

Your loving,
Puzzy

The letter signals a kind of death knell. Father and son were enjoying a delightful supper of local steamer clams with Mr. Brown. Bay was in high spirits, and seemed to enjoy himself greatly. He ate an excellent dinner and went to bed as usual. But he could not sleep, due to stomach poisoning perhaps from a bad clam, which brought on fever. The Senator searched frantically for a doctor on the almost deserted island in the middle of the night, aware that his son was fading fast. His heart

[248] His children.
[249] Bessy's.

had apparently been weakened by a childhood bout of rheumatic fever or by malaria in the Navy. In any case, the illness did not leave him; the doctor confided that Bay hadn't long to live. The Senator helplessly held his handsome thirty-five-year-old son in his arms and said goodbye to him forever. When the telegram arrived in Nahant that they (the two Mrs. Lodges) should come to the island, "they knew right away," according to Helena. The horror of having to resort to telegrams in such a crisis heightens the drama of the Senator's lonely feverish nightmare.

The Senator alerted Nannie to the danger:

August 21
Tuckanuck,
My Dearest,
Your good letter of the 19th has just come and the news of home was welcome. I am sorry that you missed seeing the President. It was friendly of him to come and we must ask him over to lunch en famille when I return. I am much obliged to you for so thoughtfully sending a telegram. The bombardment must be a nuisance. I have gained 1 and a half lbs. But poor Bay has had an upset—He was particularly well and cheerful the day Brown was here when I wrote and ate a very good dinner. But something—it must have been a bad clam—poisoned him and he had a bad night—nausea—bowels—very acute. He seemed to get better through the day and would not let me send to Nantucket for a doctor. He ate eggs and milk and took eggnogs. But it was premature. He had a relapse in the evening—sharp nausea and did not get to sleep until after two. I went across the island at 10 o'clock and telephoned to the doctor for with his heart I felt helpless and alarmed. Dr. Grouard, an excellent man, whom Dokko has told me about, promised to come first thing this morning. He has been here and made Bay much more comfortable. He is going to send his assistant over to pass the night but that is really for my comfort chiefly. He says that he might be all right in a day or two so we can come to town. When I telegraph coming, have McDermott [the Lodges' chauffeur] at South Station. The train is due at 6:55 pm. I'll write you tomorrow how he is.

Best Love,
Ever yrs,
HCL

Later that day, the Senator telegrammed for Nannie and Bessy to come:

August 21
Time received 7:55pm Bay had an acute indigestion beginning night before last. The doctor said this morning that he was rallying and ought to be able to go to town in two or three days. Improvement he has not had through the day and I do not know whether he is in danger but I am very anxious and thought that I ought to let you know. The seven twenty:five train is the only train on Sunday and the best train every day if you and Bessie decide to come. Wire me; if you come Bessie must come too. I wrote this morning but thought it better to telegraph and not wait until tomorrow.

From Tuckanuck, early the next morning, the Senator attempted to stop the two Mrs. Lodges at the South Station, sending word of the death of Bay and the uselessness of their journey.

August 22
To Mrs HC Lodge passenger 7:25 am train
Boston to Woods Hole, South Station,
Boston, MA
In case my dispatch to Nahant misses you this is to say **do not come**. Boy died suddenly 11:30 heart suddenly failed, shall return tomorrow, Sunday.

HC Lodge

And in case that telegram failed to reach Nannie, he wrote a second dispatch to Nahant:

Boy died suddenly 11:30 heart suddenly failed do not come down shall try to get on noon boat tomorrow Sunday due to arrive 655 Boston. Send Hobday [Lodge's butler] by 7:25 train to meet me at Woods Hole and wait there for me HC Lodge 6:40am.

Aug. 22
2:10 pm
Woods Hole
Mrs. HC Lodge
56 Beacon St. Boston
Leaving on special will come straight to 56 Beacon.

HC Lodge

This unpublished letter from the Senator to Dokko recounted the lonely agony of the Senator at his son's death the night of August 20; Bessy not the Senator asked that Adams delete it from his biography of Bay even though Adams had argued, "my judgment is emphatic that the last paragraph of the letter is the best possible conclusion of the book. Not another word can be added without weakening it."

> East Point, Nahant
> September 1, 1909
> *My Dear Old Friend,*
> I have not written before, because I could not summon up courage. I could write to others but not to you. My heart failed. How he loved you, you know. How devoted you have always been to him, and how much you have loved him, we all know. So I could not face writing to you. I was too crushed, too shaken, to write to you who were so near to him, and who felt his loss as I knew you would. Now John has returned safely, and I feel helped and encouraged by his presence and I write. It will be a broken kind of letter, but I want you to know everything, and from me.... Thursday the Mr. Brown of whom you have heard him speak, no doubt, who lectured on Bay's *Herakles* to his classes last winter, came down from Nantucket to lunch. We had a delightful day. Brown is a very intelligent and interesting man, full of affection for Bay. Bay was in high spirits, and seemed to enjoy himself greatly. He ate an excellent dinner and went to bed as usual.
>
> In the night I was aroused by his passing through my room. I asked him if he did not feel well, and he said that he felt restless, and was going down to move about, and get the air. I went off to sleep, and was aroused again by his return. It was then daylight. I asked him how he was, and he said that he had had a horrid night—a violent indigestion, vomiting, diarrhea, etc. He thought he had eaten a bad clam, and the doctor subsequently said that he seemed to have been poisoned acutely enough, he thought, for ptomaine poisoning. He went to bed and slept,—got up, and took his bath, and then began to feel better. He drank a glass of milk. I read to him. Then he took an egg beaten up in milk with a little cream. When I had my lunch, he ate two soft-boiled eggs. In the afternoon, he ordered tea, and had tea and toast. When I dined, he said he felt hungry and would have three soft-boiled eggs, which he ate with toast and milk. In short, he seemed all day to be recovering normally, and quite quickly as one would from a sharp indigestion, and I felt no uneasiness. After dinner, toward nine,

he suddenly began to feel worse. The nausea returned with retching, and accompanied by distress in breathing. I became alarmed and went down and aroused Ed Barrett who drove me across to the telephone. I could not get the doctor over there but Grouard promised to come early in the morning. It was the best I could do. He had an awful night. I tried chloroform,—no effect. I tried a mustard plaster,—it seemed to have no effect but it made him nervous. He would not keep it on. Toward morning he went to his room and got a little sleep. At eight, Grouard appeared. He was with him an hour,—rubbed him,—put on mustard,—gave him some morphine to quiet the stomach,—then nitro-glycerin and digitalis to be taken alternately through the day,—also calomel. He told me that the heart was bad, but that he had responded well to treatment, and he thought that he would be able to go to town in two or three days. Grouard advised me not to telegraph (to Nannie or Bessie,—said it would only alarm them, and would excite Bay,—advised me to write them cheerfully, which I did). He said that he would send his assistant down to pass the night. Bay seemed much better after the doctor's visit,—said he thought he should sleep, and asked me to leave him. In an hour I went back. The improvement was not holding. He grew worse, and when the doctor arrived early in the afternoon, although he had been taking the nitroglycerine and digitalis regularly, his pulse was up to 100. He had come down to the piazza;—more air and the sun seemed to help him. Doctor Bartlett, a physician at a life-saving station, did all that anyone could do. He was devotion itself, and over Bay every minute. He injected morphine,—then nitro-glycerine, then digitalis. I felt I could no longer refrain from telegraphing. Bartlett said, "he is in serious danger, but I think he will rally and pull through, unless there comes some sudden change." I took the boat and went to the telephone to try to talk to Grouard, whom I could not find; and to send my message to his [Bay's] mother. I had death in my heart, but I telegraphed guardedly suggesting that she come. She knew when she saw the message.

When I got back at eight o'clock, the doctor said that he had got the pulse down, that the retching had diminished, and that he was sleeping for a few minutes at a time, and was certainly no worse,—he thought a little better. He was much quieter and dozing and at ten, the doctor told me that I must lie down. I had hardly slept or eaten for 24 hours, and he said that I was looking exhausted. I went upstairs and laid myself on your bed. I did not sleep, and could hear every sound. He was quiet—groaned only a little only once or twice. Suddenly I heard the doctor call. I rushed down, and the doctor said, "There is a sudden failure." I took his head in my arms and held him,—the doctor gave him a powerful injection—felt his pulse, then applied the stethoscope. I said, "Is he going?" He listened,—then in a moment said, "He is gone!" So he died, perfectly quietly without a gasp or a struggle, in my arms, sitting in your big chair, in the parlor, by the dining table. So he died in my arms. You will know the lonely agony of that moment to me, and will pity me. I cannot write of it even without wanting to cry out as I did then. But I knew that I must hold myself together and get him to town at once,—my one thought. I sat down at the table and wrote telegrams,—a series to my wife, to catch her at different points, and prevent her from coming to Nantucket;—one to the Superintendent of the railroad for a special train at Wood's Hole. The Nantucket office was closed and Marcus and Ed Bassett started at one o'clock, and went over to Wood's Hole with the telegrams. I will tell you of the tact and kindness and tenderness of those two men when we meet. I shall never forget it.

Poor Charlie went to pieces, but he went across the island, and telephoned to the undertaker, Stanbery and Mary and Michael were all devoted and kind. I paced the piazza until three, then went to bed and slept uneasily for two hours, and then lay still until the undertaker had come, and the doctor himself had performed all the last offices, and laid him in his coffin. Charlie had done his work well. **He had reserved the biggest and the best powerboat in Nantucket. The coffin, in a box covered with a tarpaulin, was on deck. We left at noon. The doctor went with me. It was a brilliant day, a fresh northerly wind, the sea glittering and dancing, and the spray dashing over the boat and over the coffin. He would have liked that.** In four hours we were at Wood's Hole; a special train was waiting; everybody was so kind; there was no delay, and in an hour and a half, we were in Boston. I took him to your house where they all were. Of that meeting I cannot write. Nannie and Bessie behaved with a heroic courage which is hardly to be believed. He rested in your dining-room for two days. Langdon Mitchell came on Thursday morning; we gathered in the room, we three, Gus, whose utter devotion to Bessy and my wife, I cannot describe; Constance and 'Took' [probably a family nickname for Bay's brother, John]. Mitchell read some verses of Walt Whitman, and two sonnets of Bay's, unpublished; and then we took him to Mt. Auburn, and the body was burned.

There is no more to tell. I cannot express to you our sufferings or our sorrow. It is needless. The newspapers came out with big headlines the next day—columns about him and long extracts from his poems. He dies and they discover that they have lost a poet and a great intellect. Letters have poured in upon us. All have been kept, and everything from the papers for you to see when you return. I sent you the Boston papers of the next day. All my ambition's long since burned out, but now I want to live and keep my health while I can, because I can be of use to his wife and children; and I want all to rear the monument—to bring out his poems, which have crept without notice into the world, in a collected edition—you and I will do it together, for we brought out his books.

On the nightstand in Tuckanuck in one of Bay's bound manuscripts was a tragic poem written on his deathbed, no doubt to his wife, Bessy, or his mother, Nannie.

And they shall say to thee: "He died distraught,
His mind was crazed by dreaming on things past."
And so he grew in madness, till the last
Sheer height of scorn, he tottered from to naught.
His hands were weak and idle and ne'er caught
With strength of purpose at the busy world;
For low and proud he stood—Time onward whirled
And left the ruins of the things he sought.
But thou shalt understand what they despise,
Cherish what they reject; and count the few
Poor virtues dearer than the things they prize;
And weighing all the evil they have said,
Thy heart shall say, "What then? If this be true,
Be silent, for he loved me and is dead!"

My grandfather wrote in his autobiography:

Dr. Bigelow's house at 56 Beacon St., with all its works of art, its high ceilings and polished floors, was our home when we were in Boston. When my father died of a heart attack on Tuckernuck Island (off Nantucket, MA) in 1909, his body was brought there....

Nannie and Bessy arrived wreathed in black tulle so that their faces were not visible. They stood ramrod straight—Nannie stoical and Bessy brokenhearted. Bessy was brave for the children's sake—Cabot, seven, John, five, and Helena, three. A family photograph at Nahant shows Nannie wreathed in black tulle on the upper steps, the Senator perched near her, John in between; below are Helena, and Cabot, my grandfather, looking downcast and Uncle John playing with the dog Veto.

The first sentence of my grandfather's autobiography, *The Storm Has Many Eyes*, begins:

> My father died when I was seven. I remember him as a big handsome man with white teeth, blue eyes, thick light-brown hair, and a deep tan. He would draw me pictures of men on stiff filing cards, making the heads out of red and blue sealing wax. He would take me to Rock Creek Park in Washington and make little sailboats out of scraps of wood, equip them with paper sails, and launch them into the creek. He rowed me around the coves of Nahant, that lean and rocky peninsula which sticks out like a pointing finger toward Europe some ten miles north of Boston. He would row me in the summer in a dory and we climbed on the rocks examining with delight the pools left at low tide.

The Senator immediately assumed his responsibility as head of the family, his own father, John Ellerton Lodge, having died when he was twelve; and he would pass the political torch on to his grandson (Henry Cabot Lodge, Jr.), who bore his name. The face in the photograph is of a boy of seven who deeply felt a loss that appears to have only vaguely concerned his siblings. Henry Cabot Lodge, Jr.'s dignified restraint is striking for someone so young, and who might have known even then what was expected of him. Naturally, Bessy, an almost painfully private

Clockwise: Brother John and the dog, Veto; Nannie; John; the Senator; Helena; Henry Cabot Lodge, Jr. Dokko took the photo.

person, is absent from public view, but her intelligence and strength comes through in this elegant poem, written from East Point, September 3, 1909. It is the kind of poem one might imagine Psyche, the human goddess, writing to her beloved god, Cupid, from the perspective of one whose only failing was to remain rooted in the earth while to her Cupid, though abruptly fallen, could soar to such heights.

I shall grieve down this blow,
  of that I'm conscious;
What does not man grieve down?
  From the highest,
As from the vilest thing of
  every day
He learns to wean himself: for
  the strong hours
Conquer him. Yes, I feel what
  I have lost
In him. The bloom is vanished
  from my life.
For oh! He stood beside me,
  Like my youth,
Transformed, for me the
  Real to a dream,
Clothing the palpable & familiar
  With golden exaltations of the dawn.
Whatever fortunes wait
  My future toils,
The beautiful
  Is vanished & returns not.

Henry Adams wrote his Sister Anne, Nannie, first, saying that Bay was the best product of his time and moreover, was his "last tie to active sympathy with men," meaning, in an extreme sense, one could suppose, that from 1909 until his death Adams would be a shadow of his former self. Since Bay had become a son to him, how very personal a loss it was for Adams.

August 29, 1909
My dear Sister,
I could not telegraph! No words would come. I turned round at once

and came back here to see Sturgis [sic] and Mrs. Roosevelt and Mrs. Wharton and to ask what had happened. Life has not been so gay that we are without experience in suffering, but the only relief that I have ever found in it, is the sense that others are suffering too, and in this crushing calamity we are all one. I cannot pretend to say or do anything that would make this mortal blow easier to bear, except the single thought which has carried me through years of desperation, that nothing can now matter long! You have so much left you, and so much to do for them! You are not alone! To me, the sense of solitude is the hardest to bear of all the inflictions of life, and I feel almost an envy of you for having sorrows which give you a motive and a newer value for living. Bay was my last tie to active sympathy with men. **He was the best and finest product of my time and hopes. He has done enough work to place him high among the men whose names have a chance of lasting more than our day and we can even hope that his genius may throw some rays of light on us who surrounded him**. You have lived and will continue to live in him. Probably you do not much care for that kind of life, but it would have pleased him to feel it.

On September 5, Henry Adams wrote the Senator, his former protégé:

My Dear Cabot...
Of Bay I cannot speak with the smallest calm because the loss is so personal. That superb exuberance of youth which can find no outlet except its self-assertion, and no appeasement except in defiance of common-place, was the very last of my social fountains of hope. Nothing remains. I look around, over the whole field of human activity, and can see no one else to offer a ray of light.

To Elizabeth Cameron, Adams wrote of the drama of Bay's death, and of the horror of the Senator's ordeal:

September 13, 1909
Poor Cabot had to telegraph everywhere—to get undertakers and steamers and special trains, and stop Nannie somewhere on her way down—and everybody helped; and Bay was taken to Dr. Bigelow's house on Beacon Street and there, with only the family—not the children—present, they had a queer "Bay-an" service with Langdon Mitchell to read Walt Whitman and Bay's sonnets, and so finish. We know all

> that. **What we shall have to wait to know is the limit of the ruin this bomb will cause. I imagine that its first effect on Bessy was to numb all her sensations—reduce her to the mental stupor of an animal; while on Nannie it was probably to force everything inward on the heart. Cabot, I take to have felt fear—collapse of nervous energy**. This is the healthiest way of all and the quickest to pass.

But even in her sorrow, Bessy wrote Nannie heroically, quoting from Bay's dramatic poem, *Herakles*. "*Alcmena*: My boy / Is dead! –And I remember, I remember / How he was radiant and tender, proud, / Passionate, dauntless, how his eyes were grave / And clear... And I remember little things / Of him...And I believe a woman dies / When she remembers, as I do, such things, / Such simple, poignant, childish memories / Of a dead child!.... // *Megara*: She dies, I know she dies!"

In this letter to Nannie, Bessy tenderly describes Bay's affection for his mother:

> *Darling Oops,*
> I feel this too for myself what must it be for you with your memories of 35 years! The intellectual death is horror but when I think of that **sweet voice calling Poozy, of that dear shaggy head, that dear way he put his hand up when he laid his head on your breast**—All the poor little things he liked to keep, his presents to the children—these things in their way are worse. And yet for these memories, we should lose him and anything is better than that. Poor little darling Oops! I think of you so much—
>
> Lovingly,
> *Bessy*

On September 21, 1909, Henry Adams, the father Bessy never had, wrote her a brilliant condolence letter about the loneliness of grief, having many years previously lost his beloved wife, Clover, and about the illusion of that feeling of aloneness. With love and humor, he begged her not to feel too alone. Helena told me many years later that if it hadn't been for Uncle Henry, she could not have gotten through it.

> You know how much you are in our thoughts, yet I remember well how hard I found it to feel that I was not alone, and how eagerly I wanted to be constantly assured that everybody was suffering or had suffered some such irreparable loss as made them understand what you are feeling.

Even in the worst depths of solitude, I was surprised to find that almost everyone, beyond childhood, was nursing some memory, or hiding some wound, that was never spoken of, but made the deepest feeling in life. We are all together in that relation, and if it is not husband or wife, it is a lover or a child, that fills the background of life, and makes the interest and poetry of our age. **What we really mourn most is our own youth and the love it brought**. Sooner or later, it passes for us all, and we say no more about it, but the memory lives in it and in nothing else, so that when we see some new victim suffer, we feel it ourselves.

You will find half your friends who have reached middle-life quite ready to envy you for having had all that was best in the world and even now, in your solitude, for having more left to you than most of them have. Even if it is only a memory, most women would be glad to change with you. I cannot honestly say that I ever felt this idea as a consolation or mitigation of the pain, but it did certainly serve to show me what an ocean of disappointment and despondency I lived on. **We all hurry to disguise it and hide it from other people, but among ourselves it is a sort of secret society**, with pass-words and nods and jests, that take for granted all the thoughts that won't bear repeating aloud.

You have passed through the awful sense of feeling that something has happened to you that is impossible,—something that cannot be,—that is a dream,—a nightmare,—and that you will wake up, and find it all an imaginary horror. **When all the supports of one's existence suddenly give way, one writhes under it like a crushed worm**. Nothing helps except to think of the happiness we have had, and even that is a kind of self-torture. I am old enough not to try to make the suffering less. The suffering is almost a pleasure that one does not want to forget. All I care for is to help you to carry it. **You know how I felt Bay's genius and admired his art, and you will not be too jealous when I say that of all the poems he gave us, none approached the one he began with, first of all, when he gave us you. And I doubt whether all the genius that ever lived has ever produced poem or figure that could rival you when you produced the children**. You know that this is no new notion of mine, for I said it all years ago, in print, and in solemn seriousness. The woman and the child are the wonder of my old age. You are the true poems, the best he ever did.

Goodbye!
Henry Adams

My father comments in his autobiography:

Henry Adams (1838-1918), Bay's father's lifelong friend and early mentor, became one of Bay's closest friends even though he was 35 years his senior. In 1911, two years after Bay's death, he published a short biography of Bay.... George remembered Bessy well. He and his brother called her Gammy. She was the most loving and beautiful woman: self-effacing, with a "slow smile," but an iron will. Her life after her husband died so young could not have been easy, but there was never a hint of self-complaint or self-pity. Henry Adams was a good and close friend, acting as a kind of uncle to the children who called him Dordy. Aunt Helena remembers driving in Rock Creek Park with Uncle Henry in his Victoria—he hated automobiles—picking violets in the spring time.

Nannie's letter to Theodore's sister, Corinne Roosevelt Robinson, lends insight into why Bay and she were so close and why Bay was the center of all their lives. It also is a rare picture of her feelings toward Bessy:

East Point
Nahant
Dearest Corinne,
It has been hard to write to you because you are so near and dear & because your wonderful letter came so entirely from the depth of your own terrible experience. I remember looking at you last spring & wondering how you lived at all. I thought if one of my children were to die, I should fall down like a log & be dragged to bed—there to be until I died too—But here I am alive & perfectly well & able to do everything that I must do only wishing there were more I could do for all the rest who loved my darling Bay & depended upon him as I did. **He was the center of us all, the one who made things worthwhile-whom we all wanted and longed to be with & who gave to each one of us the warm living tenderness & demonstrative affection which we loved, but were too shy to bestow on each other to the same degree**. To think that we have lost that & everything else—his splendid mind & his courage & the very inspiration of his presence—is like a perpetual black nightmare. Yet what you say of him is true. He had **achieved great things mentally & physically & we have much that is tangible to love and cherish for his sake**. Of course nothing compares to the

agony for poor Bessy. The entire **confidence and dependence she had in him & his adoring tenderness and care for her—How can she live without them & bringing up those darling children. Well Cabot & I have much to live for in them & in our other children who surround us with their devotion & care**.

Bessy is absolutely courageous. I have never seen anything like it & she allows us to be with her & do all we can. Constance & Gussy & our poor dear John who hurried across the ocean to us, all help us—**We are all utterly bereft**, & no one in the world knows better than you, darling Corinne, what it means. You & I must both be grateful to have had these beautiful lives given to us for a time, & we shall think of these children who have left us as always young & strong & splendid.

It was sweet of you to want to come here, dearest, but I would not have had you travel or exert yourself-I know you are not well & long to hear that you are gaining strength. Later we shall meet, but do not think of me too sadly dear friend. Cabot keeps up well, thank heaven, & he & John join with me in love to dear Mr. Robinson & all your children & grandchildren.

Your Ever Loving,
Nannie L.

Theodore Roosevelt, who was on a hunting trip in Africa from which his health would never recover, wrote meaningfully to Nannie and the Senator:

Neri Boma
October 16th, 1909
Oh my dearest friends, the people for whom outside my own family I care more than anything else on earth, I just can't tell you of my grief and sympathy and how I mourn with and for you. I have cabled you, Cabot; and to think that my last letter, dealing with all kinds of trivial things, was written when Bay was dead, and I did not know it. I loved him dearly. He was the truest and staunchest of friends, the most interesting of companions. He was the only man I have ever met whom I felt was a genius; **I have met many men of power and talent; but he had the purple in him, he was a genius**. And geniuses aren't often fit and eager to prove the strong metal in them, the iron under the purple and gold, in battle, but Bay was. I always used to think of Cervantes at Lepanto when I thought of Bay, captain of his gun, in the heat of action. And Bessie, my heart bleeds to think of her—and her children

made with the dearest home [sic]. I have every kind of tender memory of him from the time twenty-five years ago when he and Constance and John were such friendly children at Nahant, and I told them stories my last afternoon as President, when Edith and I came to your house, and Bay and Bessie had brought their children round, and little John when leaving the room and told to say goodbye to me made a deep bow with his head pointing the wrong way. Nannie will remember. Time after time here I have seen things which I have treasured up to talk over with Bay when I got home—There is nothing in the world I can say to help you. **Nannie, you are the daughter, the sister, the mother, of fighting men; you have a valiant and gallant soul; you must let nothing, no sorrow, beat you down. You, Cabot, are blessed in that you must work hard, must strive in conflict with your fellows.** I don't suppose you would either of you wish to see me now; but I do wish I were where I could feel I were near you.

In sorrow, ever devotedly yours,
T.R.

In 1909, Edith Wharton moved more or less permanently to Paris. Bessy had apparently answered her first letter to say she understood what a loss Bay's death was for Wharton too. The oppressive sadness and loneliness of the beautiful widow with three young children alarmed Wharton. She sent eight unpublished letters to Bessy all written from Paris, embossed with the Hotel de Crillon insignia and bordered in black.[250] They show what a good friend she was and why three years later Bessy would agree to live in Paris to be near to her. One can't help but feel that Edith was speaking of herself when she writes with envy of "the great good thing" of love and happiness.

September 4, 1909
If you knew, dear Bessie [sic], how I have been longing to write again and yet not venturing to lest the tenderest touch should hurt, you would know how your few words have gone to my heart and how grateful I am to you for sending them. All these dreadful, unnatural days since the news came I have gone about thinking, if only I could talk to Bessy! If I could tell her all he was to me, who was only one among his many friends! I am so sure that, in your place, it would help me, and keep me closer to the reality of the happiness I had had, to feel that others had

[250] Two are in the main text and six others are appendixed.

understood it and felt the reflection of it in their own lives. And yet, so far off, one hesitates, one is not sure of being understood—so I have begun to write a half dozen times and then not done it.

It was sweet of you to send me that word and sweeter still to tell me that you understand what the loss is to me. It would be so natural that, in the immensity of your disaster, you should be unconscious of anything else and unable to realize that **his friends too are to be pitied**. That touched me more than anything. **But I have always thought that people who have been very happy are the only ones who have really measured human experience—qu'il faut avoir été heureux pour comprendre**. And you have had the great good thing in life and have been the means of his having it and from that wonderful **fullness of experience there ought to result a keener power of sympathy and understanding than the average cramped and thwarted life is ever likely to know**.

As for his friends, they all feel, I imagine, as I do, that you were the means of bringing him nearer, of tightening and consolidating all the ties of the little group, so that as one thought of him, one thought always in the same instant of you and one sees you still together, indissolubly part of each other, in the beautiful memory that he leaves. I am grateful to you for telling me that I was one of his best friends. Since the day that I first saw him—when Walter[251] brought him one day to the Goram Hotel in Washington, 14 years ago, at least, there never was a moment's wavering or cooling in our friendship: never one of the blank spaces that come so often in the friendliest intercourses. Whenever we met, though often after such long intervals of absence and silence, the understanding seemed completer, we seemed to be getting nearer to each other; and all last autumn, after he came back from Europe, I had more than ever the sense of the beautiful ripe fruit of years that our friendship was growing to be. There never was anyone like him; it is the exceeding bitter cry of all his friends! But it is a great happiness to have been one of his friends and to look down the long sunny vistas that always open before one at the sound of his name, down into the still depths of his nature, the nature that revealed itself only to those who loved him. Do write me again, dearest Bessy, when you like to do so. I want to talk of him, & there is no one to whom I can talk of him as I can to you. Thank you again for your letter.

Yrs. Affte,
Edith

---

[251] Walter Berry, Wharton's greatest friend. She writes "Bessie" because Bessy spelled her name both ways.

If you have a photograph won't you send me one some day?

September 16, 1909
Dearest Bessy,
I have just seen Dr. Bigelow, & had a long quiet talk with him. We are so one about Bay, and we loved the same things in him so much in the same way, that he seemed to be with us as we talked—*was* with us! It is the first time that Dr. Bigelow has been able to see me, since the day John left, but now that he is better I hope he will send for me often. I was so glad to hear from him that Langdon Mitchell was at Tuckanuck for ten days, & that he came to you afterward. I wrote him a few days ago, just for the comfort of talking about Bay. And Dr. Bigelow was kind enough to show me Bay's beautiful letter from Tuckanuck written while Langdon M. was with him. How fortunate they had those last radiant days together!

Henry James wrote Nannie a few months after Bay's death at the start of the new year, not of his hope that the bitter taste of death and the shock of it all had lessened. On the contrary, "the master" wrote that they must consider the grief "a large and constant part of your lives and that you drink deep of it and never exhaust that bitterness," because "we live with our lost" and "they must live still with us."

January 1, 1910
Lamb House
Rye
Sussex
Dear Mrs. Lodge,
If I haven't thanked you before this for your letter of a couple of months ago, nor expressed my great appreciation of your having been moved to notice my poor words at all, this has been simply from my sense of the difficulty of speaking again tenderly & understandingly enough to your stricken state. However, I am unwilling let this New Year's night pass without just intimating to you by another word that I do understand, intensely & that I have no wish or hope for you or for his Father, so misguided as to assume that you are both not living, & preferring to live, more & more with your sorrow. I hope on the contrary that it is a large and constant part of your lives & that you **drink deep of it &**

never exhaust that bitterness compared with which the appeal of things supposedly scant is poor and tasteless. So it is, & so only, that we live with our lost—because so it is that they most live still with us. I wish I were not cast away here so much, nowadays, out of the world—I might otherwise meet some friend or pilgrim who could tell me this or that about you. But I think, after all, and send no telling—& have but to hold you in my mind's eye a little to feel almost that I am near you myself & that you are letting me say to you that he has left even me—far away & after but few meetings—with the inward ache as of a sharp personal loss. It revives as I thus speak to you of him—& makes me glad to have done so & thus to be, for him, the more tenderly & faithfully yours,

Henry James

The Senator asked Edith Wharton to write a remembrance of Bay and in the New Year, she wrote Bessy of her wish to do so for *The London Times* as well as something longer for *The Atlantic*. In the end, she chose *Scribner's Magazine*.

Dearest Bessy,

I want very much to write something about Bay's work if you and his parents would like me to. You must tell me quite frankly. My idea would be to do a short article for the Literary Supplement of *the London Times*, which is on the whole, the best thing of its kind in England, & something longer for any American magazine you may prefer. My first thought was *the Atlantic*, but I should like to reach a larger public. If you care to have me do this, I should like to know by what name you wish him spoken of. Mr. Adams says, "Bay Lodge," but surely that belongs to his family and friends. One cannot use the three names each time one mentions him, & to the general public "Cabot Lodge" means his father. This is a small question, but I put it now because it happens to occur to me. I am so glad that his new volume was ready for publication. When does it appear? If you would like me to write these articles, I will send out at once to Houghton Mifflin for all the vols.... More and more as the days pass, I feel what a great gift it was to have known him &to have been his friend—what a great gift it is, for always.

Yr. Loving,
Edith

The remembrance *Scribner's Magazine* published in February 1910

Edith Wharton in 1910.

described their first meeting in 1898 in Washington, D.C.[253] Edith recalled the vivid impression he made on her. Her tribute on the occasion of his untimely death gives the reader a moving and eloquent description of Bay Lodge.

> It would be impossible, I think, for any friend of George Cabot Lodge's to write of the poet without first speaking of the man; and this not only because his art was so close to his life, but also, and chiefly, because, to those near enough to measure him, his character, his temper, the "virtue" in him, made his talent, distinguished as it was, a mere part of an abounding whole.
>
> **Abundance**—that is the word which comes to me whenever I try to describe him. During the twelve years of our friendship—and from the very day when it began— I had whenever we were together, the sense of his being a creature as profusely as he was finely endowed. There was an exceptional delicacy in his abundance, and an extraordinary volume in his delicacy. All this on the day when he was first brought to see me—a spring afternoon of the year 1898 in Washington—was lit up by a beautiful boyish freshness, which, as the years passed, somehow contrived to ripen without fading. In the first five minutes of our talk, he gave himself with the characteristic wholeness that made him so rare a friend: showing me all the sides of his varied nature, the grave sense of beauty, the flashing contempt of meanness and that large spring of kindly laughter that comes to many only as a result of the long tolerance of life. It was one of his gifts thus to brush aside the preliminaries of acquaintance and enter at once, with a kind of royal ease, on the rights and privileges of friendship; as though, one might think, with a foreboding of the short time given him to enjoy them.
>
> Young Cabot Lodge lived every moment to the full, and the first impression he made was of a joyous physical life. His sweet smile, his easy strength, his deep eyes full of laughter and visions—these struck one even before his look of intellectual power. I have seldom seen any one in whom the natural man was so wholesomely blent with the reflecting intelligence; and it was not the least of his charms that he sent such stout roots into the earth, and had such a hearty love for all he drew from it. Nothing was common or unclean to him but the vulgar, the base, and the insincere, and his youthful impatience at the littleness of human nature was tempered by an unusually mature sense of

---

[252] See appendix.

> its humours.
>
> I might pause to speak of the accomplishments that made his society, from the first, so refreshing and animating: for he was an admirable linguist, a good "Grecian," a sensitive lover of the arts, and possessed, on the whole, of the fullest general "culture" I have ever known in a youth of his age. But even as I number his gifts I see how suffused they were by the glow of his beautiful nature, and how little what he knew ever counter in comparison to what he was. At any rate, his attainments did not, even in those days, single him out as much as his unusual gift of sympathy, and the range of his response to the imaginative call. As his voice—that beautiful medium of fine English speech—could pass from the recital of Whitman or Leconte de Lisle to the vivid mimicry of some exchange of platitudes overheard in street or train, so his mind flashed through the same swift transitions, and the boy who was dramatizing the broad humours of a *tournée de Montmartre* would break off to tell how, at the end of a summer night in London, he had gone down to await the dawn on Westminster Bridge, "When all that mighty heart was lying still."[253]

She said that he was a man who kept no reserves but gave himself wholly, showing all sides of his nature—a sense of beauty, his kindness and laughter, his hatred of meanness. She set out her own aesthetic and artistic principles, contesting Thèophile Gautier's notion that artists should "sacrifice much to produce little," arguing that it was dangerous for an artist to "draw all his effects from his inner experience." She gives Lodge his due when speaking of *The Soul's Inheritance* and in particular "The Noctambulist."

> The Noctambulist is he who having "been all the rounds of repetition" in "the same old adventure of the mind," has reached a point when
>
> "Swift as passion / brutal as a blow, / The Dark shuts down… / And, O, the truth / is terrible within us!... Up from what wild beginnings, long-evolved— / The unfinished shell of our humanity…. / The night is best—for only when we fill / The total measure of our human ken, / And feel in every exercise of being / The bondage of our fixed infirmities. / Are we assured that we, in every cell / And nerve, respond to all life's whole appeal, / Known and unknown, in sense and heart and brain…."

---

[253] Edith Wharton, "George Cabot Lodge" *Scribner's Magazine*, February 1910.

> This is the writer's maturest conception of life and his verse rose with it in an ampler movement. Such memorable passages abound in 'The Noctambulist' and in its harmony of thought and form, it remains perhaps the completest product of Cabot Lodge's art. ...This power of dissociation (from the poet's own personality) and the ability to project oneself far enough for the other to focus it, is the very mainspring of the dramatizing faculty; for to draw one's neighbor is a much easier business than to draw oneself as seen by one's neighbor.

In *A Backward Glance*, her 1930 autobiography,[254] written just before her death, Wharton drew a slightly more realistic picture. The Senator was dead and his grandson (my grandfather) was launched. She could write with more detachment than she could for the memoir that was intended to please the Senator. Wharton recalled Bay as a "brilliant" but immature poet; "pathetic" is not a word she would have used in 1910:

> His fate, in fact, was the reverse of mine, for he grew up in a hot-house of intensive culture, and was one of the most complete examples I have ever known of the young genius before whom an adoring family unites in smoothing the way. This kept him out of the struggle of life, and consequently out of its experiences, and to the end his intellectual precocity was combined with a boyishness of spirit at once delightful and pathetic.... He had a naturally scholarly mind and might have turned in the end to history and archaeology; unless, indeed he was simply intended to be the most sensitive and dazzling of talkers.

This hothouse of culture Wharton refers to is otherwise known as the school of Henry Adams. Adams wrote Henry James on September 3, 1909, that Wharton was even more affected than he by Bay's death, which suggests what family sources have told me—that she had a crush on Bay.

> Bay's experience last winter completed and finished my own. When his *Herakles* appeared absolutely unnoticed by the literary press, I regarded my thesis as demonstrated. Society no longer shows the intellectual life necessary to enable it to react against a stimulus. My brother Brooks insists on the figure of paralysis. I prefer the figure of diffusion, like

[254] Edith Wharton, *A Backward Glance* (New York: D. Appleton-Century Company, Inc., 1934), 149-151.

that of a river falling into an ocean. Either way, it drowned Bay, and has left me still floating, with vast curiosity to see what vaster absence of curiosity can bring about in my Sargasso Sea. Mrs. Wharton, in spite of her feminine energy and interest, is harder hit, I think, than I by the loss of Bay Lodge, but she has, besides, a heavy anxiety to face in the uncertainties of her husband's condition.

In 1909-1910 Wharton's marriage was breaking up. Her love affair with Morton Fullerton, which took place in 1909, was disappointing and her husband, Teddy, was losing his mind. She writes her friend Bessy of her enduring memories of Bay.

On June 20, 1910
53 rue de Varenne
Dearest Bessy,
[...]I shall never, never forget that warm afternoon on the thymy hill-side over the little blue lake. Not that I shall ever forget *any of it*, or that his absence will ever leave less of a void in my life; but that particular sun-drenched fragrant hour was so full of him, so like him in its warmth & brightness & abounding sense of life!— I am waiting eagerly to see what Mr. Adams writes.[255] When is the edition to come out? How I want to have a long talk with you, to hear all these things, & many many more, & to sit with you, & feel he is there with us!—Yes, I say to you again, what you have had was worth paying any price for. You have had life in the round, & for most of us it is such a poor lop-sided thing. And you have your children, who are part of him; & I can imagine what that must be.[256]

I know it doesn't make the long hours any shorter, or the empty evenings less empty; & I realize the full force of the contrast between having *him* & having any other companionship; & yet I say that you have been blessed among women....

[...] I think so often of the day when Walter first brought Bay to see me, at the Gordon, in that far-off spring; & the very first words we exchanged made us friends, & we never lost a single precious minute afterward! I wonder if anyone ever had just his gift of reaching to the essential things in his relations with his friends, so that there were no dead moments in one's communion with him, but every one connected, & left a trace, & forged a link?—And then I remember the evening

[255] *The Life of George Cabot Lodge* would appear in 1911.
[256] The children: Henry Cabot, eight; John Davis, seven; and Helena, five.

when he & Walter were going to the theatre with us, & Walter said, "If you want to make Bay perfectly happy, ask Miss. Davis"—and I asked you & Bay *was* perfectly happy!

I am hard at work at that short novel which I have taken up since Teddy went to Switzerland,[257] & I hope to have time to get well started while I am here alone. It has been impossible to work except spasmodically these last months, & more & more I find that salvation is there, & there only....

Adieu, Chère, Je t'embrasse tendrement,
Edith[258]

The Lodges, overcome with grief, found comfort in another friend, Cecil Spring-Rice: "In a touching letter of consolation, Spring-Rice wrote at length, never once mentioning the death of their son, telling only of the virtue and promise he had found in him.... As he learned later, the Lodges prized the letter, which they read and reread many times. It was such a tribute that even Henry Adams, for all his detachment from life and death, was moved by it."[259]

In November 1909, Bessy and the children returned to their house in Washington, D.C., at 2346 Massachusetts Avenue. Adams writing of Bessy to Mrs. Cameron in January of the following year, explained the environment which eventually led to Bessy wanting to leave for Paris. He also wrote of the Senator "befor' the wah" (before the Civil War), and of the fixed idea he had about Roosevelt, probably referring to the Republican split. Adams was Nannie and Bessy's closest friend and he returned their affection. Bessy asked Henry Adams to write a biography of Bay, and told him he was the person she most cared for but Adams feared that she, the Senator and Nannie would have a heavy hand in his biography.

From Bessy:

January 1910
Dearest Uncle Henry,
I can't begin to tell you what it means to me to have you here. Apart from your sympathy and comprehension so rare, you are something brilliant and fine for me to care for. Now that the beauty has gone form my life, I tremble at the intrusion of the sordidness that tries to rush in.

Always Affecly,
Bessy

---

[257] A sanatorium near Lake Constance.
[258] This letter is published in *The Letters of Edith Wharton.*
[259] Butler, *Cecil Spring-Rice: A Diplomat's Life*, 58.

Henry Adams to Mrs. Cameron:

> January 18 & 20, 1910
> [...][Bessy] is very sad and chokey and teary, as she should be; but sleeps and eats and is very much occupied by the children who are again in boisterous health. Knowing exactly what Bessy feels, I had no trouble in understanding exactly what she wants and needs. It is chiefly to be left alone and in peace. For a year or two, she best see no one but those who do not get on her nerves and she can find those out only by degrees...
>
> ...I sat for an hour with Bessy yesterday and Cabot dined here. Bessy asks much about you, and misses you, as one of the few people she would feel pleasure in seeing. Her family naturally tire her, as families always do. They have that odious way of wanting one to "make an effort." I thank God I never made an effort in my worst moments. Cabot is shrunk and shrivelled, like me, and talks like a senator befo' the wah. He has a true idée fixe about Theodore which turns up regularly in his conversation; but he is as clear-headed and keen as ever and sees the future in a way quite new for him.
>
> Luckily nothing matters and no one cares. America is a vast mud flat.... Poor Bay's poems are to be republished in a collected form. Bessy wants me to do a volume of *Life*. I assent readily knowing that Cabot will do it and will not let anyone else do it, however hard he may try to leave it alone. Edith Wharton's notice is very nicely done with fine appreciation and feeling; but all the notices from today 'til doomsday will never make an American public care for poetry—or anything else unless perhaps chewing gum.

What Adams wrote and what was published are two different things and offer a fascinating glimpse of the relationships between the players. In 1906, with the publication of the Henry Cabot Lodge portrait in *The Education*, Adams feared that Lodge, then president of the Massachusetts Historical Society, would change his text. Four years later, Adams playfully expressed to Mrs. Cameron his fears that Cabot would change his text of his *Life*: but when it came to writing history, Lodge was Adams' respectful student, and an excellent historian; nothing in the family papers indicates that he changed anything. Adams' cold rendering of George Cabot Lodge— so unlike his natural style as seen in *The Education*—is a mystery until one realizes that ironically, it was Nannie and Bessy and not the Senator who altered the memoir. Bay's letters to Bessy and to Marjorie Nott are not included in the book. Bessy's willful insistence on cutting Bay's love letters was also against the judgment of Edith Wharton. In a letter to Bessy from Paris July 29, 1910, almost a year after Bay's death, Adams pleads with her *not* to cut the most vital, personal parts of the biography:

> I see no need of any explanation of anything I have said or inserted or omitted. You will understand! I regret only that my fear, as responsible intermediary, made me timid in speaking of you. I should have pitched the key much higher, if I had not been afraid of your going back on me. Women always go back on each other, or on themselves; it is their weak point; and they weaken the man by refusing to stand up to his standard for them. Much as I dislike notoriety or publicity, I never refused to challenge it or to accept it, when I thought it a duty, and I expect my friends, whether men or women, to stand by me, and insist on their rights too. In this society, made up of forms of social cowardice, we must do as Bay did,—insist on recognition,—or submit to be swamped. In this last case, we had better leave biography alone. Bay would be ashamed of us, and I should be ashamed of myself, if we deserted his standards; the highest standard he had, was you.

At Bessy's request, Adams excised the impassioned love letters. It was *Nannie, not Bessy,* who wanted Bay "to appear at least adequate and cheerful to the world." Adams could have written brilliantly about Bay's manic side, alternating between morosity and optimism, since he himself was moody. Nannie insisted that Adams pay tribute to *Herakles* rather than dwell, as Wharton did, on "The Noctambulist."

Nannie Lodge wrote in October, 1910: "Dear Brother,... I should advise omitting all reference of failing health or discouragement as it would have been intensely distasteful to Bay. He wanted it meant to appear at least adequate and cheerful to the world." Marjorie Nott's letter to Henry Adams implied there were quite a few letters from Bay to her but that she only had time to bring a portion of them to show him in France.

Bessy was too modest to accept the role Henry Adams wanted for her as "inspiratrice." If to Adams she was Bay's inspiration, she didn't want it known. She probably realized other women served him better in that role—Nannie, Edith, perhaps Marjorie, among others. Bessy struggled to control her destiny, but fell victim to the whims of others. First, those of her own mother who was cruel to her by giving her a poor education and who also embarrassed Bessy with her love affair with President Chester Arthur. Second, egotism dominated Bay, who loved the image of his goddess "Beatrice," both her reflecting glory and her fecundity; and third, she was surrounded by dominating Lodges; and fourth, as the dependent of Senator Lodge after the death of her husband, she was subjected to his eccentricities and often made miserable by them. Her shyness or refusal to cause a scene with the Lodges made her seem colder than she was.

Adams' "sister" grew steadily weaker after Bay's death. Although both the Senator and Nannie were powerfully affected by their son's death, family sources have said Nannie never recovered from it. Her little circle of friends tightened. In February, 1910, Adams wrote Elizabeth Cameron that "...Nanny looks to me uncommonly shaky in the hands and head. I see shakes and snakes in everyone...." And in March, Lizzie Cameron wrote, "Dear Dor, I saw Nanny Lodge yesterday and was shocked at her weakness. Even her voice trembles and she looks *terribly*."

This March 24 letter from Adams to Cameron puts a new twist on an old story. Could Roosevelt have decided not to run for President in 1908 out of loyalty to his best friend, the Senator? In the same breath as Adams spoke of Nanny's condition, he spoke of Cabot's anxieties:

> I turn green at leaving Nanny and Cabot and Bessy. Between us all, we know quite well that we don't know at all whether Nanny's life is fading out or not. Cabot has got an anxious season before him, and clutches convulsively at Theodore, but Theodore himself is in an impossible fix. He must support Taft—or sacrifice Cabot.

Although he neither asked Adams to write it, nor to change it, the Senator sent Adams his ideas for the latter's biography of Bay to commemorate the poet's work. He wrote Adams in Paris of Bay's mysticism and Dokko's Buddhist influence:

> April 11, 1910
> *Dear Henry,*
> I enclose the first poem Bay ever wrote—He brought it to me—you see the date—908 I have always kept it—It seems to me to throw light on the tendency of his mind and you may like to use it as showing what he then was. I thought it a remarkable thing for a boy in college of 20 years—I think so still—not the verse but the thought working in his mind—Nannie has told me of your talk this afternoon—Bigelow had

a great influence upon him at one time—His mysticism began then—But he worked himself out and through of Buddhistic philosophy as he did through many phases—He had reached great independence and originality of thought in his last years—I speak merely as a watcher and witness. Sturgis [sic] wrote me, "I began by teaching him. It ended by his teaching me."

The poems will certainly fill three volumes of the size of the *Herakles*—probably larger—say like the current edition of Emerson—The memoir should be about the same size, I should think—300-400 pages—But space and all that is for you to judge—Let us hear from you—I shall be most curious to hear from you of Theodore's reception in Paris if you get there in time. Best Wishes for a good voyage.

Ever Yrs,
H.C. Lodge

From Bessie's April letters, we learn something of how she ran the household, that her mother supported her, what Bay's likes and dislikes were, and how independent and difficult Bay was to take care of. She mentions that a conversation her father, John Davis, had with the Senator about Bay's choice of career, the Bay Lodges' financial future and Bay's attempt to write for the stage.

2346 Mass. Ave.
Dearest Uncle Henry,
I am sending the extracts. I tried to make them as varied and significant as possible and it occurs to me that you might like to know some of the practical details of his life. After Papa's visit to his father—mentioned in the extracts—he wrote for the stage heroically even going so far as to interview Miss. Marbury and some actors. He naturally loathed it and as his grandmother's death enabled his father to give him $2400 a year he destroyed all that work and never wrote for money again no matter what our financial condition. I had $2000 a year from my mother and Bay earned $1800 at the Capitol. This was not luxury as we always paid our house rent out of it—even here in this house—and sometimes we had to live with our families for a while to set things straight. The spirit in which we took it—all is shown on pages 24-5-6. When our bills accumulated dreadfully, we'd pull them out and choose according to our preferences for the different shopmen—it being always impossible to clear them up all at once. This we never did but they all got paid sooner or later and we seldom worried. Page 28 shows how hard it was to take care of him-he

would go his own way. I hope you will agree with me that the fewer the actual quotations from these letters the better. I could not let John typewrite them and hope you will forgive the extra trouble and strain on your eyes. Will you burn them up when you have finished and meanwhile keep them out of sight of *everyone*? I miss you more than you have any idea of and love you very much and am grateful for you.

Bessy

Adams wrote Bessy May 3 about his *Life of George Cabot Lodge*:

Bay liked his Boston even less than I do, and we shall have trouble in trying to make this clear without using some strong expressions. I foresee constant stumbling over this potato-patch; all the more because it is really the gist of the poetry. All the poems express a more or less violent reaction against Boston and ought to be read so if they are to be understood.

In May Adams wrote Nannie a commiserating letter about illness:

My dear Sister,
Have you got influenza? Grippe? Rheumatism in two backs and fourteen legs? A churchyard cough? Snuffles—pronounced feebleness of body? Total collapse of mind and memory? Have you lost all your appetite? And your sleep? And your senses? If so, you are excused for not writing to me! The condition is mine....[260]

Nannie's amusing reply to her "brother" mentions that Cabot would never change the text but that he would like his friend Theodore to write the preface. Bessy evidently thought it would bring it a publicity which she found distasteful, something which Nannie attributed to the temporary insanity of grief.

June 12, 1910
Dear Brother,
In truth, I have all the diseases you mention with the addition of writer's cramp, which is the reason I have not written.... Bessy spoke to

[260] Adams to Cameron May 19: "The influenza is all right as John Hay used to say. It goes on getting worse every day it gets better, and when it is quite well, it is worst of all. Just now it is in its improving stage when it feels limp and weak and legless and wobbly. But I dropped in at the opera last night for half an hour to see Mary Garden squirm Salome."

you about T.R.'s preface....[261] Bessy is very much opposed to it, poor child and, in fact, everything is very hard to bear.... Cabot would never have thought of adding to it [the memoir], or associating any other name or anybody else's work with yours.... Try to forget any annoyance & remember only our gratitude.

Yr. Sister Anne

For Bay, wrote Adams, "man became an outrage, society an artificial device for the distortion of truth, civilization a wrong."[262] Apparently the first draft of the biography was not well received nor—interestingly—did Adams know where Bessy was. Bessy's brother, Bancroft, who must have been in his late twenties, died June 11 in a New York hospital of typhoid fever and Bessy had been at his side. Their mother, Sally Davis, was afraid to visit her son on his deathbed for fear of catching the disease.

May 29, 1910
Henry Adams to Elizabeth Cameron
23 avenue du Bois de Boulogne...I have arranged Bay's letters, etc. down as far as the Spanish War (1898), with a thread of narrative and explanation. I can make nothing very good out of it, but perhaps it will do to satisfy Nanny and Bessy. Nanny, as you will see in your N.Y. Herald is to appear in the charity show on Thursday as a hatless Gainsborough. I am to dine with the Bacons and go with them in the ambassadorial box.

June 21, 1910
23 ave. du Bois du Boulogne
Henry Adams to Nannie
My Dear Sister,
Your letter of the 12th arrives this morning and gives me much matter to meditate on for it is the only letter I have received since I left. No one writes. Apparently the newspaper is regarded as sufficient.... When silence is kept, I always imagine something is concealed, and I try to break into it. Probably they are all anxious not to disturb my venerable repose.... I wrote to Bessy last week. When I have the material arranged with some little setting of narrative, I shall send it over to her and leave it to her and you to leave out, or put in, whatever you please. The manuscript is ready now except for my own corrections; but

[261] See appendix.
[262] Adams, *The Life of George Cabot Lodge,* 12.

I don't know where Bessy is to be found or how reached. I wonder whether I could send the package in the dispatch-bag. If you have more material I think you can insert it yourselves; but in any case, I think you had better send the manuscript back to me to get its final shape. Of course, if I write it, you may be sure that it will shock you.—You know my ruthless requirement that anyone who challenges publicity, should stand up to it and shrink from no assertion of his personality—but my responsibility ceases when you shall begin yours.

You have not replied to my question of how you got your Cabot name. I want to know....

Ever Affly
Henry Adams

Nannie to Adams, July 4, 1910
Dear Brother,...
Not a drop of the sacred Cabot blood flows in my veins. I was named for my mother's two most intimate friends, Mrs. [Anna Cabot] Lodge and my Aunt, Mrs. Charles Mills, both of whom were named Anna. Such is the simple tale.... Daisy [Nannie's sister, Evelyn] and Brooks [Adams' brother] looked the pictures of health when I bade them goodbye. We have been here a week and J.E. [John Ellerton] has come and gone. He stayed two days and gave us a killing account of some of his adventures. He is rather fatter but otherwise unchanged and looks rested. We are now alone and expect to be all summer and Cabot will not be away at all. Most of our family will be beyond the seas.... Bessy writes that she is settling back into her old way after the shock of her brother's death. As for me, I am such a clod that it makes no difference where I am. I have no life and no news.... We are all well, and send you love, dear Brother. I wish you were nearer.

Ever yr,
Sister Anne

Bessy took her children to Newport in the summer of 1910 and then went on to New York for the final days and funeral of her brother. She refers to his sorrow, to how "sad" his life had been—a telltale sign of a child who was not loved. Bessy's loving letter to Uncle Henry shows that she was a success—that she overcame her sadness through love.

July 4, 1910
Rhode Island Ave.
Newport, RI
Dearest Uncle Henry,
I knew you would be sorry before you wrote but you must know how welcome your letter was. My dear little brother died very suddenly. He had only been in the hospital ten days and I had made plans to be in New York on the 13th thinking that then his hard fight would begin. I got word here on the 10th that he was much worse and when I got there he was dying. His life had been so sad, so devoid of much that every man has a right to expect—but not devoid of affection for many men came into Washington full of sorrow—many men very much older—which shows that though his poor life was frustrated in some directions through no fault of his own it had not been barren. You must know the deep gratitude I feel for what you said in your last letter. You have always been so good to me and from the first, tried hard to think I was good enough for the marvelous creature I married. It always made me very proud and now think what it must be to me—what your affection has meant all this terrible year. I know life is not very valuable to you but you must try to feel it so just for the people who feel about you as I do and there must be many.

Always Affectionately,
Bessy

On July 24, Adams wrote Nannie from Paris, very much tongue-in-cheek about himself and his contemporaries, saying that he had finished the manuscript.

23 av du Bois du Boulogne
My Dear Sister,
The arrival of my affectionate brother along with your affectionate sister gives me very little information about your affectionate self, and your letter of the 4th gives me less. As you justly observed, I am such a clod that it makes no difference where I am, or what I am told, so I don't complain, but I hold to my opinions about what other people are. Mostly they are idiots—but that you knew before.... I am enjoying myself hugely because all the world has gone to the devil, and I hate everybody I see; but as I never see anyone but Americans, even that pleasure is monotonous especially in the restaurants. I've had no news about Teddy Wharton of late as Mrs. Wharton has been away, but I've

no doubt he's worse, and I hope that Mrs. Wharton will soon take to a sanatorium too but nearer Paris where I can see her. I want all my friends to be happy—in sanatoriums. Only the feeble-minded prosper.... I finished my Ms. long ago and am keeping it, like my ready-made clothes, only because I am afraid of Pig Loeb's [William Loeb, Jr., the Boston newspaper publisher] seizing it. If I can get courage, I may trust it to an aeroplane, where it will be relatively safe; but if Frank McVeagh puts a sentimental value of a million on it, like the assessors on my furniture, you will escape seeing it and be happier.

Ever Affly
HA

In the summer, Bessy wrote Nannie a revealing letter from Northeast Harbor about spirituality. It seems a French history Nannie had given her grandson Cabot was *not intended* for Helena but that she was the one enjoying it.

August 11, 1910
Dearest Oops,
I have great hopes of finding you in Nahant when we return on Thursday. I suppose the heat has been bearable lately but the mental depression must be great? Cabot and I went to Bar Harbor yesterday and saw Mama and Aunt Tilly! She looked very tired and thin but was very game and cheerful. Mrs. Cutting and her youngest daughter[263] are here for a month for the girl's health. I lunched there the other day and had such a beautiful talk with Mrs. Cutting afterwards. Sometimes you seem almost to get behind the *oeil* [eye] of life for a few moments. Of course **she has a much more tangible faith than I and really believes she is being helped by the people she loved who are dead**. I dare say that may have been encouraged by the lovely simplicity of her life. But in a case like mine it would be impossible. All you have is the beauty of memory and the larger vistas gained by deep experience and faith too which grows stronger **that this flowing dream is all a manifestation of something behind and interest to discover what it is**. It is this interest which keeps us alive in the best sense. The children are tumbling about outside—they have enjoyed it here very much. Cold and gray and dismal... the boys are out in a row-boat and are blissful. The French history [book] you gave Cabot last Christmas [an unusually charming book] **I brought them up to read to the boys [who] listen in a perfunctory**

[263] Mrs. Cutting had two daughters and two sons. The eldest son, Bayard, was the father of Iris Origo, the celebrated woman of letters, and a contemporary of my grandmother.

manner but Helena for whom the book was not intended loves it and reads the book when alone!

I see the papers here but the Records have not been forwarded from Nahant and I only get Pinky in scraps which is tantalizing. We shall all be so glad to see you both.

Your devoted,
Bessy

In this letter, the first anniversary of Bay's death, Nannie's famous sympathy for others, in this case Bessy, is demonstrated. In the summer after Bay's death, Bessy stayed away from Nahant and the memory of the death whereas Nannie could evidently live there peacefully and "sustain the burden." Helena was with Bessy, while Cabot and John were at Nahant with Nannie.

August 18, 1910
To Mrs. G.C. Lodge, c/o Miss. Frelinghuysen, Northeast Harbour, Maine
From East Point
Dearest Bessy,
Today & all these days, I am thinking of you & of all that you have suffered & are still suffering. I am glad you are away from the place with its haunting memories just at this time & hope you will come back a little better able to sustain the burden of all your cares and anxieties. **Why should we mourn except for ourselves who must still face the life of this world, when those more fortunate are removed from all the care which surrounds us. Of course, we do not know what new problems they may be encountering or whether there are any. Where they have gone.** But I like to think of Bay gay and happy as he was fifteen years ago when he went to claim you & to hope that some day there will again be happiness for you & him. The boys continue to be perfectly well & good & Cabot's going to write after the sports have taken place to tell you about them. We all send love to & Helena & I am ever,

Yr loving,
Oops

Bessy wrote back about her feelings of powerlessness with her husband and saying they must not "lie fallow." Edith Wharton's remark, "Bay was a climate," seems particularly apt, as if his aura were visible, or that the animal and the spirit in him seemed merged with nature.

My Darling Oops,
Your dear letter has just come and I believe you must know what it means to me. I knew you were thinking those thoughts but to have them put down on paper makes it so much more real. **How often I think of how he went out of the Villa door into the dark forever—over by the parlour door into the hall, he told me he had not been well and I see his face so plainly as I urged him to do different things with that feeling of impotence I always had with him, he went away**. It seems to me now as if several times lately he had been a little worried about himself but he always said so little. I still wish I had asked him to stop the next morning but I was afraid it, I, would bother Pinky. Probably in time those little things grow less poignant—I don't know. Lately I have had time to be very much alone and always I think, "If it is like this for me, what must it be for poor Oops!" But we do know that it will not last forever and to help us we have the knowledge that a great deal of the time we are doing our best and trying to profit by our great joy in having had him—**not to lie fallow now that he is gone**. Nothing like this could have happened to him for he was dependent on no one as we were on him but if everything he loved had gone he would have, as he always said, "stood up in his boots." And a great deal of the time so do we. There are so many heart-rending things that come back to me but I know that just as he always wrote me lovingly, forgetting any differences we had had (they never amounted to quarrels) so somehow I believe that for each other, our love has done a permanent thing. I don't know anything definite. I can't believe that we shall ever meet again—all I feel is that what was has not been in vain. And for you who brought him into the world and who through him—to say nothing of yourself—have contributed so gloriously to the beauty of the world how great a feeling of accomplishment there must be! But none of this compensates for the loving arms and the dear shaggy head, dear dear little Oops.

Mrs. Wharton said to me, "Bay was a climate." I think of it so often. It is a fine thing to have said. I knew I could not trust myself to tell it to you for it means too much to me. When she said it he seemed to come right back again. I hope John will straighten everything out soon.

Much love to you all from
Your affectionate,
Bessy

On August 19, Bessy wrote Adams how much she liked the biography:

> *Dear dear Uncle Henry,*
> It came today and I have just read it and am full of the grandeur, nobility, distinction, reserve, immensity with which you have treated it. Tomorrow I go for a short visit to Nahant and will tell you what they all say. Thank you for so much—
>
> Lovingly,
> *Bessy*
>
> I hope the emotions have not affected your health and yet this seems hardly possible.

The Senator also wrote Henry Adams how much he liked the biography of Bay and comments that Giles Lodge, the first Lodge in America, who came to Boston in 1792, escaping "the rising of the blacks" in San Domingo, married into Boston society. He claims it was Mary Langdon, a cousin of a President of Harvard, Samuel Langdon, descended from William Brattle but actually Giles married Mary's daughter, Abigail, whose portrait was painted alongside Giles', by Rembrandt Peale.

Henry Cabot Lodge to Henry Adams:

> *Dear Henry,*
> I have read *The Life*—I cannot find words to tell you how much I like it—No one else could have done it or given such an analysis of his character and his thought. It is the monument of all others which I should wish to see raised to his memory and I am very, very grateful.
> Of the last hours, I alone know. I wrote an account of it to Sturgis—He must have kept the letter-If you will get it from him you will have all the facts and can write the last page which nobody but you must write.
>
> I made one trifling genealogical correction or recommendation—my grandfather Giles Lodge was certainly a very new arrival. He came out a young Englishman on business for his brothers, merchants in Liverpool, to San Domingo—There he was caught in the rising of the blacks and barely escaped the massacre on a Boston ship. He reached Boston in 1792. But his wife was not English—He married Mary Langdon, daughter of John Lang-

don, whose sister was Miss. Frothingham and whose cousin was Samuel Langdon, President of Harvard—Mary Langdon's mother was Mary Walley and through her comes the descent from William Brattle and Lt. Gen. John Walley of King Williams Canadian Wars so on that side I am even more Bostonian than on the Cabots who were all Essex down to the Revolution. We go on here as usual—politics are in a perilous state-factions fighting and bad outlook—In this state, less bad than elsewhere. How will it all come out, I cannot say—we are pretty well sure—Bessie has just been here from Newport-Poor child! Life seems very desperate to her—The children, so far this summer, have kept well. What I like best about your "Life" is the extreme distinction which pervades it—

Ever Yrs.
H.C. Lodge

Adams responded:

My Dear Cabot,
Many thanks for your very kind letter of the 24th—As you evidently feel, the delicacies of handling so personal a subject as Bay and his relations in life, had made me doubtful whether it could be done so as to satisfy me,—not to speak of you—and I sent it with grave misgivings which were not removed by repeatedly recasting and especially filing the manuscript. Therefore I expected and expect of you, as well as of Nannie, John and Bessie, to use a free hand in suiting it to your ideas. The task of writing it had only one considerable effect on my literary mind;—it very considerably raised my estimate of the poems, both as poetry and as art. The selections that were made to show their quality and range were chosen with special views to bring out separate effects;—such as vigor, passion, thought and dramatic power;—but also, and equally, mere metric skill and scope of diction; so that you can easily insert other selections if you like, either in place of these, or to bring out other qualities that I had overlooked, or not sufficiently noticed. Nothing is lost by enlarging illustrations, if the illustrations count.

As I thought the letters even better than the poetry, I would follow the same course even more boldly in regard to them.

Of course, all are watching politics with great interest. I am now too old to have any just views on anything except the path to Heaven.

> I don't even intend to imitate William James on that trail. If I haven't better things to do than to talk about politics from the next world, I shall prefer to continue my present habit of not talking at all about subjects which are beyond my vision.
>
> Ever Yours,
> *Henry Adams*

In *The Life of George Cabot Lodge*, Adams drew attention to the life of the artist:

> However much he [Lodge] tried, and the more he tried, to lessen the gap between himself—his group of personal friends—and the public, the gap grew steadily wider; the circle of sympathies enlarged itself not at all, or with desperate slowness; and this consciousness of losing ground,—of failure to find a larger horizon of friendship beyond his intimacy;—the growing fear that, beyond this narrow range, no friends existed in the immense void of society,—or could exist, in the form of society which he lived in,—the suffocating sense of talking and singing in a vacuum that allowed no echo to return, grew more and more oppressive with each effort to overcome it.[264]

There was a kind of quest in Bay's work that may possibly be more than just a historical footnote but emblematic of an American culture that had not yet founds its voice. The dates of Bay's life (1873-1909) were unfortunate since he came of age just after the Victorian period had gone into decline and just before modern poetry made its mark. In 1894, the great Victorian period of Tennyson, Browning, Whitman, and Swinburne was drawing to a close, and the new creative poetic tradition led by Ezra Pound had not yet been born. If Bay had been born twenty years later (and therefore writing in the 1920s), he would have felt more at home with other poets who found a refuge in Paris from the literary wasteland life in America. Bay and Henry Adams certainly shared a feeling of being foreign and inadequate to the age and never finding one's niche. When Adams, in *The Life of George Cabot Lodge*, explained Bay's failure by saying he was writing to a future age, one gets the feeling he could be talking about himself:

> [It is] best reading them as though they were the imaginary effort of

---

[264] Adams, *The Life of George Cabot Lodge*, 145.

> some future writer to represent the probable life of an American idealist at the beginning of the 20th century.... The passion for idealism was not a popular defect of those years.

Adams' thought clearly had a distinct effect on Bay's poetry—suffused with the life of the spirit outside of experience. Henry Adams, in his biography, said Bay's aim was *not to become* a Nietzschean superman of the unfettered will but rather through the will, to *destroy the self* which is at the core of every human being. The theme of the search for the single, transcendent truth is found in the mystical renunciation of this world. Bay's elitest and alienated attitude nurtured by his father's friends—William Sturges Bigelow and Henry Adams—caused him to join what J.C. Levenson has called an "arrière-garde" for literature. His whole life was taken up with "a metaphysical pursuit of *the will,* a poetic drama in the line of orthodox Puritan thought refined by Emersonian neo-Platonism and the Buddhist strain in Schopenhauer." Levenson claims that both Bay and T.S. Eliot were, with varying degrees of success, part of the school of Henry Adams and that although Bay was a failure as a poet who couldn't break with the genteel tradition, he and his contemporaries anticipated the poetic revolution:

> When George Cabot Lodge uttered his second-hand convictions on the degradation of modern society, the failure of the American man, or the need for art to be bad in order to succeed, the Adamsish phrases make the older man seem to have been a corrupter of youth. If there was to have been a school of Henry Adams, it died out because the chief pupil was overwhelmed by the teacher. A weak poet embalms the influences which shape his work; it takes a strong one to keep a tradition alive. How much so may be seen in the case of T.S. Eliot, who, even in his first volume, *Prufrock*, gave a far more vital extension to Adams' achievement than Lodge ever did.[265] It is, of course, obvious that Eliot was a far stronger and more original poet than George Cabot Lodge. But, in fairness to Lodge, it should be added that if he and his contemporaries failed to escape a poetic genteel tradition, their work anticipated the poetic revolution that was accomplished by Eliot and his generation.[266]

John Crowley, in *The New York Review of Books* of March 24, 1912,

---

[265] J.C. Levenson, *The Mind and Art of Henry Adams*, (Stanford, CA: Stanford University Press, 1957).
[266] John Crowley, *George Cabot Lodge*, (Boston: Twayne Publishers, 1976), 128. See more on Lodge's legacy 274-277.

called Lodge "a New England Swinburne." For Howard Mumford Jones, the Harvard poets represented "a poetic renaissance which has been either forgotten or underestimated." Although Jones focused on Moody and Santayana, his generalizations hold for Lodge; "For them... all the primary assumptions had collapsed. Heirs to a Christian tradition without Christian belief and of a cultural tradition without any central mytho-poetic core, they lived in a universe relentlessly eroded by the advancement of natural sciences."[267]

Jones' views contrast sharply with Eliot's remark on the state of poetry at the beginning of his career: "I do not think it too sweeping to say, that there was no poet, in either country [England or the United States], who could have been of use to a beginner in 1908.... The question was still: where do we go from Swinburne? And the answer appeared to be, nowhere." Likewise, in his review of *The Life of George Cabot Lodge*, Edmund Wilson said of Bay: "One cannot say he was a bad poet: he was hardly a poet at all—though he did some service to poetry in rescuing the work of Stickney." Speaking of Adams' irony or "doubt" about Lodge's poetry and the justification of the element of violence in Greek tragedy, Wilson says:

> The better informed and the more accomplished the critic may be, who reads *Herakles* for the first time, knowing nothing of the author, the more disconcerted he is likely to be reading it a second time. His first doubts of the poet's knowledge or merits will be followed by doubts of his own.... This double-edged doubt, so characteristic of Adams—the doubt that peeled the gilt off the Gilded Age yet despaired of Adams' strength to stand up to it, the doubt which, in envying the faith that had erected the cathedral at Chartres, yet found in the weakness of the church's foundations a symbol for its own painful fears—this doubt is all through the life of Lodge, the last of Adams' published books. One feels that he dislikes Lodge's poetry. He would like to see something in it; but he shrinks—from what?—from finding in the younger man the reflection of his own sterility or from the disquieting possibility that Lodge may have really been a poet and hence have lived in some richer way than Adams had ever known? He wants to think that Lodge was a nonconformist as he imagines himself to have been; yet he meets in him all the old round of the life-cycle of people from Boston, of people like oneself; and he cannot repress a shiver. We people all come to

[267] Howard Mumford Jones, *The Bright Medusa*, (Urbana: University of Illinois Press, 1952), 47-64.

> nothing—not, of course, that we aren't better than the others.... With all this, there is even here that candor in dubiety and impotence which has the accents of a kind of strength; and the rare sensitive-cynical Adams who is himself a kind of poet, as it were, signs the little memoir... as a solitary writer weaving secret enchantments at night like a drug merchant or a magician....[268]

Van Wyck Brooks retorts:

> It is no surprise that a poet like George Cabot Lodge, devoted to Swinburne and rooted in a 'genteel' poetic tradition, proved to be irrelevant to the progenitors of modernist poetry. American poetry from 1885 to 1912 has been singularly neglected. The usefulness of reviving minor poets like Lodge has been acknowledged even by Eliot, who admitted that "we can touch the life of great works of literature of any age all the better if we know something of the less."

Although Bay never achieved a major reputation in his lifetime, his six volumes of poetry and verse drama (publshed between 1898 and 1909) elicited favorable reviews in some quarters, and he was well-enough respected to be elected to the National Institute of Arts and Letters in 1908. John Crowley, in the preface to his doctoral thesis about the poet, disputed the critics' "stifling atmosphere" theory and went a bit further about the importance of Bay. He believed that Bay's fiction, and in particular his conception of the modern wasteland, foreshadowed modernism. Lodge's poetry followed the tradition of transcendentalism and saw in the late poems an extension of Emerson's "godlike self."

> The first step toward a fair estimate of Lodge must be to bring his best work back into print.... Lodge's volumes are casebooks of the confusion and desperate experimentation which characterize a generation of poets who sensed the bankruptcy of the poetic tradition they had inherited but who lacked the genius to forge a new one. Lodge's work also bears on such areas as the vogue of muscular Christianity as apotheosized in Roosevelt's "strenuous life," the impact of comparative anthropology and scientific naturalism on the mythic consciousness of poets since 1900, the curious reputation of Whitman in the period, the dissemination of Nietzschean thought in America, and the validity of the critical cliché that has pre-

---

[268] Edmund Wilson, ed., *The Shock of Recognition: The Development of Literature In the United States Recorded By the Men Who Made It* (Garden City, NY: Doubleday, 1943).

vailed from Brooks to Ziff of the "stifling atmosphere" of the American fin de siècle. Finally, Lodge's fiction merits consideration in terms both of the tradition of American novels of manners from Wharton to Fitzgerald, and the development of American naturalism from Norris (whom Lodge so remarkably resembles) to Dreiser.[269]

The poetry of George Cabot Lodge has suffered unwarranted neglect.... Precisely because it was transitional between "Victorian" and "modern" poetry, Lodge's work was lost in the shifting winds of taste that characterized his age. This biography attempts to give a definitive account of Lodge's life in order to illuminate the achievement of his poetry. In the past Lodge's career has been used as evidence for the "stifling atmosphere" theory, a cultural thesis by which Lodge and his Harvard contemporaries have been cast as passive victims of a materialistic society. By stressing the familial and personal factors in Lodge's career, this biography places the cultural factors in proper perspective. Because by the terms of the "stifling atmosphere" theory, Lodge had to be viewed as a failure, the genuine success of his best work has been obscured. Although not a major figure, George Cabot Lodge deserves a place among the "considerable" American poets.[270]

***

On August 24, from East Point, the Senator made small corrections to *The Life of George Cabot Lodge* but otherwise left it intact. "I cannot find words to tell you how much I like it—No one else could have done it or given such an analysis of his character and his thought. It is the monument of all others which I should wish to see raised to his memory and I am very, very grateful."[271] Two days later, Nannie wrote to Henry Adams to say how deeply satisfying it was for her to be reading his biography of the poet on the day Bay had died. Women of this set taught their children the importance of an international education. Imagine a grandmother of today reading "The History of Egypt," "Ancient Rhodes," or "The Land of the Hittites," to her five, seven, and eight year old grandchildren![272]

Dear Brother,

It seems very fitting that I should be able to read your Life of Bay on August

[269] Crowley, *George Cabot Lodge.*

[270] John W. Crowley, *George Cabot Lodge* (Syracuse, NY: Twayne Publishers, Syracuse University, 1976), 127-128.

[271] See appendix.

[272] Nannie wrote Adams from East Point, in late October of 1910, news of their friends and that five-year-old Helena "talks politics a good deal with great earnestness."

21—the day he left us—This is to thank you for it and to tell you how much I value your work and your estimate of him. Nothing gave him more joy than the feeling that you understood him and knew what his life meant and what his thoughts were and I am glad you should have been willing to tell the world so and to give your time and thoughts to it all so splendidly—

Your letter of July 24th was welcome and showed that all was going as you most liked-all your friends either mad or dying or in sanatoriums, or in some other way completely incapacitated and thrown out. It is certainly in chosen conditions that the most satisfaction lies, for then one need no longer pretend nor keep up *appearances* and the temptation to scream and make an awful fuss is very strong at times. I am glad Mrs. Cameron is very near at any rate for she is a real companion and help. We are all well.... What can I tell you?... John is fishing and dealing in hieroglyphics. In the evening, I read aloud, "The History of Egypt," "Ancient Rhodes," "The Land of the Hittites" and we get through a good deal in a plodding way. Little Constance [Constance's daughter] is cheering us now and Lucy Stickney was with us for a week. Otherwise we have had no visitors. Bessy and the children are coming Sept. 20 and they will find Veto, a dachshund of the darlingest description....

Goodbye dear Brother. Give my love to all who want it, with lots for yourself.

Sister Anne

On September 4th, Adams wrote the Senator saying how writing the biography had raised his estimate of Bay's poems, their quality and range, vigor, passion, thought and dramatic power.[273] Adams conveyed to the Senator his delight that the Senator's letter to Dokko describing the death could be included. Happily, for posterity's sake, the Senator did not share Bessy's queasiness about privacy. Adams comes down firmly on the side of intimacy—that "biographies that are not intimate are no biographies at all. We cannot write about ourselves as though we were lumps of clay, though we mostly are...."

On October 13, Bessy wrote to Henry Adams of the "grandeur" of his writing style and speaks of the biography as a "monument." Then she refers to going against his wishes, withdrawing publication rights to personal passages, saying that the children (or great-grandchildren) could do it when she was dead.[274]

Dear dear Uncle Henry,

I wish it was possible for me to make you realize all the love and

---

[273] See appendix.

[274] Thankfully, therefore, I have her blessing.

gratitude that is in me as I write to you. I have read *The Life* all through for the third time and the marvelous grandeur of your style and thought strikes me more every time. I can never make you understand what it is to me to have this monument to Bay—especially when I think how he would have felt about it. Feeling as I do it is peculiarly painful to me to have gone against your wishes about so many of my letters. You will forgive me I know and though it will disappoint you—but more and more so I get my balance—I see the impossibility of publishing the personal passages. The children can do it when I am dead if they want to. Your sweetness about me touched me deeply as how should it not? We heard you were coming back next month. Will you let us know if this is true and if you prefer to have the manuscript sent back or kept til you come? I hope you are coming soon for I need you so much and love you so dearly.

Bessy

Bessy, in a letter to Adams a few days later, apologized for making him cut the love letters, showing iron determination clothed in modesty and kindness. It was a blow to him. Even as she shrivels up the manuscript, depriving it of any emotion, she also made plain what the family always said about her relationship with Adams: "She couldn't have gotten through it without him"; indeed, the fact that most of her letters were in the Adams collection and not the Lodge papers shows that he was the father she never had and belonged to him more deeply than she ever did to the Lodges or the Frelinghuysens:

October 17, 1910
Dearest Uncle Henry,
By the time you receive this, you may have read *The Life* & seen for yourself how beautiful it is—now that you can read it in a more detached way. **I know how trying it must have been to you to cut out my letters**—how hard compromises at certain times are—& I want to thank you again for your unfailing kindness & great consideration to me. I appreciate it more than you have any idea of & I can never tell you how much I have needed it & what it has meant to me. Perhaps some day you will realize how much cause I have to be grateful and devoted to you. The Life has burst upon me fresh with its great distinction & breadth. You have given it such majesty, done it in a way that only

you are master of. It must be a satisfaction to think of Bay's gratitude if he could know. That must recompense you for the many hours of work & the annoyance caused by my inconsistencies. I feel more sorry to have bothered you than I can say & I have no excuse excepting that at times the complications of life, the conflicting interests to be reconciled are too much for me.

Bessy

On October 25, Bessy, evidently after consulting Nannie, decided that Adams would have to cut one of the letters to Marjorie Nott where Bay refers to his ill health.[275] Interestingly, if Bay could have chosen a way to die, she felt he would have chosen his—"so sudden and surprising" and "with all his great faculties."

Nahant

Dearest Uncle Henry,

Now that we hear you are postponing your return, we suppose that you will prefer to have the manuscript returned to you. Some of the letters to me that I have left, you may not care to keep—without the others. Of course, I leave that to you but the very personal ones I could not publish. We feel strongly the preference Bay would have had not to have his bad health dwelt upon. He was averse to speaking of it and if he could have chosen a form of death I think he would have perhaps have chosen his—so sudden and surprising and yet with all his great faculties aware of the "adventure"—and written in his strength. **Mrs. Lodge and I both feel that his second letter to Marjorie had better be left out—after her mark on the first page. It was written in a temporary depression and was not indicative of his general state of mind. He disliked any appearance of complaining** and really was so far above the world that he was seldom affected by the praise or blame. I can't tell you how badly I feel that you should be called upon to do over any of your beautiful work. I am so overcome by the whole *Life* and I know Bay would be so glad could he know of it that it seems ungrateful to ask for any change but just because it is so superb Mrs. Lodge and I feel that there should not be the slightest blemish—and such we feel any over-emphasis of his failing health to be. I wish you were to come back soon. Washington is always pretty empty without you.

A great deal of love from Bessy.

---

[275] See letter of July 8, 1909, 240-241.

P.S. I wish I could express to you how sad I feel at the changes I ask in your beautiful work.

In late November, 1910, Henry Adams wrote of the convention dispute, and of Bay:

...It was all sad and sordid,...worse than poor Henry James' actual condition, or than the political demise of my friends, Roosevelt and Lodge and the rest. They are gone, as Bay Lodge wrote in his best sonnet—'Let us go hence lest dreadfully we die,-—before we get fairly buried.' What troubles me most is that you and I so obviously made the world which reflects so exactly our manner of thought and that we are responsible for it; which is enough to damn the archangels forever and ever.... Mrs. Wharton, Mrs. Cameron, Sturgis Bigelow and I—all chattering to keep the .... courage up.... You can imagine my brother Brooks on the elections, reproving me for my dark views, and telling me that no doubt the Republican Party is done, and Theodore with it, and Cabot is feeble-minded and society dead and rotten ....

In 1911, Nannie wrote to her friend Corinne Roosevelt Robinson a revealing letter about her lack of interest in life, her powerful role as wife, the Senator's strength in adversity and his role as father—supportive but not sympathetic. She refers to the Senator's guilt over not using Bay more as his secretary and the difficulty the Senator faced at the convention, the difficult task of getting Taft nominated for president over his best friend, Roosevelt. After Nannie's death four years later, when the Democrats swept into power, the Senator would not be nearly so adept in politics, so she is wrong in her conclusion that he would be a success without her:

1765 Massachusetts Ave.
January 27, 1911
Darling Corinne,
You always understand & say the right & true thing, although in this case, you exaggerate any part I may have played in Cabot's career. He is a man who would always have worked & succeeded & the most that can be said for me is that I have understood his requirements & have not stood in the way of his success. He is now well and happy in the result & grateful to his many devoted friends. I never saw anything more beautiful than the disinterested & absolutely honest work which

was done for him. Of course, he had his moments of agony after it was over, when he thought of Bay & what his sympathy would have meant, & all the time it was going on too when Bay would have given him such splendid help & encouragement. And that made us all feel all along how little it or anything this world could give was worth to us now—But thank Heaven Cabot has the quality of absorption in whatever he is doing & the power "to contend to the uttermost for his life's set prize," & so he stayed in to win or lose, but in any case, to do his best. He was not excited or overwrought after the very first & so he is not now tired.... He is well too & I am sure that is a help to courage and composure—If I could feel well, **perhaps I could really live again; as it is I only exist**.

Henry James.
1912.

Chapter 7

Paris, 1912

Your single beautiful presence, that immensity of nothing!

—Henry James

En pouvoir des beaux-parents.

—Edith Wharton

Bessy was a beautiful thirty-six-year-old widow when, in October 1912, she stopped in England on her way to Paris to lunch with Henry James and Edith Wharton at Lamb House. Wharton had convinced Bessy to move to Paris and James had extended an encouraging hand, inviting her to visit him in England along the way. She had made up her mind to follow the wishes of her husband, Bay, who had wanted his children to grow up internationally. They had both felt that being educated in France for three or four years was important though she would be going against the wishes of her powerful father-in-law, the Senator. Tired of being bullied, overwhelmed by the stifling atmosphere in Washington, D.C., and Nahant, always under the influence of the doting grandparents, she succumbed to Wharton's urgings.

The Lodges' relationship to James was a family affair, since George Abbot James, James' cousin, was Senator Lodge's brother-in-law, having married Lillie Lodge, the Senator's older sister. "Jabber James," as the family called him, and his cousin Henry maintained a long correspondence from 1870 to World War I. Henry James addressed Bessy as Mrs. Bay rather than Mrs. Lodge, for a number of reasons. He was a friend but at that time it was rare for friends of the opposite sex to call one another by their first names. Formality was observed but they enjoyed playing with the taboo. (Adams called John Hay "Light and Liver," for example.) Interestingly, Adams addressed Bessy by her real name and was as close as anyone could come to being a father to her. Nicknames were determined by force of character, and for James, and indeed, for everyone, Bessy was so closely identified with her overpowering husband, Bay—a force of nature—that her identity as his wife was inseparable from her persona.

> September 27, 1912
> *My Dear Mrs. Bay,*
> How shall I tell you what a charming pleasure it is to receive your gentle note?—To find it nestled in the heart of my dear old GAJ's large letter even as the very corolla (is that what the thing is called?) of that generous flower. It brings back to me those life-saving afternoons on the Nahant verandahs when you came across to tea and peopled to us for the time by *your single beautiful presence, that immensity of nothing!* Best boon of all is your intimation of your prospect of really reaching at no distant date this convenient side of the world. You must absolutely celebrate that event when it takes place, by coming to see me here as soon as possible thereafter. I am only just on a small sweet loop-line, the tiniest bit off your most appointed track. We get on to Dover so easily that breakfasting at this house at the ordinary hour we are (quite magically) in Paris by about five o'clock and so the other way around.
>
> I think ever so rememberingly of your exquisite, appealing children, and tell myself what a much mixed savour they must give your cup. Little fear for you of that's not always tasting—! I send them my earnest blessing and am yours, dear Mrs. Bay, all faithfully,
>
> *Henry James*[276]

After lunching with James and Wharton, Bessy and the children crossed the English Channel and took the train into Paris. Walter Van Renssalaer Berry, an international lawyer, active in Europe and the Middle East and Wharton's best friend, helped to pick them up at the station. Walter took the children with him while Bessy rode in Edith's car. In 1992 I spoke with my Great Aunt Helena, Bessy's daughter, about the day eighty years earlier, when she was six: "Everyone told me how lovely the Place de la Concorde was, I thought it would have all been done up in pink and blue bows. Naturally, I was *very* disappointed," she said with a laugh that rose very high and then descended, known in French as a *ris perlé*. "It was gossamer, un espace du matin," Helena added, "don't touch it," as if in speaking of it, the magic would somehow disappear.[277]

---

[276] Lodge Collection, MHS.
[277] "Un espace du matin" is a brief interlude.

The horse chestnut trees in autumn, having shed their white summer blossoms, gave forth the fruit. A spray of large glossy brown nuts carpeted the ground. Bessy had taken the apartment at 55 ave Marceau, in the 8th arrondisement, in the same building in which her dead husband had spent his post-graduate years in the late 1890s. The building near the childrens' school made the corner at the rue Bassano and faced west, close to the American Cathedral of Paris—a new neighborhood circa 1900 around the Etoile favored by American expatriates.

Edith Wharton described Bessy Lodge as a "marsupial seraph" with her three children around her. Henry Cabot Lodge, Bessy's son and the Senator's grandson, was ten in 1912. In his autobiography, he wrote:

> Edith Wharton, the novelist, was a most loyal and devoted friend to both my father and mother. My father's death had left my mother with three small children of whom I was the oldest. In 1912 she decided to take us to Paris so that we could learn a foreign language—a decision which, although I did not like it at the time—has stood me in good stead all my life. It was Mrs. Wharton who made all the numerous arrangements—finding an apartment (55 ave. Marceau), a good school, domestic help, and putting my mother in touch with all of Mrs. Wharton's many French friends. The school which I attended in Paris from 1912-1914 was ahead of its time in France, with respect to physical exercise and recreation. But by American standards we were required to work very hard—all morning and all afternoon until suppertime, except for a thirty minute airing in the park. It really pressed me and taught me how to concentrate.
>
> Mrs. Wharton lived in a magnificent eighteenth century apartment on the rue de Varenne with a perfect staff. Later she gave this up and had two enchanting houses, one at St. Brice outside of Paris and, for the winter months, at Hyeres, a most picturesque onetime medieval convent—Sainte Claire—with terraced gardens high up overlooking the Mediterranean.[278]

Bessy was reserved but not shy and men played a part in her peaceful and reclusive world. There was a limited bank account but always enough for a valet, a cook and a chambermaid, in addition to various tutors for the children. Edith Wharton's friend, Walter Berry, acted as her intermediary in paying her bills "with the tradesmen, you see dear," Aunt Helena told me, so that, even though the money was hers

[278] Lodge, *The Storm Has Many Eyes*, 22-23.

she never actually had to touch it. Edith arranged for her to meet one of the outstanding young bachelors in Paris—Jean du Breuil de St. Germain—who had accompanied Edith and Edith's friend Rosa Fitz-James on a motor trip to Spain. Jean was one of the founders of the French-American Chamber of Commerce in Paris. Helena had only a blurred memory of him—"a big, tall, handsome Frenchman." What stands out is his unusual political inclination—he was an advocate of the education of women, women's suffrage, and charitable causes. He was therefore something of an anomaly in French society. Bessy, born into a family devoted to public service, was evidently drawn to his activist spirit. After having given birth to three children in four years, she was a firm advocate of birth control.

During Bessy and her childrens' Paris stay between 1912 and 1914, du Brueil became a regular visitor. He never could have aroused the response in her that Bay did—no one could ever have replaced Bay—but she and du Breuil were "madly in love." Still they would never have married, according to Helena, and it is unlikely that their passion was ever consummated.[279] "She wouldn't have wanted to be dominated by a Frenchman. Nobody could have dominated her the way Bay had!" But Jean was a man after her own heart and unlike Bay, committed to social activism. Bessy would like to have stayed in France but re-marriage would have been a threat to the future of the family. After Bay's death, Bessy's power base was her children but without her husband, she found her rights threatened.

Her father-in-law, the Senator—self-centered and spoiled as he was —"was terrified" of Bessy's new life, according to the family—terrified of the possibility of her re-marrying, becoming pregnant and the Lodge heirs becoming French Catholic.

For the Senator, the idea that his grandchildren would be brought up by a Roman Catholic French aristocrat would have been intolerable as was the possibility that Bessy might have had more children. She was young and beautiful and if she had had children, his grandchildren would have been brought up in a French household. Without the vote, which women were not granted in France until 1940, she would have had no influence whatsoever and she would have been entirely ruled by her new husband. What was worse, he was a divorcé, which was

---

[279] According to my Uncle Harry, it wasn't consummated. "No, not Gammy." Helena's cryptic remark underscores the ambiguity: "People behaved in every kind of way just as they do now but they envisaged it all quite differently."

extremely rare in the French upper classes; even her maiden aunts did not approve of the match. But she was unquestionably very much in love—in love in the sense of an *amitié amoureuse*.

At Christmas that first year in Paris, the Senator wrote meaningfully to his grandson, Henry Cabot Lodge. The Senator feared that Cabot, like Bay, who had become so fond of Europe, might lose his American roots. In this letter making his grandson aware of his ancestry, the Senator claimed that greatness rested with knowledge, that knowledge was power. By reminding Cabot that his, the Senator's, library would one day be his, he was informing Cabot of his family duty. The library is a metaphor for the ancestral title conferred on the heir.

Henry Cabot Lodge, seated, ten; John, nine, at left; and Helena, seven.

I have been spending much of my holiday in my library arranging my books, not reading but just looking them over and playing with them. I hope you will like to do this same thing for all these books will be yours some day & my dearest wish is that you should love them & care for them as I do. I trust you will not only want to keep them but will be able to keep them for they make a very large family and need a very large house to shelter them. You will have to work hard & earn a good income in order to do so & hard work is the best thing for us all. I want you to keep these books, you see, because they belonged to your ancestors as well as to me. I will tell you whose books are in the library so that you may know & I will make a little table which you can understand.

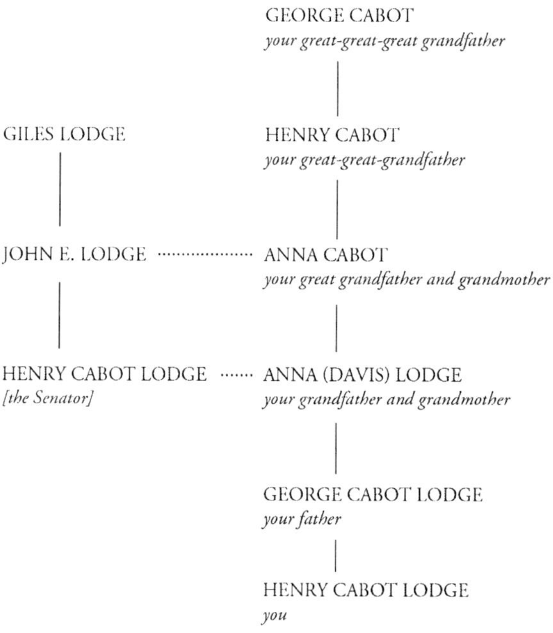

All those people from whom you are descended have books in this library—George Cabot and my father John Lodge had a great many. Then you will find too in this library a few books that belonged to your grandmother's father Admiral Davis and those you must especially value for he was one of the finest characters I have ever known. He was a distinguished naval officer and won two great fleet actions in the Civil War. He was an eminent man of science—a scholar of wide reading and a lover of books. Above all, he was a brave, high-minded gentleman.

"Integer vitae, scelerisque purus?"[280] Sometime you will know what those familiar Latin words mean but now **your mother can translate** them to you. Then your great-grandfather Davis was besides full of fun and humor and everybody loved him as you would if he were only alive with us now.... I had rather have you like your great-grandfather Davis than anyone else and so you must prize his books. The library has many rare books but it is not the library of a collector. It is a library gathered by people who liked to read. I have read most of the books in it that are not books of reference and can be read. I have read many books because it was necessary to my work and many many more which have interested and instructed and delighted and amused me but that which never wearies or passes you will find in the great works of the imagination. Poetry comes first for the great poetry is the highest work of the human intellect. But in the library you will find many friends—men and women I mean. Some of them the most real, never lived at all and live forever. I want you to have all these friends. They will never desert you and you will care for them more and more as you grow older. Some of these people were created by the great poets—Homer created a great many—Achilles and Hector are two of them. You will come to know them well. I like Hector best although he was slain by Achilles. But best of all Homer's men is Odysseus and the story of his wanderings. The Odyssey is one of the finest—I think the finest—story ever written.... Then there are Hamlet and Falstaff and a whole world of men and women, the creations of Shakespeare, the greatest genius the world has ever seen. Faust is another great figure but one never quite feels as if he were a friend. Nor can you be friends with the awful figures in Dante's Inferno or the Angelic Ones in his Paradise but his Divine Comedy is one of the great books of the world of which you will never tire. But you will make warm friends with the Don Quixote and Sancho Panza of Cervantes.... There is Dickens. He has created a whole world of people.... I love them all. You must get someone to take you to see the statue of Alexandre Dumas. On the back is seated a figure of a very gallant gentleman named d'Artagnan. He is a fine figure.... Then there are the real men who lived in history but who had such genius that they made themselves live in the books they wrote all about themselves—the great autobiographers. You will read them later—St. Augustine and Rousseau and Samuel Pepys and Dr. Johnson and Benjamin Franklin

[280] Horace, Ode 1:22, "Integer vitae, scelerisque purus" might be translated, aphoristically, as "upright in life; free of sin." The sentence from the ode reads, "The man who is upright in life and free of sin, has no need of moorish spears or a bow...."

> and George Borrow and Dumas... they all live here among their books which I hope you will learn to know and love them all. And when you read of them in these same books I hope that you will feel the pleasure which I now feel from knowing that the eyes now long closed, the eyes of those who loved me rested on these same pages. You will feel the same way I feel now and like to think that the eyes of those from whom you descended and of your grandfather and grandmother who love you dearly saw those same books and found in them the same undying friendships as you have found. Your "Gammuzzy" sends her dearest love and was delighted with your plant and still more by your thinking of her. Give our bestest love to your mother and John and Helena.
>
> Ever my beloved boy
> Your loving grandfather
> *H.C. Lodge*[281]

Meanwhile, Bessy was ensuring that her son Cabot would have an international education. Edith Wharton drew Bessy into her world, for Bessy was one of Wharton's few intimate female friends and a solace to her in the year prior to her divorce from her husband, Teddy.[282] In 1885, at twenty-three, the then Edith Newbold Jones, from a wealthy New York family often associated with the phrase "keeping up with the Joneses," had married Edward Robbins Wharton, twelve years her senior, from a well-established Boston family. Throughout their marriage and particularly as her success grew, Teddy became increasingly depressed and was hospitalized in 1912. Wharton was forty in 1905 when the twenty-three-year-old Percy Lubbock, author of *Portrait of Edith Wharton*, described his first encounter with Wharton which came as a result of his "devouring" *The House of Mirth*; his description of Paris of that time is also useful because it puts into perspective the Paul Bourgets, Bay and Bessy, and other friends.

> In talk Edith always considered the interlocutor her equal. It was the finest characteristic of her wholly civilized politeness, but on that very account, she postulated in me a range of cultures which I did not possess and I often missed the point of her rich play of allusions.... Who shall drop in to tea on a winter's evening, when the curtains are drawn and the silence of the Faubourg isolates us again in our fortress? ...this

---

[281] The Senator's namesake would inherit the Senator's library.

[282] Percy Lubbock, in his classic *Portrait of Edith Wharton*, wrote meaningfully about Edith and her circle, including Bessy. See appendix.

> is the time for a friend or two of the inner circle ...a circle naturally small, but it was also elastic—French chiefly, and then chiefly American, and English, as might happen....Their voices speak as I listen; I should know that voice anywhere, with its comfortable splutter and chuckle, and that with its low penetrating comment, and that with its suave authority; and how easily I see that face of clever experience, that of fine intelligence, that of **rare and gleaming beauty** [Bessy]: men and women, older and younger, mostly younger and mostly men.

Bessy, like Lubbock, also felt a little at a loss for Wharton's "rich play of allusions." Later in life, Bessy was to feel "her inexhaustible and delicate kindness, understanding, pity and mercy."[283]

In this letter from her house at 53 rue de Varenne, in the 7th arrondissement, she wrote Bessy early on her arrival in 1912:

> What a darling Bessy you are to have written me such a letter! But your intuition must have told you how much I need to feel a little warmth near me just now, & how every sign of affection from my friends touches & helps me.I loved Bay with all my soul. He is always with me, & always will be. I can't separate you and him in my thoughts, & having you here brings him so much nearer that I always feel when we're together that I'm with both of you—as I am!—so you see what you're doing for me. A ce soir, dear Edith.

Henry Adams, then seventy-four, was also living in Paris in 1912, and, always charmingly lugubrious, he corresponded with Henry James, his contemporary a few years younger, about being the "lone survivors." James wrote March 24, 1914: "...I still find my consciousness interesting—under cultivation of the interest. Cultivate it with me, dear Henry—that's what I hoped to make you do: to cultivate yours for all that it has in common with mine." Bay and Bessy's generation called Adams "Uncle Henry." Elizabeth Cameron, visited Adams with her daughter, Martha. The children—Martha, Cabot, John, Helena—were mad for their "Dordy." In October 1913, the Senator wrote Henry in Paris about his obsession with getting the grandchildren home again:

> East Point
> Nahant

---

[283] Lubbock, 97-98.

Bessy in 1912.

October 30, 1913
Dear Henry,
It is five weeks tomorrow since I suddenly went to the surgeon's table after a life of practically unbroken health. They tell me I am a star patient and have recovered like a young man better than most young men but they have not allowed me to attend to any business or answer any letters even by dictation. So this is my first letter. But I had to write you & thank you for your letter which meant so much to me. I am glad you liked my "memories" [*Early Memories*]. What I said of you was only a truthful utterance of my sense of indebtedness expressed with great reserve. As one draws to the end of the journey, the doubts are plentiful enough. I do not know that I have done any good. I do not think I have done much harm and I have had a busy, occupied and interesting life of it on the whole. But I have never dreamed of suggesting a word in a wilderness I do not understand to anyone else.

I am rejoiced that you are so well. I hope soon we shall meet.... **The one longing of my life is to see those grandchildren**. I have been forbidden newspapers or any thoughts of events or business so that I can tell you nothing except that Nannie and I both send a great deal of love and I am always yours,

H.C. Lodge[284]

In the winter of 1913, the Senator threatened to withdraw Bessy's allowance, an action his wife Nannie never allowed him to take. "His bark was worse than his bite, you see," Helena remarked with a little laugh. Courageously, Bessy publicly responded to her father-in-law cheerfully, calling him by his nickname. "Well, Pinky, you just tell me when you're going to do it and I'll make the arrangements" in a level and affable—but what must have been to the Senator, annoyingly immovable—way.

Privately, the letters between Elizabeth and Adams that winter indicate that Bessy's helplessness was driving her into a depression. She and Bessy became close friends and Elizabeth relates how tied the Senator had made Bessy feel with "brutal" letters about stopping her allowance and how he treated her like a governess to his grandchildren. In this letter from Cameron to Adams, in which we note that her nickname for Adams is a shortened version of the children's (also short for "adorable"), we see a bit of gossip about the fray between Bessy and the Senator.

---

[284] Adams, *Letters*.

December 4, 1913
6 Square du Bois de Boulogne
Dear Dor,
Bessy is beautiful but sad and is tied by the heels by Cabot [the Senator] who writes brutal letters when he feels like it, and threatens her with the stoppage of allowance. Bessy is good, and wants to please him & to be dutiful, but the dependence & the fact that he is *able* to threaten her galls her terribly. Cabot does not realize that she is solely responsible for herself and the children—he treats her like a nurse or governess for *his* children....

Yrs. Ever,
E.C.

Later that winter Cameron communicated to her "Dor" the new methods of manipulation that she suspected the Senator was using to try to get Bessy to return to America. First he tried the stick—threatening the withdrawal of her allowance. He never did so. But neither did she have any choice about returning to America. Second, the Senator tried the carrot of affection tied up with the stick of the threat of her never returning again to Europe; he hinted she could live with him, an eventuality, Mrs. Cameron confides, that would not work at all. Bessy never complained of her plight to anyone but shouldered her irritation without drama.

December 11, 1913
6 Square du Bois de Boulogne
Dear Dor,
I saw Bessy yesterday looking sad & depressed, I thought. I begin to suspect that her "in-laws" weigh heavily upon her, for Cabot wrote her an affectionate letter telling her how glad he is that she is coming home & adding that they will never be parted again. I wonder if he thinks that Bessy married *him*? It was I who connected the letter with the depression—not she—She always speaks of them with affection....

In this letter from Elizabeth to Adams, she tells of Bessy's beauty being noticed at the opera, has a few jealous words about Wharton, and makes the wise observation that those who have the encouragement of their friends tend to be the most successful.

January 23, 1914
My Dear Dor,

> ...Bessy and I dined together and went to the Palais Royale Farce two nights ago. **Bessy's beauty was almost startling, and she attracted attention**. She is rejoiced—so am I—that Edith is back. Yesterday I took Lady Randolph Churchill over to the rue de Varenne. There had been a séance at the Académie and Edith's salon was filled with litérateurs—the Bourgets, of course, & the other lights with Madame de Fitz-James & myself thrown in to preserve an equilibrium. What has she to make her prominent? I don't find charm, nor intelligence beyond a sort of worldly shrewdness—I overheard her say to a Frenchman who was lauding Hyde—"Il n'arrivera pas parce qu'il n'est pas appuyé par ses compatriots" which is true enough....[285]
>
> Goodbye dear Dor, Yrs. Ever,
> *E.C.*

In the summers, Bessy joined her friends in Normandy—the first summer in Le Touquet, the second in Dieppe with its Norman gingerbread houses, huge cliffs, "les falaises," bordering the coast. Dieppe was

[285] "He'll never get ahead because he is not encouraged by his friends."

the first bathing resort, before Deauville and Trouville. It was William the Conqueror's staging ground for his invasion of England. Mme. Greffuhle, Proust's friend, summered there along with the painter Jacques Emile Blanche, Edith Wharton, Minnie and Paul Bourget, and other artists and writers. Even in the summer of 1914, the air exuded peace and quiet—the kind of calm Bessy loved, gathered together with her three children, then aged twelve, eleven, and nine.

In August 1914, Senator and Mrs. Lodge, their daughter Constance and son-in-law Augustus Gardner, were vacationing in London when war broke out between France and Germany. Bessy and the children were in Dieppe when the Germans invaded Belgium. The Senator was deeply worried about his adored heir, Cabot, and still intent on not allowing Bessy to do anything so foolish as to marry a Frenchman. Cabot wrote in his autobiography:

> When the "guns of August" started firing in 1914, we were in Dieppe on the English Channel. In our household were a much loved man—Emile, by name—who was a general handyman and a companion for my brother and me, and his sister Angèle, who cooked superlatively. I can remember the newspaper stories reporting the Austrian ultimatum to Serbia, soon to be followed by the beating of the drums at every French village, announcing that general mobilization was underway. The streets of Dieppe were lined with farewell scenes as soldiers left—including Emile —never to return. In the village square, farm horses were being assembled for use by the army, each horse with a number branded on his hoof so that he might be returned to his owner when the war was over!
>
> My grandfather and grandmother were in England and anxious about us. One morning I saw a pair of tan shoes outside the door of the spare guest room which, I was told, belonged to my Uncle Gussie—Congressman Augustus P. Gardner who had married my Aunt Constance. He organized automobiles and gasoline and we drove to Le Havre where we embarked on a night crossing to Southampton, England.
>
> We had a few days there before leaving for home. On one of those days my mother took me with her to Rye, the south English town where Henry James lived. Although born an American, he had, at the end of his life, become a naturalized Englishman because of his strong feelings about the war. We sat in a large brick-walled garden containing many mulberry trees. Standing by itself in the middle of the garden was

> a one-room structure—a writing room or library. Henry James seemed to me to have an elaborate style of speech, as though he were looking for the right word. Finding the conversation rather heavy I wandered about the garden eating mulberries.[286]

On Aug 2, 1914, Elizabeth Cameron gives a valuable account of the mood at the time, writing to Dor, who was in Paris, of the panic and stampede from Switzerland to England.

> The trams crowded to literally standing room only—if that. Luggage left behind to make room for passengers in the luggage van. No through trains guaranteed. Two days ago I engaged places for this afternoon through to Calais… the banks cash no cheques…. Today all the male Swiss porters, waiters, managers, drivers, etc. leave to be registered in Berne. If they do not come back, we shall be a community of women, carrying our own trunks and foraging for zwieback. We have written to London to have money sent to us, and if worse comes to worst we can get down to Italy and possibly up through France that way….

On August 3, 1914, Bessy wrote to Henry Adams in Paris about her hopes that her visiting Aunt Lucy (Frelinghuysen) would be able to find passage to England; clearly Bessy intended to stay in France. When she speaks of the heart-breaking scenes of leave-taking, one wonders if she said goodbye to Jean du Breuil du St. Germain:

> *Dearest Uncle Henry,*
> I wonder how this terrible calamity has affected you or whether you are being bothered by all the men leaving and shops closing up. Aunt Lucy is still with me and much overwrought. I am hoping she will soon be able to go to England but for the present the boats are stopped. It is rather hard to see why. Please thank Miss. Tone for her nice letter. I was so glad to have such a good account of you. Probably your men servants have had to leave as ours have. I hope you have been spared the terrible scenes of leave-taking that I have witnessed. It is too heartbreaking to see these poor innocents go forth to the massacre. At present we have no papers which is very hard. I hope soon to have good news of you.
>
> Always Afftely,
> *Bessy*

---

[286] Lodge, *The Storm Has Many Eyes*, 24. After Dieppe, Bessy returned to see Henry James at Lamb House.

According to her daughter Helena, Bessy adamantly wanted to stay and help Wharton with her war effort—wrapping bandages and organizing women's groups and orphanages. Instead, the Senator, who was ill with diphtheria, sent his son-in-law Gussie Gardner from London to *bring Bessy back*. In a time of war, getting through the French countryside and back to Le Havre was practically impossible.

The meeting at Dieppe with Gussie was unhappy and frigid. Not wanting anyone ruling her life, Bessy greeted him contemptuously "Oh, hello Gussie," she said, looking down and away, weary and resigned. Nevertheless she set to packing her bags. If she had wanted to marry du Breuil she would have defied the Senator. But she saw that it was impossible: the danger to her children in wartime to a courageous woman like Bessy was the least of her worries, for she wanted to help Edith Wharton in an environment in which she could bring up the children freely without the stigma of being treated as if she were a governess. Yet without any financial resources of her own, she was forced to give in to the Senator's wishes.

Bessy, Gussie, and the children prepared to cross the channel for England. At Le Havre, in the rush of the overloaded boat, the three children somehow became separated from the group of two warring adults, the two servants, and the twelve trunks. They were on shore as the gangplank was being pulled away. With her iron will, Bessy somehow managed to convince the captain to delay the departure so that the three children could be loaded onboard. This story also demonstrates how powerful the Senator was, since all the boats were crowded with soldiers and ammunition and all the roads blocked to civilian traffic. Telegrams were neither being sent nor received between France and England. In this valuable letter, Nannie, the Senator's adored wife, still in London, wrote from 21 Carlton Mansions, Cheyne Walk, SW, about the drama of the August escapade to Henry Adams, with humor tinged with a slight sense of superiority:

> September, 1914
> *Dear Brother,*
> We are thankful to hear of you from Miss. Tone & have thought of you constantly. I have been remiss about writing but my hands have been full & I have waited until I could give you really good news of Cabot. He is now distinctly convalescent [from diptheria] after a very painful and trying three weeks or more....
>
> We began last Saturday to be very uneasy about Bessy but could get

> no telegram through to or from her. So Monday night Gussy [sic] went over from Southampton to Havre—no Dieppe boat running. He hired at Havre two taxicabs, filled them with petrol, & by means of passports and papers made his way to Dieppe. There he found Bessy & the children just sitting down to supper, **"comme si de rien n'était."**[287] Lucy Frelinghuysen had gone that morning in a panic, by Dieppe which did send a boat that day. But Bessy had decided there was no danger & had determined not to worry. However she fell to work to pack her twelve trunks & she, Gussy & Mlle. worked most of the night, got passports, photographs & descriptions of all & started Wednesday morning in the two taxis to make the 100 kilos to Havre. They were stopped and examined at every point but thanks to their papers got through well, and arrived in Havre in time for the night boat back.
>
> Gussy secured a cabin for Bessy in spite of the crowd so they slept & here they are. The children rosy and happy & none of them any the worse for the adventure. They have lodging at 1/2 Moon St. next door to where we once stayed—do you remember? The Gardners are at Flemings. Lucy F. at Browns & we here so we are all near together. Every hotel is full to overflowing & the town is swarming with stranded Americans with tales of privation & suffering—that is if they have come from Germany. No one coming from France has suffered anything more than the discomfort of crowded trains and boats... .Springy is working like a beaver at the Foreign Office & making himself very useful....[288] He is longing to get *back* to Washington but so far can get nothing. The strain here is very great but the courage and calmness is splendid & the desire to be useful in every possible way, very fine. The greatest good nature prevails in all the crowds & banks& offices. The White Star office is crammed all the time but you never hear a cross or impatient word, & the clerks are indefatigable in their efforts to help everyone....[289]

Brooks Adams, Henry's brother, had also only just made the crossing from France to England, with his wife Evelyn (Evelyn Davis Adams, Nannie's sister). When Evelyn became engaged to Brooks, a conventional and formal New Englander, he attempted to convince her siblings to stop calling her by her family nickname, Daisy. (One of the siblings had

---

[287] Translation: "as if nothing were wrong."

[288] Cecil Spring-Rice.

[289] The Adams Collection, MHS. Mrs. Lodge had been in London as early as February; see February 1914 letter from Henry James to Mrs. Lodge at 21 Carlton Mansions, near the U.S. Embassy, which was no. 5, where Amb. John Hay had stayed in previous years.

responded: "We shall not change the habits of a life-time at the whim of a relative stranger.") Brooks, also in Paris and London in August 1914, gossiped with his brother about Bessy's forced removal from France and traveling conditions; there was not a lot of certainty about the immediate success of the German attack which explains why Bessy did not think it immediately necessary to flee; he also mentions Nannie's bad health, failing ever since her son, Bay, died five years earlier.

Old Hall Hotel
Boxton, Derbyshire
August 18, 1914
Dear Henry,
Evelyn has taken me up here to take what may be possible of the remains of a cure. We might as well be here as anywhere until we can sail for home. Meanwhile I am extremely glad that you have not tried crossing to England. Not that the journey is worse than many I have taken but because it is tedious and wearing. On the boat the English make you show your passports twice and each time you have to stand for something like an hour. Then the train is overcrowded and you leave to get up at four o'clock in the morning. You would find it quite intolerable. I should say even if you don't have to travel in a third class car with twice the number of passengers it should hold....

London struck me as unpleasant even for London in August. It is full of distinguished Americans and very few others. Nothing is going on and tone after Paris, is like ditch water. **I saw Bessy Lodge who seemed to me very well but disgusted at having been brought from France where she and the children were comfortable to London where they were quite the reverse**. Cabot seems better than he was but, I should think, pretty well done. Nannie is as thin as a shingle but I think she is amusing herself—at any events she has decided to keep Cabot over here for the present. They fix no date for sailing. I fancy you may meet them.... Give my love to Elsie.

Yours,
B.A.

Two days previously, Brooks seemed to be saying that it was unclear whether it would become a world war; he questioned the extent of German power.[290] From this viewpoint, Bessy's cool-headed determination

[290] In the context of the time explained by Brooks Adams, Bessy's relative nonchalance seems more understandable. See appendix.

made more sense.

The Lodges returned to America on September 17, a few days after the Brooks Adams. Evelyn Davis Adams wrote her brother-in-law, the Senator, saying she was relieved to hear how far back the Germans were from Paris. Apparently the Senator was suffering from diphtheria and the entire household had been inoculated. Bessy stayed on in London through the end of September at 9 Half-Moon Street, putting some distance from the family, attempting to make a point of her independence. The Senator's actions are understandable in the sense that he felt that his grandchildren living in France were in grave danger. But in the modern age, one can't help but feel sorry for a woman at the mercy of her father-in-law who held so tightly to the purse strings, who knew his power and who exerted his control.

Edith Wharton, unlike other Americans fleeing France, managed to get back to Paris from a summer vacation in England. This letter urging Bernard Berenson to see Bessy shows how intertwined their lives had become.

> 53 rue de Varenne
> August 11, 1914
> *Dearest B.B.,*
> ...After a day or two at the Crillon I moved on to the apartment with my maid & Gross [the housekeeper] & we got a bonne à tout faire [a cleaning woman].... My sister-in-law Minnie [Mary Cadwalader] Jones was also caught here, so I have taken her in. It is all thrillingly interesting, but very sad to see one's friends going to the slaughter. There is so much to say that I won't begin now—but, oh, think of this time last year! Hasn't it shaken all the foundations of reality for you? English letters are just beginning to come & we are being told by kind friends that we can easily cross, as boats are running daily! Of course they are—trains on this side are the difficulty. In a few days it will be possible to go in relative comfort & with a little luggage. I am staying on in the hope that in another week I may prevail on the authorities to let me take my motor, a vital necessity at Stocks[291]—
>
> All well, & every one cheerful & calm. Walter [Berry] had some money, & is acting as banker for all the stranded beauties—including your affte,
>
> *EW*
>
> **If you are in London, do be really kind and go to see, at 9 Half**

[291] The country house of the Humphrey Wards. Mrs. Humphrey Ward, British novelist on Victorian values, was from a prominent intellectual family. Her sister was Aldous Huxley's aunt.

> **Moon St., poor heart-broken Bessy Lodge, en pouvoir des beaux-parents."**[292]

Edith Wharton once wrote: "Sensitive souls in those days were like muted keyboards on which Fate played without a sound." Fanny de Malrive, Wharton's character in her 1907 story *Madame de Treymes,* ironically mirrored Bessy's circumstances even though it pre-dates by five years the situation that inspired it. Bessy's was a subject that Edith knew all too well.

[292] Translation: "in the grip of her in-laws."

Chapter 8

Washington, 1915

Too much sorrow is shut up in her lonely heart..

—Edith Wharton

In late summer of 1911, Nannie and the Senator were making plans for the marriage of their second son, John, thirty-two. While hospitalized for bad eyesight, he had fallen in love with his nurse, Mary Connolly, a Catholic from the same part of Nova Scotia as the maids at East Point. In a letter to Corinne, the Senator made his disappointment clear and confirmed the supreme importance of their sons in Nannie's life—a "superannuated mother ":

September 2, 1911
East Point
Dear Corinne,
...John was married on Thursday and Nannie wishes me to give her best love and tell you how much your note and your kindness and appreciation meant to her. It would be idle for me to pretend to you that John's choice is what I should like to have seen him make. But she is a thoroughly good girl in every way and in addition she is quite pretty, fresh, simple, well-mannered and very quiet and refined so far as I can judge. He is happy and we learn to look to that first in our children. His eyes have been a heavy handicap through life but they are much stronger now and spurred by his new interest he has gone into the art museum and in six months has done so well that he has been put in charge of the Japanese department which is the great collection of our Museum—the finest Japanese collection in the world. If his eyes hold out he has a good occupation and one worth following and I hope if his eyes will permit he will also keep up his music. So the last one passes out of the house and we are left alone by the fireside as we started. You still have one of them at home. May he long be with you. No matter

John Ellerton Lodge, Jr., Bay's brother, in his mid-50s.

> whom John had married, this separation which is part of life would have come but the loss to his mother of the daily companionship is very severe.[293]

Of John's wedding, Nannie hinted to Corinne that she and the Senator had their doubts; their snobbism (toward a Catholic and from a different class) is evident in their emphatic description: "We try not to feel anxious. Miss. Connolly is charming & well-bred, very capable & quiet & well-suited to John, & they both seem as happy as possible. The work in the Museum is interesting & I think he has a chance of doing it well if his eyes hold out."[294]

John, a linguistic scholar and musician, was curator of the Freer Gallery in Washington, specializing in Asian Art, and founded largely with Sturges Bigelow's magnificent Japanese collection. But art had not always been John's interest. As a child, the Senator took him to see the great Houdini who tried to persuade the Senator to allow John to become his assistant, claiming that he could make him into a great magician. John spoke twenty languages including ancient Aramaic and Sumerian; he also played every instrument in the orchestra and had ambitions to conduct. He once wrote a symphony that was played by the Boston Symphony Orchestra. "He was a genius," my father told me. Thanks to John's knowledge of linguistics, he was part of the team who broke the Japanese code—an ancient Mongolian dialect—during World War II. The effort of doing so killed him—combined with his habit of smoking countless cigarettes. Such was his habit that when my father visited him on his deathbed under an oxygen tent, Uncle John pulled the tent up and snuck a cigarette.

On June 7, 1911, in the second year of her widowhood, Bessy wrote dutifully and cheerfully to the Senator, thanking him for her allowance:

---

[293] All the correspondence with Corinne Roosevelt Robinson is courtesy of the Houghton Library. Theodore Roosevelt Collection, Harvard University. In a letter to Corinne Aug. 27, 1911, Nannie wrote to congratulate her for the publication of one of her poems in the August Scribner's and of her precious gift. In a June letter Nannie wrote charmingly about her friend, Frances Theodora Parsons, an early advocate of women's suffrage, friend of and advisor to Theodore Roosevelt, and author of the wildly successful book, "How To Know The Wild-flowers." Later that summer, Mrs. Parsons recited her best friend Corinne's verse, "By-Ways," to Bessy, who was visiting her Aunt Lucy in Northeast Harbor. (Frances Theodora Parsons, a great friend of Theodore Roosevelt, was also my husband's great grandmother). "Dearest Corinne: ...How often I have thought of that morning when you and Mrs. Parsons floated in and floated out too full of ethereal loveliness to require or even accept anything so gross as food! You had your will, but Cabot and I felt greedy and guilty when we sat down to chops a little later!"

[294] Anna Cabot Mills Lodge to Corinne Roosevelt Robinson, August 27, 1911, Houghton Library.

Nahant, Massachusetts
Dearest Pinky,
I have thought so much about you these stifling days & I only hope that this cold wave has reached Washington & that you are using a wood fire too. Thank you so much for the cheque. How could you remember it with this heat? John is back and better than I have ever seen him—so happy and well. I read of your doings every day in a rapt manner, & am glad that your energy does not flag. We are all so proud of you & Helena practices every day shaking her finger like yours. It's a great gift!

Much Love from Bessy
[John signs]

It is so lovely here & I love it so if only there was some prospect of your visiting us! We have room if you care to come!

The summer of 1912 at Nahant, on the third anniversary of Bay's death, Nannie wrote her friend Corinne of how difficult life continued to be for both her and Bessy: "These last few hard days,—not that every day is not an anniversary, but the return to this place with all its associations—every rock & every tree suggesting some poignant memory & the season of the year & poor Bessy with her lovely children in the house where they hoped to have so many happy summers! It is almost too much."

In October, Nannie wrote Corinne thanking her for news of Theodore's health, which had badly declined in the years after his leaving the presidency due to a fatal microbe from a disastrous expedition to South America. Although Nannie didn't know it then, Theodore was hardly "out of the woods." Noting the imminent departure of Bessy for Paris the following month and of their final watch over the grandchildren, she exclaimed: "We are busy with Bessy & the children who leave us in less than a week & sail Nov. 2. I cannot bear to be away from them a minute, feeling that there will be time for everything when they are finally off."

A few days after Bessy's departure for Paris, Nannie wrote Corinne that her grief over Bay's death did not wane and she expressed her anger at Theodore's failure to win the nomination: "I am steeped in a very anguish of grief & nothing grows better or easier—only harder & more & more & more of a struggle. I am sending you Henry Adams' memoir because I want you to have it from me. I am so mad that he did not get the nomination. This is all Saints Day when my thoughts are more than ever with the departed.... Bessy and the children left us Monday....

***

In late September of 1914, after the "gossamer" period—Bessy's two years in Paris—she was drawn back into the familiar world of Washington and her old house at 2346 Massachusetts Avenue. The following February she received a newspaper report that her beloved friend, Lieutenant Jean du Breuil de St. Germain, "sociologist and traveler, a cavalry officer, was killed in action at Arras on 22 February." Whether Bessy's leaving France six months earlier had anything to do with his heroic death in the trenches is mere speculation.[295] In a sense, though she never married Jean, she was twice widowed. If Bessy had had money, she could have defied the Senator. There is no question that he used money as a weapon.

In *No Gifts from Chance*, her biography of Wharton, Shari Benstock states that Bessy's situation ironically mirrored that of Fanny de Malrive in *Madame de Treymes*. Although the author is correct in thinking that the story bore a resemblance to Bessy's situation, *Madame de Treymes* could not have been written about Bessy since the story was written in 1907 and the love affair with Du Breuil was not until 1912. It may be an exaggeration to say that Wharton "grew to detest the Lodges" for she was full of sympathy for the Senator and Nannie at the death of their son, as is demonstrated in her unpublished letters to Bessy; it would be more apt to say she sympathized strongly with Bessy's helplessness. Benstock writes:

> Edith began to lose friends to the war. The first was Jean du Breuil de St. Germain, the man who had traveled with her and Rosa de Fitz-James to Spain in the spring of 1912. He had fallen in love with the widowed Bessy Lodge, and they hoped to marry. But as he was Catholic, the Lodge family opposed the match and threatened to take away the children if she married Jean Du Breuil, a situation that ironically

---

[295] Certainly, that romance was the subject of gossip in their exclusive world. In a letter March 23, 1915, Henry James writes to Edith Wharton: "Another pang was your mention of Jean du Breuil's death with its bearing on poor B(essy) L(odge)'s history. It can't have been sweet having to write that letter to her—any more than there can be any other great douceur in her life now! I didn't know him, had never seen him, but your account of the admirable manner of his end makes one feel that one would like even to have just beheld him."

mirrored Fanny de Malrive's in *Madame de Treymes*. Bessy left France for London in August, 1914 and never saw her lover again. She settled in Washington, D.C., under the observant eyes of the Lodges, and her father-in-law began grooming her eldest son, Henry Cabot, for a political and diplomatic career. Observing from afar as Bessy raised her three children alone and scrimped to meet expenses, Edith grew to detest the Lodges, who had proclaimed such love for their son, Bay, but who provided little for his children. When news came of Jean du Breuil's death, she asked Daisy Chanler, then living in Washington, to be especially kind to Bessy: "Too much sorrow is shut up in her lonely heart"—a comment Edith might have applied to herself.[296]

On February 16, 1915, Henry James wrote Nannie a tender personal letter:

To Mrs. Henry Cabot Lodge,
21 Carlyle Mansions,
Cheyne Walk, SW
My dear Mrs. Lodge,
...I thought I already knew how deeply attached I am to this remarkable country [England] and to the character of its people. I find I haven't known until now the real degree of my attachment—which I try to show—that is to apply—the intensity of in small and futile ways.... Today for instance I have been taking to my dentist a convalesced soldier—a mere sapper of the R.E.—whom I fished out of a hospital; yesterday I went to the Stores to send "food-chocolate" to my cook's nephew at the front.... But they don't mean, please, that **I am living very intensively, at the same time, with you all at Washington—where I fondly suppose you all entertain sentiments, the Senator and yourself, Constance and that admirable Gussy, into which I may enter with the last freedom**. I won't go into the particulars of my sympathy—or at least the particulars of what it imputes to you: but I have a general sweet confidence, a kind of wealth of divination.London is of course not gay (thank the Lord;) but I wouldn't for the world not

[296] *Madame de Treymes* concerns an American woman unable to obtain a divorce from her French husband in order to marry her American lover. In France, l'heritier—"the heir"—was just as important as it was for the Lodges. We know Wharton, a visionary, drew on the dilemmas of her friends, carefully hidden in different sexes or periods; is it possible that in 1907 Bay could have had an affair with an aristocratic French woman and history was merely repeating itself in 1912?

be here—there are impressions under which I feel it a kind of uplifting privilege. The situation doesn't make me gregarious—but on the contrary very fastidious about the people I care to see. I know exactly those I don't, but never have I taken more kindly to those I do—and with *them* intercourse has a fine intimacy that is beyond anything of the past. But we are very mature—and that is part of the harmony—the young and the youngish are *all* away getting killed, so far as they are males; and so far as they are females, wives and fiancées and sisters, they are occupied with being simply beyond praise. The mothers are pure Roman and it's all tremendously becoming to every one. There are really no fiancées by the way—the young men get home for three days and are married—then off into the absolute Hell of it again. But good-night now. It was truly exquisite of you to write to me. Do feel, and tell Cabot that I take the liberty of asking him to feel, **how thoroughly I count on all your house**. It is a luxury for me to know how I can count on Constance. Yours, dear Mrs. Lodge, ever and ever so faithfully,

Henry James[297]

In September, when Cabot, thirteen, and John, twelve, were of school age, Bessy exerted her parental authority and decided that the boys should go to Middlesex, in Concord, Massachusetts. From its inception, Middlesex was intended to be different from the other academies and "church schools" of the day. Frederick Winsor, a Roxbury Latin School alumnus who founded Middlesex in 1901, wanted the school to be a non-denominational boarding school, where students from different religious backgrounds could learn. From the very beginning, his mission was "to find the promise that lies hidden" in every student.[298] The Senator and Nannie, eager to have the children back under their control, regretted Bessy's decision. Although it surely aroused Pinky's ire, they tried their best to be cheerful as this letter from Nannie to Aileen Tone, Henry Adams' companion, makes clear:

East Point, September 25, 1915
Dear Aileen,
...Bessy takes the boys to school next Tuesday & we are all trying to be very cheerful about it. They are well and Helena more of a darling than

[297] Henry James, *Letters*, 463.
[298] The design for Middlesex's campus was created by the sons of Frederick Law Olmsted, arguably the greatest landscape architect of the nineteenth century—the designer of New York's Central Park, Boston's Emerald Necklace, a chain of parkways and waterways that links Boston and Brookline, and Stanford University.

ever. Bessy has taken a little house in Boston for the winter, so we shall be very lonely but I am sure the change will do her good. Best love to all of you.

Ever Yours Afftely,
A.C.M. Lodge

Nannie had sided with the Senator on the necessity of bringing Bessy and the children back to America in 1914. The strain of another separation from young Cabot, then thirteen, the heir, and with his brother John, twelve, the focus of their attention, must have triggered a shock.

Suddenly on September 27, during the week the boys went to school, Nannie died—as elegantly as she had lived. She had been in a fragile condition since the diagnosis of a "valvular" weakness in the heart in 1899, when her friendship with John Hay may have been at its peak. The intimacy of the relationship between mother and son was such that at Bay's death in 1909, Nannie never quite recovered. The sadness of her son's death went directly to her heart where it rested and never entirely disappeared and eventually killed her. "She never got over Father's death," my Great Aunt Helena told me. There is little doubt that the 1914 voyage to England had weakened her as did the pain of the death of Bessy's friend Jean and all the young men who were dying, followed by Bessy's departure for Boston.

In this intimate letter to Corinne Roosevelt Robinson, we catch a rare glimpse of the Senator's personal feelings:

October 3, 1915
East Point
Dearest Dearest Corinne,
I have sat here and wandered by the sea these last days writing letters to you in my head—letters that would fill volumes because I want to pour out my heart to you and then I have shrunk back in fear of myself and of the impossibility of saying what I would fain write. To you I would write because you were so near and dear to her—no one outside her immediate family nearer or dearer. No wonder for in you I see impulses, qualities, faiths so alike that you and she could not but have been as close as sisters to each other....

The knowledge of your love is a stay and help and comfort. I do not thank you and my dear Douglas for all your sympathy. I should as soon think of thanking my children because they grieve with me. You understand. I am glad that you grieve with me. It helps me. Again you understand. There is great sorrow in you heart. You will cherish her memory. This is more to me than all else.

She always and often said to me that she dreaded invalidism, that when she could not live her life and do what she wished and it was all for others, she wanted to go—and go quickly—She had her wish. For sixteen years, [since 1899] she has had a valvular defect. It has grown no worse in all that time. This summer despite many cares and much work she has been very well. John and I watched her closely and we know. That evening she looked handsome and well and full of charm and talk. She went upstairs to bed last of all and I followed to bring some papers. I never left her long alone. She was in her dressing room, called me in to shut the window. No sign of anything. I went out and sat down to wait for her. In a minute she called "Cabot"—not loud. I opened the door instantly. She had slipped off her chair and was lying in a bent way against the wall. I raised her up in my arms, her head fell back on my shoulder. She was dead. No warning. No suffering. Science says not a pang. Her last conscious thought, her last conscious word was my name and I was there. I did not fail her. Fortunate in her death. She went out in a flash. Every faculty undimmed. The never failing charm at its height. All as she wished.

But to those who survive—alas it is beyond words. I wander about and wonder what I am doing here in this particular world where I have no business to be for my world went with her. I need not tell you what she was or what her death means to me for you know. But you must tell me what she was and what you felt about her. I know it all better than anyone but to have you tell me helps me and you must do it some day soon in such a way that I can lay it away to be read by my grandchildren for I want them to know about their grandmother from other lips as well as from mine because I believe that her beautiful life will be an inspiration perhaps a saving grace to those in whose veins her blood runs.

I am not a person of facile emotions nor do I open my inner self to more than a very very few. I do to you—more than to anyone although I shall write from my heart to Theodore and Bammie. To none else—and this is for you alone (and Douglas if he wishes of course)—My children and grandchildren are devoted beyond words. They surround me. They and Henley Luce [Nannie's brother-in-law and an advisor to Theodore Roosevelt], with an atmosphere of care and affection which I cannot describe. I am deeply gratified to them. It helps, it sustains me.

> I mean of course to work—to do all I can. The doctors say I am fundamentally sound and young for my age so I can work and must work. I would not have it otherwise. No one ever had a braver spirit than Nannie and she would wish it I know. But I am human, I suffer humanly, darkly, intensely. I can look to you & to Theodore and to Bammie but to you whom I can see when I come to New York & you come to me in Washington. The light of the house has gone out. In the breaking gulfs of sorrow I stretch out my hands to those I love best—so few and so dear—I want to feel in my desolate future sometimes, Douglas' faithful loyal hand in mine. I want your arms about my neck and I want to talk to you of her.
>
> Ever,
> *H.C. Lodge*

Though Nannie had been an invalid for some months, news of her death "struck like a thunderbolt," David Butler has written:

> It was 1915, and although the larger tragedy of the war weighed heavily on every man and woman, it was the individual loss, as is often the case, that brought the greatest pain. Spring-Rice [wrote] "We have suffered a great loss in the death of Mrs. Lodge. I don't know what the Senator will do." And to Roosevelt he wrote: "Poor Cabot. It is dreadful to think of it." The war and the death of Mrs. Lodge brought the senator and the ambassador closer together. Spring Rice had shared with Lodge many of his feelings about the Eastern notion of love, and the senator was aware of his mystical-poetic side. Sonnets that he had written to Nanny Lodge over the years he now gathered up and presented to the senator....[299]

On October 1, when the Senator thanked Adams for his letter, he referred to the thirty years since Clover Adams suicide, underscored the closeness of Nannie and Adams, and made an ambiguous reference, possibly to Adams' encouragement of Hay's friendship with Nannie:

> East Point
> Nahant, Massachusetts
> *My very dear Henry—*
> Forty three years ago, you wrote me a letter of the wisest advice which

[299] Butler, 58.

had led me to where I am. Now you come to me as I sit an old man with **my little world in ruins** about me, again with the wisest advice & also with words which go to my heart more directly, more poignantly than any others that kindness and sympathy have brought to me from every side. You tell me that you loved her. I knew it—But it helps as nothing else can to have you say it. **You tell me she was one of the best beloved and the tears well up unbidden** & I feel the deep relief they bring from the knowledge that you too grieve not with me but for her. She loved you well; as she could love. **For many, many years, you have filled a great place in that great heart** & there was never a moment when she did not long to care for you, to help you, **to soften the hard path of daily life. That was her nature**—You know it as well as I but to you it went out with a peculiar and never-failing force. The thirty years that you have endured have been spared to me but now my time has come & my leading two lives, the one within, the other without as you have done so long, begins. **I am not so unobservant that I have not known what you were doing and alas I know already only too well that this at least needs no education**. I shall take up my daily work, the only anodyne. They tell me that I am fundamentally sound physically and therefore I can wish & I must work. She would have it so for **there never was a braver spirit**. With a breaking heart herself, she carried me over Bay's death—I sit and dumbly wonder at the courage she showed.

I shall struggle along as best I may but the inner life will be with her & the past.

I understand what you mean when you say that I shall be my own best audience, the hardest of all to please.

But after all, what helps me most is to know that you will think of her as one of the best beloved.

Ever Yrs.,
H.C. Lodge

Corinne Roosevelt Robinson, described Nannie's talent in her obituary for *The Boston Transcript* in 1915:

So light and graceful was her touch that though the conversations were, perchance, led by the most eminent men of the country, everyone who listened subconsciously recognized the tactful and delicate guidance of her subtle and magnetic mentality. Did someone hesitate for the final line of a quotation, did another pause for the name of an old

French composer, or others still become entangled in the complexities of some intricate political discussion. Soon, the quotation was finished, the composer named, the political web unwound, and all was achieved in so quiet a way that each person only felt the situation had been suddenly clarified and, perhaps, none realized or not till much later, who had been the torch-bearer.

On October 11, Bessy's letter to Corinne thanking her for her remarks is a tribute to Nannie's strength and spirituality as well as her own:

Dearest Mrs. Robinson,
Your sweet letter has just come & I am so grateful for it. You must not be anxious about your letter to Mr. Lodge because he showed it to me & we have both talked about it many times. It is beautiful beyond words & he thought so too. I can't think what he meant—unless that you should write again. Your letter will be something for her great-great-grandchildren[300] to read—as I told Mr. Lodge—in order to show what she was. I have thought about you very often & of how you—with your deep warm-heart—were suffering. She [Nannie] wrote me Aug. 18th, this year—our wedding day—**"Why should we mourn except for ourselves who must still face the life of this world, when those more fortunate are removed from all the care which surrounds us. Of course, we do not know what problems they may be encountering or whether there are any where they have gone"** & then she went on to speak of Bay. I think that quite early in life we cease to feel it is hard for those who go—unless it is a bright young life like your boy's. Certainly in her case, it would be cruel to want her back. I keep thinking, **"To him who overcometh will I give to eat of the hidden manna"** & her life seemed to me a continual overcoming. You felt the will or duty all the time. It seems as if it must be better with her now. A great deal of love from

Your Always Affectionate,
Bessy

After Nannie died, the family gathered around the Senator and spent Christmas with him. The Senator, not being satisfied with a visit, began to exert his control again over Bessy begging that she and Helena, age ten, in pitiful, pleading, letters come and live with him.

[300] That would be me, so she was right.

November 25, 1915
Dearest Bessie,
Thank you for [your] note—so loving, so helpful—I miss you & the children sorely & am looking forward so eagerly to having you all here—Of course send anything you want for Xmas—Put on some mark so that we shall know what they are—I enclose a cheque for you to spend in Xmas presents for the children from "Oops" & myself. You can get what they want better in Boston than here [in Washington].

It was a hard home-coming to this house but yet it was soothing to be among all her books and pictures to be in a place so pervaded by her presence. Everyone is very kind. I have seen Henry Adams & Springy. Madame Jusserand, Margaritta, all so affectionate, so full of real sorrow.

I am very glad all went well about the game. The boys must have delighted in such a victory for Harvard....

Do not forget how much you are to me—how I depend on you—By and by I shall hope to have you come & take care of me as you said you would. You are one of my very own & I shall lean upon you.

Ever my dear child,
Yrs.
H.C. Lodge

When the carrot requiring her sympathy didn't work, the stick was imposed. The Senator was obviously annoyed that Bessy had rented the house in Boston both because of its timing in relation to Nannie's death and for purely selfish reasons. In 1916 the Senator withdrew payment for the boys' boarding schools, forcing Bessy to rent the house she owned in Washington at 2346 Massachusetts Avenue. The Senator told her he saw no reason to keep up two houses when Bessy was living alone in her big house. By not paying the school fees, he obliged her to give up her own house to save expenses and to live with him at 1765 Massachusetts Avenue.[301] There is a certain irony in the case of a woman who, having spurned her mother's attempt to have her marry for money, found her freedom threatened from the lack of it.

One of the Senator's grandchildren, Helena, who lived at 1765 Massachusetts Avenue from the ages ten to sixteen, was powerfully affected by her upbringing with her grandfather (and Nannie before she died).

---

[301] Now torn down to form the present site of The Brookings Institute.

Helena became the focal point of her grandfather's attention and it is said that she, more than anyone, inherited Senator Lodge's traits and strong opinions: "Mr. Endicott [their lawyer] always said that Gampa [the Senator] should have paid for the schools. And of course, had Gammuzzy been alive, he would have," she told me. The Senator made Bessy feel that it was her duty to live in his house. He never would be so vulgar as to say "I'm lonely" or "I need a hostess." He simply said, "wouldn't it be nice, dear, if you came and lived here with me."

From 1916 to 1921, a wing of the Senator's house was given to Bessy and the children. There she came in direct conflict with Constance, the Senator's daughter, tall, dark and commanding, who though she was married to Congressman Augustus ("Gus") Gardner, was nevertheless a strong presence in her father's life. Gus had been

the one, after all, who had physically brought Bessy back from France, so there was a good deal of resentment between her and the Gardners. Constance, who was intensely loyal to her father, was intensely jealous of Bessy, who in moving in with him, had moved onto her *turf*. Constance remarked on Bessy's faint air of "ingratitude."[302]

Although some winters were spent in Boston, Bessy was present during much of the League of Nations debate. To make matters worse, the Senator made her feel that it was her duty to assume his wife's role—attending to the household duties as well as entertaining dignitaries. Without Nannie's restraining influence, the Senator reverted to his boorish ways. The world into which Bessy stepped was seeped in the presence of Nannie, in a world in which the servants played a large role. Nannie was a social muse who had greater powers of communicating than Bessy did; the position in which she was placed was poisonous. These were dark days for Bessy who became the unwilling hostess for after Nannie died, the greatest example of excellence in that art died along with her.[303]

Although Bessy enjoyed the company of the French Ambassador Jules Jusserand of France and the British representatives Lord Bryce and Cecil Spring-Rice, among others, she didn't appreciate the position. To have her free will compromised meant everything to Bessy. The larger Washington community was confused by another, younger and beautiful Mrs. Lodge. She was made miserable by the misconception around Washington at the time that she was the Senator's wife. Of course, everyone gets confused and forgets and there she was living in the same house; a romantic attachment was assumed and according to family

[302] Interview with my Great Aunt Helena.

[303] Louis Auchincloss remarked in an interview with the author, "Pity she lost her place in history."

sources, *that* was what she minded most of all!

Bessy's failure to recognize her social power was a serious flaw. She was not a Lodge. She did not force her opinion and she detested bullies. The servants were still loyal to Nannie and begrudged Bessy the role of head of household. The steely Constance constantly found fault with whatever Bessy did. Constance was the spoiled cherished daughter—living off her father's generous personal allowance and handsome presents of furs, jewelry, and later, real estate—the Villa, Bay and Bessy's house at East Point. Some evenings, Constance brushed right past Bessy. "Then we got to the red rose treatment," Aunt Helena said, laughing, for after the embarrassment became too great, Constance would send a huge bouquet of red roses. My father's brother, Harry, Bessy's grandson, who helped me so much in the research for this book, exclaimed with typical brio and a great guffaw:

> Her life with the Lodges did not make life easier. The Lodges were not kind and she was easy prey. If you are faced with someone who always wants to be good, is kind, isn't splashy, jet-setty, isn't good at quick repartee, the temptation is to tease them, be cruel, at least that was the Lodge temptation. They went after her tooth, hammer and nails. She had her strong moral principles about right and wrong: Sometimes ridiculous things. The children ought to do this, ought to be brought up to do that, well; her in-laws were very worldly, quite nasty and very witty; everybody adored seeing Miss. Goody-Goody Prude miserable.

Constance, left, in black tie, with Bessy in large formal hat and eyeglass, and Cabot, in long curls, walking upstairs. In the foreground, Veto.

Here was a woman tired of being bullied, living in one end of the house, with the Senator reading Shakespeare aloud to her in the evenings; made miserable by servants whom she couldn't control, servants who had been there long before her birth and a cut-throat sister-in-law who was nasty to her. In addition, she was embarrassed socially. Despite frequent trips to see her aunt in New York and to Nahant in the summers, she was a prisoner of her situation. When she did manage to leave, the Senator used the occasion to attempt to make her feel guilty:

> April 21, 1917
> *My dearest Bessie,*
> It was a great satisfaction to receive your letter this morning & to know that all was well with you & Helena. I miss you both sadly for your presence has given me great happiness this winter & I hope your coming will be renewed next year if I survive....

1916 saw the beginning of the half-century rivalry between the Lodge and Kennedy clans and interestingly, a woman was at the center of it all. In the Senate race of 1916, the Senator defeated John "Honey Fitz" Fitzgerald, whose daughter Rose had married Joseph Kennedy.[304] Rose's son, Jack, avenged his grandfather when he defeated Henry Cabot Lodge, Jr., in the 1952 Senate race, and in the 1960 Presidential race, when my grandfather ran as Vice President with Richard Nixon. Ted Kennedy defeated my father in the 1962 Senate race.

Between the spring of 1916 and that of 1917, during the time Bessy had settled into her new life in the Senator's house, it seems that Nannie's best friend, Corinne, had become a greater friend to the Senator. Bay's verse play, Herakles, had sold out and was going into its second printing, an obvious occasion to connect with his daughter in law, Bay's widow. Instead, the Senator shares his delight about that success with Corinne:

> May 27, 1916
> *Dearest Corinne,*
> You are one of the few among the many who really knew her, who will

[304] "Fitz could not even count on the united support of the Boston Irish, for 'Hinnery Cabin Lodge' (as 'Mr. Dooley' called him) had led many a St. Patrick's Day parade and was the nation's chief puller of the British lion's tail. Michael Hennessey of the Boston Globe quoted a Democrat as predicting, '...he'll bury Fitzgerald so deep that the entire membership of the Shovelers Union will have to be called upon to dig him out...' Lodge ignored his opponent and ran instead against Woodrow Wilson." Stephen Hess, *America's Political Dynasties* (Garden City, NY: Transaction Publishers, 1997), 458.

always remember and who understands. It is such a grief to me that I cannot see you face to face and repeat to you all that is pent up in my heart. Time makes it no easier to bear. The desolation of my inmost life seems ever more complete-I wonder how I struggle along-Yet I do and shall. You help me but alas how few there are who do. But you always will help me if there is no one else.... **I had a long letter from Edwin Arlington Robinson about Bay's poems—He thinks the Herakles one of the greatest, if not the greatest of modern times and that it means assured fame. The first edition has been exhausted and the publishers said the verse warranted another which they have printed. This means much to me....**

Early in 1917, President Woodrow Wilson made his "Peace Without Victory" speech in which he advocated the establishment of an international organization for peace, backed by force. The Senator in the spring of 1916 had applauded the "utopia" of "united nations" and in which he also expressed concerns about defining the limits of international cooperation. "They seem to want to bind us to all kinds of things which the country would not hold to," he wrote Sturges Bigelow.[305] Privately he confided his doubts to Corinne Roosevelt Robinson. His letter reveals that since Nannie's death, he no longer socialized in the evening, commenting on the difficulties of working without Nannie's help and guidance. Had Nannie been alive history might well have been different.[306]

1765 Mass. Ave.
January 2, 1917
My Dear Corinne,
...I am glad that you are coming to Washington.... My evenings are all disengaged so you have only to say what you wish in that respect.... The Wilson Peace note was a wretched piece of business—He has made us ridiculous, destroyed any influence we might have had and delayed rather than advanced peace. His main object was as always of himself, to figure as the mediator and peace-maker with I suspect hopes of a third term—But neither side will have anything to do with him. Perhaps fears of complications if war continued also spurred him on. The whole situation and outlook are dark and depressing—**I find it hard work to face it for the emptiness of my life seems more oppressive**

[305] Lodge to Bigelow, April 5, 1916, Lodge papers.
[306] See appendix for the details of Lodge's opposition to the League of Nations.

than ever—But I must do my best which is little enough and there is no sustaining hand at my side....[307]

The Senator confided his aversion to Wilson to Corinne, in whom he found a truer companion than Bessy, concerning literature, politics, and world affairs. Still, it is clear from the correspondence that Bessy, who was already in Nahant in May of 1917, remained on affectionate terms with her father-in-law—the surest way to pacify him. She sent him roses on his birthday and a birthday sketch from Cabot, and he wrote to say that he hoped to get to Nahant in July, that he could imagine the memories it evoked for her and how pleased he was by Cabot's present. "I am so impressed by his idea of thinking of such a present. Best love to Helena." But for Corinne he saved his concerns about France and England and his true feelings about Wilson, "our supremely selfish man." The Senator felt the hand of fate knocking very loudly.

January 6, 1918
United States Senate
Dearest Corinne,
...It all turns on whether France and England can hold on until we can throw in enough weight to turn the scales and it does not seem probable that we shall throw enough weight in the scale really to tell before a year hence. We shall win I firmly believe but if the war is lost it will be lost here in this town by our supremely selfish man and the little subserviencies whom he puts in great offices. When Beethoven wrote the Fifth Symphony he said the opening bars were the "hand of fate knocking at the door." **In this distracted world, filled with awful discords, the hand of fate is knocking very loudly--I wish it did not sound so in my ears but when the door opens, I have a blind faith that victory will come forth....**

August 25, 1918
My Dear Corinne,
...I went home early in July when the Senate recess began and when I settled down with a sigh of relief I found all at once that the work of a long year had left me very tired-more tired than I realized and I had but one thought—to rest and let the vast ocean by which I have always

[307] All of the letters from HCL to CRR in the Theodore Roosevelt Collection at the Houghton Library refer to the call number MS Am 1785 (831).

Corinne Roosevelt Robinson. [308]

[308] Call no. 87M-102; at the time the image was used, the collection was uncataloged.

> lived soothe me and wipe away the wrinkled lines of care. I bathed and swam and fished and hawled and split driftwood and talked with John and Constance and Dr. Bigelow and the grandchildren and let the world slip.... I dwell a hermit at Nahant and eschew Boston.... Then came the terrible news of Quentin's death [Teddy and Edith's son was killed in action] which wrung my heart for he was like one of my own and I could think only of Theodore and Edith to whom I wrote helplessly not with any hope of comfort to them but to relieve myself haunted by the thought night and day of their sorrow and suffering. I think of those I love, those I have lost and those who are in danger until it becomes almost unbearable. The only relief—the only anodyne is work, a dreary but effective palliative and duller of the emotions. I stumbled in my vagrant reading last spring on a letter from Pliny to his wife and in it he says: "Aestina tu, quae vita mea sit, cui requies ni labore, in miseria, curisque solacium."[309] It came sharply home to me for I do not imagine I know what life is in which the only rest is in labor, the only solace in anxiety and cares. And yet, I am very fortunate at my age to have a place of labor, anxiety and cares where I can at least think that I am of use to the country.

Almost as an afterthought in his letter to Corinne he added that Bessy *remained* in Boston that winter. She had gotten out from under for some time, to be near the children, no doubt. The Senator confessed how alone he would be in "this big empty house" and urged Corinne and Douglas to come for a rest and a change whenever and as often as they would like.

In December of 1918, the Senator traveled to New York to confer with the ailing Roosevelt. The record of the conversation between them came to light in a 1920 letter to Corinne but I place it here within its actual chronological time, for the important light it sheds on what transpired that fall.

> Nov. 5, 1920
> Nahant
> *My Dearest Corinne,*
> ...The Lynn [Massachusetts] correspondent of the "World" came to me with a telegram from the "World" just after I had finished speaking at a great meeting in Salem. The telegram said that you had stated that the [Lodge] reservations [about the League] were prepared in Theodore's room. Of course I knew you never said anything of the sort, and what

[309] "Through work one finds solace and release from misery."

you did say was exactly right and the truth—that the essence of the reservations, the principles which they embodied, were considered by Theodore and by me in the conversation which you heard...I made the same statement two months after Theodore's death [at the Middlesex Club in a debate with Lowell]....

In this letter of Jan 5th, 1919, the Senator declared that he felt for her what amounted to a romantic friendship, that his own family –as loving as it was—was not present enough and that he needed a strong woman at his side, during the long fight over his reservations regarding the League of Nations.

My Dearest Corinne,
...You must know how much you have been to me for a long time and especially in these later years. My note was simply an expression, not to be avoided, of a very strong feeling, seldom uttered because I suffer from the reserve of my race very strong in a New Englander. I came to New York in a mood of great depression something not at all to be defended but at times unescapable. I am very keenly alive to the many conditions of my life which have my constant gratitude. My children and grandchildren are devoted to me, I am fortunate in a position when I could be of use in these perilous times, a rare gift at my age and I have worked hard which has been my salvation. But John and Bessy and her children are separated from me most of the year and the two Constances who are here and give me all that love can suggest have as is right their own lives and interests. I have necessarily many solitary hours although I have abundant resources in books and work. Best then is the mental solitude not to be avoided. It is grim to realize that one has no personal future and that one may go over the edge into helplessness or suffering or into the great silence at any moment, that one only has the happiness of others to look forward to, great as that outlook is. So it comes to pass that a wave of gloom and depression, of reflections of what has been lost, of the joys of the past, engulfs one now and then. In this way, I went to New York and being with you cleared the clouds, soothed and comforted me. It was enough to know that you were there. When I came away and sat in the train, I felt exhilarated... hence my stumbling words of loving and heartfelt gratitude. It is hard that fate should compel me to dwell in a town where you are not and see you only at intervals when I have no time to spare for intervals so little time remains.

I have had Cabot here for the holidays-You were right about nature's absorption in the growth of the last year. The rapid increase in mental and physical activity is very noticeable and his loving devotion to me and willingness to be with me very happy gifts.

After Theodore Roosevelt, Corinne's brother and the Senator's dearest friend, died on Jan. 6, 1919, the Senator wrote of the depth of feeling he had for his friend:

Dearest Corinne,
I am groping in the dark. A great blow has fallen and I cannot take in what has happened to me. I do not seem able to understand or realize. A great piece of my life—all accepted, all a matter of course, has suddenly been swept away and there is vacancy and darkness.

Nearly 40 years and never a difference, never a regretted word, never a cloud in the sky... No brother could have been closer or dearer-In the darkest hours-always he was there-Cultivated and a scholar his English and French literature –utterly modest—full open-ending humor—always charming—above all loveable—Gone in a flash.

I was about to write and tell you for I craved your sympathy and then last night it came to me of its own impulse as it always does from you—I am so grateful to you....

The dreadful news shocked the tiny circle of the Senator's friends. From his oldest friend William Sturgis Bigelow, came this condolence letter:

56 Beacon
Boston
Dear Cabot,
This is very bad news for us and for everybody. He was an absolutely honest man and he had the highest ideals and always acted up to them. He was perfectly unselfish. He was sincere and real through and through. There was not a shade or trace of sham, hypocrisy or pretence about him. Whatever he found to do, he did it with all his might. His energy was incredible. That, I take it, is what killed him. If he had been able to sit still instead of going on that ill-fated South American expedition, he at any rate would not have picked up that fatal microbe down there, which I suppose was at the bottom of it. His one thought was what he could do for the country—the exact opposite of Wilson's—"What can the country do for me?" It's not clear what we are any of us

going to do without him.

Yours,
WSB

As the Republican leader of the Senate, Lodge was obliged to say a few words at Woodrow Wilson's death on February 3, 1924, which he managed to do without offending anyone. Because of his position, he was appointed a member of the committee to attend the funeral. On the 4th he received a brief note from Mrs. Wilson:

> I note in the papers that you have been designated by the Senate of the United States as one of those to attend the funeral services of Mr. Wilson.
>
> As the funeral is a private, and not an official one; and realizing that your presence there would be **embarrassing to you and unwelcome to me**, I write to request that you do not attend.

The late great historian John A.Garraty comments in his biography of Lodge:

> What an invitation to one of his haughty, sarcastic retorts was this studied insult! Yet for once Lodge restrained his biting pen. He replied: "I have received your note in which you say that the funeral services of Mr. Wilson are to be private & not official & that my presence would be unwelcome to you. When the Senate Committee was appointed, I had no idea that the committee was expected to attend the private services at the house. I had supposed that the services at the church were to be public. **You may rest assured that nothing would be more distasteful to me than to do anything which by any possibility could be unwelcome to you**.

When Bessy's Aunt Tilley died in 1921, Bessy, then forty-four years old, finally inherited money –enough for her and the children to move back into her own house at 2346 Mass. Ave. She lived there from 1923 to 1946 when at age seventy, she sold the house and moved into an elegant apartment. In 1924, she had a suitor in Judge Oliver Wendell Holmes, Jr., 81, (1843-1936)—still one of the most eminent

1922 passport photo.

and attractive men in Washington. But Bessy announced to a grandchild, "I am not going to wear lipstick and go to teas." She was too busy with her charitable causes—translating books of literature into Braille for the blind for the Library of Congress (Helen Keller wrote her a thank you letter) and washing the incurables (for whom she reserved a separate wardrobe.)

In 1931, when she was fifty-five, she donated a 4th c. BC Greek vase, depicting the classical ideal of dignity and restraint in the face of death, a symbol for all that she stood for, to the Smithsonian Museum.[310]

Uncle Harry: "She was forty years old. She had had two great loves; neither had worked out. She went into retirement. In 1920, a forty-year-old woman was only twenty years from death. She was freed from the mess of cooking and housekeeping and went to work washing the incurables [lepers], and working with the blind. She enjoyed being the matriarch, had an intellectual life in Washington, and delighted in Pa and Uncle John's successes. John tried very hard to be a support for his nephews and nieces, and to a great extent succeeded. While Gammy appreciated her brother in law's efforts, it was very hard for her to let anyone into her inner world. I think she felt safe only with elders or people with whom she had an intellectual friendship."

John A. Garraty, writing about the Senator's last years, commented on his closeness to his grandson, Cabot:

> He devoted a great deal of attention to his grandchildren, particularly to the offspring of Bay Lodge, for whom he felt a special responsibility. He had high ambitions for his namesake, Henry Cabot Lodge, Jr. just as he had had for the boy's father, and was immensely proud of him. He hoped the youth would follow in his own footsteps, and tried to instill in him the same qualities that had produced his own success. When young Lodge was ten, his grandfather wrote him:
>
> "You know how at Nahant in autumn we see those long lines of birds flying South. Well one of those migratory birds as they are called came over the ocean the other day & whispered in my ear that you were lazy at school. I do not like to hear that...You must not be lazy. Work at your lessons & learn all you can. It is not so important what you learn as that you should work at your task, whatever it is. Whatever you try to do—do it with all your might & do your best."
>
> Several years later, when the boy's schoolwork had picked up, Lodge

[310] See appendix.

> wrote: "What pleases me...is the knowledge that you have had the will and determination to regain the place which you had lost through carelessness and indolence. You have shown, what I never doubted to be true, that you are able to control your mind and apply it to any subject that you choose. This is the most important thing in education."

Garraty explains the Senator wanted his beloved grandson to succeed him in office.

> After young Lodge was graduated from college, he went to Europe armed with letters of introduction from his grandfather which gained him access to the homes and offices of the Continent's leading statesmen. He then went into newspaper work as a reporter for *The Boston Transcript*. The Senator approved, for he considered this admirable preparation for the political career he hoped the young man would eventually follow. In the spring of 1924, before the Republican convention, he called Theodore J. Joslin of the Transcript to his office and said: 'I want Cabot to go to the Convention. I could, of course, take him with me, but I would prefer to have him go there as a working newspaper man. I make this personal request to you: Handle him as you would any other man. Be hard on him, for I want him to learn everything he possibly can there. Cabot thinks that he wants to be a newspaper man. He believes that some day he will have a newspaper of his own. That may be his calling, but I want to confide in you by saying that I hope the day may come when he will be sitting where I am sitting...My fondest hope is that the time will come when he will see his future as I believe that I foresee it.
>
> Twelve years later, long after Lodge's death, this 'fondest hope' was fulfilled, and later still his other grandson, John Davis Lodge, also entered the political arena as a Congressman from Connecticut.

In the summer of 1924, two operations for prostate cancer were successfully performed on the Senator. He was recuperating well. On his nightstand were volumes of Shakespeare, detective stories and Bernard Shaw's St. Joan. ("Whether we like him or not, he is always clever," the Senator wrote of Shaw, something which could also be said of himself.) On November 9, the family story is that he was standing in the library in Nahant when he was struck down by a cerebral hemorrhage and toppled backwards onto the floor; that evening, he died. He was seventy-four years old and like Nannie at her death, he was in full command of all his senses.

The Senator was certainly a bully—unusually arrogant and selfish—but he could also be a devoted husband and father and a scholar and a statesman with an unswerving sense of duty to his country. Without Nannie, the Senator would have had neither the grace nor the power to succeed; moreover, clearly he could not live without a superior sort of women in his life. As he himself says in the private Tribute written for his grandchildren at her death: her "rare intellectual qualities inspired my admiration for nearly half a century and taught me what was best and most worthy to know, to love and to reverence."

***

All I feel is that what was, has not been in vain.

—Bessy to Nannie, 1910

No one in my family ever spoke of East Point or if they did, it was with some mysterious sorrow. For eighty years the large octagonal shingled cottage on that rocky promontory known as East Point had served the family well. Nahant, Boston's first summer resort, stood guard at Boston harbor. Although roses still climbed on the wide veranda, the oil lamps were now dim, the white curtains in the upstairs bedrooms were frayed and a fine film of dust and cobwebs had settled over the elegant drawing room. Somehow it lacked the same luster and vigor of life after Bay's death. John, Bay's brother, and Bessy had rowed out in the dory and flung the small urn containing his ashes into the sea.

John inherited East Point at the Senator's death, but between 1924 and 1938, it was rarely used and in 1939 the government bought it and tore it down to build a big gun emplacement to protect Boston Harbor in the coming war. My Uncle Harry remembers his Uncle John throwing the artifacts for the tricks Houdini had given him off the Nahant cliffs into the sea. Nothing would remain. The memory would be effaced. The magic was gone. Helena barely had enough time to make off with some of the more valuable childrens' books. Because John had married "beneath his class", the Senator, in his will, left the bulk of his money to him in trust and he lived frugally on the annual interest of his inheritance. John E. Lodge was a lovely man and while very bright, was not full of *sturm und drang* like all the others. For example, he brought his wife, Mary, a present every day of his life, even if it was only a pencil or eraser, picked up on the way home from work.

At John's death, the inheritance was divided equally among Bay's and Bessy's three children, the Senator's grandchildren. Although the Senator had given the couple a "swell" house in Washington, in the Senator's will, Bessy inherited nothing; and to her chagrin, even her house in Nahant, the Villa, a small red-brick house where she always stayed while in Nahant, was left to the Senator's daughter, Constance. While Constance was well provided for during her marriage, the Villa was all the Senator left her. Bessy's eldest son, 'Crown Prince' Cabot, inherited the library and the paintings.

Bessy's life typified the kind of social heroism, embodied in Edith Wharton's heroes and heroines: "True love doesn't conquer all, nor is life a cabaret but one can make the best of it with dignity and determination."[311] Evidently Bessy wanted to keep up the appearance of a family existence that was entirely peaceful and happy. My late Great Aunt Helena, Bessy's daughter, wrote of her mother:

> People have not spoken enough about our mother's intelligence, her splendid sense of values, the passionate courage with which she met life, her tremendous love for her children and her great unselfishness. She was deeply religious. When I was about twelve, she started making books in Braille for the blind, saying that in this way she could work for others without leaving home. She kept this up more or less all her life and, as she grew too old to go out and work for charities, she reverted to it more and more and worked hard almost until the day of her death doing books in Braille for the section for the Blind at the Library of Congress. She got some touching letters-one from Helen Keller for instance. She gave us the most lovely, peaceful and happy childhood in spite of her sorrow and indeed, when I think of it and also of the relations and friends who tried to help, stimulate, protect and guide us, I feel we were blessed indeed. My mother's house was full of order, peace, and thoughtful kindness--a place where one could live and laugh and think. Everything looked lovely and smelled fresh and delicious and brought one comfort."[312]

Stephen Luce, a cousin by marriage with the Adams[313] once wrote my grandfather, "She was the bravest woman I've ever known." She fulfilled her family obligations as mother and daughter in law. She encour-

---

[311] Scot Lehigh, in "Soul Proprietress," "Edith Wharton's renaissance reflects an enduring fascination with the quiet war between self and society." A *Boston Globe Focus* writer.

[312] Henry Cabot Lodge, *The Storm Has Many Eyes,* W.W. Norton & Co.: 1973, 25

[313] Brooks Adams married Daisy Davis, Nannie's sister, and another sister married Henley Luce, whose son was Stephen.

aged her three children to become what the Senator always wanted for them—to be public servants. The Senator saw in his adored grandson, his heir, a worthy successor to family eminence. Some see the Senator as being as "foul" in foreign affairs and he was in personal matters. But he must be seen in the context of the age he lived in—an imperialist whose mission was to make America as great as her European competitors in the Pacific, something he saw as his political duty to Massachusetts, where the American Navy had been born by his great grandfather.

From the time young Henry Cabot Lodge was age fourteen to twenty, the Senator's house on Massachusetts Avenue was his home. My grandfather's recollections of those years are vivid and explain that the library was the place in which he had been brought up.

> My grandfather was a grand companion and in the winter when we were in Washington on vacation from school or college, he would take us on walks in Rock Creek Park. His house in Washington was actually two houses, combined into one. **It had an enormous high-ceilinged library** which we entered through a door in the west wall. To the right of the door was a fireplace six feet high which burned logs of cord length. There were two long windows facing south—onto Massachusetts Avenue. The east and north walls were completely lined with books. There was also a gallery leading to other galleries, which we reached by a small staircase. These galleries were also lined with books. In the main gallery, one could look down into the room. I remember long evenings spent in front of the fire alone with my grandfather, from 1918 until his death in 1924. He would talk to me at great length about public questions: the League of Nations, of course; but many other subjects as well, notably practical politics, local, state, and national; the functioning of the Senate, national defense, the tariff and civil rights.
>
> In this room, family life went on. My grandfather had tremendous powers of concentration and used to sit working at his desk, sometimes with a secretary, while the rest of the family and friends had tea in front of a big Italian painting which ran from floor to the ceiling. When some remark caught his attention, he would stop work at his desk and would join us, taking out a book of essays or poetry or a volume of Shakespeare to prove his point. I remember him often standing with a book in his hand, reading some passage and obtaining our complete attention. We three children had the run of the library and I believe we all still feel that just being in a library is a happiness and a strength, although using it occasionally has its advantages too, as our grandfa-

ther never tired of pointing out. A stream of distinguished persons—congressmen, senators, journalists, diplomats, and old friends dropped in for almost every meal so that all the days were fun.[314]

Bessy encouraged her children and grandchildren to have an "active" life. She did her duty to the family, loyal to the last to the old Senator's insistence on the importance of public service. Bessy may not have been as well-educated as she wanted, nor as clever as the Lodges according to Adams' definition, but she was equally courageous and had an emotional intelligence the Lodges lacked. She never used her intelligence to hurt anyone. Neither did she suffer self-pity and she worked hard to advance her childrens' careers and for charitable causes. Measured by her children's immense self-confidence and achievements, she was a success. The Senator's hopes and dreams were realized by grandson Cabot who had a career to rival that of his grandfather, with a liveliness of spirit he inherited from his charismatic father.

To Bernard Berenson
Sainte Claire
January 15, 1924
Dearest B.B.,
I will begin this often planned and long-deferred letter to you by telling you that young Cabot Lodge, Bessy's eldest boy, who is staying with me, will be in Florence in a few days. He is such an attractive and intelligent youth, & will be so fully alive to the privilege of seeing you both, & the Tatti, that I feel its not indiscreet of me to send him; & as he is to be in Florence for a very short time, I have told him that he may telephone on arrival & ask when you can conveniently see him. Above all, make no *"frais."* A cup of tea & an hour by the library fire will be something for him to remember for a long time. He has been "oriented" toward politics by his grand 'pa, & I think his natural bent is toward that, & history, but he has an eager respect for letters, has read a good deal, speaks French and German, & is on the staff of *The Boston Transcript* (having to earn his living.) I know you will like him or I shouldn't send him....

Well, bless you, dearest B.B. Forgive my long silence, set me a good example by answering this very soon—

Edith

***

[314] Ibid, *The Storm Has Many Eyes*, 26 and 27.

As an eight-year-old, I dimly remember Bessy, or "Gammy" as we called her, the year before she died. She was sitting alone in the large square gravel walled courtyard in front of the "big house" in Beverly. The cars normally parked there under the large copper birch tree whose shade on summer days was among the best. If that day, the cars were not there, my grandfather had probably banished them so that Bessy could have some peace. She was immobile in that space with just the faint smell of lilies of the valley from a corner, sweetening the air in the courtyard which was enclosed by brick walls with the ivy climbing, and with the sounds of laughter coming up from the beach. She may have been thinking of the previous night's dinner after which her son, Cabot (Grandpa), always tapped a little soft-shoe.

I remember a strong presence—a steely gentleness and presidential dignity as if one of the figures from Mount Rushmore had come down from its granite perch and sat breathing beside me. She was wearing pearls and some organza finery of a lavender color and I remember being conscious of being underdressed in a simple pastel cotton shirt and shorts with flat slippers. She gave the impression of blindness, so deep was she in some thought or sorrow. She wasn't socially dexterous nor did she exude the gaiety of my grandmother. But in previous years, she had loved funny books and movies and laughed until her sides ached.

The author at about ten in Beverly in June.

In 1959, my great grandmother was eighty; my grandfather said I reminded him of her. But in that year before she died, she was transcendent as if the present and the past had merged and she was finally at one with the passage of time. She was so much herself that, to an eight-year-old child, she stood out as a curiosity. Even in the heat of summer, she was always a lady. If she went sailing with my father and uncle she would be fully dressed as if for tea at the White House, in white gloves and hat, smiling broadly. My last image of her, captured in a snapshot, shows her seated beneath the horse-chestnut tree on the lawn running down to the sea, holding the heir, the new crown prince, my brother Henry Cabot Lodge III, a smiling-one-year old.

Front court at Beverly.

Bessy (Gammy) with my brother Cabot.

The "Big House" in Beverly, Massachusetts.

Edith Wharton's Pavillon Colombe. Photograph courtesy of the Reverend Joanne Coyle Dauphin.

Chapter 9

Emily and Cabot

Ancient trees lined the gravel driveway of the "Big House" in Beverly, Massachusetts. Brick walls surrounded the front courtyard on three sides, and a massive copper beech tree with elephantine branches guarded the entrance. Through the heavy wood and brass door, small feet would find relief on the marble floor of what was our second home. The long front hall, with three crystal chandeliers, was painted in pale gray with white panels, to complement the large white and small gray squares of marble. They drew the eye into the dining room, which had a gray and black stone floor and was framed at the far end by a crescent of French windows. It looked out on a marsh attended by white herons. At a young age, I remember wondering who we were, so surrounded by beauty and precious objects.

From the time I was four until the age of ten, my family and I lived in Washington, D.C., and in summer we lived in a house built on the ruins of a potting shed on the Sears estate in Beverly. When my father ran for the Senate in 1962, we began living there year round. My grandmother, Emily Esther Sears, had married Henry Cabot Lodge in July 1926. Dr. and Mrs. Sears gave the young couple the house and the twenty acres, an L-shaped brick mansion with a square gravel courtyard in front. Mrs. Sears was so awed by her daughter's mother-in-law, Bessy, that she inverted the tradition of the groom's mother paying a visit to the bride's mother and made the trip to Washington, D.C., to pay her respects to Mrs. Lodge.

Edith Wharton, Bessy and Bay's intimate friend, inspired them to model their house in Beverly after her own house in the south of France at Hyeres and her Parisian suburban manoir, Pavillon Colombe at Saint-Brice-sous-Forêt.

The wedding took place at the Episcopal Church in Beverly with a lawn reception stretching to Beverly Cove at Dr. Sears' sixty-acre summer estate. A family photograph shows elegantly dressed ladies with top-hatted gentlemen conversing on the lawn.

"It was the North Shore's social event of the year. Great tents were spread on the green lawn, an orchestra played; several score guests toasted the young couple in prewar champagne from Dr. Sears' ample cellars. The wedding united the Cabots and Lodges with another famous old Boston family. Dr. Sears was the grandson of David Sears, who, in the words of one descendant, 'owned half the West Coast and all of Alaska' and whose great mansion at 42 Beacon Street (now the Somerset Club in Boston) was one of the last great Georgian houses in America."[315] The North Shore of Boston, particularly Nahant, Beverly and Manchester, were, along with Newport, a part of New England known as America's first "Gold Coast."

Two oval portraits of Alexander Hamilton and Fisher Ames by Gilbert Stuart[316] hung on the dining room wall of the Big House. Mrs. Giles Lodge and Mrs. Elizabeth Cabot (c.1810), by the American painter John Singleton Copley, hung in the front hall over crescent-shaped *directoire* tables with green marble tops. Just before the dining room to the left, a red-carpeted spiral staircase led upstairs to the bedrooms. To the right, an enormous room was walled floor to ceiling with mahogany bookshelves full of rare leatherbound books—old Senator Henry Cabot Lodge's library—which brought together the books of George Cabot, John Ellerton Lodge and other ancestors.

Sears estate in Beverly before it burned.

At the end of the room, three French windows allowed sunlight to shimmer on the green and gold furniture. Double doors led outside to a

[315] William J. Miller, ibid., 72.

[316] Stuart (1755-1828) is widely considered to be one of America's foremost portraitists. His best-known work is the unfinished portrait of George Washington, which appeared on the one-dollar bill for over a century. The portraits of Alexander Hamilton and Fisher Ames by were given to George Cabot by Ames who, along with Hamilton and Cabot, was an early advocate of federalism; the three were founding members of the Federalist Party. These two portraits were inherited by George Cabot's granddaughter, Anna Cabot Lodge, then by her son, grandson, and great-grandson, respectively, Henry Cabot Lodge, Sr., George "Bay" Cabot Lodge, and Henry Cabot Lodge, Jr. who donated them to the National Portrait Gallery in the 1970s. Both portraits are in the National Gallery along with the John Singer Sargent portrait of Henry Cabot Lodge, Sr.

Emily Esther Sears and Henry Cabot Lodge.

grass patio bordered by gigantic seashells, big as bushel baskets, which china merchant John Lodge had used as ballast on his clipper ships. Above the doorstep, purple wisteria laced a trellis.

Through my child's eyes, the library was imposing, even intimidating, full of grandeur, beauty, mystery, knowledge, and power. At one end of the room hung a colossal sixteenth century Siennese painting of the Virgin and Child by Gian Giaccomo Macchrino d'Alba. At the other, niches in the massive amber-colored wall above housed small ancient statues of Chinese monks in prayer, standing guard above an identically-colored seventeenth century Florentine marble mantelpiece.

To the left on entering was a grand piano where my great uncle, John Davis Lodge, played bawdy songs he composed about Helen of Troy and Menelaus. Great Uncle John stood out in the family's eyes for having starred with Marlene Dietrich in *The Scarlet Empress*; he later distinguished himself as Governor of Connecticut and an Ambassador to Spain, among other things.[317]

There was a large Louis XV desk in front of the French window. Nearby, a small round chess table made of mother-of-pearl and papier mâché always seemed too fragile for general use. An Anders Zorn[318] sculpture of Venus rising from the sea was on the table. The implicit suggestion was that women derived their power from the vital familial function of giving birth to the heir, the Lodge woman's first and primary role. Was the tradition encouraging physical toughness and literary excellence for the boys also meant for the girls? Was the Senator's magnificent library—a metaphor for the belief that knowledge is power—intended for both sexes?

Author, right, as a child with her sister, Nancy, in the library at Christmas.

American history infused the walls of the house. In the basement was the cannon used by Nannie's father, Admiral Davis, at the Siege of Vicksburg. On the windowsill next to the large spiral staircase leading down to our grandfather's study, was a white marble bust of John Ellerton Lodge, the Senator's father.

The "white room," a small sitting room to the right of the library, had chic. Black art deco ceiling moldings contrasted the white silk furniture. On round Louis Seize tables were white and blue pieces of Ming porcelain, setting off a modern portrait of Emily and Henry Cabot Lodge by Louis Bouché, and behind the door leading to the library hung John Singer Sargent's portrait of the Senator. The room looked out on a rose-garden bordered with flat-topped box bushes framing a profusion of color—deep red, fuchsia pink, and bright yellow.

---

[317] See appendix.

[318] Anders Zorn (1860-1920), Swedish painter and etcher, was internationally famed as one of the best genre and portrait painters in Europe at the end of the nineteenth century.

From left: Uncle Harry; my father, George; my mother, Nancy; holding my sister, Nancy; the author held by her grandfather, Henry Cabot Lodge, Jr.; Emily Sears Lodge. Courtesy of Life Magazine.

June was a particularly lovely month for roses in Beverly. Beyond the French doors, one stepped onto an interior lawn interspersed with exotic Japanese bushes and bordered with pansy beds. There was no woman more elegant than my grandmother, Emily, yet she loved to get her hands in the dirt. Even after weeding the pansy beds, laughing with her granddaughters, or cleaning out the drain in the sink, her hands always smelled of orange blossoms.

To the left of the house was a Pompeian swimming pool—a twenty square foot cement pool framed by a meter-wide shallow pool for goldfish (and small children). Two huge copper beeches stood guard on either side. Beyond the interior lawn space and a set of little steps leading up to the sea, a beloved horse-chestnut tree provided respite from the sun. We often lunched in its shade on summer Sundays, and in the fall, we collected the fruit for roasting in the library fireplace. Farther down, shallow steps hedged by thick pines, cut low to form an overhead arch, led to the sea. The cold of the stone on tiny feet and the sweet smell of green fir mingling with the hot sea air advanced the excitement of getting to the beach.

"I love Emily. She's the thing that makes me live." That's what "cousin" Germaine, a French friend, said of my grandmother, Emily Sears Lodge (1905-1992). "Fortune and opportunity are her muses," wrote my sister, Nancy.[319] My father said his mother had more self-confidence than anyone he knew—her elegance was bold and simple at the same time. She was alert, compassionate, and so frank and unassuming that she could make anyone laugh. Her tall, slender form—5-foot-10 and 138 pounds—remained constant throughout her adult life (she made sure to tell me). At the reception following my grandfather's funeral, she stood radiantly beautiful in a simple black turtleneck and large gold necklace—a daring *parure*, for women in our set put on their pearls every morning. My grandfather and I had been exceptionally close and I had wept during the entire service. As I approached her in the library where the reception took place, she looked at me steadily with intense brown eyes, and her strength came into me. Though weakened by her husband's death, she yet possessed a magnetism that drew me to her. In short, she taught me the meaning of dignity. "She was like a wonderful drug which makes everything soft and bright and infinitely forgiving," recalled Nancy.[320] At big family lunches, she mostly sat with the grandchildren and great grandchildren, preferring their honest conversation.

Emily used to joke that her family, the Searses, considered the Lodges "upstarts." Richard Sears, who built dories, and later engaged in trade, had emigrated from Colchester, England, to Chatham, Massachusetts in 1630, ten years after the arrival of *The Mayflower*. The first Sears to move to Boston was Daniel and he died, leaving his wife, Fear, with one child, David, born in 1755. David married Anne Winthrop, a descendant of Governor John Winthrop, and became an extraordinarily successful financier, owning considerable real estate in Boston alongside Bullfinch, Harrison Otis, and Paul Revere. He secured much of the European capital to finance both the American Revolution and the reconstruction that followed. David's son, David II (1789-1870),

---

[319] "To Grandma Just Before Her Second Honeymoon, From Nancy," by Nancy Lodge. Unpublished essay, 1987.
[320] "Memories," by Nancy Lodge. Unpublished essay, 2004.

married Miriam Mason, from a prominent Boston family, and spent his honeymoon in Paris at the time of Napoleon's coronation; in the 1830s, the family rented Hotel de Clermont at 69 rue de Varenne. Miriam's father, Jonathan Mason, a descendant of the first Senator from Massachusetts, was a developer of Beacon Hill as a residential center in Boston, and Mason gave David and his daughter a "country place" on Mount Vernon, which later became the famous street. David Sears was an early developer of Newport with a large "cottage" that he sold in the 1850s, before the big houses were built. Sears was the richest man in America until John Jacob Astor overtook him.

Jean Struthers Sears.

His descendant, our grandmother's father, Dr. Henry Sears of Boston, a pathologist whose specialty was infectious diseases, married Jean Struthers when she was thirty-three and he was forty-two. They had met in Paris, married in Vevey in 1904, honeymooned at the Beau Rivage hotel in Lausanne and were deeply in love all their lives.[321] My father inherited the gift of clairvoyance from Jean, his maternal grandmother, whom my father called "NyenNyen," a sound formed by his infant mouth. Jean Irvine Struthers (1871-

[321] George C. Lodge, *Paths Are Made By Walking*, an unpublished autobiography. Jean's grandfather, William Struthers, owned a marble quarry and donated the marble for George Washington's tomb.

1942) from Philadelphia, was adventuresome and mystical, though she rarely went to church. Her paternal grandfather was descended from the Irvines, from the highlands of Scotland and from southwestern Scotland, Ayr and Kirkmichael, Galloway. My father speaks of himself in the third person in his autobiography:

> She read to George by the hour, as he nestled beside her at tea time, brushed by the ostrich feathers of her gown. The books she chose, oddly dissonant with her delicacy, were rough and ready adventure stories about the American frontier—the exploits of Daniel Boone, Fremont, Lewis and Clark, Buffalo Bill and the like.... She was a firm believer in ghosts, about which she told George at length with sound effects where appropriate—the yowl of the banshee at a friend's house in Bryn Mawr—a mix of a baby crying and the hoot of an owl,[322] announcing the death of her friend's brother on a sailing ship going around Cape Horn; the maiden in bridal gown at the castle of her Warwick ancestors in Scotland, who appeared before family weddings; and the knight in black armor clanking down the stone stairs as death came to a family member.[323]

Jean's mother, born Savannah Durburow (1851-1911) of Georgia, was twelve years old when General William Tecumseh Sherman forced the family to have tea with him during the period of his Civil War march to the sea.[324] The Struthers built "Moss Cottage" at Jekyll Island, Georgia, in the mid-nineteenth century before the Island became a club. Jean spent a good deal of her childhood there thanks to her maternal great-great grandparents. In the early 1750s, a Scot horticulturalist named Dr. John Trumbull married Gracia Maria Rubini of Smyrna, Turkey, the granddaughter of a Venetian Doge. Along with two thousand Greek immigrants, they settled just above what is now Cape Canaveral, Florida, on the border with Georgia—no man's land, at the time. They brought the first oranges to Florida, the Trumbull orange, and established the town of New Smryna. Jean inherited an old oak chest full of Venetian fabrics—rich silk, velvet and satin materials—and passed them on to her daughter, Emily, making whole days of dressing up as princesses possible for her granddaughters, my

---

[322] A female spirit in Celtic folklore believed to wail outside a house as a warning that a death would soon occur in the family.

[323] *Paths*, 3.

[324] Ibid.

sisters, and me.[325]

Jean, my great grandmother, an independent person with flaming red hair and blue-green eyes, was a crack shot who accompanied her father hunting.[326] He recounts in his diary how, one day at "Moss Cottage" while Jean was teaching Sunday school, an alligator crawled out of the swamp and threatened one of the children. According to his account, she pulled out her pearl-handled twenty-two caliber six-shooter and shot it through the eye. (It was the largest ever taken in Georgia at the time). She also brought apples to Geronimo, the great Apache chief, while he was imprisoned in Florida. When she told him she had learned how to row, he made her a paddle, explaining that that was the only way to properly move a boat.[327]

She had many admirers. As my father recalls,

> One of the more memorable was Lord (Freddy) Athlumne, a northern Irish Earl, who was an aide to the British general Lord Kitchener, in Cairo. On a family trip down the Nile, Jean rode off into the desert with Freddy. The Earl, who never married, came to 86 Beacon Street, Boston, to visit her every year until his death. Each time, he brought a small silver leaf like the ones that grew along the banks of the Nile. NyenNyen's husband obliged by leaving them alone for Saturday lunch while he went up the street to the Somerset Club. On one occasion Jean seems to have run off a bit too far; her father dispatched a camel brigade—and Freddy perhaps—to bring her back. They found her being feted by the notorious Mahdi, the local native leader who later became famous for killing General Gordon at Khartoum. The Mahdi presented her with the eye of the barbecued sheep that lay at the center of the tent, and, of course, she ate it, realizing the honor he had done her.[328]

In 1942, fifteen year old George was playing "Coming through the Rye" on his clarinet to her—a World War I song about soldiers meeting one another on the fields of battle ("When a fella meets a fella comin through the rye...")—when suddenly she sat straight up in bed as though she had seen her deceased husband standing at the foot of her bed and said, "I'm coming, Harry." She dropped back and was dead. The gift of clairvoyance may have been passed on to my father at this

---

[325] Ibid., 4.

[326] Ibid.

[327] Ibid.

[328] Ibid., 6-7.

time for in 1984, eighty years after his grandparents' honeymoon, on a lecture trip, my father found himself at the at the Beau Rivage Hotel, the same hotel where they had honeymooned; resting after his lecture, he saw the ghosts of Harry and Jean, his grandparents, for a few seconds—a woman with long red hair down to her waist and a man in a starched white shirt, in a semi-embrace by the window, with the filmy curtains of the open French doors blowing in the wind. On returning to America, he discovered that they had spent their honeymoon in that suite.

Jean's daughter, our grandmother, was more than a conventional wife and mother; she was a public figure. The popular belief is that rich women had French or German governesses, were taught at home and were not expected to know the word *weltanschauung*, or "worldview." This belief isn't quite accurate, however. Emily, for example, attended Miss May's school in Boston until she was nine; thereafter, she and her sister, Jean, received a "private education." Subsequently, she and her family traveled the world. Governesses were hired for French and German, supplemented by tutors for math and the sciences. Music lessons and art appreciation were provided by teachers and curators from the conservatories and museums of Boston, Paris, Rome or wherever they happened to be. Her mother taught English and American literature and poetry, while her father taught history, particularly ancient Greek, Roman and European. Marcel Proust and Aldous Huxley had a home on her bookshelf. There were no vacations, but their time was rarely spent in Boston. Rather, it was divided among Philadelphia, Paris, Jekyll Island, Georgia, and Beverly.

Women like Emily Sears Lodge were a refuge and an inspiration, running the family from behind the scenes. Yet they were not treated as equals. Although she entertained Presidents, Chief Justices and Secretaries of State with ease, and her education rivaled that given by the best universities, she admitted to a secret insecurity that she had never gone to college. She used to tell my sister, an art historian, "You know, Nancy, I'm a great 'fakaa.'" She meant that she gathered information for charming dinner table conversations. "Now, I'm lunching with Joe Alsop, so you must tell me everything about that enchanting Piero Della Francesca. I want to be able to turn to my right and say, *'Aren't Domenico Veneziano's colors heavenly... and that extraordinary linear perspective in the St. Lucy altarpiece....'* Dinner conversations were endless and very important.... To be a success I had to learn to play bridge, tennis, and make conversation with both dinner companions. 'But never go on and on about a subject and please don't contradict him. Look at him as though he's the most fascinating creature you've ever met. Flatter him, let him talk; after all, *he's a man*.'"[329]

When we would sit on the sofa with my grandmother, volumes of Dickens, Thackeray, Baudelaire and Shakespeare surrounded us. In summer her house always smelled of fresh flowers and the sea. My sister, vividly describes the scene:

> Even on the hottest summer days, the library in the big house stayed cool and fragrant. Its colors were moss green, pale gold, and brown. It smelled of leather books, oil paintings and flowers. The big French doors swung open, letting in fresh smells of the horse chestnut trees, newly mown grass, the pool, sounds of people talking and children playing. Grandma sat in the far corner of a sofa surrounded by piles of stuff—letters, pads, knitting (she was always making one of us a blanket or bandages for lepers), several books, a large tackle box in which she kept sewing and magazines. She gave the illusion of simultaneously having nothing to do but play with me and being extremely busy; if there were no one around, Grandma would garden, read, fix flowers, make green soup or a new skirt for herself, or visit the sick. When I was with Grandma, I felt truly busy. I still think that if you are with her enough, some of her magical charm, her innate happiness with herself and with the world will seep into you.[330]

I often stayed in the "pink room" at the Big House. With its pale pink walls, white furniture, thin white cotton blanket covers and white satin comforters, as well as its crescent of French windows offering an eastward view of the sea, it was fit for a princess. As a child, I remember lying next to Grandma in bed while she had her breakfast, brought to her on a tray with white linen and small roses made of Meissen china—a soft-boiled egg, wheat toast without crusts, fresh orange juice, and espresso coffee with hot skimmed milk. When the cook came back for the tray, she would give Emily the menu for the evening meal. Her favorites were poached salmon with green mayonnaise or poached chicken with hollandaise, recipes which would also become firsts in my own repertoire of favorite recipes. She would read the newspaper and comment on the advertisements from Lord and Taylor or Saks Fifth

---

329 "Memories," by Nancy Lodge. Unpublished essay, 2004.

330 "To Grandma on her Second Honeymoon," by Nancy Lodge. Unpublished essay, 1987, written seven years before our grandmother died on the occasion of her second honeymoon.

Avenue for the fashions of the day—the line of the skirt, the cut of the jacket—and add, in her New England drawl, "Isn't that prettai!" I suppose I first came to love clothes because of her. She taught me the word "chic," and though she bought designer clothes, she made do with less, relying on the same simple straight-cut black or pink suit and adding a flower or in the evening a satin stole for effect. She was absolutely without pretension or excess. She gave her clothes to the shelter she had founded for homeless women. She traveled light and her trademark gold charm bracelet made a lovely sound when she moved. She wore the kind of perfume that made her presence in the room unmistakable—some rare flower had suddenly entered. Her charm was that she was unassuming—personal, yet detached—claiming to be lazy yet incisively making her mark. She was the final judge of any speech that had been written and the person to whom one always rushed for an opinion. She never made waves, and she enfolded us in her presence.

Our grandmother's greatest gift was her ability to find humor in everything. Her self-effacement and humility were part of what it meant to have good manners. If an unfortunate guest drank the finger bowl thinking it was soup, she would have done the same so as not to embarrass the guest, as did the queens of England. If something were spilled on the tablecloth, it would not be noticed. She was fearless, opinionated, and she despised people she disapproved of, especially phonies and tyrants, to whom she delivered clever barbs coated with obvious sweetness.

***

Henry Cabot Lodge, Jr., my grandfather, completed Harvard in three years then worked as a journalist from his graduation in 1923 until 1932, when he was elected the Republican State Representative from Massachusetts. Fulfilling the destiny intended for him, he served as U.S. Senator between 1937-44 and 1947-53.

At the outbreak of World War II in 1940, his sister, Helena, escaped Belgium and went to stay with family friends in France. In the middle of the night, the telephone rang, and though it was not the custom to answer the telephone in someone else's house, she knew that it was her brother Cabot and picked up. He gave her instructions about how to make her way to Genoa where Bessy awaited her on a boat to America.[331] With the help of an American diplomat Cabot had dispatched,

[331] Photo available.

Bessy was able to hold the boat three days until Helena's arrival, in wartime. That was the kind of power Bessy exercised!

In early 1942, my grandfather, with the rank of major in the 1st Armored Division, took a three-month leave of absence from the Senate to lead a small detachment of tanks in the Libyan desert to evaluate their performance against the Germans. He resigned his seat in 1944 to return to active duty in Italy and southern France, the first Senator since the Civil War to do so. Fluent in German and French, his role in the French campaign was chief liaison officer between General De-

Emily and Cabot in the early years of their marriage.

vers, Commander of the U.S. invasion force, and General Tassigny de Lattre. Promoted to lieutenant colonel in the fall of 1944, he single-handedly captured a four man German patrol. In March 1945 he was decorated with the French Legion of Honor and the Croix de Guerre with palm. He flew reconnaissance missions behind German lines intercepting messages and received the American Legion of Merit and the Bronze Star. After the war he resumed his political career but continued as an Army Reserve officer where he rose to the rank of major general (two stars). In 1946, he defeated Democratic Senator David Walsh and became a spokesman in the Senate for the moderate, internationalist wing of the Republican Party. In 1951 he helped persuade Eisenhower to run for president, and became his campaign manager, angering the Republican candidate, Senator Robert Taft, and losing his own Senate race in 1952 (receiving 48.5% of the vote) to John F. Kennedy (who received 51.5%)—who thus reclaimed a seat that Kennedy's maternal grandfather, Honey Fitz, had lost to Henry Cabot Lodge, Sr. in 1916. In 1953, Lodge was considered for Secretary of State but Eisenhower opted to name him Ambassador to the United Nations, creating a cabinet post for him. Supportive of the UN as an institution for promoting peace, he famously said, with characteristic brio, "This organization is created to prevent you from going to hell. It isn't created to take you to heaven."

During the UN years they lived in a luxurious suite on the top floor of the Waldorf Astoria where they entertained, among others, Danny Kaye and Hoagy Carmichael. My grandfather served at the UN until his 1960 run for Vice-President with Richard Nixon that he again lost to Jack Kennedy by a razor-thin vote.

In that 1960 race, I remember my grandfather standing, his head bent in concentration, in the brief minutes before being interviewed for television by Huntley and Brinkley. The library had been invaded by the chaos of large cables crisscrossing the room, and two large cameras like small dinosaurs stared blankly toward the sofa. Grandma looked the conventional part, pouring tea, something I'd never seen her do before, while Grandpa composed his thoughts at the large desk by the far window. I watched him closely and noticed he needed just ten minutes to collect his thoughts. Clearly he had a well-trained mind, was good with the press, articulate, a good judge of character, and able with details.

I was nine during his Vice-Presidential campaign, and I recollect my sisters and I sitting in pretty dresses in the back seat of a Cadillac,

During the UN years: Emily in strapless gown with flowers and satin wrap and Ambassador Lodge on her right.

awkwardly waving to the crowd. When reporters came to the gate of the house in Beverly and asked what we had eaten and what we had discussed, Emily delighted the press with quizzical one-liners: "My dear boy, read Thomas Aquinas. Goodbye!"

President Kennedy named my grandfather Ambassador to Vietnam 1963-64. While serving, he won the 1964 New Hampshire presidential primary against Goldwater and Rockefeller in a write-in vote. LBJ reappointed him in 1965. He was Ambassador at Large 1967-68 and Ambassador to Germany 1968-69, and he also headed the unsuccessful delegation to the Paris Peace Talks in 1969. From 1969 to 1977, Lodge served occasionally as an envoy to the Vatican for Presidents Nixon and Ford. My most vivid memory of the Vietnam War years were the Sunday lunches when our grandparents were home, when my Uncle Harry, Aunt Eleanita, and their children—Freddie, Harry (now Dr. Harry Lodge), John, and Felicity—would sit down with my father and mother, and all of us—Nancy, Dossy, Cabot, George, David, and me—to poached chicken with hollandaise sauce; my grandmother would bellow across the table at my grandfather, "Cabot, you've got to stop the bombing!" He came to see the uselessness of the war and the anti-war protests, particularly as they concerned him, depressed him.

When my grandmother, Emily, died in 1992, Richard Pierson of *The Washington Post*, wrote a tribute to her describing her unique diplomatic skills and citing a *Post* reporter's take comparing her to the wives of the other candidates (Jacqueline Kennedy, Pat Nixon, and Lady Bird Johnson):

> [Mrs. Lodge is] the most fascinating character of the quartet. She is the **oldest, tallest, slimmest, vaguest, and the one with a built-in sense of humor.... Her intelligence, her skill in dealing with people from all walks of life and her love of travel, (made her) the most unobtrusively sophisticated and stimulating companion of the four."**
>
> Mrs. Clark [Emily Lodge], who also spoke French, assisted Lodge in his diplomatic assignments. She was prominent during his years as U.S. Ambassador to the United Nations during the Eisenhower Administration, acting as the official hostess to the wife of Soviet leader Nikita Khrushchev during the Khrushchevs' famous and often stormy tour of this country in 1959. In addition to her years in Bonn, where her husband served as ambassador in the late 1960s, she lived in Saigon during her husband's first tour as ambassador to South Vietnam. During his second tour, spouses generally were discouraged from living in Vietnam, and she ran their household from Bangkok. During the first tour, a time of increasing diplomatic tension and possible physical danger, she was a notable success. She not only handled the "official" duties of an ambassador's wife of her era with dignity and style, but made her mark in other ways as well. Early in the tour, her husband's personal aide came upon her near the servants' quar-

> ters chatting away in French to a half-dozen Vietnamese children. She turned to the aide and asked him why the children did not play on the broad embassy lawn. The aide stammered something to the effect that he supposed there were "rules." She told the aide: "I have 10 grandchildren, you know. I adore them, especially when they are naughty. These Vietnamese children seem very well behaved. Tell them to come over and play on the grass often. I like to watch them." They played on the grass, and she continued to converse with them in French. She once told a reporter that she had tried out some of her "new" Vietnamese on them, but had succeeded only in reducing them to laughter. Henry Cabot Lodge died in 1985. Three years later, she married Forrester A. Clark, a retired investment banker.[332] Mrs. Clark, who was born in Beverly, grew up in New England and France. In recent years, she had become active in efforts to assist the homeless and had worked with a shelter in Boston. In addition to her husband, of Beverly and Hamilton, survivors include two sons, George and Henry Lodge, both of Beverly; ten grandchildren; and sixteen great-grandchildren.

Our grandmother was very different from the pensive Bessy (Gammy) and my father's memories of his mother, written at her death, are the ones, I sensed, everyone hoped we girls would inherit:

> I remember [your] Grandma as full of joy and love with a fine sense of humor and a most generous spirit. She lived to help other people, especially her husband and family. Looking back on my childhood, I am struck by the extent to which she allowed me independence. I was free to follow my own excitement. Even at a very young age I was allowed to venture far from the world of adults—sailing, hiking, working at odd jobs. She was anything but strict and yet her example showed me what I should strive to be, caring about those less fortunate, and seeking to right wrongs. She found great fulfillment in helping my father in his political and military careers. For her his job came first. This attitude was in no way sacrificial. She was not giving anything up to follow him. It was the way she saw life and she genuinely enjoyed every minute of it except when the danger of being with him in Vietnam forced her,

---

332 Grandma observed the traditional mourning period of three years, and afterwards married Forrester Clark, a marriage that she, at 80, naughtily claimed was "for sex" and to "pay him back" for financing my father's campaign. In the Bermuda church where they were joined in marriage, when the minister asked them to please kneel, she replied with characteristic charm, "I can kneel but I am not sure if I can get up again."

> along with other Embassy wives, to live in a hotel in Bangkok. But she never failed to speak her mind and she had substantial influence on my father. For example, I think she caused him to question our policies in Vietnam sooner than he otherwise might have. In spite of his accomplishments, she never lost her sense of perspective, her humility, her sense of human insignificance in the face of God. She was religious not in a creedal or churchy way but in her belief in a higher power that shaped our lives. She was energetic, intelligent, well-read, and quick in her movements—never lazy. She was always busy whether it was entertaining grandchildren, serving lepers in Vietnam, the poor in Washington, or flood victims when the Merrimack River topped its channel, or acting as a relaxed and friendly hostess to the great and near great wherever she went. She laughed a lot, seeing humor in most everything, even the most banal. All in all, she was a happy person and radiated happiness to those around her.

When Grandpa died, we didn't see Grandma cry and it was then that her stoicism and sense of duty became most apparent. A few weeks earlier, he had woken as if from a coma very close to his death; he had not had any water for days, as he had wanted it. I knelt and took his hand and put my cheek close to his: "It's Emmy, Grandpa," I softly said. "The sun is shining through the bedroom windows and glistening on the sea. Grandma has gone to Harry's for lunch," I told him. His eyelids fluttered, and gathering together all the strength of his courageous spirit, he rasped, "I love you," and then fell back deep inside his already forward journeying soul. The visit to the coffin seemed to me to be a mere formality. Grandpa had always told me, with a humor that made him beloved by all, "When I shuffle off this mortal coil, make sure I fit into the slot." The grand old man in a simple pine box was slid into the Lodge tomb at Mt. Auburn Cemetery built by the Senator's mother, Anna Cabot Lodge. Great Uncle John wanted us to accept the government invitation for a funeral in the National Cathedral in Washington but our grandmother insisted on a private ceremony in our simple Beverly parish. Years later, I asked Grandma which of her two husbands she would be with in Heaven after death. She paused, looked me straight in the eye and replied, enigmatically, "I think God has an altogether different purpose for me."

Top row: John de Streel; Pa; Uncle John; Grandpa; Uncle Harry; Quentin de Streel. Seated: Aunt Eleanita holding older sister, Nancy; Aunt Helena de Streel; Grandma; Mummy holding Cabot; Aunt Francesca Lodge with daughters Beatrice and Lillie; Elisabeth de Streel. On the floor: Dossy; the author, Emily, at five.

Courtesy of my aunt, Edith Kunhardt Davis. The author, Emily, with her mother.

EPILOGUE

When after three girls, my brother, Henry Cabot Lodge III, was born, my parents' relief and excitement was ancient and palpable. I was meant to be the heir, and as the second girl, I strove to understand how to be a success. As late as the 1970s, going to college, having a career, serving in the military, and navigating sailboats were meant, in our world, for men. I remember my grandfather arguing with my grandmother about his granddaughters going to college. My father insisted that his daughters go to college, but our grandmother won the debate.

Every afternoon when my father was at home, he threw a football with his three sons. We girls were dressed up and shown off. I remember one particularly lovely blue velvet party dress that I wore with my blond hair tied back with a blue satin ribbon. Our conversation seemed to be meant to provide entertainment for higher authorities and greater minds.

Dubbed the "philosopher" by my father who had read my palm at birth, I was an eager and devoted sounding board for his vivid ideas. He delighted in repeating the Greek definition of happiness: "The exercise of vital powers along lines of excellence in a life affording them scope."[333]

Most of what is written about White Anglo-Saxon Protestants (WASPS) is a cliché and the generalizations are often inaccurate. But there did seem to be a standard that was to be kept up. It consisted of giving birth to the heir, cherishing one's children, anticipating a husband's and other peoples' needs, being self-sacrificing and charitable in every way, being intelligent well-informed on every topic and making a house and garden look lovely, smell fresh and bring people comfort. In our family, women were also trained diplomats. My grandmother said she enjoyed the political role of tricking everyone into believing they were right, and that she was on their side. Much of the childrearing was

[333] Edith Hamilton, *The Greek Way* (New York and London: W.W. Norton & Co, 2010), 27.

left to the Scottish or Irish servants; my father was very close to Nellie, a strong, funny, gentle Irish nurse. There was a code and standard to being a good wife and that code was not always forgiving, as Abigail Trafford wrote,[334] for the trouble came when a wife was sick or widowed or had no money.

> The secret in most families was that the WASP way of life depended on the talents, energies and sacrifice of the women. They often ran separate households in summer and winter, managed a staff, monitored large numbers of children and grandchildren, and generally created an environment in which the WASP male could flourish. After World War II, WASP women, many now armed with college degrees, put on aprons for about a decade and then decided they would rather be lawyers or bankers or holistic massage therapists. Once the woman revolts, the whole way of life collapses. All the while, an increasing number of third and fourth generation WASPS simply broke the code that had become corrupt, repressive, sexist and silly. They broke the code by moving out, marrying out, divorcing out, dropping out and opting out.... The downward fall was accelerated by the revolt of the WASP women. The traditional escape routes had always been scandal (love) and **mental illness**.

As a child in Washington, I remember being terribly in love with my mother. Nancy Kunhardt Lodge was funny, bright, talented, and beautiful. My memories of my her are as lustrous as the photograph of the greenhouse at Dumbarton Oaks where we went together on one of our "special treats." She adored her children and took pride in them. At night, when she swept out of the house for dinner in a blue chiffon dress with our handsome father, she was a picture of loveliness. Doves nested on my parents' bedroom window.

As a young woman, our mother resembled Vivien Leigh, and she shaved her eyebrows in order to better effect the arched eyebrow of Scarlett O'Hara. After graduating from The Brearley School, a private high school in New York City, Nancy was admitted to Yale Drama School but her parents convinced her that she would find a better mate at Harvard and so she abandoned acting to instead earn her Masters in Education at Harvard. My father fell in love with her in English class—

[334] Abigail Trafford, "How the WASP Crust Crumbled," *International Herald Tribune*, February 23, 1993.

her glossy dark hair, white skin, green beret and matching coat—and he rode her around on his bicycle handlebars.

As a child, I remember our mother's Meserve grandparents, who lived in a brownstone at 78th Street and Lexington Avenue in New York City. Lunch was formal with finger bowls on white linen on a polished mahogany table. Frederick Hill Meserve (Gampy), (b. 1865), gentle and friendly with children, reveled in describing the Upper East Side of his youth when he could see cows grazing in Harlem. Writing illustrated biographies of Lincoln is a family passion that began when Gampy discovered a treasure trove of glass negatives on warehouse floors in Jersey City and built them into the Meserve collection of Matthew Brady negatives, America's most valuable portrait collection of Abraham Lincoln.

Gampy's daughter, my maternal grandmother, Dorothy Meserve, married the gentle Philip Kunhardt, who became the director of the Morristown Hospital in Morristown, N.J. The Kunhardts had immigrated to Claremont, Staten Island, New York, from Hamburg, Germany in the 1840s. Dorothy Meserve Kunhardt had a comically macabre sense of humor but she kept her family afloat during the Great Depression by writing the celebrated childrens' book, *Pat The Bunny*, (the bunny belonged to my mother) and is also remembered for her illustrated histories of Lincoln.[335]

As a child visiting our grandparents in Morristown, NJ, I recall books and Lincoln memorabilia piled high to the ceiling and even up the stairs so that there was a tunnel for passing through. My mother showed me the glass vial she kept as a girl of the breath of one of her favorite nurse's, Anna. The vial was labeled "Anna's breath." Toward the end of our grandmother's life in the 1970s, Dorothy Kunhardt lived with us in Beverly and I took time from my job at *60 Minutes* at CBS News in New York to visit her. I remember her sitting propped up in bed connected to various tubes and devices. As I was leaving to return to New York, she said, "I am sorry to see you go this way." And without hesitation, I replied, "I am sorry to see YOU go this way." And a slight smile began to curl around her mouth and broadened into a grin. Other

---

[335] *Twenty Days: Matthew Brady and His World*, co-authored with her son Philip B. Kunhardt, Jr., managing editor of *Life Magazine* from 1978 until his retirement in 1982. My late Uncle Phil wrote *My Father's House: A New Birth of Freedom*, and of my personal favorite, *Lincoln: An Illustrated Biography*, a great work of art co-authored with his sons, Philip B. Kunhardt III, Distinguished Scholar in Residence in the Humanities, New York University, and Founding Director of The Center for the Study of Transformative Lives at NYU, and Peter W. Kunhardt, executive producer of Kunhardt Productions, and winner of three Emmy Awards.

family members, hovering at the doorway, tried to stifle their laughter; she knew I was giving a nod to her odd humor.

We grew up in Washington in the fifties, when trolleys still ran up Wisconsin Avenue, and Georgetown was a slow southern town where gracious elms folded lazily into O Street. As a young reporter for *The Boston Herald*, my father interviewed the Secretary of Labor, became his speechwriter, and worked his way up to becoming Assistant Secretary of Labor. On the way to school in our Nash, our father taught us funny songs he had learned in the Navy, planting a tiny seed in me that grew into a lifelong passion for music. My father became friendly with Bobby Kennedy. JFK, then Senator from Massachusetts, sat at our mother's feet when she was pregnant with my brother, George, and Ethel Kennedy competed with her over who could have more children, while my father played touch football with Bobby.

When my father ran against Bobby's brother, Ted, for the U.S. Senate in 1962 our mother was unable to fulfill the challenging role of the Lodge political wife and was overwhelmed as the mother of six children. She was sentimental (as much about animals as children), an innocent who remained so her entire life; inherently good, but flawed, and her contradictory behavior produced a lot of fear in her children. Her descent into mental illness and alcoholism made her increasingly and profoundly self-centered and unable to cope with life so she withdrew into her own world, which was a tragedy because she was capable of compassion.

My childhood yearning for trust and consistency grew into a fascination for other, more dignified role models within the family—other, that is, than our powerful black housekeeper, Beatrice, and our life-giving Dutch governess, Anna Marie, both mothers to us. In our house, our father, not our mother, read to us—memorably, *A Christmas Carol* by Charles Dickens, every holiday season.

The sea runs to the heart of the family. At the age of six, my father, George Cabot Lodge, was already sailing his dory twelve miles from Beverly to Gloucester with a ten-year-old friend. He seemed to have the eighteenth century George Cabot in his bones as well as the nineteenth century John Ellerton Lodge, and the half-models of John E. Lodge's clipper ships used in the China trade lined our living room walls. Prior to reading about the great voyage of his *Mayflower* ancestor, John Howland, my father dreamt of his having been washed over by a wave, and managing incredibly to swinging himself back onboard. Yet, though it was only a few miles from our house, he never took us to visit John Cabot's house (now the Beverly Historical Society), a large square red brick mansion perched atop Cabot Street in the center of Beverly, with a lawn which, in the eighteenth century, ran right down to the harbor.

Ours was a simple house, for my father had built its walls on top of preexisting brick garden walls. His first job was picking carrots beside a deaf and dumb Polish immigrant, a summer job he sought out to avoid tennis and dancing lessons. He wanted to strike out on his own and never spoke of family, teaching us the value of independence and the importance of humility. His first memory marked him for life. In 1930,

Senate campaign portrait of my father, George C. Lodge, in 1962, at thirty-five.

when he was three years old, he recalls: "I was standing on Fifth Avenue in New York, waiting for my uncle to take me for a picnic. [Uncle Harry Sears, Commodore of the New York Yacht Club]. A limo came by with the chauffeur uncovered in the rain and a woman in back sheltered under a roof, wrapped in furs. The image stirred a lifelong interest in why the two people found themselves in such different class positions."

If the family passion has been for conflict resolution, then my father has been carrying the torch. He inherited his grandfather's daunting double name, George Cabot Lodge, and a love for good government. When he became a candidate for the Senate in 1962 against Teddy Kennedy, we moved permanently to Beverly, our summer house in Massachusetts. His father, Henry Cabot Lodge, Jr., had been groomed to be a Senator from Massachusetts by his grandfather, the Senator, who had been inspired to do so by Senator George Cabot, a family tradition dating to the eighteenth century. Yet my father would consider calling our family a "political dynasty" extremely bad taste.

After his unsuccessful run for the Senate he became a professor at Harvard Business School, where he taught for forty years and wrote fourteen books, including, notably, *The New American Ideology*. My father set forth the theory that we, as a nation, are moving away from the cherished historic roots of our country—namely, private property, the limited role of the state, and individualism, toward an ideology which cherishes the values held by the community, toward responsiveness to community need. Communitarianism, an idea that he helped to develop, is now a watchword in the political arena.

At the Harvard Business School my father helped to create a new course in the required first year of the MBA program called Business, Government and the International Economy. It was the only course with no businesses in it. It sought to help students understand how the world works. It was built around the concept of national strategy and sought to compare the strategies of many countries, ranging from Japan and China to Germany, Brazil, Mexico and the United States. His special field of interest was ideology and his many books on the subject used ideology as a way of comparing nations and understanding change within a nation, especially the United States. In addition, he sought to understand the introduction of change in so-called underdeveloped countries. His book on this subject, *Engines of Change*, and several *Foreign Affairs* articles led to the establishment of the Inter-American Foundation, of which he was vice chairman during its first seven years. It is an independent government agency dedicated to finding and fueling engines of change in Latin America. His most recent book, *A Corporate Solution to Global Poverty*, proposes a World Development Corporation to facilitate corporate investment in poor countries to provide jobs and raise the standard of living. He has taught literally thousands of students solutions to the dilemmas business and governments encounter in the global economy. From the standpoint of family history, it is interesting how he was able to successfully merge the meditative and active life that his grandfather, Bay, struggled to achieve.

In his autobiography, my father writes of the unusual experience in 1963, when his father was Ambassador to Vietnam, of seeing and "conversing with" the Senator's ghost. The Senator's love for and protection of his family, as well as his love for history, state, and country, was so great that even after his death, he made his will known to his great grandson (my father, George), asking for news of his adored heir, my father's father, Henry Cabot Lodge.

> [George] had just given a speech at Tremont Temple and was returning to his car which he had parked in front of the State House. As he climbed the steps out of the Common he looked up and saw the figure of Senator Lodge as he must have looked in the prime of life [1890]: reddish hair in wiry waves close to his head, a short well-clipped beard, sharp brown eyes, a slender, well-knit figure, smartly dressed in a long jacket. His demeanor was of a man in a hurry.
>
> 'You've been to Viet Nam,' it said, or at least that was the message communicated to George.
>
> 'Yes,' George replied.
>
> 'How's Cabot?' it asked.
>
> 'Fine.'
>
> 'Give him my love when you write.'
>
> And it was gone. After the ghost's departure, George yearned to revive it. He crossed the street to where the Senator's statue stood but it was as dead as the bronze of which it was made. He wondered what had restrained it. Why didn't it go to Saigon and see for itself? Why was it in such a rush?[336]

How could the Senator exist posthumously? What was it about that place in Boston that enabled my father to "speak" to his great grandfather? Was it through the power of love or the love of power that the Senator could appear before his great grandson?

***

[336] George C. Lodge, *Paths Are Made By Walking*, 28-29. My father speaks of himself in the third person.

Part I of this book traces the ancestral threads that bring together the central characters of Nannie and Senator Henry Cabot Lodge. When speaking of those ancestors, my Great Aunt Helena, the Senator's granddaughter, intoned, "They were good and tough." Part II turns attention to the next generation, where Bay, the rebel poet in the Gilded Age, struggled to create a new poetic genre while his wife, Bessy, masterfully managed their burgeoning family, Cabot, John, and Helena, who in the end succeed at the destiny chosen by their the powerful grandfather.[337]

Daughters of admirals will recognize themselves in Nannie Davis Lodge. While Charles Henry Davis was fighting the Battle of Vicksburg during the Civil War, his wife was lovingly encouraging her children to train their minds, inculcating in them the importance of service to country, and instilling in them the importance of self-restraint. From the age of twelve, Nannie was reading Shakespeare and three years later, had memorized it all; at sixteen, while a student in the first class at Wellesley College, she went on to discover the philosophical genius of Samuel Johnson and Edmund Burke. Her maternal grandmother, Harriette, wife of Senator Elijah Mills, regaled her with stories of the Monroe administration, on how to be a Senator's wife, while at the same time, bringing up the children and running a farm. By the time she got off the train at Lynn at eighteen, she was ready and she recognized in Henry Cabot Lodge the kind of person who would amuse her and challenge her and not be a bore. She was his anchor and his rock.

Bessy Davis Lodge came to her education on her own as a form of sustenance. As my grandfather told me when I asked who the lovely woman was in the portrait on the stairs,[338] he replied, "That was my mother; she had a difficult life." This long journey into the past has been an attempt to understand why it was so. Though she suffered from her mother's neglect, she was deeply admired by her father, who taught her "to read by the mile." Bessy, Bay Lodge's muse, his virtuous Beatrice in Dante's firmament, embodied, according to Adams, his highest standard. She couldn't convince the Senator to let her stay in France, but she fulfilled her place in history by instilling in her children the widest possible education including an international one (French grammar school) and a non-sectarian one (Middlesex school).

Like Isaac Davis, the Minute Man, and Theodore Frelinghuysen, the Dutch Reform Minister, when Bessy set her mind on something she was

---

[337] See appendix for more about the lives of John Davis Lodge and Helena de Streel.

[338] See cover photo.

(Brother) Henry Cabot Lodge III dancing with the author at her wedding in the library at Beverly.

immovable. And, as we have seen, this did not always sit well with her father-in-law, the Senator. The reader will perhaps agree with Henry Adams when he wrote Elizabeth Cameron in 1901 about the Lodges that Bessy would end by "ruling them." Just as my grandfather was inspired to political office by his grandfather, his mother instilled in her son, the importance of common sense and being charitable to others. The family was amazed by her courage in response to the early death of her husband, Bay, and later, of her admirer, Jean du Breuil de Saint Germain. But we also laud her for great unselfishness, for bringing books in Braille for the blind into being so that a woman like Helen Keller could find something to read at the Library of Congress—and, as my grandfather's sister, Helena, reminds us pointedly she did so without leaving home.

In the end, it can certainly be said also of Emily Sears Lodge, our grandmother, that, according to Helena, they were not only intelligent but their houses were full of order, peace, and kindness, where "people could laugh and think and everything looked lovely and smelled fresh and brought one comfort." It is difficult to underestimate the life giving, soul binding, nation building power that serenity brings.

Interestingly, the two Lodge women who dominate this book are both descended from a man named Dolor Davis who came to this country in 1630. Though his first name means "sadness," Dolor nevertheless created over the centuries two remarkable women, both muses to their husbands, friends, and family. As if sadness was a kind of kindling for the hearth of the soul, they managed with courage what was required of them.

> *Spirit, that made those heroes dare,*
> *To die, and leave their children free...*
>
> — Ralph Waldo Emerson

Appendix

Chapter I

Henry Cabot Lodge, in his first book, *The Life and Letters of George Cabot*, pgs. 63-64, shows his gift for political oratory: "But to Jefferson and his followers belongs the sole glory of introducing foreign influences into our politics. Adoration of France produced worship of England; and both brought a curse upon our politics, and warped public sentiment among men of every shade of belief for the next twenty-five years. [...] With Gênet, this wretched business began. The contagion, under the benign influence of the French envoy, spread rapidly... To these men, friends of order who had just rescued the country from the anarchy of the Confederation, came the specter of French democracy. Not of constitutional freedom which they venerated; not the well-ordered State which they sought to construct; not the liberty for which they had fought the War of Independence—none of these principles were supported by France. The French liberty... preached license not freedom; substituted names for realities; and, redressing wrongs by indiscriminate massacre, set up a tyranny much worse than the one she had thrown out. To the Federalists in America, comprising many of the best political thinkers of the age, the spectacle of French anarchy seemed to betoken the coming of French despotism. And it was this sham liberty beginning in fine words and ending in confusion, shame and tyranny, which they saw imported amongst them. As they watched these delusions spread, and Jacobin clubs rise up with all the vile paraphernalia of liberty poles and red caps, the Federalists roused to a vigorous and bitter resistance. 'Anti-Federalists' now changed to 'Jacobins' and 'Anarchists' was retorted to the accusations of monarchy.... Mr. Cabot was of the opinion that it was no time for sentimental and baseless gratitude, when the interests of property or liberty were threatened... try to imagine what our own feelings would have been at the time of the French Revolution—when its horrors were actually at our doors, and threatening entrance; when the ambassador of that polite nation preached his crusade in our country, appealed to the populace against the government, and spread his pernicious doctrines far and wide.... The President (refused) to hold any further communication with Gênet...."

***

WASHINGTON TO CABOT
(Private and Confidential)

Philadelphia, 7th Sept., 1795
DEAR SIR,
The enclosed letters (which after reading, be so good as to return to me) will be the best apology I can offer for the liberty I am about to take, and for the trouble, if you comply with my request, it must necessarily give.

To express all the sensibility which has been excited in my breast by the receipt of young Fayette's letter, from the recollection of his father's merits, services and suffering, from my friendship for him, and from my wishes to become a *friend* and *father* to his son, are unnecessary. Let me in a few words declare that I *will be his friend*; but the manner of becoming so, considering the obnoxious light in which his father is viewed by the French government, and my own situation as the executive of the United States, requires more time to consider in all its relations than I can bestow on it at present; the letters not having been in my hands for more than an hour, and I myself on the point of setting out for Virginia to fetch my family back, whom I left there about the first of August.

The mode which, at the first view, strikes me as the most eligible to answer his purposes and save appearances is to administer all the consolation to the young gentleman that he can derive from the most unequivocal assurances of my standing in the place of and becoming to him a father, friend, protector, and supporter. But secondly, for prudential motives, as they may relate to himself, his mother and friends whom he has left behind, and to my official character, it would be best not to make these sentiments public; of course that it would be ineligible that he should come to the seat of the general government, where all the foreign characters (particularly that of his own nation) are residents, until it is seen what opinions will be excited by his arrival; especially, too, as I shall be necessarily absent five or six weeks from it, on business, in several places. Third, considering how important it is to avoid idleness and dissipation, to improve his mind, and to give him all the advantages which education can bestow, my opinion and my advice to him is (if he is qualified for admission) that he should enter as a student at the Univ. of Cambridge, although it should be for a short time *only*. The expense of which, as also of every other means of support, I will pay, and now do authorize you, my dear sir, to draw upon me accordingly; and, if it is in any degree *necessary* or *desired*, Mr. Frestel, his tutor, should accompany him to the University in that character. Any arrangements which you shall make for the purpose, and any expense thereby incurred for the same, shall be borne by me in like manner.

One thing more, and I will conclude: let me pray you, my dear sir, to impress upon young Fayette's mind, and indeed upon that of his tutor's, that the reason why I do not urge him to come to me have been frankly related, and that their prudence must appreciate them with caution. My friendship for his father, so far from being diminished, has increased in the ratio of his misfortunes, and my inclination to serve the son will be evidenced by my conduct. Reason which readily will occur to you and cannot be explained to him will account for my not acknowledging the receipt of his or Mr. Frestel's letter.

With sincere esteem, I am, dear sir,
Your obediant and obliged,
GEORGE WASHINGTON

P.S. You will perceive that Lafayette has taken the name of Motier. Whether it is best he should retain it and aim at perfect concealment or not depends upon a better knowledge of circumstances than I am possessed of; and therefore I leave this matter to your own judgment, after a consultation with the parties.

***

"Can the Suffering of Humanity Be Justified?" George Cabot's journal, 1796:

Appointed to a state wherein there are various and abundant sources of pleasure and pain, man is naturally induced to survey the present scheme of things and form some judgment of its economy and justice. Taught alike by the voice of nature and human lips to adore a God of perfect wisdom and goodness he is content in infancy to rest with the conviction that all things are ordered for the advantage of mankind. He beholds the sun as made to minister with its light and heat to the comfort of the human race—the moon and stars as lamps hung out in heaven by a kind Father to supply the absence of the bigger light—in short, the whole arrangement of human affairs as under the immediate providence of a merciful Creator. But the brief season of unclouded joy and unbroken confidence yields to coming doubt and discontent—he begins to perceive that there are thorns as well as flowers in the way of life—and perhaps by degrees, learns to be blind to the sunshine and have an ear only for the tempest. So that his youth and old age are commonly in the opposite extremity—if he trusts too fondly in the spring of his existence, he enjoys too coldly and admires too insensibly in the latter days of his abode on earth.

The child seldom sees anything but beauty or hears ought but music. Experience teaches him that there is good and evil—virtue and vice—appiness and misery. He contemplates the great plan of human affairs and dares to measure its excellence and scan its imperfections. What then is manifest in the condition of humanity? Does the good or evil preponderate? Is there any evil? If there is how can it be explained consistently with the perfect knowledge and goodness of the Creator?

No one who observes the condition of mankind with a desire of truth can deny that the majority pass the greater portion of their lives in real enjoyment—existence itself is a blessing—the mere ordinary exercise of the senses is a great privilege and an ample satisfaction. Of this, there is strong proof in the natural cheerfulness of children when they first are able to use with tolerable freedom their faculties of sight and hearing. Pleasure is the constant companion of the early acquisitions necessary to the welfare and preservation of life. Health must be admitted to be a positive source of exultation and it is the common legacy of the parent to the child.

Go forth into the public streets—see the signs of happiness in the active step, the easy laugh, the careless countenance—you will see misery also but so little that it can hardly be discerned in the general aspect of joy. It being admitted that good is the prevailing power (and no reasonable man can doubt it) it is yet to be determined whether evil can be justified—for there surely is evil—men do suffer—suffer most acutely and that, often with no apparent desert of its infliction. Why should not good be the only influence of a perfectly good power? Is it because God has not the ability to make a constitution of things free from evil? Or does he not wish to do it? Is it a necessary part of any system? The answers to these questions has baffled the strongest endeavors of human curiosity and wisdom—yet many get some satisfaction from his own contemplation on this interesting problem.

It may be answered first that it is of little concern whether God is able to destroy all evil—God is all powerful but without further information it is by no means clear that this is not an impossibility. God cannot make a whole less than a part—perhaps the existence of evil is absolutely essential to the existence of good. Indeed, there seems good authority for this opinion. Everything is good or bad by comparison—our estate is measured by the new loss or gain. He who has been tortured by exquisite pain finds excessive joy in the relief from it—while he who is in full possession of health prizes not the blessing but toils for some distant and unattained object of desire.

Evil is a necessary thing to our continued existence—for in the present condition of our bodies, if we were not used to avoid the destructive circumstances which ever threaten us, we should soon learn to be. If the heat of the fire did not inflict pain on our bodies, we would soon be consumed in it. Our character would be nothing conceivable in the event of no evil in the world—it is made up of desire and fears which must cease when the objects excite them are removed. The existence of evil is essential to the existence of good. Let it be remembered that without difficulty there could be no victory—without pain, no congratulation—without perplexity, no deliverance—without deformity, no beauty, without discord, no harmony—without sorrow, no sympathy—without distress, no consolation. The calamities of the mortal life may be beautifully reconciled with the mercy of God—both in the supposition that they are a necessary portion of humanity and they are designed as monitors on our conduct and the forerunners of perfect joy.

***

James Hamilton has preserved in his *Reminiscences* an anecdote which illustrates what our ancestors meant by an after-dinner conversation:

> This story of Gouverneur Morris reminds me of what George Cabot told me when I was staying at his house in Boston:
>
> "I never give dinners but Morris came to Boston and having known him well in the good old times, I felt it due to him to make up a party for him. I invited Fisher Ames and Harrison Gray Otis and others of that stamp. After the cloth was removed, I introduced as a subject of conversation, 'How long can Great Britain sustain her load of debt?'

I briefly expressed my own views. All waited to hear Morris who with great force and knowledge of the subject, presented his. When he had finished there was a pause: we drank and all eyes were turned to Ames who was admitted to be our best talker. As you know, he was then in feeble health. He began in his low melodious tone to express his views which differed widely from those of Morris. He was thoroughly acquainted with the subject, which, by the way, was very frequently discussed at that time. He talked in his best vein with singular clearness and eloquence. Morris was all attention. The first indication on his countenance of what was passing through his mind was, 'he talks well.' The next, 'he talks as well as I do.' And as Ames warmed to his subject, 'he talks better than I do.' Cabot, I remember well. He was one of the best talkers of the day and one of the most intelligent, upright, amiable and excellent of men."

***

Anna Sophia Blake Cabot's Travel Journal

10 June 1823-24

Left Leghorn[339] in the Rockford on June 10th, arrived the 11th, early morning at Elba where we anchored in anticipation of sea sickness, happily dissipated by an enormous breakfast of tea and cold beef.

Visited the house which was once the residence of Napoleon.

15th Set sail early in the morning through the channel of Pirnbrio and arrived in the Bay of Arballette early in the morning.

19th Arrived in the Bay of Naples early. Magnificent view.

20th Established myself at the Via Vittoria, no. 29.

Party at Mrs. Hamilton's in the evening.

21st. Dined onboard the Rochford with a large party of Italian princes and princesses. Supped afterwards with the same party at the Villa di Roma.

22nd Dined with the Duchess Deboli.

23rd Dined onboard the Rochford.

Ball in the evening at the Academia.

24th Dined with Monroe—ball at Princess Noia.

26th Dined with Sir Henry Lushington, English consul. Very unwell.

---

[339] Livorno is above Elba on the way south to Naples and below Genoa.

29 Attended first representation of a serious new opera by Donizetti. Violent headache and indigestion.

July Engaged an apartment in Vico Freddo 37 (Rome) from Princess Caetani.

Sunday, July 21 Went to see Duke of Casperano's pictures.

22nd Dined with Princess Caetani, removed my effects with some regret from Vico Freddo, 37. After dinner, received certain direful warnings from an old stump of a tooth. Ventured however in the evening to St. Carlos to hear Spontini'sVestate. Obliged to leave the theatre with violent paroxyms of a toothache.

29th Has seized my whole face. Took two glasses of sulfur water.

31 Cheek swelled even into deformity. Obliged to wear a piece of flannel over it although the thermometer is about 80 in the shade. Thunderstorms, every peal as loud as an explosion of a powder magazine or somewhat more noisy perhaps.

1 August

2nd Finished correcting the introduction to *Berenice.*[340] Began Dante.

Felt myself well enough to go to St. Carlos.

5th worse. Teatro di Fiorentina.

6th Return of the King. Illumination, beautiful effect.

7th Post day and yet no letter. Found a letter from a miscreant of a servant.

Went to hear Spontini's *La Vestale* again. More and more delighted with it.

Ballo of Sesastri, splendidly got up but rather unintelligible in terms of plot.

8th Began to bathe. 1st warm water to be agreeable.

18th Princess Caetani in the evening.

21st News of the Pope's death.[341]

23 Long morning of Handel with Blyh.

25th Went to St. Carlo to hear a new opera by Salieri—tolerably good.

30th Paid for my lodgings. Finished finally the first act of *Berenice.* Had a row with the tailor. Weather pleasantly cool.

31st Church. Dined with Blyh. Supped afterwards at the Villa di Roma.

13-14 Went to the Dardenelles.

[340] She wrote a play based on Racine's play.

[341] Pope Pius VIII.

17th Commencement of the autumnal rain. Thunder made such a row all night that I could not sleep.

18th Post-day and still no letter.

Saw apartments at via delle belle donne.

Took them. Went to see the Duke of Casperano's pictures.

Dined with the Princess Caetani. Removed myself with some regret from Vico Freddo to No. 6 Nicoletto Delle Belle Donne, find that so far have not gained by the exchange.

23rd Breakfasted with the Duke of Casperano, cold wet day.

24th Concluded negotiations for tea cups and saucers. Miserable weather.Dined with Munroe.

25th Breakfasted with the Duke of Casperano, went with him afterwards to see Prince Colonna's pictures, a fine head by Leonardo da Vinci and a Salvator Rosa among them.

29th Monday Wrote last bars of *Lucio Vero.*

30th composed a duet for harp and piano for Miss. Caetani at Teatro Necorio.

1 Oct. News of Pope's election (1824) Friday wet cold day.

27th Opera

1 October News of the Pope's election Friday wet cold day.

Sat. Oct.4th Opera by Mayer called *Medea*, magnificent music.

17th Large party at Mrs. Hamilton's. Heard Guiliani, the famous guitar player. Dismissed the French master whom I began to find a bore.

18th Ball at Lady Lushington's.

19th Went with Mr. and Mrs. Hamilton to the palace to hear a *Te Deum* in honor of the King of Spain.

Fatigue walking in vineyards.

Pozzuoli explored site of ancient Cicena.

29th Stiff as a poker, unable to move from sofa, torrents of rain.

Largo castello. Went to the Academia where there were 6 ladies.

26th New opera at St. Carlos by Merradante entitled *Castenza and Almeriska*. Music not worthy of the singers.

27th Post day and no letter.

4 December Made arrangements to go to Rome. Pangs at the idea of leaving Naples.

Understood that Mr. Earle after amusing me for a week with the promise of going to Rome with me, had decided to go to Benevento. Luckily there was a place left in Perelli's carriage which I reserved for 21 piastres.

23 Transferred my affairs to Hotel Vittoria.

Monday, 8th Breakfasted with the Duke of Casperano. Farewell visits to Academia. Packing up and bill paying. Not much of the latter thank God. Went to hear *Il Matremonia*, alas for the last time. Retired at 11, rose next morning at half past 3.

10th Arrived at Cessna at daybreak. On leaving the place, met a large sow in the very act of labor in the middle of the road.

11th Arrived in Rome at 5pm. Obliged to go to the dogana[342] to have trunks examined. Very tedious business. Proceeded to the Hotel of Europe then to Diamonti's in the via delle Croce where he found tolerable apartments at a moderate price.

14th St. Peter's.

15th Visited the Sciarra gallery with renewed pleasure.

Mr. Barton's.

17th Horribly annoyed by a rash on my face.

25th Christmas Day—church at Santa Maria Maggiore illuminated. Dined à l'anglaise[343]

25th Christmas Day—church at Santa Maria Maggiore illuminated. Dined à l'anglaise with Mr. Earle. Concert at Torlonia, his new palace. Music bad and rooms unaired.

26 Went to Baron Leiparts and thence to Balfour's,[344] played cards until half past one.

27 Dined at Balfour's.

29 Dined with Lady Dunlop. Extremely unwell.

30th Colonna palace. Dined with Blyh. Went afterwards to the Apponyi's. Obliged to leave from indisposition.

31st Feeling rather better. Bored to death by the woman of the house.

'Est-il possible' I have spent the whole year '23 in Italy. Roused in the morning by an invitation to dinner. Bracing day. Good spirits.

Dined with Blyh. Went afterwards to the baron de Redens.

8th Vatican. Went to an opera of Donizetti's. Horribly stupid.

9th Palazzo Doria. Ball at Athley's.

10th Face prodigiously swelled. Ball at Baron de Redens.

10th Villa Borghese gallery.

He attained this day the age of 23.

Took upon myself the management of the music of an amateur play.

---

[342] Customs house.

[343] Informal, not dressy, no tiaras, no longer Empire, Restoration, conventionally dressed.

[344] A Scot living in Rome. Part of the English colony who liked to entertain.

11th Face better.

12 Rehearsal for the play. Contrived after much trouble to rid myself of Mrs. Hasloe, Lady Blyh

13th *Wrote an overture for the play.*

Ball at the Austrian Ambassador, dined with Prince Gabrielli.

15th Rehearsal.

16th Dined with Mr. Earle. Rehearsal by candlelight. Play went very well. Farce about a wedding day (*Il Matremonia*).

17th Ear dreadfully bad. Ventured to go to Lord Ashley's ball.

18th Ear worse and disgusting to behold.

Grand ball at Count Apponyi. Suffered indescribable torments of my uniform and boots.

Composed some music for 'The Innkeeper's Daughter'. Went to hear a new opera by Therandante

22nd Took a turn on the Pinci.[345]

Composed "Adieu my native land." Alarmed by appearance of rash on my cheek, appeared before ear got bad.

Dined with Sir George Prescott. Went to hear new opera. Stupid music. Ear infection.

24th Ball at Palazzo Torlonia. News of death of Cardinal Consalvi[346] —it is said he was killed by his physicians who treated an infection of the lungs as gout. The body was placed upright in sitting posture in state carriage with a number of wax lights. Sighs of disrespect in the populace.

Lame due to tight shoes. Bad toothache. Sleepless night. Dr. Jenks applied leeches which bled profusely from 5 to 11pm.

24th Carnival with Sir George Prescott. Annoyed by a pimple on my left cheek. Melancholy over death of poor Fatina, my little dog.

Masked ball at (Russian) Prince Demidoff's. Very hot.

25th Dismissed Domino for inattention. Took another servant by the name of Luigi Gerti for 10 piastres a month. Annoyed by a pimple on my left cheek.

26 Boil in my ear. Hard of the Duchess of Devonshire's death from Munroe who drove up from Naples

27 Received letter from England. Awoke with a sore throat, went to Belfast's play.

1 April Torrents of rain. Temperature frigid. Ball at St. Peter's.

3rd Boil in my ear broke. Received a severe burn on my face dur-

[345] The hills above Corso.

[346] The Pope's Secretary of State.

ing the extinguishing of the candles last day of carnival. Bought a carriage.

9th Settled to leave Rome Thursday.... Packing up. Pangs at the thought of leaving Rome. Settled to leave Rome. Met with a blast of hot wind which had the same effect as the opening of a furnace.

16th In the Appenines. Beautiful scenery.

Arrived at Lens at 10:30 after a day's journey of 90 miles.

On arrival found it impossible even to procure a little milk though we were both[347] in the most unconscious state of exhaustion.

17th View of the Adriatic. Travelled along the banks of the sea to Pedero. Went to see the Cathedral at Rimini (on the way to Ravenna).

18th Arrived in Ravenna.

19th Breakfasted with Lt. Newborough. Saw Cathedral. Pictures by Guido. Figure of St. Michael in the dome fine.

St. Vitale, rich mosaics. Pliny, 70 AD to Aristophanes. Two doctors from Berlin have been lately here copying it.

Church of Apollinaire.

Opera in the evening. Bonini sang. Much pleasure with the latter.

20th Set off for Bologna at 10:30. Hotel San Marco; Opera. Theater fine and orchestra and ballet excellent.

22 May 1824 Walked through the principal streets of Bologna adorned with arcades. Cathedral in grand piazza. Magnificent pictures of 'The Murder of The Innocents' by Guido Reni, the transfiguration of Caracci and St. Anton by Raphael.

Travelled along the banks of the Brenta Canalto Venice. I am informed that this place is never too hot in summer and in winter it is intensely cold. First view of Venice startling and magnificent.... Hotel Royale near Rialto on the Grand Canal. Called on Munroe. Barbarigo palace full of dirty but invaluable Titians. Went through the Ducal palace, sat in duce's seat in Council room. Magnificent collection of Titian and Veronese. Went to Lido in a gondola. Opera. Church of San Rocco. Tintorettos. Dined with Lady Westmoreland.

4th Left for Verona in the morning with regret.

Milan new opera. Went to Lake Como—wind so high we could scarcely get to the turning of the lake. Enchanted with scenery.

***

[347] First mention of Mr. Cabot.

Newport
Dec. 12, 1875
My Dear Cousin,
I send these verses of the mysterious lady who is (I don't mind telling you in confidence) Emily Dickinson of Amherst, Mass. Her father was formerly M.C and latterly Treasurer of Amherst College. He was a stern, reticent old-fashioned New England lawyer and opened his house once a year for a college reception at commencement time—the only time E.D. ever saw her fellow creatures as she received no visitors and never went beyond the gate. He died last year and she lives there alone with a paralytic mother and one sister. I had first sent my sister Louisa's verses to my sister Anne and will ask her to copy for you those you wish. May wishes to be remembered, was hoping to see you this summer and was sorry to be disappointed.

Ever Cordially,
T.W. Higginson

Some keep the Sabbath going to Church—
I keep it, staying at Home—
With a Bobolink for a Chorister—
And an Orchard, for a Dome—

Some keep the Sabbath in Surplice—
I just wear my Wings—

And instead of tolling the Bell, for Church,

Our little Sexton—sings.

God preaches, a noted Clergyman—
And the sermon is never long, So instead of getting to Heaven at last—
I'm going, all along.[348]

Emily Dickinson's poem number 324, "Some keep the Sabbath going to Church—" (Dickinson 2567) is an anti-puritanical poem, following in the tradition of Walt Whitman's liberated verse and Emerson's ideology. It criticizes the church, espousing a more natural religion. The meaning of the poem might be that while most

[348] For proper formatting, the author has referred to R.W. Franklin's *Poems of Emily Dickinson*, considered the authoritative edition of Dickinson's poems.

people hypocritically go to service, she actually *practices* her religion—without going to church. This is a celebration of the Protestantism that formed this country that, at its extreme, renounces all need for formal or communal worship, liberation from the Catholic Church, and "free worship" which marries Protestantism with deism or pantheism.

***

Poem from Dr. Oliver Wendell Holmes to Harriette Mills (later Davis), the daughter of Senator and Mrs. Elijah Mills, Nannie's mother:

The token of a nameless knight!
And canst thou read the sign,
As gleams thy dark eye's liquid light
Along each mystic line?
No symbol crowns the champion's crest,
Nor blazon marks his shield,
Nor yet has herald's voice confest,
Nor tell-tale dame revealed
The name that was a powerless charm,
If this unbannered lance,
Now wielded by thy true knight's arm,
Full in his lady's glance,
Should strike too faint, or stray too wide
And wrong that blushing name
Once honored with the few that ride
The lists of love and fame!

***

Ages spares the green Provençal vine—
The Troubadour is gone;
The Castle crumbles by the Rhine—
The river still rolls on;
Alas! have I, while life is green,
Forgot my lyre and lay?
Have two sweet, sliding summers seen
Romance dissolve away?

No, Lady! while the lilacs spread
Their dark leaves on the stem
And low the vestal Mayflower's head
Bows with its morning gem,
This slumbering fancy spreads her wing,
The frozen fountain flows,
And greets the glowing step of Spring
In thee, her fairest rose!

When the Senator and Nannie were in Rome on their honeymoon (1871), William Wetmore Story, an old friend of both families, also an admirer of Nannie's mother, wrote Nannie, then seventeen, of her likeness to her mother, for whom he pretended to mistake her in a verse entitled "A Mistake."

"A Mistake"

O Filia Pulchra!
How your sweet face revives again
The dear old time, My Pearl,--
If I may use the pretty name
I called you when a girl.

You are so young; while Time of me
Has made a cruel prey,
It has forgotten you, nor swept
One grace of youth away.

The same sweet face, the same sweet smile,
The same lithe figure, too!
What did you say? "It was perchance
Your mother that I knew?"

Ah, yes, of course, it must have been,
And yet the same you seem,
And for a moment all these years
Fled from me like a dream.

Then what your mother would not give,
Permit me, dear, to take,

The old man's privilege --a kiss--
Just for your mother's sake."

***

From *Early Memories* by Henry Cabot Lodge

[note the politeness of the day—The Senator often employed Mr. with the surnames—compared with the modern habit of using only the last and sometimes only the first (!) names.]

Sumner

Although Charles Sumner lacked humor, he could be witty. He was staying at our house shortly after the fall of the second empire and the establishment of the French republic. He had just returned from Paris where Gambetta had called upon him and asked his advice. He said: "Gambetta rose to go and as he took my hand he said: 'Ah, Sumner, il nous faut un Jefferson! I replied: 'Trouvez un Washington, M. Gambetta, et un Jefferson arrivera.'[349]

Longfellow

I came to see Longfellow, Sumner's most intimate friend, frequently. He was very quiet, invariably gentle but usually silent since the tragic death of his wife. Occasionally I met him on his walks; he seemed so calm, so removed from the storms of life and yet, always so kind, so very gentle and so sympathetic. But the gentleness implied nothing soft or indefinite. I remember well a dinner which my mother gave for Mr. Schurz when he delivered in Boston his eulogy upon Sumner; I sat next to Longfellow. Mr. Schurz was an accomplished speaker and the mood was one of uncritical admiration. I asked Mr. Longfellow if he did not think Mr. Schurz's address very fine. "No," he replied, with decisiveness; "it was a clever speech but I do not wish to have him tell us what Sumner was not, but what he was." Under the gentle manner now and then, if he were roused by anything or if his indignation was excited there would come a flash in his eyes and a look in his face which made one feel the presence of a strong nature and strongly suggested that his own "Viking bold" was numbered among his ancestors.[350]

---

[349] "Find a Washington, Mr. Gambetta, and a Jefferson will come along."
[350] Bessie Davis Lodge, the Senator's daughter-in-law, was also descended from Dolor!

Longfellow was a handsome man, even in his old age, with clear blue eyes and snow-white beard and hair. Inseparable from him was the air of distinction and high breeding without a trace of egotism or suggestion that he was conscious of his own fame. As an English critic said at the time, Mr. Longfellow was always an artist and his respect for his art and his refined taste were perfectly apparent in the converse of daily life.

Emerson

I saw Mr. Emerson at the Historical Society on one or two occasions though I cannot say that I knew him. When I saw him I watched him with the deepest interest: tall, thin, with a face full of intellect, unscarred by passion, in a way remote in look and yet with such human sympathy and feeling in the regard that no one could call it ascetic, he seemed to me a man whose mere appearance must have impressed the most careless gazer. When I last saw him at the Historical Society, he read a little paper on Carlyle and his rather characteristic absent-mindedness had increased.... The occasion on which I remember Emerson best was at a dinner at my mother's house to which I have referred in connection with Longfellow on Schurz' eulogy to Sumner April 29, 1874. Dr. Holmes was also there and in my diary I wrote: "Longfellow as always very silent except to his next neighbor (who was myself). Emerson (was) [sic] also very quiet. Dr. Holmes was describing a dynamometer or contrivance for measuring memory, with great enthusiasm. The machine was his own invention. Emerson listened in silence and then said, in a low voice, "Such things are very disagreeable to me."

***

Letter from Elijah H. Mills to his wife, Harriette Jan. 13, 1816 Northampton, regarding life in Washington under Munroe administration:

The drawing room of Mrs. Munroe is open but once a fortnight... Mrs. Bagot and Mrs. De Neuville have open room each one evening in a week, the former on Mon. and the latter on Saturday. At the British minister's the amusements are such as you usually find in such parties, conversation, music and cards. At the French ministers dancing is almost always superadded. These are spoken of as much more pleasant though not more elegant than Mrs. B-'s and are very constantly and crowdedly attended. **Even our staid and sober New England ladies, it is said, almost always shew (show) themselves at these Sat. evening parties and readily 'join the jocund dance' on what they have been educated to consider as holy time.** These public meetings together with select parties more or less every week enable the fashionable visitors here to kill time as effectually as they can wish. I have been nowhere not even to call on the President. This I shall do however on Monday. But although I have neglected this mark of respect I have received today an invitation to dine with him on Friday next. I should certainly have foregone the society of the women to have had the opportunity of traveling with him.[Elijah begs his wife not to leave her room or get her too overtired as she's just had a baby]. I know you are too apt to be indiscreet with yourself at such times. Take good care of yourself against the cold. Pray tell me all about your domestic affairs, what difficulties you meet with and how you surmount them... Has Pomeroy sold any of her wood or corn and at what price? Yesterday I dined with the French minister in a party consisting of about 20 or 25 mostly members of Congress. The dinner was in true French style. Everything so disguised and transformed that no one knew what to ask for or what was before him whether ham or jelly, mutton chop or pudding no one could tell until he had put his knife into the dish. The first course consisted almost entirely of cold meats in various forms pickled, hashed and minced as well as whole. Turkeys without bones and puddings in the form of fowls fresh cod disguised like a salad and celery like oysters all served to excite the wonder and amazement of the guests. It reminded me of an anecdote told by Horace Walpole when giving an account of a dinner of a great man at which he was present. He said, '**Everything was cold but the water, and everything was sour but the vinegar.'**

Excepting however the perplexity of finding out what was upon the table I had a very pleasant time. **Mr. and Mrs. de Neuville are decidedly the most pleasant and the most popular of the foreigners residing here.** Pleasant and affable in their deportment, they take great pains to please and to avoid the ceremony and cold politeness which distinguish almost all the intercourse which takes place here. Although of a frivolous nation, they both seem very considerate and sufficiently grave and have much less of frivolity than the other ministers resident here. **Their kindness seems unaffected and their piety, it is said, is equally so.** In the evening there was an immense crowd of ladies and gentlemen, their house being open for that purpose every Sat. evening. **The usual insipid interchange of idle questions and heedless replies, gazing, lounging, card playing, and dancing occupied the various groups as fancy or caprice might dictate.** And the evening closed with a waltz by the daughters of the Spanish minister and a few others mostly foreigners.

The death of the queen of England [Queen Charlotte] has kept Mr. and Mrs. Bagot out of society for the last fortnight and thrown all the foreign ministers and families into a mourning dress. The intensity of their grief has however almost worn off. When amends will be made I presume this a temporary seclusion.I dined too the other day at the President's and had a much more pleasant and less reserved intercourse than I had ever witnessed when Madison was President. Mrs. Hull, the wife of the Commodore, who is now in the city, is said to be the reigning beauty here. If you have seen her therefore you may be able to form some idea of the others. She is not a beauty to my taste. Too insipid and too much like waxwork. But I did not intend to fill this whole letter with nonsense and will stop.

***

Sen. Henry Cabot Lodge's tribute to his wife:

On both sides she came of English Puritan stock. Her father was descended from Robert Davis, who with his sons, Dolor[37] and Shubael, landed in Massachusetts with the first Puritan emigration in 1630. Robert Davis moved to the Plymouth colony and there his descendants intermarried with families of Pilgrim ancestry and in this way she traced her descent from John Alden of *The Mayflower* and Priscilla Mullins, and from Constant Southworth whose mother became the second wife of Governor Bradford. Her grandfather married Miss. Freeman and in this way the name Constant which has passed through eight generations since the days of the Pilgrims came into her family's family. Her great-grandfather Daniel Davis, born in 1713, was a Judge in Plymouth; her grandfather, also a distinguished lawyer, was United States District Attorney, appointed by Washington, and afterwards for thirty years Solicitor General of Massachusetts.

Her mother's father was Elijah H. Mills, from Northampton, Mass. He was a graduate of Williams College and became the leading lawyer of the Connecticut Valley, went into politics, was chosen Speaker of the

Massachusetts House of Representatives, then a member of Congress and then U.S. Senator. After 8 years in the Senate, he was forced by ill-health to retire in 1827 and died prematurely two years later, at age of fifty-three. He was personally handsome and distinguished in his public career. His wife was Harriette Blake (through whom she was descended from John Howland and Elizabeth Tilley of *The Mayflower*), the youngest sister of (Senator's great-grandfather) John Welland Blake, children of Joseph Blake of Boston; in this way, Senator and Mrs. Lodge were related. John and Harriette Blake were descendants of William Blake, a cousin of Robert Blake, the great English Admiral in the days of Cromwell[351] who came to this country about 1635 and settled in Dorchester where for forty years he was Town Clerk.

Your grandmother's father, Rear Admiral Davis, was born in 1807 and *bred* in Boston schools, Admiral Davis entered Harvard in the class of 1825 but left college at the end of his sophomore year to become an officer in the navy. His career in the navy was long and distinguished. He engaged the first work of the "Coast Survey" and was one of the founders of the Nautical Almanac.

When the war of Secession broke upon the country, he was eminent in the group of young officers who came at once to the front and upon whom the burden of our decisive naval operations fell. He was fleet captain with Dupont; they were intimate friends and they carried out the expedition under the latter's command which resulted in the capture of Port Royal, one of the most important, as it was the first, of our great naval successes. Admiral Davis received rapid promotion, and not long after succeeded Foote in command on the Western rivers. He fought and won the battle of Memphis where he destroyed the rebel flotilla, and soon after was again successful in the fight at Fort Pillow. For these victories, he received the thanks of Congress. Some day you will, I hope, go to Vicksburg, and there see his statue, which, with those of Farragut, Porter, and Foote, stands at the base of the great monument to the Navy of the United States. Broken down by river fever, he was obliged to return to Washington where he was put at the head of the Bureau of Navigation and toward the close of the war, appointed superintendent of the Naval Observatory, the highest scientific post in the navy.

With strong, handsome features, erect in figure, of pronounced military bearing, I have never known any man more charming or more

---

[351] In the 1650s, the Isle of Jersey Cabots may have fought on the side of Charles II after his father's beheading against Blake in Cromwell's navy.

lovable. In his perfect simplicity, in his absolute courage, in his purity of mind and generosity of spirit, he always makes me think of Colonel Newcome. But, unlike Thackeray's hero, he was a man of the world in the best sense, of high professional ability and exceptional intellectual force. His manners were not only delightful but were quite perfect. I have always thought the phrase "a gentleman of the old school" a misleading phrase, involving the error of confusing the incidental with the permanent. Differences in manners—and by manners I do not, of course, mean customs, but only those purely personal attributes which are the result of training and tradition, such as are implied in the words "old school"—are the superficial, accidental differences of time and place.

Really fine manners must have been and must always be the same. I never saw, for instance, finer manners than those of the famous Chief Joseph, a blanket Indian, in his full panoply of war-bonnet and paint, one night at a White House reception. Good manners, whatever the outward changes and differences at different periods in history, must be sympathetic, considerate, and, above all, distinguished; and if they have these qualities in high degree, then they are good without regard to details of dress or morals or form of expression.... Admiral Davis... loved literature and learning in every form... was a scholar in the old-fashioned sense and the Latin classics were more with him almost more than that of his own speech or of any of the modern tongues in which he was versed, for he was an accomplished linguist. This love of letters never waned. He told me he meant to take up Greek again... his favorite author was Shakespeare, whom he seemed to know almost by heart, the fruit of long voyages when he read and re-read the few books which he could take with him on his ship. His second love was Virgil and the Virgilian lines were constantly on his lips. The grace and distinction of the gentlest and most refined of Roman poets particularly appealed to him....

No mean or low thought ever crossed his mind. High-minded to the last degree, it was a positive pain to him to hear, still more to believe, anything ill of any one. His gentleness and kindness were not those of the weakly good-natured, but of the man of strength and courage who would do his duty without fear or favor, and who hated evil and evil-doers. He had infinite humor and a wholesome love of nonsense and fun, ever among the most endearing qualities... As Steele said of Lady Elizabeth Hastings (with the slight change which the sex commands), "to know him was a liberal education."

As Emerson said of Samuel Hoar, where he sat "there Honor came and sat beside him." He had the secret of perpetual youth, that gift so rarely bestowed and which has such perpetual charm. With all his experience of life, with all his labors and activities, he never grew old in heart or mind. Age and years appeared to have no relation to him.... When he suddenly broke down at the age of seventy, it seemed to all that he had died prematurely and in the flush of youth.

The marriage of Admiral and Mrs. Davis, your great-grandparents, was a love match, and so it remained to the end. Despite the exacting demands of his profession and the narrow income of a naval officer, no happier people in their marriage and in their children could be imagined. Your great-grandmother retained to the last her beauty, the rare beauty which seems to adapt itself to age, as well as the attractions of voice and manner, of sympathy, humor, wit and quick intelligence which had always made her loved and admired. They had six children. Of the two who survived, your Uncle Harry and your Aunt Evelyn who married my lifelong friend Brooks Adams, I shall say nothing for you know and love them both. (Constant Davis, his tutor was the eldest, then Frank, Anna Cabot, the eldest daughter, Louisa, wife of Henley Luce, son of Admiral Stephen Luce.)

My own family was a very small one—my mother, my sister, and her husband; but your grandmother, when she married, made her family mine—a great and precious gift, for her father and mother, her sisters and brothers, were all unusual people and their loyalty and devotion for me has been one of the best of my life's possessions. There was among them all an intensity of affection which I have never seen equaled... a family quarrel although they all had strong convictions and very independent opinions, was unthinkable. They were all clever, all cultivated, all with a strong sense of humor and a wholesome liking for fun and nonsense. They were all musical, some wrote cleverly in prose and verse; all were fond of books and art and at least one drew and painted so well that in later years he became a successful artist.

Like all sensible people, they realized what money could buy and above all, what good could be done with it when properly applied but money as a standard and object of life, as a dominant purpose in living, never touched them. The successes and ambitions they saw about them had no connection with moneymaking but were far higher and nobler, for they concerned public service, science, literature, learning and art. In such an atmosphere and amid such influences your grandmother (and her siblings) were brought up. I cannot imagine surroundings more refining, more ennobling, or better calculated than these to infuse into children a high and fine conception of the meaning, the purposes and the conduct of life.

...Toward the close of the war, after he had been put in command of the Naval Observatory in the winter of 1864-65, they joined their father in Washington. Your grandmother was in Washington when Lincoln was assassinated; she watched the passing of the funeral procession and saw the great review of the Union armies after Victory had been achieved. Although only a child, these great events occurring before her eyes made an impression on her that was never effaced. From those days came the intensity of love of country, of her passionate feeling about the Union and the men who fought and died to save it....

They lived at the Observatory until 1867 when her father was ordered to the command of the South Pacific squadron and he took his two oldest sons. After the death of Constant, Mrs. Davis and her youngest daughter went out to join the Admiral in Brazil and your grandmother returned to Cambridge to live with her aunt, Mrs. Charles Mills.

When she was 16, she came to Nahant to stay with Cabot's mother. "I had scarcely seen her since we were little children," he says in *Early Memories*. "I drove over to Lynn and met her at the station. That day is very vivid in memory. I remember she had a book in her hand which she had been reading in the train. I asked what it was and although I was fond of books and had read more than most boys of my age, I was surprised at finding that a young girl had been casually reading Boswell's "Life of Johnson," one of the masterpieces of English literature, instead of some obvious novel. Even then she had widely and instinctively what was best to read. So it was through life. She read constantly and always well. Born with a good taste that never seemed to err, she developed and refined her critical judgment, ever learning as the years with their increasing cares and many interests went by. She never would admit that she knew anything; she always with an extreme of modesty deplored her own ignorance, but it was that ignorance which is born of wide knowledge, of the sense of the petty done, the undone vast, which is the surest proof of knowledge of the highest and finest kind. She had the family aptitude for languages. She spoke French and Spanish and read Italian and German. It was one of the disappointments of her life that she had never studied Latin and Greek so as to command them both and that she could know the great classical literatures only through translations.

Before that summer of 1869, the most memorable of my life, had ended, we were engaged. Two years later, on June 29, the day after I had received my degree at Harvard, we were married at Christ Church in Cambridge. She [had] all the great attributes which we cover by the word "character" in the emotions, the impulses, the love which come from the heart, and which guide the life and make the happiness of those for whom they are expended.

Nannie's particular love was poetry and she had a wide and intimate knowledge, sensitive appreciation and judgment of the poetry of all nations and tongues. It was not merely "the bards sublime"—these, beginning with Shakespeare, the household divinity, she knew almost by heart. But not content, she was always searching everywhere for a sound of the true note. All the latest poets, all the newest verse, she brought within her ken, patient with mediocrity and failure, searching at all times and everywhere in the hope that "amid the huddling silver little worth," she might find, "the one thin piece, pure gold." Her patience is often rewarded, "the spirit, dumb to us, would speak to her," and even if it were only a line in which the true note could be heard, there would come the joy of a fresh sensation of beauty in the wide world of imagination."

It was the same with all the fine arts. Whether it was a Cathedral, a Greek temple, a great gallery of pictures or statues, always there was the same intensity of enjoyment, the same discriminating taste, the same eager and unwearied desire to see and know the beautiful in the handiwork of man. In art as in poetry she watched with intense interest all that was being produced, ever seeking even in obscure exhibition of some unknown artist to find a glimpse of a new beauty or of a genuine aspiration and effort.

But her greatest intellectual and emotional happiness was found in music. She played the piano extremely well, although what she did herself never absorbed her. Her passion was for music, the best music, and wherever the highest and finest could be heard, there she went. She knew music with a comprehending sympathy and knowledge and when sorrows fell upon her she turned to it as the one great solace left to her.

Hand in hand with the love of poetry, art, and music, went the love of nature and all its beauties and splendors. From the beloved flowers, from the flight and song of birds, to the clouds of the sky and the shadows on the grass, nothing seemed to elude her. The sun uprising from the sea, the "dropping of the daylight in the West," the path of moonlight on the waters, the stars which she knew as the child of an observatory, never passed her unnoticed or unloved. They went by in long, recurrent procession and no beauty escaped her vision or failed to give her the keen happiness which every expression of beauty, every sensation of the beautiful always brought. And with all this passion for beauty and power in nature and in art went not only a keen intellectual curiosity, a profound interest in abstract questions and in the mysteries of the universe, of life and death, but what is not common in such combinations, the quickest wit, a hearty love of nonsense, and the most complete, perfect and unfailing sense of humor.

These rare intellectual qualities inspired my admiration for nearly half a century and taught me what was best and most worthy to know, to love and to reverence. From these qualities so imperfectly set forth by me you may learn in part the secret of that magical sympathy with others which made her so deeply loved and admired by all who knew her or who felt her influence.

Chapter 2

"When through the feast-litten halls"
by John Hay

When through the feast-litten halls my lady goes,
A sudden, tender brightness fills the place;
    Joy radiates from her beauty and her grace,
    Round her a softened splendor ebbs and flows.

Her cheek, a lily dreaming of a rose,
    Her eyes, which deck with light that heaven, her face,
    Draw to her every heart in love and praise.
    As cornfields bend to dawn when the west wind blows,

So to my lady turns the glittering throng
    With smiles and flattery and light whispered loves,
    And neither envy or hate my spirit moves,

Such tributes unto her of right belong.
    She needs must hold all hearts in that sweet thrall,
Let them all love—I love her more than all.

***

Quartette in B Flat,
Opus 18...........................Beethoven

Andante Con Variazione,
From quartette in D Minor......Schubert

Quartette in G Minor............Grieg

"Love and Music"

I gazed upon my love while music smote
The soft night air into glad harmony;
Lapt on the ripples of a silver sea
I heard the bright tones rapturous dance and float.

Hearing and sight were wed; each flattering note
Meant some perfection of my love to me.
Caressed by music, it was bliss to see
Her form, white-robed, the jewel at her throat,

Her glimmering hands, her dusky, perfumed hair,
Her low, clear brow, her deep, proud, dreaming eyes,
Bent kindly upon me, her worshipper;

The dulcet, delicate sounds that shook the air--
As if love's joy rained from the starlit skies--
Seemed all sweet, inarticulate thoughts of her.[352]

***

10 p.m.
"An Idle Question"

I, looking on my darling's picture where
All charms of soul and sense in beauty vie,

[352] The two are published in *The Collected Poetry of John Hay.*

Ask in love's idleness, nor wait reply,
Whether her body or spirit be most fair.

What can be lovelier than her heaven of hair
Her low, white brow, her love-compelling eye,
That mouth of ruby and pearl blent cunningly—
Is all not fair and sweet beyond compare?

But then, that spirit, gentle, firm and bright,
The lambent mirth, touching all with glee;
The loving heart that wreathes those life with light,
Kisses and blessings their divided fee;

The soul that through those eyes shines warm and true,
Clear as the light of stars, and pure as dew.

***

Enough of thunderous passion
That clouds life's weary way
Bid now in merrier fashion
The jocund pulses play

Welcome the airy fanciesThat charm and pass away,
The light loves
The bright loves
The loves that last a day.

Too rude for mortal bosoms
The storms that rage for aye;
Ask not from frost the blossoms
That deck the laughing May.

Bid welcome all the gay loves
That wither if they stay—
The sweet loves
The fleet loves,
The loves that live a day.

***

"Goodnight my tantalizing goddess," Hay wrote Elsie Cameron in 1891. "A dozen times this day I have been on the point of believing that you are not really so complicated as you seem, but that last half hour threw me into the wildest confusion again. I give it up. I will not try to comprehend you. Still less can I criticize you. I shall never know you well enough to do either. After you were gone, the usual outcry of admiration broke forth. S. said "she had an absolutely different manner of speaking to each man in the room." I thought—then the goddess is seen. Upon my word, I believe if you spoke to a thousand men, you would naturally by some divine gift of sympathy—or else by some malign science of cruelty—assume to each one of them the form, the eyes, and the voice of his ideal. And yet, it seems to me that you cannot be to others anything different from what you are to me. A form of perfect grace and majesty, a face radiant with a beauty so gloriously vital that it refreshes and stimulates every heart that comes within its influence; a voice, a laughter so pure and so musical that it carries gladness in every vibration of the air. You sweet comrade, you dear and splendid friend, who is worthy to be your friend and comrade? I am humbled before you."

***

In this unpublished poem, Hay, in a bit of fun, expresses his passion for Lizzie and their restraint: "The First Kiss" or "Through the Veil":

"Through the Veil"

So long as I on earth shall stay
I never can forget the day—
Till life and heart and senses fail,—
When under blue and vernal skies,
Lured by the springtime in her eyes,
With trembling hope and glad surprise,
I kissed her through her veil.

The short voilette of filery lace,—
It seemed to guard the radiant face,
As safe as bars of Milan mail;
Remote as stars and angels be,

She in her beauty seemed to me,
Yet tenderly as reverently,
I kissed her through the veil.

Glad years have passed; my love is mine,
O'er all my life her dear eyes shine,
My guiding stars through calm or gale;
But through long days of tranquil bliss,
There comes no purer joy than this—
The memory of that swift, fond kiss,
The first kiss through the veil.

***

March 18, 1892, from John Hay to Lizzie Cameron:

"Obedience"

The lady of my love bids me not love her.
And I must bow obedient to her will.
And so, henceforth, I love her not; but still
I love the gold bronze hair that glitters over
Her proud young head; I love the smiles that hover
About her mouth; the lights and shades that fill
Her beryl eyes; the low sweet tones that thrill
Like thrush songs gurgling from a vernal cover.

I love the fluttering dimples in her cheek;
Her cheek I love, its soft and tender bloom;
I love her sweet lips and the words they speak,
Words wise or witty, full of joy or doom.
I love her shoes, her gloves, her dainty dress—
And all they clasp, encircle and caress.

Chapter 3

While Mr. and Mrs. Lodge were on their European tour in 1899, the Secretary of State propositioned Mrs. Cameron to meet him in New York:

Department of State
July 18, '99
Dear Mrs. Cameron,I wrote this between statesmen to say the weather here is delightful. It will grow worse every hour from now till October. Why then delay? If you are too haughty to come to my house, there is Mr. Adams next door longing for you: and your own house vacant across the way: and the Lodges awaiting you with servants en manches de chemise on the doorsteps whenever I pass....I am hideously busy and woefully tired and I would fain refresh my worn and weary eyes—bleared with too much diplomacy, contemplating something more attractive...Even if you came I could not dedicate to you more than 24 hours par day. Yours Faithfully, John Hay.

Department of State
July 24, 99
...I have an excellent idea. I want very much to see you but I fear your hotel—the haunt of statesmen. Could you not happen to be in NY anywhere Tuesday morning at a given instant. I would be there too crammed with questions to ask you. Then we would lunch somewhere and drop a parting tear and take trains for opposite quarters of the sky. Don't be haughty but charitable and tell me where and when. Yours Faithfully, John Hay.

July 26, 99
...Where shall I see you and where shall we have lunch? In the Metropolitan Museum by the Rembrandts...It seems unreal and impossible that I am to see you again—if I am. Are you as beautiful as ever and as heartless? I hope so. It would be such a pity if you grew kind. Men are so numerous and so unworthy...

800 16th St.
Sept. 5 1899
My Dear Mrs. C...
Dante understood the true precedence of states of mind. He put the

Inferno first and Paradise last. You having the same divine genius follow the same method. I got your telegram saying you were not coming before I got your letter saying you were. It is too vile, my fate. I have been waiting for you here a week in an air like glue-refusing to make an engagement, hoping every day to see the coming of your feet, beautiful upon the asphalt.

***

"The Path That Leads to Nowhere"
by Corinne Roosevelt Robinson

There's a path that leads to Nowhere
        In a meadow that I know,
Where an inland island rises
        And the stream is still and slow;
There it wanders under willows
        And beneath the silver green
Of the birches' silent shadows
        Where the early violets lean.

Other pathways lead to Somewhere,
        But the one I love so well
Had no end and no beginning—
        Just the beauty of the dell,
Just the windflowers and the lilies
        Yellow striped as adder's tongue,
Seem to satisfy my pathway
        As it winds their sweets among.

There I go to meet the Springtime,
        When the meadow is aglow,
Marigolds amid the marshes,—
        And the stream is still and slow.—
There I find my fair oasis,
        And with care-free feet I tread
For the pathway leads to Nowhere,
        And the blue is overhead!

All the ways that lead to Somewhere

Echo with the hurrying feet
Of the Struggling and the Striving,
But the way I find so sweet
Bids me dream and bids me linger,
Joy and Beauty are its goal,—
On the path that leads to Nowhere
I have sometimes found my soul!

***

Editor's Preface
The Education of Henry Adams

This volume, written in 1905 as a sequel to the same author's *Mont Saint Michel* and *Chartres*, was privately printed, to the number of one hundred copies, in 1906, and sent to the persons interested, for their assent, correction, or suggestion. The idea of the two books was thus explained at the end of Chapter XXIX:— "Any schoolboy could see that man as a force must be measured by motion from a fixed point. Psychology helped here by suggesting a unit— the point of history when man held the highest idea of himself as a unit in a unified universe. Eight or ten years of study had led Adams to think he might use the century 1150-1250, expressed in Amiens Cathedral and the Works of Thomas Aquinas, as the unit from which he might measure motion down to his own time, without assuming anything as true or untrue, except relation. The movement might be studied at once in philosophy and mechanics. Setting himself to the task, he began a volume which he mentally knew as 'Mont-Saint-Michel and Chartres: a Study of Thirteenth-Century Unity.' From that point he proposed to fix a position for himself, which he could label: 'The Education of Henry Adams: a Study of Twentieth-Century Multiplicity.' With the help of these two points of relation, he hoped to project his lines forward and backward indefinitely, subject to correction from any one who should know better."

The "Chartres" was finished and privately printed in 1904. The "Education" proved to be more difficult. The point on which the author failed to please himself, and could get no light from readers or friends, was the usual one of literary form. Probably he saw it in advance, for he used to say, half in jest, that his great ambition was to complete St. Augustine's "Confessions," but that St. Augustine, like a great artist, had worked from multiplicity to unity, while he, like a small one, had to reverse the method and work back from unity to multiplicity. The scheme became unmanageable as he approached his end.

Probably he was, in fact, trying only to work into it his favorite theory of history, which now fills the last three or four chapters of the "Education," and he could not satisfy himself with his workmanship. At all events, he was still pondering over the problem in 1910, when he tried to deal with it in another way which might be more intelligible to students. He printed a small volume called "A Letter to American Teachers," which he sent to his associates in the American Historical Association, hoping to provoke some response. Before he could satisfy himself even on this minor point, a severe illness in the spring of 1912 put an end to his literary activity forever.

The matter soon passed beyond his control. In 1913 the Institute of Architects published the "Mont-Saint-Michel and Chartres." Already the "Education" had become almost as well known as the "Chartres," and was freely quoted by every book whose author requested it. The author could no longer withdraw either volume; he could no longer rewrite either, and he could not publish that which he thought unprepared and unfinished, although in his opinion the other was historically purposeless without its sequel. In the end, he preferred to leave the "Education" unpublished, avowedly incomplete, trusting that it might quietly fade from memory. According to his theory of history as explained in Chapters XXXIII and XXXIV, the teacher was at best helpless, and, in the immediate future, silence next to good-temper was the mark of sense. After midsummer, 1914, the rule was made absolute.

The Massachusetts Historical Society now publishes the "Education" as it was printed in 1907, with only such marginal corrections as the author made, and it does this, not in opposition to the author's judgment, but only to put both volumes equally within reach of students who have occasion to consult them.

HENRY CABOT LODGE
September, 1918[353]

---

[353] Henry Adams, *The Education of Henry Adams: An Autobiography*, (private published 1903; Boston: Houghton Mifflin, 1918), Massachusetts Historical Society. Original from Harvard University, Digitized 2006.

Chapter 4

In "Dramatic Verses," a sonnet written in 1898 in defense of poets, shows the extent of Trumbull Stickney's disagreement with Bay's admiration for the active life:

You say, Columbus, with his argosies
Who rash and greedy took the screaming main
And vanished out before the hurricane
Into the sunset after merchandise,
Then under western palms with simple eyes
Trafficked and robbed and triumphed home again:
You say this is the glory of the brain
And human life no other use than this?
I then do answering say to you:
The line
Of wizards and of saviors, keeping trust
In that which made them pensive and divine,
Passes before us like a cloud of dust.
What were they? Actors, ill and mad with wine,
And all their language babble and disgust.

Chapter 5

22 April 1903
Henry Adams to George Cabot Lodge on fiction writing:

...To me, the story-teller must be a trivial sort of animal who amuses me. His first quality should be superficiality; for this quality, as fundamental, I take Miss. Austen and generally the women-women, not the men-women like George Eliot, as examples, and Dickens, if you like, as a warning of what happens when one tries to be serious in order to fill up the holes in one's mind. Balzac tires me from the instant he becomes moralist....

Art comes in at the corner of F and 20th, when you want to get a moral into me without my knowing it. You've got to do it because that's what you are for; you won't grin through a horse-collar just to make the clowns laugh. Yet, when I get to the corner, I tell you to go to the devil. How are you going to grab me by the throat after the strenuous presidential manner, and jam your pill down? That is the whole subject of dispute. That is art. One man tries to do it one way; another man fetches you a hit in the stomach; and a woman tickles you behind your left ear; but an old, hardened, vicious reptile like me just runs off—to Paris, if possible. You have got the hardest kind of a job to find a new trick for me.... To make Saint Thomas [Saint Thomas Aquinas was Adams' nickname for Henry Cabot Lodge, Jr.] smile, though the object of all our ambitions is not easy, but once discovered, the old trick will always fetch him unless he has a stomach-ache; whereas the old trick does not fetch me any longer. The New Yorker bores me in real life; how can he amuse me in fiction? Doubtless it can be done; but I am singularly on my guard against his tricks. You have got to study me,—not him. If I know myself, the only possible way of interesting me in a New Yorker would be to make him funny and sympathetic because I never should recognize him in that light; but, as New Yorker—no! in my opinion, you can't make me swallow that pill,—art or no art; no –, not even the diabolical cunning which your mother attributes to Sargent's portrait of the President can make me swallow it. Brute, fraud, mountebank, millionaire, cheat or philanthropist, all is one to me. I won't swallow him....

In the face of this stupid and mulish obstinacy, what are you going to do? I am a pig; I am sorry for it; but I am a public too; I want to be amused. Make for me a comic Mrs. Hull, braining her son-in-law with a rocking-chair, and probably you would amuse me to the end; but I don't care a straw whether one New Yorker brains another, or how he does it; and the more accurate the types, the less I care. You can't make me care. No art could ever make me swallow that pill. This is my solemn conviction. Of jelly I am nervously suspicious. As a cocktail, it has ceased to deceive. Pure brandy I loathe. Even with a crowbar it won't go. Your only chance is to make me laugh, and slip it into my mouth while it's open. For this reason I say, as I began, that I want you to reflect on what you are trying to do. Remember that, after all, I am or have been, human and that nothing human has any longer the slightest interest to me, if it resembles myself. That particular form of boredom, in all its varieties, can only be saved by putting into it what never was there—a sense of the ridiculous.

***

In his biography of William Wetmore Story, Henry James attributed Story's failure as a sculptor to his dividing his artistic concentrations between sculpting versus writing. "The master's" viewpoint about the artist's life is crucial to understanding Bay, who also lived a double life.

> We mean by insistence, in an artist, the act of throwing the whole weight of the mind, and of gathering it at the particular point (when the particular point is worth it) in order to do so. This, on the part of most artists—or at least on the part of those who are single in spirit—is an instinct and a necessity, becomes in fact the principal sign we know them by. They feel unsafe, uncertain, exposed, unless the spirit, such as it is, be, at the point in question, "all there." Story's rather odd case, if I may call it so, was that when he wrote prose or verse he was "there" only in part—not, we infer, as completely, as anxiously, as he might have been. And this, in spite of a great and genuine love; it was not at all as if prose and verse had been for him perfunctory cares. It was impossible to be more interested in the things of the mind and in the forms and combinations into which they overflow. The question of expression and style haunted him; the question of representation by words was ever as present to him as that of representation by marble and bronze... Inevitably we are not able to say what a lifetime of Boston would have made, in him, or would have marred; we can only be sure we should in that case have had to deal with quite a different group of results.

***

Bay's love poem to a mysterious C.L.G. was written in the year before his death. Verses one and four follow:

"To C.L.G."
With the love of George Cabot Lodge

O say! In the splendor of days that await us, the scope and desire ofmidnights to be,The fruit of what fearful, fierce passions shall sate us, what truthMore effusive shall make us more free?What new depths of the soul shall we seek and discover, what strength of the body, what heat of the heart?In the dream of the seer, on the lute of the lover, what secrets shall yield or what melodies start?In what wise shall the lips of our new loves grow fervent, what dreamed—Of stresses lie warm in their hands?Than the Gods who made Sappho their priestess and servant, what lovelierGods shall inflict their commands?When the altars of love are heaped up over measure, when the passion ofLove grows intense as despair,What embrace shall afford what unbearable pleasure—on what breast, in theperfume and dusk of what hair?

Chapter 6

Six unpublished letters from Edith Wharton to Elizabeth (Bessy) Lodge; unfortunately Bessy's letters to Edith were evidently destroyed:

Sept. 23, 1909
Dearest Bessy,
The sonnet is beautiful indeed, & it was dear of you to wish me to have it. I think and think of that long golden afternoon in the warm thymy hillside above the lake, where we all lay among the ferns & the blue-berries, & he read my verses, & here & there shifted a word, or re-touched a line.

"Gigantic on the mist our shadows saw" is *his* in wording, & the placing of "gigantic" at the head of the line trebled its "value." (It's in one of the sonnets in my little volume—those we were reading that day on the hill, just after I had written them if I find the old habit of referring impressions & ideas to him still goes on unchecked— it keeps him so near!—And so, dear Bessy, does the thought that *you* think of me, & wish to keep the circle unbroken.

Yrs,
Edith

I hope Walter can manage to see you before he leaves. He wanted so much to go to you at once.

Oct. 6, 1909
Dearest Bessy,
Your letter & Mr. Lodge's have just come together, & I will write at once to Mr. Burlingame about the Scribner article. I do hope the early volume of poems can be found, for I don't see how I can do the article unless I first re-read him in the right order, & see the links. I don't think I have that volume at home or I should make a desperate attempt to have it found at the Mount. I have tried to find some one here who had

some of the volumes, but in vain.

My Dear, I can measure to a certain extent the degree of desolation, of deprivation, that you feel, by the extraordinary way in which at every turn, my mind reverts to him. One loved him, & felt one never "wasted" him—yet we didn't know how many crannies of one's mind he was rooted in! And the wonder of it is, the length of the reach of association, from the great grave things—the poetry and pictures & fine "gestes"—to the dear foolish nonsense, all the little human silliness... Only a moment before your letter came I took up a Scribner & there was a flaming "ad." Of a new Rex Beach novel—you remember him on Rex Beach? And there was a wonderful *forain* in the Figaro two days ago, that I started to send him—made the mental gesture to do it! And so, by all these little ways, I penetrate into your feeling, measure something of it, know the blank face that life wears to you. And I come back always to the same thought: there is joy unspeakable at the core of such a pain! It does away for you, in a very real sense, with all possibility of the deepest kind of loneliness, which is the loneliness of frustration, of the life pressed at & missed.[354] You are richer, Dear, by all of Bay—by every thought, act, sensation of yours that you would have never had but for these years with him; & that you will go on having, that will spring up, self-same, from the traces of his presence... There never was a richer more bestowing nature than his: a few of us knew it, & rejoiced in it, &it is ours for the rest of our days... My heart aches for the three children, who have missed so much that they might have had! But they have you, & the image of him in you, & the reflection of such a happiness ought to shine a long distance down their path. Please thank Mr. Lodge for his letter. I will write him soon. Send me a line or two whenever you can. I wish I were to see you, but I fear it won't be til next spring. Meanwhile, let us talk together often.

Yours Affectionately,
Edith

I go & sit with Dr. Bigelow every two or three days. We understand each other... he *knows.*

Nov. 19, 1909
Dearest Bessy,
I am so glad to get your little word from Washington. You will have

[354] Edith makes a veiled reference to her love affair that took place at the end of 1909 with Morton Fullerton who was irresponsible and dishonest with her & whom she loved even though he maddened her.

Walter there now for a week or two, & that will help, I know. He wanted so much to see you I am struck by the beauty, the *growth*, in the new poems. Walter and I read them together just before he sailed. Strength and solitude, & the Noctambulist & some of the sonnets are among his finest. How much I want to say of them!—

I will do as you wish about the name, & call him Cabot. Mr. Lodge & Lodge would have seemed equally unnatural...When it's possible I will use the three names.

Dr. Bigelow lunched with us the other day. He seems much better but he's awfully lonely. I wish you'd pack up, tuck the babies under your arm, & come out to him for the winter. It needs doing, & I don't believe he'll ever dare suggest it. You could carry him down to a villa somewhere in the south, & toast him in the sun; & Teddy and I would come down to see you, & we'd get as close to eachother as we could,—I'm not joking, you know. I believe it's the thing Bay would have wanted you to do. He is aching so for your all, poor Dokko! And he is so pathetically glad to come & talk to me because I am a link.—

Oh dearest, Bessy, when I think of you in that house, and remember the good hours we had there! What a life-giver he was! And how good it is to have been near him!

Yrs Affte
Edith

Nov. 30, 1909
Dearest Bessy,
I am sending you the article, another copy of which has gone to my typewriter in New York, to be thence transmitted to Mr. Burlingame. I have been so happy in writing it that I hope you will feel I have given some impression of what he was to his friends. As regards the critical part, I have simply given my personal view, as I often put it to him.—I knew you would not wish me to do otherwise; & I hope you will like the choice of quotations, which I tried to make as characteristic & as varied as I could.—I wanted to say much more, but I think this kind of article gains in some way by being short &, even if I didn't the inexorable magazine limits are there!

I gave practically no "biography," because that has been done in all the papers, & seemed to me less important in an article like this.—

If there are any small changes to make, will you please ask Mr. Lodge to write to Mr. Burlingame, as I believe they want to bring the article out very soon, & it might make too great a delay if you wrote to me first ?—

Next week, I am hoping for news of you from Walter—though, alas, he will not have more than a few hours in Paris.

Will you please thank Mr. Lodge for his letter of Nov. 20th, just received?—And do write me soon, just a word or two. Please!

Your affectionate and remembering
Edith

Dec. 29, 1909
Dearest Bessy,
Your letter of the 19th has just come, & I must tell you at once how distressed I am to know that little John has not picked up as quickly as the two others. I heard about the diphtheria from Walter, with whom, of course, I talked about you all the time; but he spoke of the cases as being so mild that I supposed they had ended without leaving a trace. Walter had such a bad crossing that he got to Paris too late for his Alexandria steamer, &stayed with us here a week, to our great consolation. Unfortunately, however, his mother's death and his being obliged to return to America, have made a big hole in his winter "term" & he will have to work out the lost time by staying in Cairo till well on into the summer, which is very bad for him. But then he's pursued by the fates.

Thank you very much for what you say about the article. I pitched the critical part in a *very* low key, because I didn't want the big public who didn't know his work, to say, "Oh, it's written by a friend, & of course one must discount that. I wanted the verse I cite to speak for itself, as it will, without any drum beating on my part. It needs only to be known for Bay to take his place, & then the critics can amplify and emphasize what I purposely said as quietly & briefly as possible. I do hope you liked the choice I made. That last sonnet is incomparable.

I move next week to 53 rue de Varenne, so please address hereafter to 53 rue de Varenne.

...Do write me, Bessy dear, And oh, do send the photograph! I want to see his face again. The little one that Mrs. Gardner sent is just a tantalizing hint.

Yrs Affely,
Edith

March 23, 1910
Folkstone
Dearest Bessy,
I have delayed a long time to thank you for your letter telling me the date of the photograph—I am so glad to know it—& giving me more news of your dear self & the small selves. I am so constantly hovering in thought about you all that it is a real kindness when you will write me. And I don't believe anybody can realize more intensely than I do the things *the house says to you, & the room* above all. The only speech one hears at such times in the voice of these inarticulate witnesses. There is only one comfort that I can see, & that is that a few rich incomparable years are worth paying *any* price for—*any,* believe me!

Teddy is perhaps a little better, very quiet & easy to look after, & luckily delighted with the apartment.—Dear Dr. Bigelow—partly, I'm sure, for your sakes & His—has been so kind and helpful to me, & comes often to lunch, & takes Teddy out in the motor. We are here now for a few days' change for me, & also to be near Henry James, who is not well, alas.[355] We are going over to see him this afternoon. Walter seems to be having a dreary struggle for health in Cairo, & I wish he could snap the chain & get away. The last news was that he had sprained his ankle, & had to go to court (?) on crutches!

I was so pleased with Mr. Brown's article, & I am so glad Bay read it. Of course, Dear, I knew you would like mine, but when it was done it seemed so little beside what he was & what I felt for him! Luckily people seem to have understood what it was meant to express, for I have had a great many letters about it, from all sorts of unexpected quarters; people who knew him well, saying, "How like him," & those who didn't know him, "If he was like that, what an incomparable friend indeed! "I am sorry to say that we have had to give up going home this summer as the Dr. thinks it would be too isolated for me at the Mount, alone with Teddy[356], especially as his sister is to be in Europe this summer, & can remain near us.

It is a great care to look after a big place like that, & all my business affairs besides, when I have to be almost constantly with Teddy. –

Do write me soon.

Yr Ever Affectionate
Edith

We return to Paris next week. I wish I could see you.

---

[355] In the spring of 1910, Henry James had a serious nervous breakdown.
[356] Edith gave up the Mount soon after this.

***

Preface by Theodore Roosevelt
Poems and Dramas of George Cabot Lodge
In Two Volumes
Houghton Mifflin Co., 1911

Introduction

My intimate friendship with George Cabot Lodge lasted for a quarter of a century. It began when I first saw him, a handsome, striking-looking boy, of great promise, at Nahant in the Spring of 1884; it did not end when I last saw him, on the 4th of March, 1909, at Washington, when he came through the blizzard to say good-bye. He was then in the still vigorously growing maturity of his powers, in the midst of a performance which more than made good his early promise and which was itself the promise of performance greater still.

Of all the men with whom I have been intimately thrown he was the man to whom I would apply the rare name of genius. He was an extraordinary student and scholar; he walked forever through the arch of the past experience of all the great minds of the ages. Any language which he cared to study was his, and he studied every language which held anything he wished. I have never met another man with so thorough and intimate a knowledge of so many great literatures, nor another man who so reveled in enjoyment of the best that he read. He never read for any reason except to find out something he wished to know, or, far more frequently, to gratify his wonderful love, his passion, for high thought finely expressed. A great poem, a great passage in prose, kindled his soul like a flame. Yet, he was unaffectedly modest about the well-nigh infinitely wide knowledge, as deep as it was wide, in which his being was steeped. It seemed as if he did not realize how very much he knew. He never made any show of it; unless it came out incidentally and naturally no one ever knew of it; indeed he was really humble-minded in the eager simplicity with which he sought to learn from others who had not even a small fraction of his hoarded wealth of fact and thought.

He was far more than a book-man. He loved his friends, he loved the life of human interest, and the throbbing pulse-beat of cities. He loved also the breath of the open; and he knew the joy which comes in the strife of hardy adventure. As a boy and young man he was a bold and good rider; he was equally at home hunting alone on the vast Western plains, and also alone, wild fowl shooting in the dangerous winter seas off the New England coast. His combination of idealism and bodily prowess made it inevitable that he should strain every nerve to get into the Spanish War. He came of fighting stock; his forefathers had fought in every great American War; kinsfolk of his were to be in this one; and he simply could not stay out. He went into the Navy as an ensign and served as captain of a guncrew. He made an admirable officer, training his men with unwearied care, and handling them with cool readiness under fire. He belonged to the gallant brotherhood of the men who have written and fought, the brotherhood whose foremost figures number, among many, many others, Cervantes at Lepanto, Sydney in the Low Countries, Koerner, the man of sword and song, in the war for German freedom. But here again what young Lodge did seemed to him so natural that, so far as his friends could tell, he never even thought of it afterwards. It was to him a matter of course that he should serve when his country called, just as a generation before young Shaw and young Lowell went forth "to dare, and do, and die at need" when the nation girded her loins for triumph or ruin.

To him was given the greatest of all blessings, the love of wife and of happy children; and his delight in the house where he was husband and father in no way dimmed his delight in the house where he was son. He cared little for the perfunctory part of social life; but no man was ever more beloved by his friends, by the men and women to whom his soul was open.

It is not my province to more than touch on his writings. His first volume of poems showed extraordinary strength and originality, and an extraordinary wealth of thought and diction. Indeed at first there was almost too great strength and wealth; the depth and wide play of the thought were obscured by the very brilliance of the way in which it was set forth. But with each succeeding volume his mastery over his own strength grew. In his last volume, *The Soul's Inheritance*, he had fairly begun to come into his own. He had begun to find adequate expression for the teeming wealth of his mind, for his surging, thronging passions, for "the high and haughty yearning" that burned within his soul. He cared only to do his very best; he demanded only the right to be measured by the loftiest standards, to be judged by the keenest and most serene minds; he could be swayed from the course he had marked out as little by love of general approval as by love of gain itself—and in his case this is the strongest statement that can be made, for no man lived more incapable of mixing sordid alloy with the gold of his work.

In abounding vigor, his task well begun and stretching far ahead, his veins thrilling with eager desire, his eyes fronting the future with dauntless and confident hope, he stood on life's crest; and then death smote him, lamentable, untimely.

> He lived detached days;
> He served not for praise;
> For gold
> He was not sold;
>
> Deaf was he to world's tongue
> He scorned for his song
> The loud
> Shouts of the crowd."

—Theodore Roosevelt

Chapter 7

Percy Lubbock describes the intimate world into which Wharton drew Bessy:[357]

> I devoured *The House of Mirth* on the spot, and there and then, before having met her, my intimacy with Edith began. At that first stage of my literary apprenticeship Bourget was my great 'task-master,' and, as in the Miltonic sonnet, I was ever living in his eye.... As I was imprudent enough to mention to him, no less than to Minnie, my unbounded admiration for *The House of Mirth*, he decided, with the irresistible authority which never forsook him, that I was to translate the book, and that by trying my hand at it I should at least prove whether or not I had a hand. And so it was, when a few weeks later the Whartons arrived in Paris, that I was presented to Edith as the eventual translator of her first masterpiece.
>
> For the youth that I then was the predicament was a rather formidable one, and in our first encounters it did not lead on my part to ease of intercourse: the less so that I had not then the slightest idea that

[357] Percy Lubbock, *Portrait of Edith Wharton*, (NY and London: D. Appleton-Century Company, Inc., 1947), 51-56, 86, 87.

Edith was *shy*—that shyness to which she herself alludes more than once in *A Backward Glance*, which I was to identify soon after, which remained in her an inveterate trait, and which constitutes the key to all her social demeanor outside the circle of close friendship....

Edith, when she accepted a familiar companion, accepted that one thoroughly... he wouldn't be there, I safely generalize, if he hadn't two things to offer—that which answered her humanity, and that which met the precision of her mind.

She was neither shy of her work nor in love with it...Certainly she had a dread, not unwholesome, of appearing in her world as a social muse, admired as a curiosity among her kind; and this reluctance, I dare say, she might push to an extreme that was ungracious. But with those to whom she did open the history of her ever-active art she was frank and free in all simplicity, always ready to show and consider her hand, to listen and learn.

The few clever critical people who made the inner circle that she drew around her—tightly and closely, and by this time more and more so—could never have taught her, had she needed it, to break her new ground with such decision; and as for the society of the profession in general where her work belonged, it was never, oddly enough, to know her familiarly or retain her long...She spoke just now of her pleasure in the company of London and Paris, but of course it was Paris that really came first, with London for a long while far behind....we all know how much less amusing it is, or was in youth, to make new friends within the family than beyond it; for within the circle of the blood they are too apt to accept you naturally, to take you for granted and new friendships, to be interesting, should create more circumstance and need more care...

But in the fullness of her energy, there could be no question: it was Paris for her. It must be the right Paris, however: by no means the city of the general settler from overseas, where he installs himself among his kind and calls it Paris. Not in any quarter of new smartness, of spruce and polyglot modernity—in a very different region is the place for one who looks for the best in the art of manners and communications. Across the river, in the discreet old recesses of the Faubourg—more and more penned, the fate of distinction everywhere, in a shrinking space encroached upon from all around—tradition, noble and composed, still lives, or did still live when this affinity from the new world brought to it her fine understanding of its quality.

The narrow streets, the retiring 'cités,' the closed portals of the great houses within their courts, the tree-tops leaning over the walls of their hidden gardens—among these is the spot, if you are seeking for the heart of civilization, where you end your journey. France in the world (if all the world is open to you), Paris in France, and the Faubourg St. Germain in Paris—you can evidently go no further; and a dignified little apartment in the rue de Varenne, with a row of rooms looking toward the sober and elegant privacy of the past behind it, will be a home to abide in.[358]

Her life was centered there for a number of years—years fruitful in work and interest, years shadowed by troubles and anxieties of her own, years finally overarched by the vast cloud of war. She had all the company about her that she needed...between the worldly and the literary lay her range, touching no far extremes in either direction... since this was Paris, they could all talk...here in Paris she found prepared for her a world of men—a society in which the men were as plentiful and as civilized as the women, to say the least of it. More than one of her friends have already noted, without surprise, that she preferred the company of men; and indeed there were some obvious reasons why she should, two of the more so being that she had a very feminine consciousness and a very masculine mind.

She liked to be surrounded by the suit of an attentive court, and she liked to be talked to as a man; and both likings were gratified in a world of men and talk. The friendships that will go far and last long with a little impersonal dryness in them, the salt of independence, were those in which she was happy, and it was mainly with men that she found them... She felt perhaps safer with men—safer from the claims and demands of a personal relation: from some of which she shrank so instinctively that intimacy, what most people would call intimacy, was to her of the last difficulty.

One of the women who knew her best, an old friend and contemporary, recalls and confirms what Paul Bourget always said of her, 'To understand Edith one must recognize that she is '*une sensitive*'—so much so that the presence and proximity of people, were they even the most familiar of friends, seemed to check or chill her response, and to the end they might scarcely know, unless sometimes her letters showed them, that she needed and returned their warmth. It is hard to speak of a chill, a check upon the swiftness of the sympathy that so many found in her; but certainly those who looked to her for a flow of deep

[358] I am thinking of the house, 53 rue de Varenne, where nearly all her Parisian life was spent. There was a short prelude in another house, on the opposite side of the same street.

communion, heart to heart—wouldn't find it....Henry James once remarked, ' Ah, my dear, you have made friends with Edith Wharton. I congratulate you. You may find her difficult, but you will find nothing stupid in her and nothing small...."

***

Brooks Adams Letter to Henry Adams about the beginning of World War I:

August 20, 1914
Dear Henry,
...Berhadi says bluntly that Germany may probably have to fight alone, France, England, Russia, and that their (the German) hope was intimidation. How near the Germans were to succeed this correspondence, I think, shows. It was the turn of a hand with England. Germany probably seized on the Serbian issue because in no other way could she be sure of Austria, though, by so doing she alienated Italy. She wanted to fight this year Russia and France, but she counted on intimidating England, and she did up to the very end. There was a point at which France and Russia surely would resist; but to the last day, neither to friend or enemy would Grey say one decisive word. And I believe it was only when the German chancellor pointed out that the annexation of Belgium to Germany would be futile without Holland, a remark that Grey quoted in parliament, that Grey made up his mind even to give a serious intimation that Great Britain might be driven to war. Hence I incline to think that if Great Britain had been as solid with her friends as France, the war might perhaps have drifted over for another year or so—though it was bound to come at last. The impression I receive is that the cabinet was, at last, kicked into a war by the notice that both Holland and Belgium were to be absorbed, but that they would have crawled out, as they did with Denmark for anything less... the Belfort frontier is too strong for a great and sudden stroke, but that Belgium was thought, by the staff, relatively easy. This would be precisely in line with Bernhadi, and, on the whole, my inference is that the soldiers in Berlin have been also the diplomats, and the whole administration, in fact.

The Emperor, I judge, would not have had the courage or the tenacity for such a plan—but I have very little doubt that throughout he has been a figurehead reduced to absolute submission by fear of imprisonment as a lunatic. The financiers have been thrust aside with hardly a word of notice—fifteen years ago they owned the Emperor and Germany. Thus we come to the logical result—the attempt of the only really cohesive force in the world to attain to supremacy. My instinct is that this force itself is already ceasing to cohere. We see it now in its bewilderment at the first stroke. It behaves, mutatis mutandis, just as the financiers did in America in 1912. I look for somewhat the same result—but we shall soon see. Evelyn sends love.

Yours,
B.A

Chapter 8

The Senator was opposed to those articles in which America would have to cede her national sovereignty—articles that Wilson felt were necessary to make the concert of nations effective. If a league could be constructed to be effective and still not infringe on American sovereignty then Lodge would be for it. His position was entirely consistent with his other views: his doubts over immigration; his veneration of the Monroe Doctrine and profound nationalism combined to make him suspicious.[359] Specifically, he was particularly opposed to Article X of the proposed League of Nations that would have committed American troops to foreign wars without the consent of Congress. His arguments are also completely consistent with, for example, his earlier objection to the Hay-Pauncefote treaty of 1900, based on the argument that America should never permit an enemy fleet to use the Panama Canal. "I will not put my hand to a treaty that promises to do things which we know we would not do," he told Roosevelt in 1911; "that is not advancing peace but promoting war and trouble."

By the summer of 1918, with the end of the war in sight, the Senator, in direct opposition to President Wilson, took the position that the League of Nations should be put aside until the peace treaty had been signed and Germany stripped of her powers. That winter, while Wilson was in Paris wrestling with the problems of the Peace Conference, the Senator was carefully working on the opposition. The President committed a fatal error by including neither any members of the Senate nor

[359] His long campaign for the restriction of immigration finally succeeded in 1917 when a literacy test was written into law over Wilson's veto.

any Republican politicians. The delegation included Wilson, his friend Colonel Edward House, Secretary Lansing, General Tasker H. Bliss (all Democrats) and Henry White who was a good Republican and former diplomat, the most accomplished Republican in the group but not an active politician.

The Senator, in a detailed memorandum, told Henry White, a member of the League of Nations delegation and an old friend, that while he did not think the league was practical, he did not want the United State to adopt an isolationist attitude toward the rest of the world. America, he believed, should be an active partner in the realignment of European boundaries and a guarantor of the results.[360]

***

Washington
Nov. 30, 1915
Dearest Corinne,
I have been trying to get a moment to thank you for your letter—So helpful, so grateful to me as all your letters are but I have been constantly occupied, mercifully so, not only with public work but with an infinity of work in the house-papers, letters, all that belonged to her which must be arranged for those who come after us. Coming back to this house was hard but it has brought compensations-I like to be with her books and pictures, all her things about me—It is soothing and quieting—The work is an anodyne-Goethe in his hard wisdom said "Man must resolve to live not only for Truth and Beauty but for the Common Weal" ...Edith Wharton's note was very sympathetic—She has written to me more than once and been to see me, full of affectionate sympathy—She really feels deeply I think.

Ever Yrs,
H.C.L.

Mrs. Douglas Robinson
9 East 63rd St.
Nahant
Sept. 11, 1916
My Dear Corinne,
You asked me to send you any of my speeches that were printed and

---

[360] Garraty, *Henry Cabot Lodge*, 348.

now you see what you have brought upon yourself. One is the speech I made at the unveiling of the Statue of Lafayette at Fall River,a very great occasion for all our citizens of French descent. Jusserand was there and everything really was very impressive and good. I spoke in French and I send you what I actually said in that language...[361]

Later, in the summer of 1918, he wrote her about the elections that year: "...Nothing could be worse than the whole of Wilson's conduct in every direction and although I am never sanguine about elections, I cannot help feeling that the majority of the American people are against him and his Administration and that he will be thoroughly defeated. The only state of which I can speak with absolute knowledge is Massachusetts, ...although I am aware that the feeling against Wilson is stronger in the East than the West."[362] After the summer recess, the Senator told Corinne that he had made a speech on what constituted Peace—"the only peace." It was aimed at the White House in the hope of doing something to prevent a negotiated peace, "a peace of betrayal." He told her he was sure the people were with him. "I have been surprised and delighted at the way all the newspapers without regard to party praised the speech." A day later, his Republican colleagues elected him chairman of the minority conference which meant the official leader of the Republicans in the Senate. "On neither side do Senators feel in the least bound to vote with the official leaders but none the less it is a post of power and responsibility and adds weight to one's words before the world. It is really a great honor and what gratified and touched me most was that the men with whom I serve, with whom I live and work day in and day out should unanimously give me the greatest mark of confidence and honor in their gift. All the Democrats too express pleasure and satisfaction."[363]

Meanwhile, events in Paris were taking shape and on Feb. 15, 1919, the American newspapers published copies of the draft covenant that President Wilson had read to the Peace Conference the day before. Before leaving Paris, the President invited the members of the Congressional committees on foreign relations to dine with him to discuss the proposal off the record; then he spoiled the friendly effort by making a speech on his arrival in Boston before consulting the Congressional leaders.

[361] Roosevelt papers, Houghton Library.
[362] August 5th, 1918.
[363] John McC. Roots, "The Treaty of Versailles in the U.S. Senate," unpublished manuscript, Harvard Archives, 25.

"Mr. Wilson has asked me to dinner," the Senator commented to the press. "He also asked me to say nothing. He then goes to my own town and makes a speech—very characteristic."

Between the Senator's personal vanity and the President's impetuosity, the result was predictable. Just as in 1899-1900 with the Clayton-Bulwer Treaty when the Senator, not consulted by Secretary of State Hay, rejected the treaty out of hand, in 1919, the powerful Senator went along with Brandegee, an "irreconcilable" enemy of the League of Nations and with thirty-seven signatures proposed that the League was unacceptable. But no Senate action could separate the Covenant from the Versailles Treaty. The opposition could not reject the League without also destroying the Treaty and delaying the peace. As it was, Wilson told the French Ambassador, "I shall consent to nothing. The Senate must take its medicine."[364]

Regarding President Coolidge's move for the world court: the Senator was not against a world court—the Hague Tribunal already existed—but he was against a League court and he clearly did not think it was right for the U.S. to join the League.

***

The Senator's Letters to Corinne Roosevelt Robinson about The League of Nations:

Feb. 23, 1919

My Dearest Corinne,

...I cannot express to you what it was to me to have you with me during those two days which meant so much to us both. Merely to know that you were in the house, that you would be there when I returned in the evening gave strength and comfort and held me up. It seems hard, left as we are with so many sorrows and so many memories in which we share, that Fate puts the separation of earthly space between us.... There is a great fight on over the League but I think we shall win and save the country from the traps and pitfalls of which it is full... remember that your letters are very precious to me and that I miss you grievously-

With all love,
Ever Yrs.,

[364] Thomas A. Bailey, *Woodrow Wilson and the Great Betrayal* (New York: 1945), 15.

May 3, 1919
My Dearest Corinne,
...The new League is no better really than the old but it leaves the Faint Hearts an opening to say—"It has been amended and all is well." What will come out of it I cannot tell. I am as Nannie used to say as a "one-idea-ed" person and my first idea and first step is to get a Republican organization of the Senate-Without that, we can do nothing that I think is safe. Until that is part—I will not go beyond general conversation which are useful but we shall try for some real amendments and make the thing safe if we can. I wish I had you here to talk over my difficulties day by day.

With dearest love,
Ever Yrs,
H.C. Lodge

Oct. 19, 1919
My Dearest Corinne,
...I believe I now have our 49 agreed on effective reservations and six Democrats in addition and that we shall put them on and make the treaty safe for our country and so better for the world. You have the right to hope... Bessy and Helena are just established here for the winter so I am no longer alone. I have had very sweet and affectionate letters from Edith once or twice and they have been a comfort. Alice discourses on Wilson and joins me in the treaty fight in what I may call a vigorous manner, very good to hear and very amusing.

How I wish instead of this wretched scrawl I could be with you and talk it all out!

With dearest love,
HC Lodge

United States Senate
Nov. 10, 1919
My dearest Corinne,
...The fight is drawing toward an end here. The first two days on the reservations were very successful. We carried everything before us. I hope and pray the rest may go as well but I utter no shouts until I get out of the woods. If we succeed in getting those reservations on, it will be a victory for Americanism worth talking about.

Dec. 25, 1919
United States Senate
...I have much to say. We have won-we have won a great battle and hold a strong position. I think that we shall retain it and have a complete victory. I am certain that those who come after us will think we served the country well. Lord Grey sails on January 3rd. I am sorry to say. He has talked to me a good deal about that and made a speech about it at Harvard. I shall try to get copies of it for you and me. He has learned much here I think, has done all the business he can and cannot see the President. So he goes. The President cannot see the British Ambassador, has not seen Lansing since he returned last July. The list is a long one-but he can find time to give an hour last week to Barney Baruch—He is a "real nice man"—I mean Wilson—What is the matter with him no one exactly knows but that he has had and has some very serious affliction no one doubts. Meanwhile, the Government of the United States cannot function but limps and hobbles along. As I reflect upon the miseries that man has brought upon the world, the harm he has done his own country, all to satisfy his own selfish desires, I cannot expose myself in a way fit to print. More of this anon...

With dearest love, Ever,
HC Lodge

Feb. 20, 1920
...We started the treaty today and when it will end I cannot say. Ere long I trust. Nor can I tell how it will end. Not badly I think in any event for I have tried so to arrange it. Wilson's abominable letter to Lansing seemed crazy enough but following it up by his renewed interference in France seems really mad. It is believed here very generally that he is mentally worse than anyone supposed and quite unfit for responsibility. The situation is certainly grave. He may easily bring on war between the Slavs and Italy...Helena and Bessy both send love, My dearest love always—I miss you very greatly—

Ever Yrs.,
H.C. Lodge

May 10, 1920
My Dearest Corinne,
...The vote in Massachusetts was, naturally, very gratifying to me, as you may suppose. It was an opportunity to get the direct opinion of my own people on the work I have been doing, probably the only oppor-

tunity I shall ever have, and nothing could have been more complete. There were about ninety-two thousand votes cast and I received over 75,000. The whole result in Massachusetts was satisfactory to me in many ways...

I do not know whether I am to be chairman or not, although it seems probable I shall be the temporary chairman and make the opening speech. I want to do it, not that I care a button for convention honors, which I have had more than once, having presided over two conventions and been chairman of resolutions in two others—but I want to complete my work on the treaty. I want, so far as I can, to lead the party into a right position and win at the polls. Wilson's letter this morning is very helpful to us...After I have voted for Coolidge, my first choice, as you well know, is Wood... Harding is another man I am personally fond of but he has I think been pushed out of the campaign by the quarrel in Ohio which was so intense that he barely carried the state....

Aug. 5, 1923
The death of President Harding was to me a real grief. I shall miss him personally for he was always kindness itself to me in all our relations....

May 14, 1924
My Dearest Corinne,
...There is a move for a world court. There has been no opposition to Mr. Coolidge's suggestions, because all he did was express the hope that we should take favorable action. We have not taken any action yet, but the Committee as a whole is opposed to the League Court; that is, they are opposed to the League, and the effort to get us into the League is nine-tenths of the movement for the League court. We are at work on that very subject now. The League court is not a world court. It is a court made and supported by members of the League and the fact is that the great majority of our people here do not mean to get into the League. If you were to drop off tomorrow all connection of the League with the Court, you would see Mr. Wickersham and these other gentlemen lose all interest in the Court like a shot. It is also never remembered by those people who are talking about the League Court that we have now in existence over fifty arbitration treaties, made with individual Powers. In addition, we are members of the Hague Tribunal, which is the world tribunal....

July 15, 1924
In my work of editing the letters... I have come to 1909, the year of Bay's death. You remember that Theodore wrote a preface for the collected edition of the Poems which appeared at a somewhat later time. It is I think one of the most beautiful things that Theodore ever wrote and I mean to print it with the correspondence of that year... I should be gratified to have it included in the great Scribner's edition of Theodore's complete works....

Chapter 9

Great Uncle John Davis Lodge (October 20, 1903—October 29, 1985) graduated from Harvard University in 1925 and from Harvard Law School in 1929. On July 6, 1929, he married actress and ballet dancer, Francesca Braggiotti. They had two daughters, Lillie and Beatrice. He was admitted to the New York Bar in 1932. He became a movie star between 1933 and 1942, appearing in *Little Women*, *The Scarlet Empress*, and *The Little Colonel*. He served with the United States Navy as a lieutenant and lieutenant commander August 1942 to January 1946 and was a liaison officer between the French and American fleets. He was decorated with the rank of Chevalier in the French Legion of Honor and with the Croix de Guerre with palm by General Charles de Gaulle. He was elected as a Republican from Connecticut's 4th congressional district to the 80th and 81st Congresses, serving from January 3, 1947 to January 3, 1951. He was elected Governor of Connecticut, serving from January 1951 to January 1955 and was unsuccessful for reelection in 1954 (the Connecticut Turnpike is now named after the former Governor.) He was a delegate to the Republican National Convention from Connecticut in 1952 and 1960. He then served as United States Ambassador to Spain from January 1955 until January 1961. He was an unsuccessful candidate for U.S. Senator from Connecticut in 1964. United States Ambassador to Argentina, 1969 to 1974; United States Ambassador to Switzerland, 1983.

Of the three children, Bessy's daughter, (our Great Aunt) Helena—intelligent, humorous, and strong-willed—may have been most like the Senator. But like her female predecessors, she never wanted the limelight. Mother of three—Jean-Paul, Quentin and Elisabeth—and wife of Baron Edouard de Streel, the Private Secretary to Queen Elizabeth of the Belgians, she contributed to life at Court and was revered in her small circle.

Inspired by my father and grandfather, I too became in a journalist. In 1975, I lived with my grandparents for a year when Grandma was seventy and Grandpa was seventy-three. She made it possible for me to work, for had I been living at home with my mother, I would have been expected to cook and clean up; with a demanding job as a police and court reporter, arising at five am, attending trials during the day, and writing at night, I depended on my grandmother's uncomplaining selflessness. She thrust a drink into my hand when I returned home and the three of us watched the news. In a feature for *The Beverly Times*, I had interviewed a Boston police officer and Beverly resident charged with the desegregation of Boston's schools in which he had stated that the white children picked fights with the black children as much as the reverse is true and that if they lived together they would come to understand one another better. Once at dinner, I announced—"Grandpa, the Ku Klux Klan say they are coming to Beverly to burn a cross on our front lawn"; unperturbed, he went on slurping his soup. Grandma shuffled out to the pantry in her flat slippers that she always wore so as not to appear too tall, and I watched as she taught me how to load a dishwasher properly so that everything fit. "See, my pet?" she would murmur. "I only saw Grandma cry a few times," my sister Nancy recalls. "Listening to Richard Burton sing the last song in Camelot, 'for one brief shining moment'—that always made her cry. Another time was after *Out of Africa* for the heroine embodied by Meryl Streep, closely resembled her. She cried when she laughed and when she sneezed. She always sneezed 13 times...."[365]

[365] Nancy Lodge, "Memories of My Grandmother."

Bibliography

Grateful acknowledgment is made to the Massachusetts Historical Society for lending me copies, while a resident of Paris, France, of the six volume edition of *The Letters of Henry Adams*, Harvard University Press, edited by Ernest Samuels, Charles Vandersee, Viola Hopkins Winner, Jayne N Samuels. Copyright 1982 and 1988; and to the Harvard University Press for permission to publish and from the four volume *Letters of Henry James*, edited by Leon Edel, copyright 1974, 1975, 1980 and 1984. Quotations from the Lodge and Adams Papers are from the original letters, by permission of the Massachusetts Historical Society. Quotation of John Hay's poetry is by permission of John Hay Library, the Brown University Library. Quotation of the Henry Cabot Lodge-Corinne Roosevelt Robinson letters is by permission of the Theodore Roosevelt Collection at the Houghton Library, Harvard University.

Adams, Henry. *The Education of Henry Adams: An Autobiography*. Henry Cabot Lodge, ed. Boston: Houghton Mifflin Co., 1918. New York: Bartleby.com, 1999. http://www.bartleby.com/159/. Lodge signed the preface at Adams' request but it was actually written by Adams.

___. *The Letters of Henry Adams*, Vol. 1-6. Ernest Samuels, Charles Vandersee, Viola Hopkins Winner, Jayne N. Samuels, eds. Boston: Harvard Univeristy Press, 1982; 1988.

___. *The Life of George Cabot Lodge*. Boston: Houghton Mifflin, 1911.

Amory, Cleveland. *The Proper Bostonians*, New York: E.P. Dutton, 1947.

Auchincloss, Louis. *Theodore Roosevelt*. New York: Times Books; Henry Holt and Company, 2001.

Bailey, Thomas. *Woodrow Wilson and the Great Betrayal*. New York: Peter Smith, 1945.

Benstock, Shari. *No Gifts from Chance: A Biography of Edith Wharton.* New York: Charles Scribner's Sons, 1994.

Boorstin, Daniel. *The Americans: The National Experience.* New York: Vintage, 1965.

Brands, H.R. *T.R.: The Last Romantic.* New York: Basic Books, 1997.

Brooks, Van Wyck. *The Writer In America.* New York: Dutton, 1953. Reprint New York: Avon, 1964.

Burton, David Henry. *Cecil Spring Rice: A Diplomat's Life.* Rutherford, London: Associated University Presses, 1990.

Carter, Harold Dean, ed. *Henry Adams and His Friends: A Collection of His Unpublished Letters.* Boston: Houghton Mifflin Company, 1947.

Chanler, Margaret Terry. *Roman Spring.* Boston: Little, Brown, 1934.

Chastellux, François-Jean, marqus de. *Travels in North America.* London: Printed for G.G.J. and J. Robinson, 1787.

Crowley, John W. "George Cabot Lodge (1873-1909)." *American Literary Realism 1870-1910*, Vol. 6, No. 1 (Winter 1973), 44-50.

___. *The Education of George Cabot Lodge: A Literary Biography.* Submitted to the faculty of the Graduate School for the degree Doctor of Philosophy in the department of English, Indiana University, September, 1970.

___, *George Cabot Lodge.* Boston: Twayne Publishers, 1976.

___, "The Suicide of the Artist: Henry Adams' Life of George Cabot Lodge." *The New England Quarterly*, Vol. 46, No. 2 (June 1973), 189-204.

Dalton, Kathleen. *Theodore Roosevelt: A Strenuous Life.* New York: Alfred A. Knopf, 2002.

Decker, William Merrill. *Epistolary Practices: Letter Writing in America Before Telecommunications.* Chapel Hill, NC: University of North Carolina Press, 1998.

Dickinson, Emily. *The Poems of Emily Dickinson.* R.W. Franklin, ed. Cambridge, MA; London: Belknap Press of Harvard University, 2005.

Garraty, John A. *Henry Cabot Lodge: A Biography.* New York: Alfred A. Knopf, 1953.

Green, Martin. *The Problem of Boston*. New York; London: W.W. Norton & Co., 1966.

Hatch, Alden. *The Lodges of Massachusetts*. New York: Hawthorn Books, 1973.

Hay, Clarence Leonard. *The Complete Poetical Works of John Hay, Including Many Poems Now First Collected*. Reprint: Lake Stevens, WA: Foster Press, 2008.

Hess, Stephen. *America's Political Dynasties: From Adams to Kennedy*. Garden City, NY: Doubleday, 1966.

Higginson, Thomas Wentworth. *Descendants of Reverend Francis Higginson. 1910*. Massachusetts Historical Society.

James, Henry. *The American Scene*. New York: Penguin Classics, 1907; reprint, 1994.

___. *The Letters of Henry James*, Vol. IV (1875-1916). Leon Edel, ed. The Belknap Press of Harvard University Press, Cambridge, Mass. London, England, 1984.

___. *The Letters of Henry James*, Vol. II. Percy Lubbuck, ed. London: Macmillan and Co., 1920.

___. *Selected Letters*, vol. I. Leon Edel, ed. Cambridge: Harvard University Press, 1987.

Jones, Howard Mumford. *Guide to American Literature and Its Backgrounds Since 1890*, second revised edition. Cambridge: Harvard University Press, 1959.

___. *The Bright Medusa*. Urbana: University of Illinois Press, 1952.

Kohlsaat, H.H. *From McKinley to Harding: Personal Recollections of Our Presidents*. New York: Charles Scribners, 1923.

Lawrence, William. *Henry Cabot Lodge*. Boston: Houghton Mifflin, 1925.

Lee, Hermione. *Edith Wharton*. New York: Vintage, 2008.

Lewis, R.W.B. *Edith Wharton: A Biography*. New York: Harper & Row, 1975.

Lewis, R.W.B. and Nancy Lewis, eds. *The Letters of Edith Wharton*. New York: Collier Books, 1989.

Levenson, J.C. *The Mind and Art of Henry Adams.* Stanford, CA: Stanford University Press, 1957.

Lodge, George Cabot. *Paths Are Made By Walking.* Unpublished autobiography, 1999.

___. *Poems and Dramas of George Cabot Lodge.* Two volumes. Boston: Houghton Mifflin, 1911.

Lodge, *George and Craig Wilson. A Corporate Solution to Global Poverty: How Multinationals Can Help the Poor and Invigorate Their Own Legitimacy.* Princeton, NJ: Princeton University Press, 2006.

Lodge, Henry Cabot. "The Anglo-Saxon Land Law." In *Essays in Anglo-Saxon Law.* Henry Adams, ed. Boston: Little, Brown and Co., 1876.

___. *Early Memories.* New York: Charles Scribner's Sons, 1913.

___. *Life and Letters of George Cabot.* Boston: Little, Brown and Co., 1877.

___. "Tribute to Anna Cabot Mills Davis Lodge." Unpublished.

Lodge, Jr., Henry Cabot. *The Storm Has Many Eyes: A Personal Narrative.* New York: W.W. Norton and Co., 1973.

Lodge, Nancy. "Memories." Unpublished essay, 2004.

___. "To Grandma Just Before Her Second Honeymoon, From Nancy." Unpublished essay, 1987.

Lubbock, Percy. *Portrait of Edith Wharton.* New York; London: D. Appleton-Century Co., Inc., 1947.

Miller, William J. *Henry Cabot Lodge: A Biography.* New York: James H. Heineman, Inc. 1967.

Morris, Edmund. *Theodore Rex.* New York: Random House, 2001.

Morison, Samuel Eliot. *Maritime History of Massachusetts, 1783-1860.* Boston: Houghton Mifflin, 1921.

Origo, Iris. Leopardi: *A Study in Solitude.* London: Hamish Hamilton, Ltd., 1953.

O'Toole, Patricia. *The Five of Hearts: An Intimate Portrait of Henry Adams and His Friends, 1880-1918.* New York: Simon & Schuster, 2006.

___. *When Trumpet's Call: Theodore Roosevelt After The White House*. New York: Simon & Schuster, 2005.

Pound, Ezra. *An Examination Of Ezra Pound.* Peter Russell, ed. Norfolk, CT: New Directions, 1950.

Riggs, Thomas. *Trumbell Stickney, 1874-1904*. Unpublished Doctoral dissertation, Princeton University, 1949. MHS.

Samuels, Ernest. *Henry Adams: The Major Phase.* Cambridge, MA; London: Belknap Press of Harvard University, 1964.

Santayana, George. *The Letters of George Santayana.* Daniel Cory, ed. New York: Scribner's, 1955.

Schriftgiesser, Karl. *The Gentleman From Massachusetts: Henry Cabot Lodge.* Boston: Little, Brown, 1944.

Smith, Bradford. *Bradford of Plymouth*. Philadelphia: J.B. Lippincott and Company, 1951.

Spring-Rice, Cecil. *The Letters and Friendships of Sir Cecil Spring-Rice: A Record.* Two volumes. Stephen Lucius Gwynn, ed. Boston: Houghton Mifflin, 1929.

Stickney, Joseph Trumbull. *The Poems of Trumbull Stickney*. Boston: Houghton Mifflin, 1905.

Thomas, Evan. *The War-Lovers: Roosevelt, Lodge, Hearst, and the Rush to Empire, 1898*. Boston: Little, Brown, 2010.

Tocqueville, Alexis de. *Democracy in America*. London; New York: Longmans, Green, 1889.

Ward, Humphry, Mrs. *A Writer's Recollection*. London: W. Collins & Sons, 1918.

Wharton, Edith. *A Backward Glance.* New York; London: D. Appleton-Century Company, Inc., 1934.

___. "George Cabot Lodge."*Scribner's Magazine* 47, (February 1910), 236.

___. *The House of Mirth*. New York: Scribner's, 1905.

___. *Madame de Treymes*. New York: Scribner's, 1907.

Wilson, Edmund, ed. *The Shock of Recognition: The Development of Literature in the United States.* Recorded By the Men Who Made It. Garden City, NY: Doubleday, 1943.

Zimmerman, Warren. *First Great Triumph: How Five Americans Made Their Country a World Power.* New York: Farrar, Straus & Giroux, 2002.

CPSIA information can be obtained
at www.ICGtesting.com
Printed in the USA
FFOW01n0644110314
4171FF